350

U.S.A. CONFIDENTIAL

Previously Published

by *Jack Lait and Lee Mortimer*

NEW YORK CONFIDENTIAL

CHICAGO CONFIDENTIAL

WASHINGTON CONFIDENTIAL

by *Jack Lait*

HELP WANTED (*a play*)

THE BIG HOUSE

BROADWAY MELODY

BEAST OF THE CITY

PUT ON THE SPOT

GANGSTER GIRL

BEEF, IRON AND WINE (*short stories*)

GUS THE BUS

OUR WILL ROGERS

WILL ROGERS' WIT AND WISDOM

A PRACTICAL GUIDE TO SUCCESSFUL WRITING

by *Lee Mortimer*

NEW YORK BEHIND THE SCENES

U. S. A.
Confidential

BY *JACK LAIT*

AND

LEE MORTIMER

CROWN PUBLISHERS, INC.
NEW YORK

Printed in the United States of America
American Book–Stratford Press, Inc., New York

The Confidential Contents

Introduction: U.S.A. CONFIDENTIAL   ix

Part One: THE PEOPLE (Confidential!)

1. ALL OF US   1
   Screwballs, politicians, good Joes, millionaires, paupers,
   white, black, yellow and albino. What makes us tick and
   what's wrong with the main spring.

2. MISS AMERICA   6
   She's the national dream-boat, but only this age could make
   her.

3. CROOKS AND RACKETEERS   8
   Despite Kefauver they are still with us. This tells what
   Estes didn't tell, also why.
   A. The Sicilian Benevolent and Blood-Money Society.   8
   B. Crime but no Punishment.   15
   C. Hoodlums' Hoppy Hunting Ground.   21
   D. Wave of the Future   31
   E. Hope of the Future.   34

4. WOMEN CONFIDENTIAL   38
   What Kinsey Won't Tell.

5. MEN CONFIDENTIAL   44
   What Kinsey Didn't Tell.

6. THE RIGHT TO GO LEFT   46
   Americans are overeducated boobs, no longer taught the
   three R's, which are "bourgeois and old-fashioned." Now
   we learn how to conform while the schemers and dreamers
   overrun our schools and colleges.

7. REDS IN CLOVER   52
   Commies, pinkos, welfare statists, progressives—whatever
   they call themselves they smell the same.

8. OUR AFRO-AMERICAN BRETHREN   57
   The Second Emancipation.

9. "LABOR"—THE ONLY LEGAL MONOPOLY   66
   There's no anti-trust law against union goons who sleep on
   silk and sip champagne.

Part Two: THE PLACES (Confidential!)

10. NEW ORLEANS—PARADISE LOST   74
     Every man a King—but not enough men.

11. NEW ENGLAND CONFIDENTIAL—CODFISH
     AND CONMEN   86
     Maybe Plymouth Rock should have landed on the Pilgrims.
     A. Boston Baked Beans and B-Girls.   88
     B. What They Raise on Providence Plantations. 95
     C. St. Tobey Confidential.   100
     D. Connecticut—New York in Pink Pajamas.   106

12. NORTHWEST CONFIDENTIAL   112
     Where men are men—and women, too.
     A. Carry Me Back to Old Minnesota.   114
     B. Seattle—Skidrow on the Sound.   121
     C. From Portland, Maine to—Portland, Ore.   127

13. INDIANA—POLITICS ON THE PRAIRIE   131
     Home of the new President-maker.

14. CALIFORNIA CONFIDENTIAL   137
     Where it's ham-and-eggs every Tuesday, but every day is
     Tuesday.
     A. San Francisco—Bridgeport on the Golden Gate. 141
     B. Los Angeles—City of the Lost Angels.   151
     C. San Diego—Springboard to Mexico.   169

15. DETROIT CONFIDENTIAL—CRIME ON THE
     ASSEMBLY LINE   171
     Socialization in flower.

16. THE LOST FRONTIER   181
     We found it, but why?
     A. Denver—Mile High Monkey Business.   181
     B. Nevada—Punks' Paradise.   187

17. THE LONELY STAR—TEXAS CONFIDENTIAL   191
     We fought Mexico—for what?
     A. Dallas—Culture and Fairies.   195
     B. Houston—Hustleton on the Canal.   201
     C. Where the West Begins: Fort Worth, San Antone. 209
     D. Galveston—The Free State.   213

18. PENNSYLVANIA—THE CAPTIVE KEYSTONE   219
It holds up the underworld.
   A. Philadelphia Confidential.   221
   B. Pittsburgh—Steel and Steal.   224

19. MILWAUKEE AND WHAT NEVER MADE IT
   FAMOUS   228
Gals, gats and gemutlichkeit.

20. MISSOURI—STATE OF TRUMANKIND   232
Principal product: Jackasses.
   A. Kansas City—Suburb of Independence.   235
   B. Don't Meet Me in St. Louis.   243

21. DEAR ALBEN'S OLD KENTUCKY HOME   246
Why they burnt down the co't-house.

22. KEFAUVER CON CONFIDENTIAL   253
Tennessee—from Old Hickory to Estes, the coonskin-er.
   A. Chattanooga—Uncle Estes' Cabin.   257
   B. Memphis—Cramped by Crump.   263
   C. Top Secret—They Make More than Atomic Energy at
      Oak Ridge.   266

23. THE BIBLE (NOT CHASTITY) BELT   271
Nothing in the middle of everything.
   A. Iowa—In and Out of Death Moines.   272
   B. Omaha—Beef and Bookies.   274
   C. Bloody Kansas—Silos and Sex.   277
   D. The Arkies.   280
   E. Drought in Oklahoma.   284

24. OHIO CONFIDENTIAL   288
Home of the "Gang."
   A. Cleveland—Hard Heart of Hickland.   290
   B. Cincinnati—You Go There to Get Away from It   294

25. NEW JERSEY—THE UPTOWN FLORIDA   296

Part Three: LOWDOWN ON THE BIG TOWNS, ACT II
(Confidential!)

26. NEW YORK CONFIDENTIAL (ACT II)   300
Since the Best-Seller.
   A. Sidewalks of New York.   308
   B. The Empire State.   318

27. CHICAGO CONFIDENTIAL (ACT II)   320
     Brought up to date.
     A. Chicagoland Confidential.   325

28. WASHINGTON CONFIDENTIAL (ACT II)   330
     New dynamite to blast America's dirtiest city.
     A. White House Gang—Past and Present.   330
     B. The Pentagonians.   333
     C. Probe Bono Publico.   337
     D. Truman Sickness.   343
     E. Politics as Usual. (How to win by losing.)   352
     F. The District of Confusion.   357

29. BALTIMORE CONFIDENTIAL (ACT II)   360
     Another chapter of infamy.

Part Four: THE EMPIRE (Confidential!)

30. HALF-BAKED ALASKA   366
     The not so frozen north.

31. HAWAII—HULAS AND HAOLES   372
     The unwanted pearl.

32. PUERTO RICO—MANHATTAN'S INCUBATOR   382
     Love and votes for sale.

33. TEMPORARY EMPIRE CONFIDENTIAL—
     PROCONSULS IN JAPAN   386
     Every man a Mikado.

Part Five: "ONE" WORLD (Confidential!)

34. UN—THE GLOBAL BOONDOGGLE   392
     The East River Debating Society.

CONFIDENTIAL INDEX   397

INTRODUCTION: U.S.A.
CONFIDENTIAL

*P*SS-S-T!

For the fourth time Lait and Mortimer want a word with you —Confidential!

We dissected New York, we turned Chicago upside-down and Washington inside-out. With each of these books our acceptance grew until, in 1951, of some 11,500 titles published, *Washington Confidential* stood No. 1, and all three books are still in high demand.

They were written with a rifle, each aimed at the bull's-eye of a great metropolis. This is a shotgun book, splattering heavy-gauge ammunition all over our country. We traveled 75,000 miles before we pulled a trigger.

In each of the cities to which we gave the treatment heretofore we were blackguarded by our confreres of the local press, though many critics elsewhere relished us. Now we expect denials and damnation from everywhere. We encountered threats, offers of bribes and other pressures, to which we have become accustomed.

The picture we present is not pretty. We do not offset it with the fine and wonderful American institutions, which we love with patriotic affection; library shelves groan with panegyrics on the glories of our country, and we cannot improve on them.

We have assumed the function of uncovering what the sight-seeing writers don't know, even about their own communities.

Teddy Roosevelt denominated such endeavors muckraking; the muck is there, deep and dirty; the rake digs into it and turns it up. It's your muck, not ours.

As we have proclaimed throughout the Confidential series, we are reporters, not reformers. We have nothing to sell but books. In not one instance did we interview a police official, a prosecutor, a Mayor or a Governor. We had no reason to tell them; our sole business is to tell you. And from them we would get nothing but alibis and whitewash and invitations to see the nice new water-works and the doctored public records.

We have our own methods and our own contacts. Wherever

we lit we were anticipated. Also, in many places we were trailed and watched. So there will be denunciations pointing out that in some towns we spent little time. That is true. To others we gave weeks. But in the one-night stands our information had been prepared for us and we checked it and beat it.

We could not apply this process to every burg that has a city hall. But do not ponder between the lines for mysterious reasons which led us to discuss certain places in some detail and to ignore others. Some we saw but dismissed as not our kind of copy. Others we skipped because routings and timetables barred us from making every crossroads. For instance we went over the Southeast states lightly and found nothing much that would not be repetitive of other Dixie territory. As for Miami, it is the winter Chicago. The job was breathless rather than measured with pedestrian research aimed for an all-inclusive compendium designed to grow dusty in reference cases, awaiting the scrutiny of future generations of historians and scholars.

We got our training on fast dailies. And this is hot journalism, gathered and knocked out to be fresh in these rapidly changing times. These pages were rushed to press, poured in up to the last minute that mechanical processes permitted. As in many first editions of newspapers, there may be some minor errors, such as misspelled strange and intricate names and designations of unfamiliar streets. These will be rectified in later printings, and we know from the advance demand that there must be later printings.

But we apologize for nothing. We have winnowed the forty-eight states and all our territories and dependencies. No more exacting search could affect our conclusions.

We learned that the conditions of vice, crime, graft and organized racketeering have spread over virtually the entire nation, rural as well as metropolitan, much of it even more revolting and alarming than the shameful corruption of the three major cities. The tax cheating which has come to general light is only the surface scum.

Differing only with climate, population and other local and regional circumstances, we found prostitution, perversion and protected political extortion in hamlets, counties and states as rotten as in the big cities; north, south, east and west have adopted varied shades of extortion, larceny and the gangsterism and bribing and assassinations which make and keep them possible and profitable.

The effects of the Kefauver television circus are negligible, the whole ballyhooed binge of publicity and melodrama laughable. Gambling and whoring slowed down temporarily, but came back in full scale.

The country is in the grip of the Mafia, tighter than ever, and with new "improvements" and closer control all the time. Politics on all levels everywhere we found crooked, raw and shameless. Minorities are bought in blocs and paid with privileges and power.

The Reds feed on conspiracy, pressure groups and the imbecility of naïve, myopic "liberal" suckers, who are allied willynilly with traitors, mobsters, panders and dope-pushers.

Our youth is unbridled, hopped up, sex-crazy and perverted.

We have demonstrated through three successive books in three years that we are not sloppy workmen at our trade. We could write a book about what we have exposed which was later forced out through official channels and became page one banner news (without acknowledgment) because we have the unique will and skill and guts to get and to publish what no one else seems able to handle. The rewards are substantial. A few feeble imitators have tried to cash in on our successful system. They didn't know how or where to begin. Some even stole our title and copied our format, but they all flopped miserably. All they had was formula —ours—and the half-baked boobs will never understand what they didn't have.

This will be our story of America—man's bravest dream—and how greedy groups and misguided ninnies are turning it into a nightmare.

That's why we were born—to dig and to disseminate the McCoy —Confidential!

PART ONE

THE PEOPLE
(*Confidential!*)

1. ALL OF US

THIS richest and strongest of nations, conceived in a bloody revolution, has given up its elementary liberty: the right to get mad.

That was the salt in our blood on which the framers of our Constitution based our entire inspired system. They depended on our will as well as our liberty to change, to amend, to fight and to uproot laws and men inimical to the common well-being. It worked as fairly well as any institution dependent on the rectitude and resiliency of humans could, until, some score of years ago, a panic-stricken flock of some 150,000,000 sheep fled into a pen at the command of a daring rustler.

Since then we have been shorn and clipped and we have huddled, shivering and scarcely bleating—sluggish and torpid, groggy and tired. Lethargy has displaced the lusty spirit to resist and to rebound.

Not only in our political doldrums have we shed our character. We have forgotten how to play. We grub for fifty-cent dollars which are snatched away from us by the talons of an insatiable horde of harpies. We are content to be amused with the vicarious vibrations of mechanized, standardized, commercialized pap.

For our own spontaneous pleasures we turn to our vices in a surreptitious sense of guilt, bereft of that fire of open rebellion which prompted us to go on that long, glorious drunk in defiance of a law which our manhood could not stomach. Now we stand meekly by while the burgeoning bureaucrats send the same snoopers out to police gambling by a legislative atrocity which attacks

1

it with our most fearsome weapon—taxes. This is done by the party which destroyed Prohibition in response to the outcry of the people. Now there is no outcry. We are being pushed into the subjection of socialism by all its rules and devices. We don't want socialism. But we drift along without sail or anchor or rudder, without enough gumption to even call for help.

The 80th Congress was elected in a mild upset when the women —not the men—struck a spark of indignation over regulation of prices and supply of necessities. Our last lone hope lies in house-wives who may again get hot over the cost of hamburgers. But they are susceptible to capricious crushes on handsome males— like Kefauver—and they're sorry for a little geezer like Truman.

America has become a matriarchy. Women own it and run it. There are more of them and more of them vote. They have come into their own—also to our own. Instead of less crime there is more. Instead of less corruption there is more. Instead of less war there is more, but now it is called something else.

Doting mothers raise soft sons, plump for laws so they can't work in their youth and don't have to in their manhood. America is becoming a land of manicured hermaphrodites, going the way of Rome.

The crime and political unorthodoxy which grip the nation stem from the same roots of frustration and egotism. Until he wins the revolution, the rebel is a criminal. Organized revolutionary undergrounds are criminal in the beginning, with no marked dividing line. Hunted scum, like Stalin, gather into gangs and live by theft, blackmail and murder. Few rebel for the good of humanity. Few are Washingtons and Jeffersons. Most are thugs like Hitler and Bridges and the Russians, who want something someone else has. Costello and the Capone boys are more forthright about it.

This is the United States in 1952:

The government spends—as usual. And it taxes and taxes—as usual.

The defense effort is impaired by strikes—as usual.

Inflation spins and spirals—as usual.

The State Department secretly appeases while pretending a bold front—as usual.

Russia and its satellites draw off American dollars and American products—as usual.

"Liberals" decry Communists and fight anti-Communists—as usual.

In Washington, as well as in every state capital and city hall, influence is peddled, crooks sell contracts and immunity, and high office-holders take, from minks to money—as usual.

And the President, governors and mayors deny it—as usual—until the scandals become so odoriferous that even the captive citizens hold their noses; then they say—as usual—"This is an individual case. This is smear technique."

The casualties in Korea are frightful—and Treasury figures show Truman taxed America more between July 1, 1945, and July 1, 1950, than the entire national tax bill from the founding of the government in 1789 until he took office, including two world wars, the Civil War and thirteen years of Roosevelt. Twenty billion dollars more in five years than all his predecessors exacted in 156 years.

And yet Washington demands billions more. It issues fraudulent figures indicating that 20 per cent of the population earned 47 per cent of the income (but this was before taxes) while another fifth only got 3 per cent. This is to justify new bites. No one mentions that if all individual incomes over $20,000 were confiscated completely it would only add a billion, and if no one were permitted to keep more than $6,000 a year that would bring in only four billion—which we send in cigarette money to Greece and Turkey.

States, counties, municipalities and everyone with the power to tax digs merrily. As these pages unfold, we will show that crime, corruption and handouts, criminal and political, as well as the cost of narcotics and sexual perversion annually rob the taxpayers of more than the cost of war.

We are rich—in deflated dollars. The average income for each man, woman and child is $1,436—over $5,000 a year per family. The pet theory of the Socialists and settlement-house workers that when poverty is ended crime will go has exploded—as a new criminal class arises—the overprivileged.

There are alive and at large in the land 9,028,535 individuals who have been arrested for crimes serious enough to involve finger-printing. Many were never convicted, of course, but the nationwide average of convictions is about 50 per cent, which would give us almost 5,000,000 ex-cons on the streets. Many who were acquitted or not tried were guilty also. Few innocents are convicted, but many guilty escape.

Many have relatives and families. Add them to millions of non-criminals in the half-world who make their living in secondary connection with some criminal enterprises, such as bartenders, chefs, waiters, bouncers in gambling dives, mechanics who repair slot-machines, cab-drivers who steer to whore-houses, etc., and you have 15,000,000—a tenth of the population—with an equity in crime.

America's biggest business is liquor. More than 50 per cent of the booze is moonshine. There are more illicit stills in operation than there are individual outlets of any other form of business. The total revenue from legal and illegal liquor far surpasses the gross income of any other industry. Recently increased liquor taxes are estimated to cost the government more than $7,000,000 a day—$2,500,000,000 annually—in revenue now diverted to moonshiners.

All forms of crime and vice, including rum-running, are drawn tightly into the hands of a small cooperative syndicate of law-breakers dominated by the Mafia or Unione Siciliano, an outgrowth of the Sicilian Black Hand. This bandit bund actively supports blue laws, increased liquor taxes and national and local clean-ups, such as the Kefauver Committee, on the theory that when natural human appetites are curbed and driven underground gangsters can step in.

As liquor and gambling are driven out of the usual channels of trade, veterans' and fraternal organizations become the only outlets where men may drink or wager. Professionals take over as concessionaires or managers. The clubs get rich and are easily aligned on the side of the incorporated underworld. We noted this process all over the United States. It is more evident in rural communities and small towns than in the big cities. The more liberal a community's laws, the less chance that gangsters will take over these organizations.

Blue-law towns with early closings or inconsistent liquor laws are subject not only to more law-breaking, but considerably more to illicit activities in sex, natural and abnormal, precocious asocialities and flight to stimulants.

These pages will reflect a new alignment of the age-old Negro problem. U.S. Census Bureau figures indicate that more than 3,000,000 migrated in the last decade, adding to the already large colored populations in Northern industrial centers. As usual these findings are short of the facts. It is impossible to conduct a correct Negro census, as millions lose themselves in the white community and other millions fear any man with a badge, refuse to be counted.

The rural population sinks, the city population is static, but the big city suburban population is growing at five or six times the rates of the metropolises, as Negroes push whites out of the cities and replace them. These newcomers are usually ill-educated and poor. They bring problems of health, relief and crime. They are often and easily colonized by their own and white exploiters who vote them in blocs for the underworld. The prosperous whites, driven to the suburbs, lose interest in the cities. They join churches in their new towns, vote and pay taxes there, gradually cutting all ties and losing all weight in the metropolis.

Rural America is changing, too. Farmers are no longer yahoos. They have all the latest means of communication and convenience. No longer do they buy gold bricks. Their moral fiber and business morality is as low as any. In the Ozark country they have a gag: "How do you make a thoroughbred out of a cow that's too old to give milk?" The answer is, "Cross it with a Missouri-Pacific engine."

Farmers are on the make like everyone else, to rob the railroads, beat banks and gyp consumers. There is more crookedness, cussedness and sex excess in the tall grass than on Park Avenue, but the home newspapers don't print it and the big ones don't get it. Most rural areas have no law whatever—when they do it's an aging constable or neighborly justice of the peace making a good thing of shaking down motorists from the cities. Prosecutors, judges, village selectmen and police wear earmuffs and blinders.

Farmers pay no income taxes, take fortunes from the government and prate the rottenness of the cities while their kids join sex clubs, their hired men sleep with their wives and they chase the neighbor's daughters. Their youngsters break all the traffic laws in hot rods, they raise fighting cocks and dogs and match them openly in pits while the sheriff looks on, and almost all make their own liquor.

The Ku Klux Klan, though disorganized, is arising and active in Georgia, northern Florida, Mississippi, Kansas, Nebraska and Oklahoma under a half-dozen different fronts. The populace goes in for faith-healing, naturopaths, chiropractors, new thought, psychoanalysis, ghost-raising, fortune-telling, yogi and yogurt.

The man with taste is suspect. He who wants to choose his own friends is a "Fascist." We have been browbeaten for so long we speak in fear, apologize when we tell dialect stories, shudder at the word "conservative," and regard "reactionary" like a four-letter word in *From Here To Eternity*.

It is a sin against the new world of mediocrity to be distinct or distinguished. We are in the chain-store, neon-lighted era. Almost every city looks the same. The same people all dress the same—kids as Hopalong Cassidy, men with loud sportshirts and Truman suits, women in slacks. Sometimes you can tell whether a trousered individual before you is a man or a woman only by the width of the buttocks. Only a few cities have individuality. They are the seaports, New York, New Orleans and San Francisco. Boston reeks of decay, and not genteel. The rest are all Cleveland.

Each year America becomes more uniform and standardized. Our schools no longer teach children to learn to fight their own way. They are educated to be part of the "community." Their personal likes and dislikes are supposed to be subordinated to the welfare of the group, the school, the city, and in the final analysis, the mass. Schools are in the grip of this insidious trend of education actively sponsored by Communists, Socialists, Eleanor Roosevelt and other welfare-staters, who are bringing about the "revolution" painlessly, through our children.

The pinks have infiltrated the entertainment, reading and thinking of an entire nation, aiming to make us all canned sardines.

We give you U.S.A. CONFIDENTIAL.

2. MISS AMERICA

IN ALL foreign lands the familiar symbol of the United States is the Statue of Liberty. Miniatures are displayed as souvenirs and Americans are expected to palpitate with patriotic pleasure on beholding the reduced reproduction of their country's emblem.

The old iron gal has long done her bit. We have no disposition to dispossess and retire her for old age alone. But she has outlived her primary purposes: to beacon our freedom and to welcome the poor, the miserable, the oppressed of the world. Our liberty has shrunk since she first went up on her pedestal and we don't want others' peelings and leavings unless they are Puerto Ricans, who can vote, or Sicilians, who can be enlisted into the good works of their older compatriots, or members of special groups who have relatives here who know members of Congress.

So we suggest, respectfully, even tenderly, that the aged bimbo step down—and in her place we erect a statue of Virginia Hill, holding high a jimmy instead of a torch.

For Virginia is the all-round American girl who made good in the modern arts, crafts and industries:

The Sweetheart of the Syndicates;

The greatest attraction in television;

The apotheosis of the modern methodology, which beckons us to get rich without working;

The prototype of our political and commercial slogan of the day—"Honesty is no substitute for experience."

We have written of Virgie before, not always with indulgence, but always with admiration.

Until she attained her zenith, as a Kefauver witness, we had not yet plumbed her full greatness. She was magnificent—the voluptuous heroine of the star bout, the Juno rewriting mythology by defying the lightning as millions heard and beheld the Great Performance.

She was not the typical gunmoll, flamboyantly fascinating, tough as a bullet-proof vest, chewing gum, smoking a cigarette and answering, "Yeh—an' what're youse gonna do about it?"

She was cool, calm, coherent. She took the play away. She rambled on with her great story of how so many powerful men had given so much money to so helpless and hapless a little girl, confused by the big cities, taken under the protection of the strong and the wise.

All this time we knew what she had told the Senators in executive secret session. We knew the answer she had flung back at the beatified bulldozer, Tobey, when he asked her in effect how it had come about that these hard hoods had all pushed dough into the soft palm which had once slung hash in Chicago.

Her reply to him was that of a true champion; in fact, she claimed the championship of the world. At what, we are not going to reveal. Tobey may want it for his memoirs; and it would be the punch-line.

So, when she was put on display at this Mardi Gras in New York, the query was not repeated and the inquisitors let her do a monologue. She needed no rehearsal; she had been up against tough audiences before and had never laid an egg.

So far did she have her head that she busted out with a wild wallop at Lee Mortimer, which was not in the script. Mortimer was mortified. He had never done the girl a thing, except show up

her exact place in the workings of the international mob and
elucidate why she was in Europe when Bugsy Siegel was bumped
off in her Beverly Hills love-seat. For that she spat Chanel No. 13
at him, this Alabama whistle-stop kid who had never worn shoes
until she was sixteen, and whom Uncle Lee had pictured not as
Juno, but as Mercury—the winged messenger of the Mafia.

This spirit she had first displayed when she tried to take a sock
at Mortimer in a New York saloon. Mortimer, who had been
bopped by the best, ducked. Fools don't live to write best-sellers.

It was only later, however, that we mulled over the case of
Virginia and voted her Miss America of 1952.

We summed up her skills, her success story, her self-made
stellar eminence, her triumph over the nation's "best brains," and
her immunity against all harm.

And it was so up-to-the-minute!

Her medium was TV, which is conquering the country, which,
they all say, will make future Presidents.

Her tale was one that no passé charmer could have recited, for
it was of the system yet unknown to the multitude, dealing as it
did with fearsome but fearless figures of that type of current
manipulators who are wrapping up our money and our power.

She represented the toppling of old virtues and old habits and
the ascendancy of the new, the living, the dynamic now.

That is why we nominate her to stand as our national symbol:
the Statue of Larceny.

3. CROOKS AND RACKETEERS

A. The Sicilian Benevolent and Blood-Money Society

*L*AIT AND MORTIMER did not foresee, when they revivified
the Mafia some years ago, that they had created a new national
industry. The term, almost forgotten by the present generation,
expunged from the glossary of its own members because of its
fearsome international reputation, lay dormant. But the Mafia
not only was still alive, it had reached heights and depths un-
dreamed of by its ancient progenitors. We said so; and that set off
a Mafia wave.

Scores of investigators—Federal, state and municipal—district attorneys, crime commissions, newspaper and magazine "experts," writers of "fact" and fiction books, movie scenarists and broadcasters moved in and ate at our table, swiping material verbatim, distorting it, embroidering on it, sneering at it, speculating over it.

The chiselers, with no independent means of their own, all made the same boner when they tried to expand the drama in our brief chapters—those who accepted our copy and those who derided it. They assumed we had pictured the Mafia as an established enterprise with a suite of lavish offices and a gold-lettered front door inscribed: "Mafia. General Headquarters. Please Enter." Those who pilfered most flagrantly proceeded from that premise. Those who tried to cash in by spoofing at our revelations asked how such an institution could exist, with no one hep to it except us.

We never said it was an open going concern. We traced the birth and growing pains of the Crime Syndicate through three books. We pinned it on organized Sicilians in America. We called it the Mafia, which it is. But we did not portray it as listed in the phone book or holding open house for uninformed suckers.

Because of the crass stupidity of the Kefauver Committee—we will call it that in lieu of a more actionable noun—and the billions of words of tripe, most of it unfounded and much of it sheer fake, circulated since then, we will recapitulate a little and expand a lot on the topic, bringing it up to 1952. This is what Kefauver did not tell you about crime:

"Mafia," we will here interpolate, is a Sicilian localism applied for centuries in fear and whisper to the Black Hand extortionists who terrorized the island.

Omerta is the secret and unwritten code of the Mafia. Mafiosi and decent Italians—even Italian-Americans—and of course, ALL Sicilians, whether they are in Sicily or elsewhere, live in mortal fear of violating Omerta.

This is Omerta:

"If you are wronged, NEVER seek the help of legal authorities; NEVER render help or aid of any nature or description to properly constituted authority seeking to solve a crime, even if that crime is committed against you or yours; WHEN you take the law into your own hands, with the knowledge and consent of all MAFIOSI, be assured THE MAFIA will stand by you ALL THE WAY;

"NEVER forget that ANY violation of Omerta ALWAYS is

rewarded by your own death, or the death of a loved one—administered surely and swiftly by Mafiosi duly chosen by the top council of the Mafia;

"NEVER reveal the identity of a Mafiosi known to you, either by sight or reputation, for this constitutes the gravest of crimes against the Mafia;

"REMEMBER ALWAYS that no hand can stay the swift hand of Mafia retribution and so conduct yourself and your affairs that you cannot possibly be accused of violating Omerta."

Sicily is not Italian by origin. It has been absentee-owned since the dawn of history—by Phoenicia, Greece, Rome, France, Italy and even Britain. It is the original Ireland; the Black Hand began in the first instance as a movement of unorganized patriots who burned and destroyed homes and plantations of rich landlord owners and slew with stilettos and bombs.

Over the course of years the project went crooked, as did some Confederate guerilla bands after 1865. As time went by, if one saw the right local politician or paid off the right leader, the Black Hand letter didn't come to him but to his neighbor or competitor.

There always were and there are similar terroristic secret societies all over the world; but they are especially numerous in Mediterranean countries, where passions are strong and government transitory. They existed in great number on the Italian mainland, too. Every kingdom, dukedom and principality had its own. After the unification, most of them were destroyed. Their members fled to Sicily, where they were absorbed by the Mafia, or abroad, where they made contact with far-flung Mafia units. One of the largest so taken over was the Camorra, of Naples.

Similarly, there were terrorists in the Balkans, especially in Greece and Serbia. Racially and historically, Sicilians are closer to Greeks than to Italians. Fugitives from those countries also found welcome in Black Hand circles. In the beginning these all preyed on their own people, through primitive shakedowns. From time to time they were employed for political assassinations. When these miscarried, thousands were rounded up and sent into exile, other thousands scrammed while they could.

As early as 1850, there were Black Hand cells operating in every American city and in most parts of the world. Wherever there were Sicilian immigrants there was sure to be a Black Hand chapter, living off the proceeds of legitimate labor. Because of overpopulation and poverty, the Sicilians, like the Irish, moved on to more fertile fields.

When the 18th Amendment found an eager underground ready to take over the distribution of potables, crime was not yet organized—except into neighborhood gangs. During the early years of the booze-rush there were many independent contractors in the illicit trade who competed on equal footing with local mobs; but, as the business grew to undreamed-of proportions, the merging process set in, as it earlier had in gasoline, steel, utilities, etc.

But there was no J. P. Morgan to act as catalyst. The rum trust was fashioned the hard way, with guns and barrels of cement, when temporary trust and trade agreements were broken. In this effort the Sicilians had a head start, though they didn't know it. There were other racial mobs, too: Irish, Jews, Poles, Mainland Italians. They had no more than neighborhood ties between them. But all Sicilians were related, intermarried, or had ties from the home towns. Every Black Hand local was connected by blood with every other local; and, though they break all laws and commandments, Sicilian hoodlums are almost maniacal in their love for family.

The Sicilian conspiracy to master the underworld, with its finagling, killing, torturing and treachery, is history. The individual crimes will never be solved; most of the torpedoes who committed them and the bosses who ordered them are dead. Such puzzlers as who ordered the execution of Vincent (Mad Dog) Coll, or did Abe Reles jump or was he pushed, are now academic—minor patterns in an over-all mosaic.

After the Black Hand became rich and powerful and some of its members "respectable," the old terms for the sinister brotherhood were interdicted. It became dangerous to use them. What the peasants and serfs referred to fearfully as the Mafia came to be known in more genteel circles as the Unione Siciliano. At first the Unione did not embrace all the individual Black Hand groups, some of which remained in independent competition all through Prohibition.

During the period of Sicilian amalgamation, the non-Italian mobs realized that for their own protection they'd have to organize, too; which they did. But the best each usually could do was to set up an organization in one town. The New York Irish mob might or might not work with its opposite number in Chicago, but the Italians always did. Furthermore, there were many non-Sicilian groups which also fought each other as well as Mafistas.

During the 1930's, when the boys began to move their Prohibition wealth into other enterprises, legal and illegal, there naturally was another outbreak of violence. But Al Capone had been sent to Alcatraz and Prohibition had been repealed after a wave of public nausea over gangsters. The more far-seeing among them realized something would have to be done to bar a repetition of the mob wars of the twenties.

That was where Louis "Dutch" Goldberg, also known as Pop Shomberg, came on the scene with the brilliant idea that the underworld should appoint an impartial arbiter, as did baseball, Hollywood and the needle trades. The papers were drawn up at a meeting in Atlantic City, attended by the big boys from all over the country, at which Frank Costello presided. Goldberg was the first underworld Judge Landis. This *modus operandi* worked well for a number of years. So well, in fact, that during most of the 1930's the public forgot that gangsters had ever existed, though they were richer and more powerful than they had ever been. Goldberg also conceived the idea of supporting candidates for Federal jobs, as local gangsters long had done on ward and municipal levels.

Thus, as impartial umpire, he levied on the entire national underworld to raise a boodle fund to slip to the Democrats for Roosevelt's first re-election, in 1936, and for Lehman's tough gubernatorial fight against Tom Dewey in 1938. The Lehman money was doled out to Charlie Poletti, then Lieutenant-Governor, who returned the favor by pardoning mobsters out of Sing Sing during his month as Governor.

Lehman, now a stuffy and sanctified U.S. Senator, is fully conversant with the fact that he got underworld support in all his elections. During one, before we got smarter, Lait and Mortimer did some volunteer promotion work for his campaign committee. Mortimer happened to mention to Grace Flexner, Lehman's personal private secretary, that mobsters were again active and had raised a huge fund to back Democrats. Miss Flexner was sincere, upright and honest. She asked Mortimer if he would go to Albany the next day and give his information to Lehman. She set the appointment. Later she called and canceled it, because "the Governor had told Poletti about it and Charlie vetoed the idea." Poletti then was Lehman's legal adviser.

These were lush days for the boys, while they were making billions in legal liquor, extortion, labor rackets, etc., as well as legitimate businesses, which they were beginning to infiltrate.

But the greedy Mafistas did not keep to the arbitration agreement. Over a couple of years they eliminated all major non-

Sicilians—some through violence—*vide* Dutch Schultz and Chink Sherman—and some by helping the law take its course—as with Lepke, Gurrah, Owney Madden.

Thereafter there was no longer need for an impartial arbitrator. Poppa Goldberg was deposed and kicked out. All he has today—with permission of the Mafia, of course—is a couple of saloons and cocktail bars in New York, one on Madison Avenue, in the smart upper sixties, and the other on the tough West Side. The coppers and the liquor board know he's got them, but they shrug their shoulders. Who wants to tangle with him?

Thus, when the Sicilians took over, everything was smooth and organized and running for them, just as if a criminal syndicate had taken over baseball by capturing the Ford Frick office.

Non-Italians were given the choice of doing business or getting out. Those who did neither were disposed of. And that is how the organized underworld stands today.

This giant conspiracy has two facets. One is a loosely organized group of interlocking enterprises which we shall call the Crime Cartel, but which is also known as the Syndicate, the Big Mob, the Outfit, etc. The other is a secret blood-brotherhood with a strong centralized government and a disciplined membership. This is the Mafia, a word the members never utter, or the Unione, which they do.

One can be a member of the Crime Cartel without being a member of the Mafia. But all Mafistas are, per se, members of the Cartel. Included in the Cartel are tens of thousands of non-Sicilians as well as many Sicilians who have not taken the blood oath to the secret society. Many of the non-Unione cartelers are high in the criminal councils, may even be in equal partnership in some enterprises with top Mafistas. In some favored cases they are permitted to run some of their own operations without kickbacks.

Included in the Cartel are many of the brains of the organization, such as mouthpieces, accountants and auditors, advisors and management front-men, such as chain hotel owners, distillers, bankers, etc. Virginia Hill, the message center, is a full stockholder.

But while all members of the Mafia are members of the Cartel, not all Mafistas engage in criminal enterprises. Many are elder statesmen, practically on the retired list, enjoying their profits. Others have inherited their ranks or positions in the Mafia and live off legacies from deceased relatives. Many of the most im-

portant men in the Mafia are not actually "card-holders," a stunt
also utilized by the Reds. These are prominent and respected
Italians of whom the public hasn't the slightest suspicion, and
they include leading bankers, contractors, politicians, judges and
foreign-language newspaper publishers.

The Mafia, like all secret societies, is under strict discipline.
It also "enforces" it for the Crime Cartel, which has no such
agency of its own.

Human nature in the netherworld is pretty much as you find
it up above. There are factions, cliques and parties in the Unione
Siciliano, just as there are New Deal Democrats and Dixiecrats,
Republican internationalists and isolationists, Communist Stalinists and Titoists, and orthodox and "liberal" co-religionists. As in
Moscow, disagreement with whatever faction is ruling at the moment usually means death, though many who kick over the traces
are first offered exile and retirement.

In addition to factional fights there are frequent private feuds,
when one gangster or local group of them tries to "cut in" on the
perquisites or molls of another affiliated bunch. This happens too
in private business, where ambitious employes try to snag others'
jobs; or in politics, when a former machine member suddenly
becomes "independent" and enters a primary contest.

But in the underworld this usually results in violence, though
every effort is now made to settle the fights at high level.

A new rule now being enforced provides that a member of a
Jewish gang affiliated with the Crime Cartel may not "take" an
Italian without the permission of the Mafia, nor may the Sicilians
kill a Jew without consultation with the Jewish leaders. The same
applies to the other semi-independent mobs. The purpose is clear
—to stop indiscriminate warfare. The culprit's own group is supposed to give satisfaction to the aggrieved, and usually does. But
there is a stop clause which provides that after continual failure
to ban overt acts the "oppressed" side may kill not only the trou-
blemaker, but leaders who supported him as well. This has yet
to be used on a large scale.

Most of the recent gang rub-outs were acts of enforcement
within the Mafia itself. If a member draws too much publicity
or gets "hot" due to questioning by law enforcement authorities,
he not only is no longer of value to the organization, but becomes
a positive liability. In such instances he may be rubbed out for
the good of the group, sometimes tearfully, it is true. The big
guys also resent glamor-boy hoodlums. They are afraid they will
bring the law down, or at least the press.

The hierarchy of the Unione Siciliano is organized and complicated, like degrees in Masonry.

At the top is a Grand Council presided over by a Grand Councilor. Neither the Councilors nor the Grand Councilor are necessarily the most important members of the organization; they are the board of directors, chosen by powerful constituents and subject to change and rotation.

This year's Grand Council is composed of:

1. Vincent Mangano, New York—Grand Councilor.
2. Joseph Profaci, New York.
3. Joe Bonanno, Brooklyn.
4. Frank Milano, Akron, Ohio.
5. Vincenzo Triana, Brooklyn.
6. Paul de Lucia, Chicago, alias Paul "The Waiter" Ricca.
7. Stephano Margardino, Niagara Falls, New York.
8. Antonio Rizzotti, Los Angeles, California, alias "Jack Dragna," who sits for a brother.

Though listed as No. 2, Profaci appears to be "Mr. Big" of the Mafia—the man behind the man who is behind all the publicized "Mr. Bigs" whom naïve dabblers in the underworld like *Collier's* and CBS fall for.

The operating departments are presided over by the following:

9. Charles (Lucky) Luciano, president, International Unione Siciliano, Sicily, Italy.
10. Francisco Seriglia, president, Unione Siciliano of U.S.A., alias Frank Costello, New York City.
11. Tony Accardo, former "enforcer," succeeded the late Charles Fischetti as president of the Unione Siciliano of Illinois and vice-president of the national organization.

B. Crime But No Punishment

Under such a set-up as is described in the above section the organization controls practically all crime in the United States. That does not mean every holdup, heisting or second-story job is acted and voted on by a select committee in advance. What does happen is that, sooner or later, every underworld independent who does well enough to make a living has to join forces with or cut up with the Crime Cartel or one of its members. Crooks who make less than a bare living do not last long anyway.

All forms of dishonesty lend themselves to organization, before the act or after it. Whores need protection from arrest, bail and counsel after that. Burglars cannot operate without "fingermen" who stake them out and fences who dispose of the loot—jewels, furs or hot money. All these things must be arranged for before the crime to insure success.

Anyone who schemes up any kind of profitable racket—from crooked bookkeepers to pimps—is eventually forced to do business with the boys. If they don't, they are turned over to cops or black-mailed out of existence.

The Outfit has such terrific lines of communication, it is sure to learn about businessmen who cheat on OPS allocations or in-come taxes; merchants who sell "seconds" in place of articles as advertised; saloon-keepers who refill bottles with inferior booze; company officials who rig their stock, and servants who steal from their employers or bank tellers who take home samples. Once the Syndicate gets the word, a couple of impressively tough guys turn up. The wrong-doer suddenly discovers he's got a partner.

It is almost impossible these days to break a law more serious than a traffic offense without becoming entangled with the Crime Cartel, and one of its branches even takes care of cops' tickets. The boys have their greedy fingers out for the prominent man or woman who kills in a fit of passion as well as for the thugs who do it for a living. Once you get pinched you are on your way to be-coming a part of the machine. The criminal lawyer who defends you is probably on the mob payroll.

Perhaps you ask why all this is tolerated and how do Lait and Mortimer know about it if Kefauver couldn't find it.

The Crime Cartel raised a slush fund of more than $100,000,-000 to be used in national, state and municipal elections this fall.

The word to "dig" was sent along the line all last year by Vice-President Barkley, Howard McGrath and Joe Nunan, former In-ternal Revenue Commissioner. Democrats have had such an ar-rangement with the underworld since 1932, but the Kefauver Committee—with two Republicans on it—shied away from that hot potato.

In *Washington Confidential* we explained the formation of the committee; how Kefauver, ambitious to run for the vice-presi-dency, which he is disguising with a campaign for the top job, jumped in with a resolution to investigate the underworld, not realizing its tie-ups to political brass.

After it was too late to head it off, Barkley saved the day by naming the probers for both parties—a violation of unwritten law. He chose, in addition to Estes, Democrats O'Conor of Maryland, from a corrupt machine, and Hunt, of Wyoming, a small-town dentist; Republicans Tobey, of New Hampshire, a puritanical faker, and Wiley, of Wisconsin, sincere, but one Barkley knew could not be at meetings, because of more pressing interests.

For chief counsel the committee hired Rudy Halley, a cold, shrewd and scheming New York attorney with safe political connections. Halley was picked by Judge Ferdinand Pecora. Charges that Pecora was Frank Costello's choice for Mayor and that Halley had represented a traction company in which gangsters had oodles of stock were never convincingly refuted. A special act of Congress permitted Halley to retain his $76,000 annual law practice which included actions against the government.

As soon as the committee went to work, it became obvious to insiders that rumors of payoffs to some of its key personnel were not far-fetched. One investigator told us $50,000 was passed in Miami to keep one witness off the stand. We know that another $50,000 was handed over to immunize the Hollywood movie industry. We know $100,000 was collected in Chicago. The Costello mob turned over another $100,000 to insulate Costello so his ordeal on the stand would amount to no more than window-dressing for the circus. Meanwhile, he was asked certain planted questions which now, under Supreme Court rulings, make him immune against Federal prosecution on old tax raps. The most that will happen to him is an easy contempt conviction—a misdemeanor. We were advised to bet he never serves a day.

From this vantage point, a year later, try to remember the hearings. It sounded swell and exciting then—with Tobey calling down the wrath of heaven, Kefauver, stern and judicial, giving every man his chance, and Halley, the relentless prosecutor. But what did they bring up? Nothing that was not already known and in print; and very little of that. The sexomanes had a field day with Virginia Hill; Bill O'Dwyer was sweated, and Costello didn't come up as smart as he'd been painted, though he put on an act requiring forethought and rehearsing to keep the show going without incriminating him.

We have intensively studied the eighteen-volume record of the hearings—printed at government expense—and found nothing beyond rhetorical mentions of the Mafia and the Big Mob. Not one of its important figures was bothered beyond an anemic contempt citation.

Many were subpoenaed, but newspapers were told in advance, and prospective witnesses scrammed. No other cops tip their mitts

until they've made their collars, but Halley and Kefauver tele-
graphed their punches.

Many of those Halley said were missing weren't; they could
have been picked up in fifteen minutes. During all the hue and
cry, Irving Sherman was staying at the Saxony Hotel, in Miami
Beach. Joe Adonis dined at Lindy's in the midst of the man-hunt,
then visited a yacht anchored off Brien McMahon's bailiwick in
Connecticut. The yacht belonged to one of McMahon's supporters. At the height of the search for Longie Zwillman, he dined with
Costello at the Waldorf Men's Bar, then went visiting in Engle-
wood Cliffs, New Jersey. We published the foregoing in newspaper columns while Keystone comedy sleuths were supposed to
be looking for the lamisters. No attempt was made to follow our
leads. When the committee announced with fanfare that it was
determined to question Charlie Fischetti and Sam Maceo, both
suddenly died "natural deaths," in the same week. Some suspicious
souls are unkind enough to suggest that if the boys didn't help
nature along, maybe they substituted other stiffs while Charlie
and Sam went to live under assumed names and plastic-surgically
assumed faces in Italy, Morocco or Mexico. Could be.

No important Mafista was even worried. The few brought before the committee to make it look good were asked innocuous
questions—all planned in advance—and were cited for contempt
(also per plan) with causes so flimsy the courts or juries would
throw them out.

We got the legal lowdown on what the Kefauver Committee
was doing while it was going and told Kefauver, in our suite at the
Carlton, in the presence of attorneys, that Halley's questions were
covering the rascals with a blanket of immunity. He denied it.
The record shows we were right. In only a few cases did any malefactor run into serious trouble.

In *Washington Confidential* we told how Bill Drury, former
Chicago police captain, who had been fired from the crookedest
force in the world because he was too honest—tried to cooperate
with the committee. Bill and his ex-partner, Captain Tom Connelly, knew more about the organized underworld than Kefauver
will know if he lives to be a hundred. Halley vetoed their appearance after he learned they had been investigating the mob tie-up
in the traction company he had represented. A few days later,
Bill Drury was ambushed and murdered.

We spoke to Drury shortly before that assassination. We know
why he was killed. Though we are not cops, we offered to give

the facts to the committee. We were not called. We publicly dared the committee to call us. Nothing happened. We sought no publicity, were willing to talk in an executive session. We still are.

Shortly before the road-show came to New York, an agent of Senator Kefauver called on prominent businessmen, suggesting they "contribute to Kefauver's vice-presidential campaign." We know the man had acted as an agent of Estes, who had introduced him to us as such. "Why, he practically elected me Senator," Kefauver told us.

Among those this Kefauver advance man approached was Clendenin Ryan, heir to the copper fortune. Ryan devotes his time and money to purifying Gotham. He was told that for $5,000 he could sit on the dais at Foley Square with Kefauver and take credit "for cleaning up New York."

Now let's see what's left of crime since the plumed knight from Chattanooga "destroyed" the underworld.

The only tangible result of his comic opera on video was a nationwide wave of raids on penny-ante poker games, park-petters and ginmills that sell drinks after hours. Blue-noses are temporarily in power. In some towns they closed the plush gambling casinos, though more often they devoted themselves to picking on pinball. The vice dicks take it out on operators of amusement park games, such as rolling balls, which were closed up at Savin Park, New Haven. Gumshoes are having a field day chasing mashers and shaking them down. But the organized underworld is unmolested in the things that count, like dope, union rackets, protection, hijacking, counterfeiting, smuggling, blackmail, bootlegging and moonshining, and political shakedowns, while the authorities drive out amateurs and independents. When the heat is off again these lone wolves will have disappeared, leaving the way open for the big mob to pick up even the formerly unorganized petty vices if it wants them.

In our former books we showed how the crime syndicate has invested billions in legitimate enterprises. That process is still going on. The boys suddenly fell in love with petroleum and are funneling great sums into Texas and Oklahoma oil fields.

Now that they are firmly entrenched in Wall Street, through stock ownership in important companies, they are discovering profitable tactics in playing the market their way. Some of their gimmicks:

They milk treasuries of companies in which they infiltrate.

They promote strikes in big industries, to break stock market prices and to buy in on them.

They use their huge holdings in legitimate securities to rig the market, making prices go up or down as they will, a felony. The SEC knows about all that, but takes no action.

Underworld holdings in the liquor business probably represent the greatest single concentration of wealth in the entire world. Considerably more than three-quarters of American, Canadian and Scotch distilleries and French and American vineyards, as well as many breweries, have come into their possession. They own also most of the state distributorships and local wholesalers.

The syndicate recently discovered another profitable source of "legitimate" enterprise—the small loan business. This is right up their alley, because many graduated as street-corner, waterfront and factory shylocks. They are buying stock in some nationwide personal loan companies and setting up their own independent ones in states where laws are liberal. The traffic is a set-up for them. Not only do they milk unfortunates with all kinds of trick commissions, interest, insurance, bonuses and investigation fees so a borrower never gets out of hock—but they make it a perfect cover and front to finance illegal operations.

Top mobsters have given up personal operation of the rackets, acting instead as bankers. They "lend" money to actual entrepreneurs, who pay back profits as interest and bonus on notes of hand. This keeps the boys in the clear, because they can always claim they did not know for what the money was to be used.

New tax laws and other drives have made it necessary that the entire bookmaking system be reorganized. Small loan banking is handy. Runners no longer act as agents for bookmakers. Each conducts his own piker book—and settles up with the overlords at the end of the week or month, turning over profits as "payment on a note" or taking money to cover losses—as "a loan." It is just humanly impossible to track down every elevator operator, cigar store clerk and newsboy who keeps his bookmaking office in his hat.

The boys also infiltrated into broadcasting. Former Governor James M. Cox, of Ohio, testified that Arthur McBride, Cleveland wire service operator, was a friend of Al Capone, but the FCC issued a license permitting the transfer of radio station WMIE in Miami to the Sun Coast Broadcasting Company, principally owned by McBride.

They love show business because that's one field they're used to from days dating back to when they owned most of the major cafes and backed a lot of Broadway legits. The hoodlums are tied up with some of the larger theatrical booking agencies and take percentages running as high as half the earnings of some of the new $10,000-a-week video and film stars whom they plugged on the way to fame in plush night clubs like the Copacabana. A photo of Sinatra with two noted racket boys was extracted mysteriously from the files of the Kefauver Committee. But we have the original.

Sinatra has always been a mob property, but he costs them money, always suffering from the "shorts" as a result of his heart-troubles and other indiscretions. But the gangsters get a full return from him by using him as a stalking horse to make themselves and their enterprises respectable. Sinatra, a great favorite of young Henry Ford, introduced the auto magnate to some of the infamous Fischettis. It is probably a coincidence that many of the Ford agencies in the country are now owned by hoodlums. Another business the mob is interested in is undertaking and mortuaries—don't laugh. They're not in it because they manufacture their own corpses, either. One advantage is easy disposal of bodies by including them in coffins with innocent stiffs and performing burials with legitimate death certificates. Contraband such as dope, smuggled jewelry and hot money can be moved as bodies are shipped from town to town. Also, graves and mausoleums provide ideal places to hide money, stolen goods, and the books of illegal enterprises. For long concealment these are buried in coffins. They can always be retrieved by having a "relative" decide to move the remains to another cemetery. Short-time stuff is put on ice in family fire-proof, burglar-proof vaults that can be entered by the owners at any time. An officer of a textile company, who made millions in the black market through deals with Frank Costello, hides his loot in such a place. He goes to visit it on moonless nights. His only fear is that when he goes, he *will* take it with him.

C. Hoodlums' Hoppy Hunting Ground

As 1952 dawned, the American underworld was a nation within a nation, supporting a population larger than that of Canada. This well-organized and semi-sovereign state was happy and prosperous. It had weathered a rash of investigations, probes and shutdowns in good fashion. It was still rolling, probably more powerful than ever.

Like all huge enterprises, the criminal empire was flexible and knew how to adjust itself to changing conditions, technological improvements and the march of time. Wherever public demand

or conscience decreed that a particular form of misdeed was verboten the underworld pulled in and sent its forces out under new
alignments.

From the very beginning, the Kefauver probe—and its local
copies—was sighted against gambling; a misdemeanor easy to dig
up without effort or skill, because it exists everywhere. It conveys
no moral turpitude in the public mind. The Big Mob arranged
that it should be that way—they knew the taxpayers would not
support a shutdown on wagering. In truth, the organization benefited by temporary clean-ups, which drove the few remaining independents out, leaving the field open for capture by the Mafia as
soon as the agitation wears off.

The underworld continued to learn and profit by the lessons of
1951. It began to smell that horse-racing may be on the way out
as the prime source of betting. Even before the Washington hearings, chumps in many parts of the country had ceased betting on
nags—were trying to outsmart point predictions in basketball and
football instead. In the Southwest this had far surpassed the racing take. In Wichita, Kansas, football bookmakers were running
raw; you couldn't even get the odds on a pony.

In many communities citizens are beginning to sour on tracks,
seeing them as the source of all evil. A powerful movement is
afoot in California to repeal the law permitting racing and pari-
mutuel betting. Governor Warren and Los Angeles' Mayor Bowron are sympathetic to the idea, as are many merchants and
bankers who contend that when tracks run they absorb the loose
money in the vicinity.

The new tax laws aimed at bookmakers will undoubtedly affect
the course of betting. People will find other outlets for their gambling urges. When the man on the street loses interest in the sport
of kings, first-class tracks and huge stables will go busted. With
this in mind, the mob held a meeting in Cleveland, around the
first of the year, and considered closing the tracks they own,
though it would be a windfall for ministerial, civic and reform
groups, always panting to ban racing by law.

One of the mob's prime considerations is that tracks and bookmakers are taking money out of saloons, and indirectly out of the
liquor industry, almost a criminal monopoly. While the books
were going good they provided so much money that the liquor
angle was secondary, but now, with certain forms of gambling
hedged in with restrictions which make them unpredictably unprofitable and possibly dangerous, the big boys would as soon
get out.

Gambling was the last major racket they organized and they were never too happy about it. After Repeal, the Mafia devoted its energies to unions, moonshine and extortion. Its next field was narcotics. After that had been absorbed, it restlessly sought new worlds to conquer. Many members of the Crime Cartel were gamblers on the side. Until 1946 there was no over-all attempt to tie gambling up into a trust. The unification process did not succeed until 1949.

Gambling has many disadvantages. It calls for tremendous overhead, vast organization and terrific leaks in the form of ice and protection to every guy with a badge from a cop on the beat to state troopers. But it held a populous criminal organization together and provided out-of-season work for hundreds of thousands. Another use was to disguise the transfer of hot money. Bribes, payoffs, kickbacks and other funds which must be moved can be pushed over a crap or roulette table to make it look as if the remittee won the money, instead of being paid off. Similarly, the horse-wire is utilized to send money from branches to Mafia headquarters by making it appear sums so transmitted are rental fees for the use of the wire.

Do not think the Federal tax act has ended bookmaking or policy-slip selling. The latter is not concerned as the transactions are small and any salesman sells so few, evidence is scarce and dealings are picayune, though they add up to fantastic takes. In many big cities, most of the numbers pushers are Negroes—so that doesn't count.

The bookmaking industry was vitally affected by the new tax. It is meeting the menace to its vested interest in different manners in various parts of the country, depending on the local situation. When the new bite took effect last November, almost all large operators temporarily went underground. The big boys took their vacations. To them a shutdown of even a year or longer is just a hazard of the trade, discounted in advance. The errand boys, runners and pushers could not take it that way. Most of them make up to $100 a week when it's good. A few kept on going in the beginning, chancing a pinch. Others became dope-sellers, accounting for the new wave of narcotics. Others bought guns and became stick-up men and burglars. Some crime categories leaped up 20 per cent. This process had begun as soon as Kefauver publicity caused some local authorities to knock down gambling.

The only victim of the Kefauver Committee or of any other drive was bookmaking. The more serious and profitable crimes were not touched, are not touched and will not be touched. It is almost as if a huge nationwide conspiracy of "law enforcement" officers, congressmen and legislators had decided to pick on gambling so more venal felonies could operate without peril while the public's mind was engrossed with the spectacle of bookmaking being eradicated.

The Federal gambling stamp and 10 per cent tax were not designed to raise revenue. The end purpose is to kill gambling, which it will not do, but which will cost Uncle Sam more than $3,000,000,000 a year in income taxes that gamblers used to pay. Now they will pay neither their income taxes nor the tithe for excise, on the theory that it will be as easy to fight a rap for both as for one.

A dozen different dodges have been set up and are being developed to beat the law. We have explained how runners are becoming independent contractors and "borrow" from their bosses, who are now "bankers." Instead of having central locations or fixed spots, bookies now make "social calls" on patrons and accept "friendly" bets. Phone wagers are no longer called in. The bookmaker phones his customers at set times from booths. Transactions are no longer payed off by check, only in cash. Regular customers are allowed charge accounts and settle periodically.

The problem of suppressing gambling is like all others as to vice and crime: where local authorities can be reached, bookmaking will continue to run; in such jurisdictions they will take out Federal $50 stamps, knowing the local cops will not act, though their addresses are published. The police always knew where they were—especially on Saturday nights, when they came around for the gravy. The stamp will prevent Federal prosecution. Their returns will declare only a small part of their business, keeping special books for the purpose.

Wyoming, home of Senator Hunt of the Kefauver Committee, is an example of how these things work. During the first month of the new tax, professional gamblers took out 181 Federal stamps in crime-buster Hunt's back yard—about ten times as many as the total sold in all of wicked New York state. These 181 are still violating Wyoming laws. Hunt does not hunt them down. Despite the planted publicity that bookmakers had thrown in the sponge, more than 7,000 stamps were sold in the first two months, indicating that more than 100,000 are still in business.

In other jurisdictions, where gamblers do not take out stamps, the payoff price to local bulls has doubled or tripled. If gamblers are taken to court and get a suspended sentence or nominal fine,

Feds will get their names and nail them for operating without a "use" stamp. Arrests for bookmaking have fallen all over the country—not because there is that much less gambling, but because there is that much more payoff.

Gambling is a human appetite, like sex and drinking. No law will curb it. The more law, the more violation and the more profitable the rackets, despite even more bribes to officials. Prohibition taught us that.

Table gambling is exempt from the new tax, so bookmakers are now going in for craps, faro and poker, stud and draw.

When Congress passed the law forbidding the interstate transportation of slot-machines those who proposed it tried to hamstring J. Edgar Hoover and the FBI. They tossed it into his lap as they now want to give him the enforcement of all street-level vice, not because they want to clean up the country but because they think they can take him off subversives and set him chicken-feed-chasing. Reds, pinks, all degrees of progressives and traitors hate the FBI, their prime enemy. They will go to any extent to destroy it. They want it to be a national police force, hoping that when it expands overnight, with inexperienced and untested agents handling juicy things like gambling, sex and liquor, the now honest, fearless FBI will go the way of the revenooers in the 1920's. Once that happens, America will be a pushover for the fifth column.

Hoover is the only man in government who, since 1933, consistently realized the extent of the Communist menace. If the Reds can send his men snooping on streetwalkers, as they now have them hunting slot-machines crossing state lines, those who would sell America to the Marxists will have won a victory beyond any on a field of battle. Hoover knows it. He opposes a national police force, seeing it as an arm of Fascism. He fights attempts to saddle the FBI with duties that belong to local authorities. When they slipped him the hot slot-machines they thought they'd embarrass him. But Hoover sent his boys out and closed the interstate traffic so fast they're still blinking. But there is no law, can be no Federal law, stopping slot-machine makers from decentralizing and setting up factories in every state. That is what they are doing.

There are some 300,000 machines on which the Federal "use" stamp has been paid operating post-Kefauver. Save in Nevada, they are illegal all over.

The new law took one-armed bandits out of army posts and

officers' clubs here, but air force planes flew them to overseas bases in Guam, the Azores, Europe and Asia, where our expeditionary forces still contribute to Frank Costello.

We were accused of exaggeration in our previous books when we told about the narcotics menace. We were the first to talk about it openly and we were branded liars by public officials, settlement-house workers and frightened old ladies. But we cannot overemphasize the diabolical evil now. Since our last publication, only a year ago, it has tripled.

Government and municipal officials try to underplay it, but once in a while official, but confidential, figures leak out. Experts employed by the Public Health Service secretly estimate at least 300,000 school-age addicts in the country. That's the number they know of, who have been arrested, observed, reported or who have taken treatment. The total may be a million. It takes from one to five years for a user to become an addict, so there are no statistics on undisclosed juvenile or other users.

Your average healthy American refuses to face these facts. When we were in Omaha, the *World-Herald* editorially castigated us, said there was no reefer-smoking in its schools. Our figures are that at least 25 per cent of the teen-agers in Central High School alone smoke the weed from time to time. When we were in Wichita, the neighboring *Topeka capital* agreed that Wichita was probably full of dope-fiends, but not Topeka. Yet we saw a pusher selling junk to two kids around the corner from the Governor's office.

Dope is big business. Though its gross is considerably smaller than the booze turnover, in actual profits it is among the world's richest. Narcotics require little handling, overhead and manpower. The uncut dope that sells for $10,000 in Asia will bring $1,000,000 on the retail market and can be carried into the country by one man. The industry does not need warehouses, cases, trucks and retail outlets. The stuff is peddled on the street. There is no payroll; each step in distribution is done by an independent contractor, buying outright for cash, down to the pusher, who sells $1 heroin caps for $1.50 in Harlem.

The big boys never come in physical contact with the contraband in this country. They act solely as bankers. They lend money on notes to traders who go abroad to make purchases. They get theirs back when the junk arrives here and is resold to wholesalers. The Mafia's hand cuts in on the dope at several points. The first comes after the trader arranges for its purchase abroad, then

Mafia agents in Italy or the Orient arrange for its shipment here via smugglers and couriers in its employ—usually seamen on merchant ships.

Though little dope is produced in Italy, that country is to narcotics what Holland was to diamonds and England is to casualty insurance; the world exchange or bourse for dope is there. It is now Italy's single largest source of revenue.

The Italian government frequently bluffs it out by pinching operators caught sending stuff to the U.S. and convicting them, which is duly recorded here; the next day the sentences are commuted or the felons are pardoned. "Lucky" Luciano, deported New York vice overlord, is the richest man in Italy and pays off half the government and most of the cops.

Though he will probably deny this for "policy," we can assure you that Harry S. Anslinger, Commissioner of the U.S. Bureau of Narcotics, has often called on the State Department for measures to cut off the flow of dope from Italy. Acheson's dumb daisies reply that we cannot do that: Italy needs the money it gets from junk and if we don't let them keep their "little racket" it might go Communist. What the boys mean in English is that if the Italian politicians can't keep their gold mine they might sell out; but since when does State care if "agrarian reformers" take over?

Actually, the Italian government works hand in hand with Commies on the importation of the dream powder. All white stuff, i.e., morphine and heroin, etc., is derived from opium. The major source of opium is behind the Curtain, where Italian Mafistas buy it with good American money.

The close ties between the Italian government and the Mafia were startlingly shown, but not printed or openly discussed during the recent American fund-raising tour of Premier de Gasperi. In almost every city he visited, noted members of the Mafia sat on the dais with him at official parties. In Detroit, four Sicilians cited by Anslinger to the Kefauver Committee—but not bothered, natch —were at his elbow.

Junk-smuggling is closely tied up with other forms of border violations, such as movements of aliens and jewels into the U.S. and transportation of money, securities and gold. The Mafia owns private airports in all parts of the country where their smuggling operations will not be observed closely. Shipping unions work with them. The Customs and Immigration Services can be "seen." One manner in which the rake-off works is to permit Customs to seize a certain amount of contraband, then sell it back to the crooks.

These are some sidelights on the dope situation in America:

Dope-peddlers operate in hospitals, jails and asylums as well as in schools. There is not a prison in the country where inmates cannot buy junk. Some of the worst are Joliet, Canon City and the Federal Big House at Leavenworth. The same sources that sell dope to prisoners supply booze and girls. At the Cook County Jail a guard will deliver a dame for $25.

Negroes have been organized into a ring to steal government checks from mail boxes. This is a colored man's closed business, because so many are employed as apartment house janitors, elevator operators and handymen. They attract no attention around the mail boxes. In return for the checks, which are turned over to the Crime Cartel through crooked cashing services and neighborhood grocery stores which the mob has been going into in a big way, they are given dope, the acceptance and possession of which is a crime, so the secret is doubly protected.

One of the tie-ups between dope and gambling is through the stickmen in the casinos who, themselves, are usually addicts and almost always pimps. Most croupiers and dealers usually have from three to five girls in their stables, kept in line by putting them on junk and in return taking all they make for drugs.

As profitable as dope is, it also enables the Crime Cartel to recruit and keep together a tight underworld organization. School-kids are started out with free samples. The eventual purpose is not to get their few pennies when they become addicted, but to force them into prostitution and crime to support their addiction. It costs from $200 to $500 a week to keep up with a heroin habit and up to $1,000 a week for cocaine. Once a victim is really hooked, the money must be raised, regardless of the consequences. Boys become killers, burglars, stick-up men, dope pushers or anything; girls are turned over for prostitution, blackmail or extortion. In every case, the Mafia garners almost all their earnings as payment for the dope, on which they control the price.

This fits nicely into the ideas of the Reds. They not only get fortunes for having supplied the dope in the first place, but it helps them promote civil disorder here. A definite tie-up exists between Communists and the narcotics traffic. In some instances they are allied directly with the Italian underworld mob; in other cases they have working agreements.

The Kremlin will, of course, work with anyone who serves its purpose. Likewise, the underworld will do business with anyone who pays.

The key tie-up is Frank Costello's association with Marcantonio, through "Three-Finger Brown" Luchese.

These are not isolated coincidences:

1. Lucky Luciano's defense attorney in Havana was the official head of the Cuban Communist party, a senator.

2. Tactics of all would-be conquerors include flooding the prospective enemy's country with drugs, to weaken the will of the people. Japan did it in China, Germany in Poland.

3. Drugs represent the most easily portable form of wealth. One man can carry a million dollars' worth of uncut narcotics in a belt. Importation serves two purposes, providing money to support an extensive underground and bringing gold and dollar exchange back to Russia, transfer of which is arranged in reverse through the same route by which the dope got here.

4. New York dope-peddlers are imported from Puerto Rico to sell junk and vote for Marcantonio. Some are kept here three months, sent back and replaced by new imports. If pinched, they never open their mouths; they'd be knocked off if they did. For every one seized, two more are brought from Puerto Rico and sent out to peddle on the day of arrival.

With the organized gangsters working on one side and the Communists and pinks on the other to turn Americans into addicts, one is not surprised to see from what exalted sources the junk-ring gets aid and comfort. The late Fiorello La Guardia, New York's pink little stink-weed, commissioned a committee of dizzy do-gooders to report on the reefer situation. They came up with a statement that looked as if they were on the hop themselves, which La Guardia issued under his imprimatur. It said marijuana is not harmful or habit forming—less dangerous than cigarettes or coffee. As will be shown in another chapter, La Guardia was, despite his comic opera protestations to the contrary, on close personal and financial terms with the Mafia. The worldwide dope headquarters are in his old East Harlem district, which he turned over to his faithful secretary, Marcantonio.

The *New Yorker* magazine, noted for its pro-Red bias, recently did what was supposed to be an exhaustive survey on narcotic addiction in East Harlem among Negro and Puerto Rican children. Their families do not read the *New Yorker,* but rich and impractical leftists do, and they have become molders of public opinion. The *New Yorker* reporter questioned a Dr. Zimmering about the use of heroin by teen-age boys, who, the reporter said, had tried the drug several times and not been hooked. (Note the subtlety of this inference, that it is possible to use drugs without becoming addicted.)

"It's no sign of abnormality if a boy tries drugs once or twice," Dr. Zimmering said. "It's only natural, I suppose. If he's an aggressive kid—one who goes after what he wants, and finds pleasure in his daily activities, and knows he has a reasonable chance of succeeding in what he wants to do—he isn't apt to become an addict. He'll just play around with it briefly, out of curiosity, and then drop it."

Catch the joker? It infers that it is natural for boys who are going to get ahead in the world to use the filthy stuff.

Early in 1952 the left-sympathizing *Harper's* magazine came up with a typically inspired piece claiming the present dope scare is a phony—that there are only half as many addicts now as there were a generation ago.

One result of the abortive Kefauver hearings, which ignored narcotics other than to glamorize a couple of thirteen-year-old girl addicts, is that junk is bigger than ever. Kefauver and Tobey advertised it so that millions of other kids were tempted to try it. Then agents had to go out and make arrests of sidewalk peddlers, addicts and children for the record, to quiet the hullabaloo. Now there aren't enough agents or city cops to go after the top men, who alone matter. You could fill the jail with pushers and there would be as many on the street as there were the day before. When you read inspired stories that wholesale raids have busted the racket, don't believe them. The major criminals are never touched, these are merely retailers.

During our junket across country we were asked by many citizens how they could spot dope addiction among youngsters. Among the give-away signs are trembling hands, shifty glistening dilated eyes, unusually sallow complexion, wan cheeks, loss of appetite and weight, restlessness and sleeplessness, itching, scratching, sudden bursts of energy when under the influence and listlessness at other times, frequent yawning and sneezing and running eyes and nose. Those who sniff are apt to have red nostrils. Those who use it hypodermically will have tiny punctures or rashes on their arms, legs or abdomens.

The following tips for spotting narcotic activity are not ours, they are from the files of the New York Police Department.

The patrolman on school crossing post shall give constant attention to:

1. Candy stores, luncheonettes, "jive" joints, billiard rooms and other places frequented by teen-agers or places where there is constant activity.

2. Rooming houses and apartment houses where there is an unusual amount of traffic in and out.

3. Corner hangouts frequented by older boys and girls.

4. One individual on a street who seems to be doing "business" with many persons.

5. Older boys or men hanging around junior and senior high schools.

6. Groups at amusement areas such as Times Square or Coney Island or parks, who seem to meet frequently and late at night.

7. Teensters smoking in groups—on street corners or in basements or hallways. They may be puffing marijuana.

8. Well-dressed "sharp" individuals who hang about and seem to have no employment.

What the police are up against is emphasized in one sentence.

"The profits derived from this illegal commerce are so enormous that the reputed profits from bookmaking and gambling seem infinitesimal in comparison."

And they said we were nuts!

D. The Wave of the Future

Second and third generations of Mafistas are in business: children and grandchildren who inherited giant underworld fortunes which require constant ingenuity and daring bravado to keep them expanding. We have seen what happened to the heirs of the Wall Street pirates who got soft. The Crime Cartelers have no such intentions.

The mob had not been in dope very long before it discovered an uneconomical leak. Those who transported junk had to travel back empty-handed for another load. Experts figured the overhead would be no greater if carriers took something out with them. From that developed the idea of smuggling gold out of the country—the only commodity forbidden by law for export. This brought another complication: you can buy gold only under license for commercial purposes.

So the boys quickly got into jewelry and other manufacturing businesses needing gold. Frank Costello tried to get his personal dentist appointed as government assayer, but the Senate turned down Truman's nomination. Other gold is bought noncommercially by hundreds of assigned dummies who purchase less than an ounce at a time, and are not required to register. When this gold is sold abroad it is worth more than its weight in gold. It brings a 1000-per cent premium in the black market.

Other experts realized many Mafistas owned interstate trucking lines. This came as a natural development, for many Italians had started as one-wagon peddlers or one-truck haulers. During Prohibition they transported booze, growing immensely wealthy and reinvesting in more trucks. This was a business they knew and liked, so they began buying stock on the exchange in big, legitimate long-haul lines like Keeshin. Still other schemers figured they were chumps to be satisfied with merely legitimate trucking profits, though with their ins they paid less taxes, got higher than market rates for government contract work and kept competitors out with strong-arm tactics or strikes. So they worked out a plan to turn the taxpayers' highways into rights-of-way for the transportation of hot gems, women and dope. Untaxed liquor is moved during the night by ostensibly legitimate firms which also have crews on the highways hijacking non-gangster-owned trucks. Drivers get $25 to deliver a whore. Dope, stolen goods and liquor bring various prices, depending on the distance, risk and size of load. Each driver is permitted to carry a little contraband on his own account.

Experts also discovered the possibilities of credit bureaus. They seduced a few key employes in many major agencies, whom they use as locators, casers and steerers for gamblers and con-men, as well as a constant source of information for blackmailers.

The Mafia had also taken over the age-old racket of running arms across the border. The huge illicit profits from this are not enough for their insatiable appetites. Instead of buying guns through regular channels, they now steal from United States arsenals. Al Howard (square monicker Al Contento), an Italian with a long record, recently smuggled $180,000 worth of guns filched from an arsenal into Mexico and the Mexican government used diplomatic pressure to prevent his prosecution here.

In our chapter in *Chicago Confidential* called "Mafia Rose" we told how the underworld had improved on the old-type gun moll through the use of an intelligent broad like Virginia Hill, who was and is used as a message and communications center.

Another parallel between the Crime Cartel and big business is the fact that the operations are now specialized, with fulltime experts retained for various jobs.

Some lawyers and others do nothing but scheme how to bring Sicilians into the country, to be used as new recruits for the machine. Others are occupied exclusively bringing exiled Italians back, legally or illegally. Through this bureau Joe Cappolo, who had been bounced from the country and was known to be operating in Mexico, left there mysteriously, and is now active in Miami.

A new trick is being prepared to bring "Lucky" Luciano back. Brilliant mouthpieces are trying to needle U.S. authorities to extradite him from Italy on a narcotics smuggling conspiracy charge. If he were brought here to stand trial and were acquitted, he could not be tried on any other outstanding charge, nor could he be deported again. The law provides that if you force a man to come unwillingly you cannot thereafter chase him out. The proper price has been passed to the right boys in Justice for an indictment with an assured acquittal. The one hitch is that Italian law will not permit the extradition to a foreign country of an Italian citizen, who may be tried only in Italy for offenses committed anywhere. If Lucky waives that technicality he must waive his right to future immunity here.

Other experts figure how to glamorize the gangsters, through association with movie stars, friendly interviews in newspapers and magazines, charitable contributions, etc. One example of how this works occurred recently in Los Angeles, when a noted woman author of children's stories was introduced through the underworld's glorifying department to Mickey Cohen. She mentioned she was going to Boston. Cohen said he had a friend there who would call her up. It turned out to be the nefarious Rocky Palladino, who took her out and told her all about himself. She thought him a wonderfully salty character. Now she writes stories for children about him and his horses.

The sport of kings is not the only interest the underworld takes in nags, by the way. The Mafia has organized the trade in horse meat masquerading as beef, with pay-offs to crooks in the Department of Agriculture. Don't be surprised if your next hamburger neighs.

The following is an example of why today's kids do not fear the penalties of a life of crime. We introduce you to Salvatore Capito, alias Sal Caputo, a beetle-browed tough from Brooklyn.

For several years he worked as a sparring partner for Max Baer; he gained entry to cafe society and was to marry Mary Kirk Brown, a publicized glamour doll, until her mother learned of his criminal record and prevailed on her to call it off.

His known record goes back to 1931 when, at the age of nineteen, he was convicted of petty larceny after an auto theft. A month later he was again arrested and pleaded guilty to petty larceny and robbery, but the sentences were suspended along with those imposed on the first conviction.

In 1940 he drew a six-month sentence in the workhouse when he stole two fur pieces from a waitress. But by 1947 he was residing in the swank Hotel Marguery on Park Avenue, buying and selling surplus merchandise in the black market and making book. He was again arrested in 1947 in connection with a framed card game in the Marguery where it was charged victims were swindled by the use of mirrors. He beat this rap.

Now comes the pip!

Sal bought a second-hand Ford and painted it to look like a U.S. mail truck. He rented two mailmen's uniforms from a costumer, got an assistant, one Ernesto Jecon Ryfkogel, and pulled up daily in front of a branch post office which handled valuable shipments from the New York ladies-wear garment center. Sal and his man jumped on the platform, loaded their truck and rode away. Before they were nabbed their loot ran into a million.

There's an old underworld axiom that you can't fool with Uncle Whiskers. The Post Office is supposed to be toughest of all. When we heard about Sal, we figured he'd get at least twenty years—impersonating a mailman, robbing the mails, conspiracy and more.

He pleaded guilty to two counts. We read that he got a "stiff" twenty-seven months. A few days later we saw him at the Copacabana with Joe Adonis and a couple of bimbos. We did a little checking to see how come he was out. After the judge sentenced him in open court, in the presence of the press, he changed his mind in his chambers and gave Sal a suspended sentence, which was not printed.

But a mailclerk is doing three years in Atlanta for stealing a registered package worth less than $10.

E. Hope of the Future

J. Edgar Hoover said, "Present-day crime no longer bears a label to separate it from honesty."

He meant that impractical idealists no longer consider lawlessness as anti-social; on the contrary, they pamper criminals and blame society. But crime does not take root in underprivilege alone. It flourishes where there is overprivilege, too. Marxists long promised crime would end when poverty ends. The Fair Dealers now tell us America was never so rich. So why is there more crime than there was when bosses enslaved starving workers? Why is there more juvenile delinquency since child labor was abolished than in the evil days when infants toiled in cotton mills?

Could it be that coddling the young has led them to incorrigibility?

The process is in the modern mood of parents who suddenly have more money to spend than is good for them, "scientific" social workers, teachers, preachers and the law.

The case histories of American communities, which follow, indicate that crime, among both whites and Negroes, is higher in rich states than in poor ones. Plutocratic New York is worse than impoverished Mississippi.

Young vandals cost the New York Board of Education more than $500,000 yearly to repair their ravages, indicating a national damage bill of $10,000,000.

Though the *New York Times* reviewer who reads these pages will probably say we are archaic, because "progressive education," which the paper espouses, alibis kid crime, juve delinqs and teenage gangs have virtually taken over some Gotham schools and turned them into iniquitous hotbeds of sin, lawlessness and violence.

In such asylums of privacy, roving gangs settle grudge fights, break windows and steal the pipes out of the walls. The yards harbor degenerates, drunks and dope-fiends. The situation is so desperate, teachers of some New York public schools are forced to travel in numbers for personal safety or risk a switch knife slashing or gang mauling.

The richer a town, the more astronomical its juvenile delinquency rate. Rich suburbs are plagued by waves of teen-age rowdyism, rape, burglary, mayhem, mugging and marijuana addiction. Well-to-do parents clamp down on police who attempt action. In many a wealthy community, like Senator Kefauver's home, Lookout Mountain, outside Chattanooga, and Grosse Point, near Detroit, as well as New York's Westchester County, pupils not accepted in the gangs are robbed, slugged, stabbed and shot.

In a high-class high school in Philadelphia a Nazi group (they gave the Hitler salute) burned and stoned synagogues and planned to attack Catholic houses of worship next.

Upper-class kids are indulged by parents. Poorer ones get kid-glove handling from professional social workers, appointed by politicians. There are more votes in hoi polloi.

An example of how this works comes from New York's Harlem, where Dorothy B. Fleming, an impractical welfare worker, got a new idea on how to change the attitude of tough kids. She figured she'd get at them through their girl friends. So she went to work on the female auxiliary of a Negro teen-age mob. When we told in detail of such gangs in *New York Confidential,* we were accused of "libeling a whole race" by our first publisher's left-wing attorney, now the sole Republican member of New York's city council.

Miss Fleming, a Negro, gushed:

"The important thing is to bring about a change in the girls' attitudes. That means their attitude toward themselves, toward the boys, toward their place in the community. That is slow work."

Even if it were possible to provide all the advantages that have been denied them, the problem of the gangs and their followers would not be solved at once, Miss Fleming spouted. She found that in Harlem many girls were not conditioned to enjoy some of the advantages available. A crust of indifference had to be worn away first. Pregnancies were a serious hazard among the girl-friends of the gang. The social worker found misinformation and superstitions about sex common among the younger girls. Some got drunk at Friday night parties, some carried weapons for their sweethearts, a few stole for them. In the main, though, sex delinquency was the biggest problem.

"In many cases the aggressive actions of the boys have their source in girls," Miss Fleming declared. "The gang boy thinks he acquires prestige with the girls. Some steal so they have money to impress the girls. There are fights between gangs because of rivalry over a girl. A change in the girls' attitudes will be reflected in the attitudes of the boys. We will try to keep constantly before these girls, through richer day-by-day experiences, the fact that there is a fuller and better life within their reach."

We blush to report that the birth-rate of Harlem bastards has not fallen off since culture came, nor has the narcotic rate declined.

Twice as many New York youths last year died from dope as from polio!

Juvenile delinquency has always been with us. So have nutty kids who've outgrown such things as Prohibition, the flapper age, etc. But only of late has delinquency been tied to drugs—which you can't outgrow. It has been protected by Democrats and splinter parties, who get funds from drug dealers; and Socialists and Reds who find youthful resentment against constituted authority and morality encouraging—to hear them tell it, junkies are merely rebels like Washington and Jefferson.

No community, rich or poor, rural or congested is free from the plague of juvenile delinquency. It is more than a fad, it is a fanatical drive tied up with religious and political overtones; a sort of secret society. Teen-agers speak their own mystic tongue, unintelligible to adults but understood by kids throughout the country.

Their cells are in juke-box joints, soda-dispensaries and hot record shops, especially the latter. Like a heathen religion, it is all tied up with tom-toms and hot jive and ritualistic orgies of erotic dancing, weed-smoking and mass mania, with African jungle background.

Many music shops purvey dope; assignations are made in them. White girls are recruited for colored lovers. Another cog in the giant delinquency machine is the radio disc jockey. This character has become the high priest of this strong cult. We know that many platter spinners are hop-heads. Many others are Reds, left-wingers, or hecklers of social convention like Barry Gray in New York.

Through disc-jocks, kids get to know colored and other "hot" musicians; they frequent places the radio oracles plug, which is done with design and malice, to hook juves and guarantee a new generation subservient to the Mafia.

Crime is now at a sixteen-year high. Arrests of minor girls show the sharpest increase, an all-time peak. Prisons and dope hospitals are overflowing with kids. The largest single segment of the law-breaking population is the under-twenty-one group, with the twenty-one-to-twenty-five next. In old-fashioned times, when youngsters shined shoes, delivered packages, sold newspapers and labored in sweat-shops, juvenile crime was practically unheard of. Those were hardship days, but they did not create child criminals. Now it starts right at the infant level. An eight-year-old was picked up in New York as a confirmed hop-addict.

One of the newest rackets schemed up by crooked orphan homes and adoption bureaus is to "lease" young children to crooks— especially conmen or those in hiding or on the lam. The brats make swell blinds. Who would suspect a young pair with a couple of kids? When the heat is off the children are returned, or retained to be trained for the trade. Crime, like all other big business (of which it is the biggest) needs experts in this technological age. Fagin would starve to death in 1952.

4. WOMEN
CONFIDENTIAL

SINCE THE last time we looked around things have changed. Now there are more dames than men. That should make it nice for us. But it doesn't. Because women have been emancipated. Now they can pursue us. And everyone knows that when you can get it, you don't want it.

From the new freedom for frails have come vital economic and social readjustments as well as changes in public and private moral codes. Just as the frigidaire put the iceman in limbo, so have modern sexual patterns caused a new order in the ancient business of peddling sex.

In *Washington Confidential* we said women are the same all over, except in Washington. That was before we hit Toledo, Tusla and Temple, New Hampshire, the home of Deacon Tobey. We now withdraw the statement. Females in farm houses, factories, furnished rooms and in furs are as promiscuous and predatory as the G-gals in the D.C.

We found non-virgin clubs among high-school lassies in Baltimore, Boston and Butte, and we could alliterate this for every letter of the alphabet from Albany, Albuquerque and Atlanta to Zanesville.

Actually the nationwide ratio of women above men is slight, only about two per cent, but the odds are longer because of the withdrawal from home circles by military service of millions of men, in the prime of life—all of marriageable or fornicating age.

As you go deeper into this volume you will discover a third strike against women. As in Washington, not all who shave are what they seem to be. An entire generation of misfits is growing up in place of the lovers, husbands and fathers the census figures would seem to indicate.

The pigeons who inherited the earth are worse off than ever

before. There exists a terrific competition for male favors. School-
girls fight in bars with waitresses and whores which plays havoc
with the vested interests of the babes in the oldest profession.

To some men, the experienced professional has a greater appeal than the simple home-girl. Many amateurs expect to be ro-
manced and entertained. That may cost more than the payment-
in-full exacted in commerce. Romance is even worse than entertainment—it may bring about lasting consequences. The prostitute is kissed, then kissed off.

A. The Decline and Fall of the Cat House

Men and women finally found out about Alexander Graham
Bell's invention. It took seventy-five years for the red light on the
switchboard to dispossess the red light over the door.

During our recent excursion across the continent we found that
in most big cities the restricted area was extinct, the bawdy
houses were shuttered or torn down for parking lots, and the
madames had scattered to wherever retired madames go.

The local police claimed the credit. The townfolk felt properly
virtuous. But there was more copulation than before. Despite
competition provided by amateurs and semi-pros, more of it was
strictly on-the-line stuff, too.

The telephone had come into its own. Whores are "call girls,"
"party girls" or "company girls." Instead of your visiting them,
they come to see you.

This resulted in a complete change in the economic set-up of
the oldest profession. Since houses are not needed, neither are
large investments. Without houses immovably located, pay-offs to
bluecoats on the beat have become almost extinct, and so, for
that matter, have raids. Only the lowest streetwalkers are collared.
Meanwhile, the price is up; the old 50-cent house girl is insulted
with $10 for a quick visit to your hotel room. The younger,
fresher and smarter talent asks $100 and frequently gets it.

Other vice is highly organized, but prostitution gets more individual. Since she needs neither location nor protection, the call
girl can work on her own from a furnished room or small hotel.
Sometimes two or three girls band together, often with a cab
driver or hotel bellhop pimping.

In towns like Chicago, where the underworld is well established,
girls often work for a central clearing house which provides
switchboard service for as many as one thousand hustlers.

Some houses still exist in isolated rural sections, and there are perambulating bagnios working the harvests and crops in California and the Northwest, traveling houses in luxurious trailers.

The few remaining red-light belts are not in class-one cities. We found them in Galveston, San Antonio and Butte and, strangely enough, Portland, Oregon, where the lady Mayor promised to drive the hussies out of town.

Houses still exist in towns like Bakersfield and Fresno, California, and Saginaw, Michigan, where itinerant lumberjacks and farmworkers come for week-ends. When the cops shuttered Saginaw's Market Street, the whores moved all over town. Then one opened a house across from the Mayor's home. Now they are back on Market Street.

Most of these small-town dens of iniquity import girls for seasonal work and special occasions. The telegraphic code is "black bag" for brunettes and "tan valise" for blondes.

Independent contractors work streets everywhere from Times Square to the Golden Gate, swinging large handbags and asking, "Want a good time, dearie?" They take their trade to rooms in flea-bag hotels or check into side street assignation joints which exist in every city in the country.

B. Company Girls

Some people call them call girls and others refer to them as party girls; because you call them when you want a party.

Since the dimming of the red lights, the best prostitutes, and by that we mean not only those who look best, but who work best, are company girls, phoned for appointments like your doctor and often paid off that way, by monthly charge account and check.

When the FBI took over the enforcement of laws against white slavery in interstate commerce, the trade, for all practical purposes, was smashed. Some continued to operate undercover. It is an axiom of police work that you can't catch all malefactors, and you can't convict all you do catch. Federal judges and juries are soft. Many U.S. attorneys hesitate to prosecute because judges throw Mann Act cases out with, "That's only prostitution. Let the local cops handle it."

In the old days babes were recruited in Scranton, Reading and other such towns, as well as in Europe, and sold by the head to dive operators. The G-Men broke that. The present day movement of such cattle is more insidious, almost impossible of prosecution. Party girls are not "sent" or transported to other states.

They cross the lines on their own, to follow the seasons, conventions, etc., in search of "jobs." They go out on "dates" and the man "seduces" them. Try and make a Mann Act case of that. It's impossible under the law.

These gals usually play circuits, working west from New York in groups of ten to twenty, ostensibly seeking work as entertainers, models, B-girls, or just adventuring. They play week-long stands in Philly, Pittsburg, Cleveland, Detroit, Chicago, St. Louis and Kansas City, where they split into two groups for the cowtowns, one going south through Wichita, Tulsa, Oklahoma City, Texas, Arizona, etc., and the other northwest through Omaha, Des Moines, Minneapolis, St. Paul, Seattle, Portland, etc.

The two companies join in California. The tour takes a year. A new group goes out each week so that every town will always have new faces. Many are lost along the way as girls find protectors, pimps, steady jobs, or husbands.

C. Glamor (And Not So Glamorous) Girls

In every community girls combine business with pleasure, for a side-line income above and beyond their beanery earnings. In New York this category includes some of the most publicized models, Copacabana chorines and video and stage stars, as well as the humble sister who slings hash.

It is impossible to distinguish them from simon-pure amateurs, because, quite often, they also do it gratis, or for entertainment, for love or fun or both. There are definite patterns in the migrations of these and other gals from farms to big cities and from one city to another. Most of New York's originate in Texas, Oklahoma, Florida, Georgia, and for some strange reason, Erie, Pennsylvania.

Girls from other parts of the deep South work their way gradually to Chicago; but most of Chicago's semi-pros come from Wisconsin and Minnesota. St. Louis recruits from Louisville, by way of Indianapolis. The Northwest draws girls from Canada and California, while Los Angeles is unique among big cities, having a preponderance of native-born hustlers, though would-be film stars from all the forty-eight states sooner or later end up in bed there whether they get the contract or no.

Boston's reservoir is Maine, Rhode Island and New Hampshire. Maryland gets them from West Virginia, while Washington's pros, as distinguished from the G-girls who come from all over, usually pop in from Virginia or the Carolinas.

There is a constant movement and interchange of this item between New York, Los Angeles and Miami; but girls that end up in Chicago usually remain there, sometimes in a barrel of cement.

D. Amateurs

This is known in professional parlance as "the hot sheet trade." Changing sexual patterns which destroyed the multimillion dollar whore-house racket built up new outlets for the ingenuity of American business men.

America's inventive genius came to bat with the motel and the drive-in movies. The former is now one of the biggest industries in the nation gradually being taken over by the underworld. The latter is so gigantic, it saved hard-bitten Hollywood just when help was needed most.

There are motels that do not go in for the hot sheet trade, but most do. Except on slow nights most tourist courts will not take you if you are a genuine tourist who plans to sleep. But if you drive up with a cutie and no baggage you are welcome—if you get out in an hour or two.

At most drive-in movies you see a better show in the cars than on the screen. The ushers in these places call themselves "auto pimps." Some supply dames for cars that drive in without them.

E. He-Women

The Sapphic lover, unless she goes to the extremes of wearing mannish habiliments and cutting her hair short, is seldom obvious. Literature, the stage, the daily papers and the smutty gags of low comedians abound with stories about effeminate men, but when did you last read about a sex crime involving two women or hear a joke about a couple of Lesbians?

This form of perverted love is as ancient as male homosexuality and probably has always been more prevalent; but women, because of their nature and the restrictions placed upon them by society, have not been so obvious about it. That is, not until 1952.

One of the most startling surprises to slap us in the face as we dredged the nation for the truth was that sexual deviation is as great or greater among the female of the species than among the so-called male.

None but the blind or those who don't want to see can fail to be aware of the diseased state of the nation's sex life. The same rock bottom factors that are responsible for the wave of swishes accounts for the epidemic of homosexuality among the maidens, though in reverse.

Under a matriarchy men grow soft and women masculine. The self-sufficient girl who doesn't want to become an incubator or "kitchen slavie" for a man is a push-over for a predatory Lesbian. The shortage of men is an aggravating factor. Marxian teachings, the examples of women in high political and social places, and the propagandized knowledge that many of the movie set prefer it that way are contributory.

The perversion begins at school age when impressionable girls are often lured into it "for fun" by a fellow student or a teacher or professor. Homosexual cells exist in many high schools, public and private, and in practically every college and university. Those at UCLA, Hunter, Barnard, Teachers' College, University of Wisconsin and the University of Chicago are famous in the third-sex grapevine.

Artistic and intellectual circles are supersaturated with queer girls, which is expected. They neutralize the faggots. But Sapphism has gone underground into the ranks of secretaries, file-clerks, telephone gals, the five-and-dimes and the female armed services.

WACS, WAVES and the other auxiliaries are paradise for Lesbians. To the woman with male attributes this is as good as if a man could get himself into ladies' night at the Turkish bath.

Large numbers of the professional peace-time female soldiers and sailors are deviates. They have built up a caste system in the services which insures promotion to other queers. Consequently many new girls are quickly seduced by oldtimers.

This is to tell you that Lesbians in heat are more combatative than the ordinary garden variety male. Uncooperative girls are often raped.

A few such scandals were too hot to bottle. Greatly sapolioed, they broke into print. But so many more are covered up. The lady-lovers are now so firmly entrenched they no longer hesitate to try to take pretty young girls away from high ranking male brass, who used to have first pick on most WAC, WAVE and women Marine recruits.

The affinity between such forbidden fruits, narcotics and Communism is well understood by law enforcement bodies, and is explained in greater detail in later chapters.

So let's all let down our hair and just be girls.

5. MEN CONFIDENTIAL

CONFIDENTIALLY, many aren't men.

You may have thought all queers who aren't on Broadway or in Hollywood are in Washington. We found them in Milwaukee, Boston, Dallas, Honolulu and Des Moines. They pursued us in Minneapolis.

In *Washington Confidential* we explained the presence of more than ten thousand fairies on the government payroll this way: Deviates are too obvious in their home towns; consequently they've got to get out where their unorthodox sexual activity will not interfere with earning a livelihood. We knew that the talented ones went to New York and Hollywood, where there were jobs for actors, designers, interior decorators. The others went to Washington, where they were lost in the anonymity of civil service. Many were actively recruited into Washington by a cell that existed in the State Department and which still, despite denials and purges, is considerably more than 30 per cent faggot.

The homosexual is likely to seek his own, because the pressures of society are such that he feels uncomfortable unless he is with homos. So he tends to surround himself with others of his kind in his social and business life. If one squirms into government, where he can influence hiring of personnel, he will place others.

So that explains three hives of queen bees.

Now we'll chuck a haymaker: the entire nation is going queer! The mayor of one of our largest cities is a swish.

What might once have been true about migrations of the intermediates is dated. Many stay at home.

And the masculinization of women, which had its counterpart in the feminization of men, is obvious wherever one travels in this nation, in all the forty-eight states and the territories. It is as pitiful a menace as the nation faces.

Communism actively promotes and supports sex deviation to sap the strength of the new generation and make the birth of another problematical—which might not be such a bad idea.

The unsophisticates who think of queers as prancing nances

with rouged lips and bleached hair will not believe us. The pansies in the State Department do not wear skirts over their striped pants. Any cop will tell you that among the fairies he arrests are tough young kids, college football players, truck-drivers and weather-bitten servicemen. An admiral tried to rape a young soldier on the street in Honolulu. Many queers are married, fathers of families. They hide their perversions from their wives and neighbors. A particularly sanctimonious U.S. Senator from an Eastern state is known to follow youths as young as his grandchildren into rest rooms. Another Eastern Senator, Democrat and left-wing, has a wife and a boy friend.

Young thugs fight over the affections of their male sweethearts with brass knuckles, knives, fists and boots, as their grandfathers did over girls. In many circles, especially the military and the more advanced big-dome set, it is considered weak and decadent to engage in normal sex. In artistic society, males glorify the male body.

All fairy night clubs and gathering places are illegal, and operate only through pay-offs to the authorities. They are organized into a national circuit, controlled by the Mafia which also finds unique opportunity to sell dope in such dives. Many gangsters like it that way, too, after indoctrination in prison.

Young men are being infected with the virus of an epidemic which was old when Spartans believed he-men and warriors should love each other, because women were merely for the reproduction of the race. The Prussian military caste thought along similar lines, and depravity became official for many in Nazi Germany. See what happened to Sparta and Germany.

Aside from the criminality and immorality, such behavior is so contrary to normal standards that persons who engage in it are regarded as outcasts by society generally. The stigma is so sinister that many perverts go to great lengths to conceal their tendencies. Thus they are frequently victimized by blackmailers who threaten exposure. Gangs make a regular practice of preying on homos.

Nazi and Communist agents have attempted to obtain information from employes of our government in the same way. Intelligence agencies the world over use this tactic. Our armed forces crawl with queers, though regulations decree that perverts may not be enlisted or drafted. If they are discovered in the service, they must be detached. But few queers are turned down. The Department of Defense itself has some deviates at very high levels, including one of almost cabinet rank.

There is an active daisy chain in every post and on every ship. Lonesome young boys are easy prey. And yet the brass makes it difficult for boys to find normal feminine companionship by putting bars where girls hang out off limits, while permitting notorious fairy joints to cater to servicemen. (We refer you to the San Diego chapter.)

When we first read Kinsey, we thought he went off half-cocked. He did err, but toward conservatism. The extent of homosexuality is much greater than even psychiatrists can know. It exists in all walks of life.

6. THE RIGHT TO GO LEFT

THERE HAS grown up in the land a superprivileged class— the teacher. As a consequence of belligerent radicalism over twenty years, we are inoculated with a completely false doctrine— that teacher knows best and we must not interfere.

This craftily created "right" flies a flag bearing neither stars nor stripes, but blazoned on its synthetic cloth is the slogan: "Academic Freedom."

It means that any and every semi-idiot, semi-man, semi-woman and all the others who fear the battle of life and take refuge in the somnolent security of instructing the young may propound whatever ideas, ologies and isms he or she chooses, and such pronunciamentos may not be disputed.

Most people who decide to train for teaching are already frustrated failures, afraid to face a constructive world; and when they are given immunity against public policy which would hold them to account in any other field, like all midgets with a bludgeon, they go haywire. They are social misfits to begin with, in a capitalist system, so they use their protected "freedom" to attack a way of life in which they are handicapped for open competition.

This was foreseen by the mongers of discontent, who realized what teachers could do for their cause if they were insulated so no metal of criticism could touch them. And with that was born the inspired dogma of academic freedom.

It was fought for by interested individuals and organizations as the instrument whereby a nation could be overturned in a generation or two by those who can most easily and most constantly influence the minds of youth.

And now the greatest power on earth is threatened by the little red schoolhouse and Miss M'Foofle, who taught third grade. Miss M'Foofle, who had trained at Teachers' College—any normal school will do, since Columbia infected them all with the mental VD virus—came out with a license and a machine-made and pattern-stamped mind, designed by a small, solid clique of insidious "moderns."

The brats Miss M'Foofle taught passed through high schools and colleges, and all along the way they met other Miss M'Foofles and some Mr. M'Foofles—who might have been called Miss at that. And when they had their degrees they, too, had assembly-line minds, all with the uniform surface glitter of pseudo-intellectualism, but without the ability to think. They took their glossy diplomas—millions of overeducated dumbells—and went out into the world to teach, preach, write and edit, compose, make fun—all the same way, singing or writing or trumpeting the same piece. It came about that the schools, foundations, newspapers, magazines, book publishers, radio stations, public forums and libraries were almost united in a conspiracy of propaganda that pounded and pounded in the word so long that the people began to believe it. Soon they were afraid or ashamed to admit to themselves that conservatism is not a crime, that nature has created people in varying colors and with different mental equipment or speech habits, that some are not as smart as others, that the government does not owe a living to all.

Capitalism, which means merely possession of private property, became a four-letter word like those scribbled in chalk on fences and walls. And yet, as citizens, the members of this new caste are no better than the uneducated slobs to whom they profess to be superior.

Socialism and statism were slipped over on us by the process which had begun in the public schools. By the time the Roosevelt gang was ready to certify it by law, schoolteachers had done the groundwork. We were too weak to resist. Their students had become molders of public opinion.

The heavy of this piece is John Dewey, a ninety-two-year-old "thinker," the father of progressive education. The central idea, despite the big words, is that children should no longer be trained as individuals but as integers in a huge, paternal, possessive state. Where did we hear that before?

Report cards are frowned on. Initiative is crushed. Accomplishment is a Fascist fallacy. Dewey wrecked the national character, but Eleanor Roosevelt, the *Saturday Review* and the *New York Times* hail him as its savior.

There were schisms in the movement—the prissy, precise former boy-wonder chancellor of the pink University of Chicago, Dr. Robert Hutchins, now managing head of the Ford Foundation, is the chief "sultan" in another harem of advanced scholars opposing the Dewey creed. But the difference is merely in the method of imparting education—not in the end, which is defined as "integrating the pupil into society." You know what kind of society.

When the rank harvest of his vile planting—juvenile delinquency, West Point honor scandals, college basketball swindles, public and private immorality—was thrown up to the venerable Dr. Dewey on his last birthday, the sage said, "Not unusual. The fault is that of parents," he continued, "not of the schools or government leaders." He said youthful narcotic addiction or athletic fixes did not indicate a declining morality. You have to have a Ph.D. to think like that.

Three generations of teachers and instructors have grown up under this system. Educators have built up a self-perpetuating priestly class. They choose their own successors. They seek to extend their influence over everything affecting schools and colleges, not only curricular, but problems in politics and economics. Such organizations as the National Education Association and various teachers' unions, especially in New York City, are left-wing. They use public schools for partisan propaganda, to poison the minds of children with social welfare gospel, backed by shaded mendacities and subversive jokers in textbooks slipped past lackadaisical parents and "conditioned" school-board members. This is the first that taxpayers in Newark, Buffalo, Detroit and Cleveland will have heard that many marms are passing out Red plugs in their schools.

So successfully have the teachers taken over the minds of the students that organizations like the United States National Student Association, representing "600,000 students in 185 colleges," are roaring radicals. The Americans for Democratic Action have student chapters on most campuses. Many schools spearhead its drive for socialism. The ADA recently declared for repeal of the Smith Act which makes attempts to overthrow the government a crime. The chief tenet of the new educational order is that the state owns the child's mind. Teachers represent the state. They

consider themselves a special, untouchable caste, not to be questioned or disciplined by others. The preceptors of progressive
education say schools should be used to build a new order. When
they are called to task they yell that their critics are "reaction-
aries." Many well-meaning, thoughtless citizens are misled by
their propaganda.

The situation in American colleges would fill a couple of Confidential volumes. We toss out a few choice bits here—merely
samples.

The basketball scandals were trifles compared to what is going
on. Football is far more vulnerable and corrupt than the cage
game ever was. Hundreds of "contests" are rigged, on results and
points. The 1950 Army-Navy upset was crooked. Frank Costello
knew the score before it happened. He placed heavy bets on Navy.
If you say such things can't be, we remind you that most of the
Army squad was later discharged for infraction of the honor
system. The West Point coach, whose son was among those kicked
out, is still employed by the institution.

Football games are thrown by players, but more are fixed by
coaches, who call the plays. The football parlay card business
turns over billions. One point in a jerkwater game may mean
millions to the operators.

Hunter College—that's for girls. No football, but maybe they
fix softball, tatting and debating. Who knows?

Hunter is owned and supported by New York City. It is a
nest of Communist filth and infection, one of the few colleges
where American Youth for Democracy, formerly the Young Communist League, operates openly in public premises. Its auditorium
is a meeting place for Reds; their fronts are welcomed. On the
faculty are professors who taught at Jefferson School. Novelist
Howard Fast, jailed Communist, was a welcome speaker, even
after his conviction.

Johns Hopkins University—once respected institution of higher
learning in Baltimore—is dominated by a radical clique which
follows the leadership of deflated Professor Owen Lattimore.
Lattimore's testimony about Communist infiltration into the Institute of Pacific Relations was so much at variance with facts
testified to by others as to raise doubts about his understanding
of common English words. Lattimore is Baltimore's intellectual
light. His preachings—we won't call it teaching—affect the mental
tone of the nation's sixth largest city, because the once vigorous
Baltimore Sun, now emasculated and "liberal," makes a hero of

this pundit. *Sun* staff members are required to attend some of his indoctrination lectures and are paid for their time while at the university.

Those with sons at Johns Hopkins might be interested in the following statement by Lattimore, published in the Soviet-loving *New York Compass*. On his activity as a State Department adviser, Lattimore said:

"As it became more and more obvious that Chiang Kai-shek and the Kuomintang were doomed, the conduct of American policy became increasingly delicate. The problem was how to allow them to fall without making it look as if the United States had pushed them. . . The thing to do, therefore, is to let South Korea fall—but not to let it look as though we pushed it. Hence the recommendation of a parting grant of $150,000,000."

Despite frantic denials, the University of Virginia is deep pink. Among left-wingers on its faculty are Alfred Fernbach, Charles Micaud, and former State Department employe John Gange. They are only surface dressing, hiding a genuine Communist cell among other professors and students. Some instructors are the commissars. The only tradition these radicals did not want to shatter was to shutter "Margueritte's," the campus cat house which was established by Thomas Jefferson for gentry "to relieve themelves."

The neighboring University of North Carolina harbors the same types. The welcome mat was out for them during the presidency of Dr. Frank Graham, later appointed to a U.S. Senate vacancy. When he ran for the full term he was licked; but Truman rewards his Socialists, so Graham won a UN appointment, as mediator in India. He was a miserable flop. The collective intelligence of the Senate is not high, but many who saw Graham in action during his brief moment of glory wondered how he could tell time to get to the sessions. While he was at Chapel Hill, the Commies literally stole the campus—what was left after the crooks got theirs. Homos were a big thing there, too, during his reign. This was considered "self-expression."

Professor Thomas Emerson, of Yale Law School, was the head of the Communist-front National Lawyers' Guild. Dean Wesley Sturges, of the same school, delivered a blistering attack on the House Un-American Activities Committee before a CIO convention. The sons of two justices of the United States Supreme Court learned law from these men.

Subversive activities at the Rockefeller-supported University of Chicago are a stench in the nostrils of even Chicago's liberal citizens. It and Roosevelt University, also in Chicago, were so bad that the Illinois Legislature was forced to investigate them for Red activities. But so much pressure came from rich and powerful "liberals" and professional do-gooders like Senator Douglas, that the committee ended its hearings with an inconclusive report, but refused to clear either institution. Roosevelt College is outright left-wing. It makes a virtue of the fact that it teaches labor and economics courses not given elsewhere.

The record of Harvard Law is long and well known. Its off-color graduates include that star, Alger Hiss.

The faculty of Columbia is overboard with Reds and pinks, undisturbed by President Eisenhower.

Despite a purge at the University of Washington, it is loaded with Reds in the faculty and student body. Communist cells on the campus throw parties at which students mix Marx with cocaine and sex.

Another hotbed is the campus of the University of California at Berkeley, where left-wing professors were able to veto the State's anti-Communist oath. There is much homosexuality.

Some professors and teachers not actually anti-American are infantile souls, lost in the unreal atmosphere of ivy-clad cloisters, who don't see the moving world. The dean of the Bible College at Wellesley tried to persuade its students to spend the summer as settlement workers in East Harlem—the sink-hole of the continent, where Puerto Rican and other morons rape and rob in broad daylight and policemen are afraid to patrol even in pairs. This is the constituency of former Congressman Vito Marcantonio, darling and protector of the Communists. In his domain is the central and protected headquarters of the narcotics ring in the United States. Other absurd professors belong to a do-gooder group called Christian Socialists, which actively sponsors attempts by young girls to break down class and race lines, with no patience for consideration of their own breakdown of morals and decent thinking.

No college big-dome will approve this book. We are not "advanced." If you question one about this chapter, he will reply, "Certainly, we instruct our students in the principles of Marx. We explain socialism and communism, as we teach about syphilis in our medical schools."

But they don't try to make syphilis the new order, a lofty American aim.

7. REDS IN CLOVER

SEX IS the subversives' secret weapon. They make communism palatable to the little faceless men and women by offering them an escape from their repressions and frustrations.

Marxism came into Russia on a wave of free love. In countries which have not yet been engulfed dreary men and pimply women are brought into the fold with promises of purple and unconventional delights. Communist families must teach their children that sexual activities are biological. There is no place for love and emotion in proletarian society. Deviation from that rule is punished by expulsion from the party unless it is applicable to uses for the state.

Female card-holders are required to show their loyalty to the cause through indiscriminate intercourse wherever it will do the most good. Judging from the looks and odor of most of the revolutionists, we prefer to remain capitalists.

Sex is offered as an inducement to comrades for attending meetings. Most soirees of the faithful end up with vodka toasts in dim candlelight. Negro men get first choice of white women. An indoctrinated girl may whimsically turn down a white man, but never a Negro; that is racial intolerance. Many Negroes join up only for that purpose and pass the word along to their friends. The Red bed-battalion is also committed to romancing unioneers in sensitive industries.

There is a vocal voluble segment of Americans, numbering millions, which claims to be anti-Communist but always hysterically attacks those who try to expose communism, while invariably leaping to the defense of accused Reds.

These people are classed under many labels, but what holds them together is their devotion to the "welfare state." They plug "security from cradle to grave." They contend that treason is excusable if the traitor became "enlightened" in or after the 1930's. They champion Hiss, Remington, Lattimore, et al. They accept socialism as the specific for all evils—and they believe Marxism differs from communism.

Eleanor Roosevelt, annually voted the world's most outstanding woman, is the chief tub-thumper for socialism. Until recently she apologized for Comrade Joe. Now, as a delegate to the UN, she "hates" communism, though she excuses socialist India for flirting with Russia. The differences between her "welfare state" and socialism, and between socialism and communism, are not in kind; they vary in extent, degree and who will be the boss, comes the revolution.

There are cliques and factions and wings and blocs among the Reds, as there are among Democrats, Republicans, unions and Wall Street trusts. Some are orthodox Stalinists. Others are Trotskyites. Some are nationalists. Like Tito, they practice communism but do not want it directed from an outside source. These "native" Communists are the most insidious. They preach against Russia but work for a revolution they will run themselves. All these forms are closer to each other than they are to us, as honest Republicans and Democrats are for the American way despite policy differences.

Holding up the rear, like a huge infantry, are the millions of "intellectual" Socialists and welfare-staters, the Americans for Democratic Action, the Fair Dealers, the liberals and progressives, etc. Among them are shrewd and ambitious politicians like Hubert Humphrey, Warren Magnuson, Wayne Morse and F. D. Roosevelt, Jr., as well as stunted visionaries like Margaret Chase Smith, Herbert Lehman, Irving Ives, Leverett Saltonstall, Paul Douglas, Charles Tobey and William Benton. These diverse elements are joined with a bottomless slush fund provided by heirs, movie stars, popular authors and others itching with guilt and inferiority complexes.

On the battle line, the shock troops of the organized Reds go to war. They have access to the nation's military and diplomatic secrets through their control of the left-wing American Communications Association, which was too malodorous even for the radical CIO. Confidential messages clear along telegraph lines manned by ACA workers. Its Red leadership has trusted operators stationed at key points. Many former ACA members are in the armed forces, operating military lines of communication, sneaking secrets to the enemy.

Communist Harry Bridges, tycoon of the West Coast shipping unions, knows every ship movement on the Pacific. His strikes and tie-ups are aimed to interfere with the flow of matériel; his members sabotage shipments to our troops. War supplies are stolen from the ships and docks and transhipped to the Reds.

The vital and key electrical industry is represented by the Red-controlled United Electrical Workers, which was kicked out of the CIO, then went back into CIO plants like General Electric's sensitive one in Schenectady and swamped the new CIO union by better than two to one in plant elections.

The chief protector of the radicals on the White House level was and still is David Niles, mystery man from Massachusetts. Niles handled all labor, minority and left-wing affairs under both Roosevelt and Truman. His "clients" provided the votes in doubtful areas and the big dough. He could not be overruled.

Niles quit under strange circumstances in 1951, when he announced he "didn't feel well" and was going to take an extended trip abroad and spend a lot of time in Israel. But this was not printed: that Senator McCarran was about to subpoena him to testify about the Communist plot. Truman pleaded with McCarran as one Democrat to another not to call Niles. McCarran stuck to his guns. Niles went off so fast he left his dirty drawers in the White House. He planned to remain in Israel until the committee ends or cools off. Meanwhile, he transmits orders through the diplomatic pouch.

While Niles sits in temporary exile in Tel Aviv, he is kept abreast of the McCarran Committee's secret files by two of his boys, whom he sneaked onto the committee as key employes without McCarran's knowledge. They tip him off in time when anything embarrassing is on the agenda.

Another who got out of the White House one step ahead of a process server was Laughlin Currie, wizard of the left-wing braintrust, who suddenly got a job, maneuvered by Truman, in the Republic of Colombia as a government expert at $100,000 a year. The fantastic salary is paid by us through ECA and secret deals.

Communists are still employed by the government in every stratum. Despite purges and the security investigations, tens of thousands of pinkos are on the payroll and dictate policy.

We are still shipping automotive parts for eventual consignment to Poland, cleared both by State and the National Resources Board in the "interests of our war effort." Try to figure that out. Other stuff is still going to China and other Iron Curtain countries.

The President's recent order banning importation of certain Russian furs mentioned mink, a dirty word in Washington now, but not ermine, sable and many other Russian furs. It happens we do not import mink from Russia; the best comes from North America. Rich commissars bring American and Canadian minks back to Russia. But other furs still give Russia dollars.

While we were seeking to negotiate a Korean cease-fire, the United States Information Service distributed publications in Formosa to "explain" the Chinese Communist movement as a "Peoples' revolt against unscrupulous warlords."

The dynamo of the left-wing movement in America has moved from the House Office Building to 1404 New York Ave., NW, in Washington, where former Rep. Vito Marcantonio and John J. Abt, ex-Agriculture Department attorney, opened a tiny office on the 7th floor. Marcantonio and his New York American Labor Party echo the Communists. He voted the straight Red party-line throughout his years in Congress. Abt was identified as a Communist cell member in testimony before the House Un-American Activities Committee. He was retained by the Communist Party to test the constitutionality of the McCarran Act.

Legal strategy for the Reds via the courts and Congress is hatched in this little office. Marcantonio avails himself of his prerogative to lobby on the floors of both Houses. He collars Senators and Congressmen in the cloakrooms. Some, like Lehman, young Roosevelt, Ives, Celler, he threatens with loss of votes. Others, like Javits and Powell, who so often play in his back yard, he talks to in understanding whispers.

It requires little effort to arouse sympathy for Reds in Washington. To a large number of people in the Administration Alger Hiss, in jail, is a martyr. He is being given special handling in the gentleman's country-club wing of Lewisburg Federal Prison, where he is secretly and illegally permitted to write briefs and do other legal work for lawyer friends. He is helping at least one Justice of the Supreme Court.

Many members of the Communist-front National Lawyers' Guild also employ him. A vice-president of that organization, according to *Who's Who*, is William Henry Hastie, former Governor of the Virgin Islands, and now, since his appointment in 1949 by Truman, the only Negro member of the exalted United States Circuit Court of Appeals. The president of the National Lawyers' Guild was Thomas I. Emerson, who teaches at Yale Law School. He was retained to represent sixteen Communists on pre-trial motions.

The character witnesses for Hiss in high places have not turned their backs on him. Some are quietly and subtly engaging in whispered propaganda to prove that Hiss was framed, relying on the great lie technique, which Reds accuse us of using, to clear a traitor's name so that after the next election, when the passions of the trial shall have been forgotten, the President, whoever he is, will pardon Hiss and restore him to full citizenship. He will return to high office a hero. The pro-Hiss clique includes the following:

Supreme Court Justice Felix Frankfurter, former law professor at Harvard and his sponsor in the New Deal.

Supreme Court Justice Stanley F. Reed, Hiss's employer in the Justice Department.

Governor Adlai Stevenson of Illinois, who was assistant to the Secretary of State when Hiss was in that department.

Gerard Swope, Jr., counsel for the International General Electric Company, Harvard Law School graduate and formerly associated with Hiss in a law office.

Judge Calvert Magruder, Boston, a former Harvard Law professor.

Dr. Philip C. Jessup, U.S. ambassador at large, who has been described as having an affinity for Communists.

Stanley K. Hornbeck, former ambassador to the Netherlands and former State Department official.

Charles E. Darlington, chief of the trade agreements division of the State Department 1937–1939.

Dr. James T. Shotwell, Columbia University professor and president of the Carnegie Endowment for International Peace.

Joseph C. Green, executive director of the foreign service board of examiners of the State Department.

Clarence E. Pickett of Philadelphia, executive secretary of the American Friends Service Committee (Quakers).

Donald Hiss, brother of Alger, and also a government official. He has denied any Red associations.

Many persons have aided Hiss through writings, speeches and letters. These included Mrs. Franklin D. Roosevelt, who set a pattern followed by many New Deal Communists and journalists. The *New Yorker* magazine ridiculed evidence of Hiss's guilt. Senator Lehman endorsed Hiss, declaring he had complete confidence in the latter's loyalty. Hiss and his wife lived with Lehman's niece during the trial. She and her husband paid most of his legal expenses.

Arthur Garfield Hays, who made a good thing of "civil liberties," is the chief legal advisor to the infamous Longie Zwillman. A few months ago Hays said, "Free speech is being jeopardized in America because Americans are too timid to speak their minds on the Communist question." What he meant was Americans were afraid to defend alleged Communists. He said, "Freedom of speech has been greatly curtailed. The effects of these red herrings is terrorizing."

8. OUR AFRO-AMERICAN BRETHREN

The Second Emancipation

OUR ANCESTORS, whom schoolchildren are taught to revere, were hard, cruel, acquisitive fugitives and freebooters on the make. They massacred and robbed the Indians. They kidnaped and enslaved black African savages. The Christian citizens of states where slaves were not useful frothed at the mouth against Negro slavery while they impressed seamen and hunted down indentured serfs of their own blood. In time there came a great civil war. After Americans had killed and impoverished and devastated and pillaged the conquered South, they left it with millions of darkies freed by force and given rhetorical equality.

Many of the ex-slaves had no conception of such blessings. Their African forefathers had never been free or equal. Centuries of slavery here had conditioned them to that estate as life-in-actuality. They were left bewildered, unlettered, shorn from their means of sustenance, thrown on their own in a region which was so shattered and shell-torn it could offer little of the primary needs for bare subsistence.

In time and through pain and want and conflict came gradual adjustments. The Negroes became servants, plantation-hands, share-croppers, railroad laborers, biped beasts of burden; some turned criminals and prostitutes; all lived in shanties much as they had before 1863. They were still slaves without the one advantage of slavery—security. The Abolitionists who had rent the air and scourged Dixie to strike off their shackles now did nothing for them. Some in the cities down South found work in the slowly growing industrialism there. The rest remained in rural, seasonal tasks. A few, more thrifty or more lucky or more sober, acquired elementals of education, entered crafts, even acquired property.

The North was swelling, multiplying its manufactures, needed

more manual workers. Negroes trickled up over the Line and settled in the centers where employment was waiting. No such city
attracted many and recognized no "problem" in those it had.

Then came organization and conflict. For certain types of labor
Negroes were recruited as strike-breakers, notably in meat-pack-
ing and stevedoring. There was resistance; there were "race
wars"; informal but inflexible Negro sections were established,
Jim Crow habits were imposed. The Negroes did not mind segregation, they welcomed it; they liked their own kind better than
they did the "ofays." Wages were high, by Southern standards,
and they sent for more of their people. Thus, gradually, settlements of some proportions formed. The newcomers were allowed
to vote, but had little effect. They were all Republicans, following the tenets of Abraham Lincoln, and most urban communities
were safely Democratic. The Negroes had little taste for politics
and did not exult over their franchise in these strange places
where, by choice and by compulsion, they were unassimilated.
White cops clubbed them and jailed them when they got too
ginned; but that was better than it had been below, where they
were beaten and locked up for nothing. They had no heavy axe
to grind. They did not take the Fourteenth Amendment literally.

World War I was burning up Europe. Our plants were smoking day and night. Every source of manpower was tapped. High
wages brought up many more Negroes. Then came Woodrow
Wilson's draft order; there were no racial exemptions. Many
thousands of colored men were trained, they traveled, they saw
new vistas. Some remained North after the victory; many more
who had come there to earn white men's wages would never return to their birthplaces.

And still the metropolitan citadels of Caucasian supremacy
scarcely noted the increase in darker inhabitants. But, in the Southern towns and cities, Negro soldiers who had come home from
abroad and from farflung camps did not again behave quite like
the docile darkies who had shuffled off to service. The Ku Klux
Klan was revived by Southern extremists. It was contagious. It
spread to Indiana, Ohio, New Jersey, Michigan, even New York.
That fomented a defense movement, loosely organized, not by
Negroes, but by Jews and Catholics, who, also, were the targets of
the Klan. These groups were strong, angry rather than afraid. So
they met the whole issue; and the first wide, deep "Negro problem" was promulgated. The Klan was rather easily decimated and
defeated up North. But the solidified indignation now took the

offensive, invaded the South, where the Klan had germinated. The attack was aimed at the most sensitive nerve of the old Confederacy—agitation for equal rights of the races.

This fired blazing ammunition in Congress and in many states. Lynchings and whippings were melodramatic; poll taxes and terror at the polls were no trumped-up injustices; mighty journals like the *New York World* investigated, then exposed, then crusaded. National labor bodies enlisted, seeing in the agitation a passionate as well as economic cause to unionize the South, fight the old families and the descendants of the carpetbaggers, the leaders of those who still took Negro freedom with tongue in cheek.

It became fashionable for liberal organizations to howl over oppression down South. Decent folks could not dispute their basic soundness, though their methods were inflammatory and sensational. The "good life" in the major cities was exaggerated and it induced more thousands of the disgruntled to tear their roots and come up after the perquisites. But the mass exodus was yet to fulminate. And, as will be told here, it was set off by an entirely new American maneuver—deliberate political proselyting, colonizing, achieved by promises of public subsidization.

This cold-blooded ersatz phenomenon distorted our entire national balance. How many Negroes were recruited to be displaced and resettled will never be known. Through the years extraordinary measures have been effected to fake or hide statistical information. By common tacit agreement all the Communists, other radicals, professional reformers and the whole fringe of fuzzy dilletanti have conspired with the political bosses who utilize and thrive on the strategy to minimize the numbers and the degree of influence swung to Negroes in the new complexion of our decisive cities. Even the remaining Southern pool for their continuing machinations is deceitfully underplayed.

The census bureau places the nation's Negro population at 15,-000,000. By our own dead reckoning it should be far more. For many reasons, blacks are not counted as such, including shifts sleeping around the clock, overcrowding of tenements beyond legal rate, fear of guys with badges, etc. Many Negroes are on the lam, others have no permanent place of residence, moving about often from one rooming-house to another. Many census-takers are afraid to visit Negro slums, so they guess. Colored census-takers don't even bother—they turn in a round faked figure and collect their fee.

The Census Bureau's statistics indicated that the Negro population in the thirteen Southern states stood still from 1940 to 1950. This would mean a net loss proportionately for them, because in the decade in which they stood still in the South the whites increased about 5,000,000, or 16 per cent.

Negroes multiplied by natural processes, of course. The overall gain was reflected in the Northern invasion. Even the inaccurate census showed it. The bureau admitted that more than 300,000 had moved into California in a decade. (It was almost 500,000.) The shift to many other states was equally vigorous. Negroes rapidly became a major factor even in Oregon, Washington and Minnesota.

New York, New Jersey, Pennsylvania, Ohio, Illinois and Michigan first felt the tidal wave during the depression. By 1940 it had drowned out many white localities. But cities like New York, Chicago, Philadelphia and Detroit continued to attract more Negroes during the last decade. Their already swollen little sections grew, burst, and in every case overflowed. Harlem can't expand, but New York's colored contingent jumped the river to Brooklyn and the Bronx where the non-white increase was 308 per cent in the decade. According to the census, the over-all rate of Negro increase in Northern cities was 500 per cent greater than the rate for whites.

Most colored men who left the South came North in search of better earnings. Few set forth in pursuit of civil liberties. That came later, whipped up by rabble-rousers.

To the typical Southern Negro segregation is the accepted way of life. He knows no other. Apparently, he is happier with it than he would be mixing with complete equality with white folk, whom he considers stuffy. Because he does not want or does not expect equality, the Southern darkie has less emotional stress than have those north of Mason-Dixon, who had many expectations and got few realizations. The unregenerate Southern whites, still flying the Stars and Bars, helped drive them northward—which they now deplore because it robs them of cheap and submissive labor. As the supply of unskilled workers grows smaller in a South rapidly becoming industrialized, the problem reaches major importance. And so even the Dixie Negro finds himself courted by employers who prefer him to the poor white leavings, unsteady, unreliable and unintelligent.

On the other hand, most of the Negroes in the North are now much worse off than they ever were back home, despite their gains. They are lost in a strange land where the climate is harsh and cold and where they are outcasts, unwanted even by other Negroes who came before them. These citified blacks resent the new influx and call them "niggers," a word now forbidden in white conversation. They are kept out of settled colored residential areas with the same kind of coercion and violence that whites show when their neighborhoods are block-busted by Negroes.

Each new arrival in the North lessens the value of other Negroes in the labor markets, where they are still forced to do menial labor and are barred from the better commercial jobs. And yet they come—the North is a magnet which seems destined to virtually empty Dixie of blacks within a generation, thus solving the racial problem in the South while bringing a different kind to the North.

Much of this movement northward is directed, as it was initiated, by superior brains from above. Very little is impromptu. The Democratic Raw Dealers, fighting desperately to keep control of the country forever, conceived the idea of mass movement of potential voters into weak or doubtful spots. The device was first used on a big scale as a political tactic by LaGuardia, New York's maverick Mayor, who arranged for the importation of hundreds of thousands into Harlem, guaranteeing to put them on relief. He and his successor in Congress, Vito Marcantonio, later repeated the process with hundreds of thousands of Puerto Ricans.

The success of these large-scale directed migrations awakened other politicians to the gold-strike, and they sent colonizers down to the deep South, loaded with big talk and money for bus-fares. As the new voters arrived in the North they were put on welfare rolls or given government or municipal jobs. When these weren't available jobs in private industry were commandeered.

The colonizing agents are often CIO or NAACP field officers, with assists from the Americans for Democratic Action, Eleanor Roosevelt and the other tune-callers of the crackpot set, who dished up the advance propaganda to get the Negroes into the proper mood for the major move, which means cutting off family ties, uprooting from land lived on for generations and facing a new civilization—all hazardous for unskilled, uneducated minorities.

In the South the Negro vote is wasted; even where they are permitted to vote they now go Democratic, which until now has not been needed in Dixie. In the North, however, these new Democratic ballots can be counted on to cancel out Republicans, so they were and are moved into GOP congressional and legislative districts, where they swing elections.

Meanwhile, the reverse process occurred to the masterminds who figured that many CIO and AFL votes were no longer needed in highly industrialized Northern communities—so why not send the white faithful, through plant dispersal, to Dixiecrat Southern states, to insure elections? That is one reason why the white Southern population is increasing.

When the Negroes come to the North they are told they have equality and can go to white men's schools. Shrewd politicians woo their votes with FEPCs, anti-lynch bills and other utopian Federal legislative measures which will not be adopted, and if they are will not be enforced. But the black man is still ostracized, forced to live in old ghettos or new ones, and to accept inferior types of employment. Only in one respect is he equal—rather superior—to Caucasians. That is in rigors of law enforcement.

By common consent all Northern police departments overlook all Negro crime unless a white man is involved. In that case the white man is frequently made the goat by rabid racists and over-enthusiastic, unrealistic equaters in a hurry.

In New York City a Negro, a twenty-one-year-old dance-band drummer, leaving a mid-Manhattan jam session at 3 o'clock in the morning, stepped into a waiting taxi and ordered the jehu to take him to a Harlem address. White cabbies are afraid of such hauls at such hours. This one refused. The passenger kicked out all the windows and with obscenities ordered the driver to carry him or have his throat cut. The taxi started. But the wise nighthawk pulled up before a police station and ran in. The enraged fare followed him. A white detective confronted the pursuer inside and held him off from the driver. The Negro drew a dagger, which he had carried in a tailor-made harness on his suspender, and stabbed the officer right where his blade would have penetrated the heart. But the point struck a 10-cent pocket-comb, and the detective was wounded instead of being murdered.

The maniacal musician was overpowered. Hospital tests showed he was loaded with alcohol as well as heroin, a homicidal combination. But already a frantic round-robin was being circulated, signed by Dashiel Hammett, Vito Marcantonio and dozens of others of their rabid persuasion, demanding the discharge of the cop because of "police brutality unprecedented in the annals of the world." Public meetings were called, resolutions were screamingly voted, circulars were passed on the streets, and a defense fund was raised for the prisoner.

Twice he was tried and twice the jury disagreed. The testimony of a half-dozen eye-witnesses seemed to have made out a prima facie felony case. After the second disagreement, an assistant prosecutor approached a white woman, not connected with any organization, who had stood out on the jury for acquittal, and asked her why. With bland brevity she replied:

"I would never convict a Negro. Never—no matter what witnesses say!"

As you turn through these pages you will see that in no instance is a Northern Negro colony closed up, regardless of how tight the curfew is on in other parts of town. Regardless of the community, drinking, doping, gambling and whoring are permitted in all of them, blatant, unashamed and around the clock.

Actual arrest figures show that Negroes, with one-tenth of the acknowledged population, commit about 50 per cent of the nation's crimes. Mind you, these are crimes for which arrests were made. But any cop will tell you that less than one of five Negroes is apprehended. In many big cities all Negro murders are put down as traffic accidents. Negro knifings are disorderly conduct, usually not even that.

Lottery flourishes openly in all colored settlements, always backed and banked at the top by a white member of the national Crime Syndicate. Negro pushers are used to sell marijuana and harder dope in every town.

Northern Negroes are getting education as good as or better than whites. More colored students than whites attend the District of Columbia public schools, from kindergarten through junior college. After graduation, they are too advanced for the common jobs—but white employers will not hire them for what they have been qualified to do. Negro stenos, accountants, secretaries, technicians, etc., rarely get jobs in white industry. So they are forced into the civil service, where they can get in because of their Northern bloc voting power. Anyone who has not had occasion to visit a public building—state, municipal or Federal—for years will be surprised at the change, with Negroes conspicuous. They are becoming a special ruling caste of government servants who will in time control civil service at all levels, except in the top directing echelons, and there they are making great, rapid inroads. They are not yet represented proportionately in such rarefied strata as the courts, Congress, heads of bureaus, etc., but all that and more is on the way.

Mathematicians who study immigration and population movements in respect to voting estimate that by 1960 there will be more Negroes than whites in Chicago. They say that by 1965 the combined Negro and Puerto Rican population of New York will exceed the Caucasian. These figures are based on the experiences of the last decade, which show whites moving out to suburbs while Negroes flock into the cities. These experts say Chicago will have a Negro Mayor in 1965; New York in 1970.

It is estimated that by 1970 the colored population in Dixie will have sunk from its present 10,000,000 to 2,000,000, while the North will have more than 25,000,000.

Already the inroads in the North have made great changes in the cultural pattern as well as in politics and urban living. The African motif becomes more and more emphasized in art, music, literature. African décor is quite the rage in smart shops. Music was captured years ago. Colored writers are entering the best-seller lists. The stage and concert halls show similar trends. A Negro ham is a star doing what a white man can't sell. It is considered smart and intellectual to patronize Negro arts, associate with colored performers and jump the racial fences sexually. The white girl who repels a Negro's advances is called a snob and Fascist. But white men who chase colored girls are called "degenerates" by the Negroes, who resent their women who sleep with whites.

All this while the great mass of Negroes, North and South, are innocent victims of political chess-players. As a race and as a group, they are less interested in political ideologies than is any other segment of the American population. These still happy-go-lucky folk are more concerned with a full meal today than civil rights tomorrow. Even in the upper brackets, $5,000-a-week colored stage and movie stars are usually in hock. Big band leaders draw their salaries from day to day. Snappy clothes, snappy gals and snappy cars are their criteria of success. That is chiefly the reason why efforts to Communize the Negro have failed. They don't give a damn, except for a small minority, about the promised manna, nor are they excited about discriminations, which to them are natural. Few want to mix. Most whites aren't fun.

But the Fair Deal is another thing. That is real. They vote Democratic not because they believe in or even know what the party's principles are, but because white men tell them to vote that way, and in return give them concrete financial returns—government handouts, government housing and government jobs. They stop to count the eventual cost no more than do whites.

Southerners see the changes a different way. For decades they've said the solution was to "send all the damn 'Nigras' back to

Africa." Now that they're leaving, planters and merchants are desperate. Southern Negroes are taking advantage of their superior bargaining power. The Negro is getting a better break there—not because of the Fair Deal, but in spite of it. The problem is working itself out.

Yet there are many tensions and problems still to be solved. Southerners resent uppity Negroes per se, with inbred hot hatred.

It is a common practice to stop and rob Negroes with Northern license-plates and good-looking cars who travel back to see their friends and kin. This abuse is most flagrant in the Carolinas.

Highway troopers flag such parties, force them to get out and show their papers. They grill them on where they got such fly autos, what they are doing so far from where they "belong," and say something to this effect:

"We don't stand for fresh boogies down this way. You act suspicious. More than likely you're wanted and making a getaway. You'll be held till we can verify who you are, make sure you didn't steal that car."

The terrified Negroes are soon robbed of their money as a bribe to avoid being locked up and "lost" in a Southern calaboose, and they are in luck if they don't get a pistol-whipping or blackjack battering, "for luck."

There is little balm in recourse to minor courts or officials in the you-all country for any Negroes, and none for those who live outside the immediate area.

But violence against blacks has decreased, almost vanished, despite publicity to the contrary, served up by Reds and Northern firebrands. During the last five years, there were seven Negro lynchings in the U.S., 1.2 per year. Many times more white people were lynched by union thugs in the North. Thirty Negroes ran for public office in the South in 1951—without violence. Five were elected, others only narrowly defeated.

Yet the FEPCers yell for anti-lynch laws, not to cure an evil (which no longer exists), but to give the Federal government "force powers" to supersede the police prerogatives of the Southern states at will. Granted that Negroes have rights. But so have states.

9. "LABOR" – THE ONLY LEGAL MONOPOLY

YOUR REPORTERS carry three union cards between them. They were dragooned into CIO and AFL join-or-no-work organizations.

Thus they are part of the 15,000,000 the mandarins of "labor" claim to "represent." And we go on record here to state that the gangsters, Reds, extortioners, political leeches and bribers do not speak for us.

The only union to which we pay homage is the Union of the United States.

Labor unions are now openly waging class war. They have long since passed their primary purpose: to right the wrongs of workers, which even at its best was un-American in concept, if not always in execution. We feel that all combinations set up for special privileges of groups, unobtainable by individuals, are trusts, though supine Congresses have exempted labor unions by arbitrary legislation from penalties for restraint of trade, restraint of competition and restraint of life, liberty and the pursuit of happiness.

It is against all principles of our Constitution that two men—or any number—should be entitled to do what one man may not do.

And such preferred bodies, armored with extra-legal rights, have found they can seize many other rights because they have become rich, can influence mass votes, and attract venal leaders who become captors and who now rule our economic lives with a grasping, greedy grip on prices of everything, and with enough political weight to bar any curb on their power. Bosses of unions, unaccountable to anyone, overrule the President, defy the Supreme Court, control our national defense and in many instances finance, and betray us to our enemies.

Members of most unions are as voiceless and as voteless as Stalin's serfs. They have nothing to say about the running of their mutual organizations, or the spending of their money, or the choice of their officers. The broad picture of unionism in America in 1952 shows that most unions are organized rackets with all that the words imply, owned outright by a small group of evil men, many of whom are as morally putrid as the gangsters and polluted politicians with whom they do business.

These unions, with approval of laws slipped over for their benefit by vote-hungry politicians, keep themselves and their friends and relatives in office and in sole secret control of the vast union treasuries for life. Any who rebel are maimed or murdered, or, if given mercy, only deprived of a livelihood.

On the one side, the self-elected and perpetuated union czars have strait-jacketed the workers. Their enforced contributions first built up the huge wealth of the unions, which now aggregates twenty-five billion dollars, untaxed, often withdrawn without itemized vouchers at the pleasure of the commissars who control them.

The working stiffs, who by entrenched unioneers are thought of and spoken of as "dogs," are kept in line with a few crumbs and bones. They are held together with promises of "breaking the bosses," always a popular battle cry to the bitter.

Meanwhile, union leaders get together secretly in expensive watering places and divide the booty. Depending on the industry, special concessions are made to the employers who play ball—come through with kickbacks at the expense of the stiffs or competitors. There is hardly a union in the country which cannot be dealt with. The consideration is not always graft—a few small professional unions are operated by dreamers who think they are being realistic when they give special concessions.

As this book unfolds you will read some specific examples of practical unionism at work, such as Dave Beck's infamous Teamsters Union, some members of which control Seattle prostitutes as a sideline, or Walter Reuther's United Auto Workers, some officials of which are partners in a billion-dollar gambling racket.

In a recent issue of her syndicated slop, the widow Roosevelt approvingly opined, "The union seems to have adopted as its slogan: 'What is good for us must also be good for the country as a whole.'" What profane impertinence! Not what is good for the country must also be good for the union, but what is good for the union must be good for the country! In one sentence, she gave the whole racket away.

For example, Jimmy Byrnes lost out to Truman for Vice-President (and President) at the 1944 convention because he stepped on the toes of the railroad brotherhoods, and while "Assistant" President, vetoed their raise.

This has not been printed: Before the historic Chicago con-clave, the Brotherhood's Whitney phoned FDR and laid down the law. Roosevelt, the Aladdin to all unioneers, who cleared every-thing with Sidney (Hillman, of the Amalgamated) folded up, though Byrnes was his first choice. Truman got Hillman's okay.

Similarly, on atomic energy projects, the United States Employ-ment Service, an organ of the government, takes lists of prospec-tive employes from the unions and transmits them without change to management, who must hire as written. Prospective workers do not get on the list because of merit. It is usually necessary to make a special under-table payment to a union heeler who bosses the particular project. The worker may not be able to do the work. But he goes on the public payroll automatically. Bad security risks get work this way; it takes many months before the overburdened and understaffed FBI can catch up to them. Then they have ap-peals and appeals from appeals.

While these words were being written, the American Guild of Variety Artists, which holds sway over night clubs, vaudeville, etc., was being investigated by the New York State Insurance Depart-ment for unlicensed policy writing and unauthorized kickbacks. AGVA is one of the loosest unions on the horizon. A former officer was convicted for extortion from employers. The manage-ment kicks around a staggering fund in the form of cash "per-formance bonds," required from all employers. Jack Irving, pres-ent national czar, overlooked gangster operations in Chicago—his home bailiwick.

Most beverage and liquor unions are mobster-owned from top to bottom, their chief duty being to keep manufacturers of non-gangster liquors and beers out of locations. Strikes are called on bars and stores which do not sell hoodlum-approved spirits, or which feature non-mob stuff.

In another instance the Sailors Union of the Pacific notified the Federal Maritime Commission that it did not approve of the interior design of two new freighters. Though sailors' cabins are as large as those for first-class passengers on Atlantic greyhounds, the union said its men would be cramped, and laid down its own requirements, or no ships would sail. These included certain types of inner-spring mattresses, a particular make of swivel chair, etc., all pointing to the fact that certain union officials know certain furniture contractors. The Maritime commissioners knew that—yet few words were printed about it.

Members of the Red-dominated United Electrical Workers operate the pools and bookmaking in their plants. The GE factories in Schenectady are worth millions a year to top UEW bosses.

When union officials are arrested for breaking the laws of the community or the land workers are levied against to meet their legal expenses. Jack Hall, Hawaiian regional director of Bridges' unions said, "The time is rapidly approaching when unions will have to demand cost of legal increases as well as cost of living adjustments." That time will not be far off. And the NLRB will probably grant them. It has forced employers to provide free hams, lunch money and Christmas bonuses. So why not defense against gambling and pimping raps?

The holier-than-thou United Auto Workers, some of whose kings split a billion-dollar gambling plum, pretend to be against gambling in the auto plants. The gullible *New York Times* falls for their declamation that union members "convicted of breaking the laws" will lose the union's bargaining support. But the union has set up a "clearance committee" to try all suspected cases first. Those "unjustly" accused will be supported with the union bankroll. You can be sure that no shop bookmaker who kicks in will be accused, except "unjustly."

There is no end to this criminality of some unioneers. A full report would include every felony from extortion, blackmail and assault to enforced servitude, white slavery, dope and alien-smuggling, piracy and murder.

Politicians play ball with union goons for the same reason they do not touch important gangsters. The unions pay off, too; they lay it on the line in graft and they come up with campaign funds. The union chiefs and the gangsters are so intertwined that in many unions and in many instances they are one and the same, and the gangsters are affiliated with the office-holders of both parties in every city and state.

We have room here for one classic example—the International Ladies Garment Workers Union, AFL, with more than 400,000 members, most of them in New York City, a personal pocket property of David Dubinsky, sage and seer of the labor movement.

With its sister union, the late Sidney Hillman's Amalgamated Clothing Workers (men's wear), the ILGWU spawned modern gangsterdom and was directly responsible for Murder, Inc. Its story has been recited so often, in so many different ways, we will not repeat it; but none who told it ever traced the sluggings, maimings and killings to the upper echelons of the two unions.

Much of New York's giant needle trade industry—the great

city's largest—is mob-owned and mob-ridden, not only with the connivance of the unions, but in partnership with them. This is the garment center situation as of today, something you will not learn from the tinselled probes of the terror-struck Truman.

Many, if not most, of the larger houses are owned by underworlders, or are under their protection. In each house one or more union officials also own stock. Such factories are exempt from the stringent regulations the unions enforce against the rank and file of small manufacturers.

For instance, Irving Sherman, Costello pal, is an owner of Courtshire Fashions, one of the giants of the industry. It operates ostensibly as a union shop, but Sherman is secretly given waivers on practically every point in the contract, so that in fact he is nonunion even to the extent of being allowed to manufacture in scab shops out of town.

But small manufacturers are forced to operate under strict union conditions, carrying heavy handicaps as against the big mucky-mucks who made deals.

This industry was once entirely Jewish. Now Italians have come into it on such a large scale almost half the workers are Italian, and many of the biggest corporations also are Italian.

The channels of contact in the needle trades are these: Italians work through Joe Straci, alias Joe Stretch, of the important firm of Zimmet & Straci. Jews work through Tom Cutlow, alias Tom Cutty. These gentlemen pass the word on through Joe Bresslau, head of the ILGWU's Pressers Union, who sends it on and up to the department in charge of the particular situation.

If the matter has to do with the transportation, rather than manufacture of ladies wear, the fix is sidetracked through John Dioguardi, business manager of the AFL United Automobile Workers, not to be confused with Reuther's CIO-UAW. Dioguardi's union comprises men who work on the autos. He is better known to the police as Johnny Dio. Though a union official, he is also on the payroll of the Truckers' Association—the employers—and is czar of both.

The lovely part of this arrangement, for the crooks, is this: nonmobster manufacturers cannot operate unless they obey all union rules. If they refuse to sign up, thugs help them make decisions. Several murders a year still take place in the cloak and suit market, but are not publicized as union killings, because newspapers are diverted with false reports to police on causes for the crimes.

A recent cause celebre involved Benjamin Macri, who was arrested for the murder of a union organizer after a long manhunt and a $25,000 reward offer by Dubinsky. He claimed his man had been killed by hoodlums in the employ of strike-breakers. Actually both the deceased and the defendant were thugs and the slaying involved a battle over bookmaking profits.

Many gullible newspapers preached a crusade against the "evil men" who wantonly slew a Dubinsky stooge. But the jury quickly acquitted Macri who at once went to work for Benny Levine in his non-union cloak shop in Hazleton, Pa., which the union exempts in appreciation of Levine's past services to the ILGWU in the days of Murder, Inc. Levine has no trouble underselling manufacturers who are signed up with Dubinsky.

Frank Hogan, New York's fearless and imaginative District Attorney, has a confidential squad working on the needle trades where the boodle and graft make the waterside-take penny ante stuff by comparison. None has ever dared tangle with Dubinsky before. If Hogan "gets" this union it will make him Governor, and he will deserve it.

Many top unioneers have become millionaires through kickbacks and as partners in the big houses; Dubinsky, however, does not need such take, because, in addition to his lifelong salary of $25,000 a year he has an unlimited and unitemized expense account—tax free. And he has one-man say over the union's $160,-000,000 available as a political slush fund, including the $80,000,-000 welfare fund turned back to it by the State of New York, which also gave the right to levy taxes to some unions, including the ILGWU. No accounting need be made to the State either, but Dubinsky can check employers' books and veto their business expenses.

The manner in which that fund is used and how it is enhanced is best illustrated by New York's recent election for President of the City Council. But first we must go back a year, to the Kefauver Committee hearings there.

Now that the hoopla has been forgotten, the record is clear. Rudy Halley, the video avenger, was an ambitious young man. He shouted, he shrieked, he yelled; he demanded the forthwith appearance of Frank Costello's bosom companion, Irving Sherman. But he did not look for him with a magnifying glass. When the committee finally got him, it asked nothing of any consequence.

Meanwhile, through days and nights of expensive grandstanding with Virginia Hill, Mayor O'Dwyer and a couple of $50-a-week policy-slip peddlers, the committee at no time and in no

manner connected Dave Dubinsky's union with the scores of un-
solved gang murders that took place in the garment center.

Dubinsky saw a great future for a fellow with a head on his
shoulders. Why, Rudy might even become Mayor, which is now
being planned as part of the greatest union-underworld-political
steal in the history of the country.

Halley was given the councilmanic nomination by the Liberal
Party, a New York splinter outfit supported by this union and
thousands of rich and silly left-wingers, but dominated by
Dubinsky, Luigi Antonini and other shrewd union professionals.

Rudy wasn't given an outside chance to cop the election against
the regular party nominees; but, all at once, several factors turned
up which made the old-line politicians blink.

Rudy's newspaper and radio advertising ran about ten to one
compared to both his regular opponents put together. Someone
had to pay for that. Then word went up and down the line, among
New York's million-odd union members, that they'd better vote
for Rudy or else. Most of them are uneducated, unread naturalized citizens who believe the shop union bosses when they are told
that they can tell how you vote, even on a voting machine. They
believe that because they know it happens in the old country.

Then the high-pressure boys got to work. Irving Sherman or
one of his tough associates would put in a call to a manufacturer
and suggest that he contribute to Rudy's campaign—and name an
amount. A few minutes later Charlie Zimmerman, Dubinsky's top
lieutenant, would also call—and quite by coincidence name exactly the same amount.

These strong-arm methods were effective. Both the Dems and
GOP were broke, but the Halley campaign fund was so well-
heeled that about $2,000,000 was returned to contributors after
the election! Though the official report will show no such thing, between $3,000,000 and $4,000,000 was spent on his campaign or
pocketed by some campaign collectors for the mob, the union and
themselves, and paid for indirectly by every woman in the country who will find the cost of electing the daring young man on her
next new frock.

Dubinsky is feared. Few dare cross him. The penalty may be
painful. But he gets good publicity, too. Barry Gray, a particularly
raucous and objectionable specimen of disc-jockey with a large
night following of prostitutes and pinks, is a hot booster of unions,
and of Dubinsky's especially. It is probably a coincidence that
Barry is sponsored by Nat Sherman, who runs a big cigar store

in the garment center. Sherman's store is patronized by all the expensive Havana-lovers among the big-shot gangsters and cloak-and-suiters. Nat Sherman happens to be a brother of Costello's dearest pal, Irving Sherman, who happens to be a dress manufacturer, who happens to be friendly with Dubinsky. Conviction by association? Of course not. That's un-American!

PART TWO

THE PLACES
(*Confidential!*)

10. NEW ORLEANS—PARADISE LOST

THE ONE spot which two hard-hearted wreckers of illusion had hoped to treat with chivalry and reverence, such as gentlemen might lavish on a dazzling woman or rare old vintage, shattered any such gallant diversion from our hob-nailed methodology.

We remembered New Orleans. We were conscious of the destructive changes which have coarsened and corrupted our national manners, our spirit, our sense of beauty, our love of romance and adventure entrusted to us as our heritage. But we dreamed that somewhere some of the remnants would resist and remain. And if there were such a place, it would be New Orleans.

This was the old world in the new; Paris, Madrid and Trinidad; flavored with deep Dixie, throbbing to its savage African music with obbligatos serenading love behind the filigreed grills where dark eyes burn. This was where wickedness did not quite seem to be vice.

This was the city where men kept their voluptuous octoroons but dueled with sword and pistol at the slightest reflection on their wives and sweethearts; where square miles of bordellos were maintained by picturesque madames who had their own newspaper to report the social affairs of their doxies and to portray their enticements; where curtained couches were appurtenances of private dining rooms in the last American refuge of exotic cooking; where drinks were concocted by knowing and loving masters of mixing who handed down the formulas to their descendants; where, in the shadow of the old slave market, the Negroes were humble but happy—servants with affection for and pride in those who understood them, indulged them, let them enjoy their lives

74

in their own ways, instead of striving to bleach them in the image
of the white reformer and exploiter.

We realize that to many today such sentiments may appear
blasphemous. We, too, have been exposed to the propaganda of
"progress." Equal opportunities for all is an irresistible slogan in
theory. But if the pursuit of happiness is also a true human ob-
jective, we know that in the process of forced marches toward
leveling all mankind onto a single plane life may become a
cruel and distorted actuality. We see it in the ruptured relations
of races and classes, fomented by hatred and too often incited by
professional meddlers to whom smiles and songs and love and
mutual tolerance must fall before the regimentation of a faceless
proletariat composed of identical machine-parts, molded for
eventual world communism.

Millions who sincerely believe they are helping to lift up the
underprivileged are agitating them out of contentment into a vor-
tex of angry strife in abortive movements that violate the funda-
mentals of social gestation, which were meant to take their course
like the winds and tides. Not to be impatiently hurried by the
pressing of buttons which tempt the thumbs because they are
shiny and because they would set something in motion which they
can see and hear.

Men must and will go forward. Even though they were to set
themselves against that, wars and floods and earthquakes and the
very rust of time will force the new where was the old, no matter
how much beloved. But history has proven repeatedly that self-
seeking man is a destructive animal; invents bulldozers and blasts
with dynamite. He has reached his eighth heaven on earth with
the atom bomb.

This grisly modernization obliterates everything within its
radius, and the first to die are the primary ethics of human relations. These are not analyzable or translatable. They cannot
exist unless many individuals have agreed and concurred that they
want them so; their gist is in those wishes, not in rules or laws
except by common consent, without influence or interference of
truculent minorities or interloping intruders.

New Orleans is an extreme example because it is far from the
industrial belt, was far from the trampling hordes that, having
never seen or known gracious living, scrambled and screamed only
for the immediate tangibles, and thus quickly saw the leverage
of mass-organization, political and economic. For the powers that
these could exact they enlisted numbers—and everything that

walked on two feet was another potential number. And to hold them all and use them all, they had to give them something. The easiest thing to give them was what they did not have to give—equality.

Since there is no such thing and never will be, and since the shrewd, acquisitive leaders, such as crop up in all groups of men, knew that they could not uplift the ignorant and moronic by quick action under the American system, they began to pervert that system more and more, in various degrees, toward the Marxian foreign concept of a Soviet state.

In New Orleans that was impractical. The people were rooted in the society which had flourished for three centuries, during vicissitudes which came and went and left little mark. So it had to be done from within, by a crude, coarse, conscienceless, native upstart who raised the inflammatory battle-cry of revolution:

"Every man a king!"

It reverberated through the bayous, along the levees, through the oil fields and pecan-groves, among the share-croppers, into the shanties of the cotton-pickers and the cabins of the white trash. These were the congenital have-nots, long overripe for a flaming confidence man with the relentless ferocity that could germinate in only one of their own.

Huey Long lied and harangued and became the czar of Louisiana. Only New Orleans brushed him off. Its people despised him. So his Louisiana took over their New Orleans and crushed it in his clammy clutch.

The Crescent City had survived pestilence, floods, sieges, bombardments, devastating fires and the tortures of Reconstruction. But this was revolution. The aristocracy which had ruled and driven with a light rein was rudely yanked out, and into its place leaped the vulgar, venal crooks with shibboleths of democracy and all the terrorisms of a totalitarian oligarchy.

The old families, whose social dominance had been undisputed and had spread over political behavior which preserved the unwritten tenets of deportment and relationships in this balmy, semi-tropical cosmopolis, became the object of attack by the empowered rabble. Fortunes were decimated by vicious taxation to build roads into swamps and erect grotesque public buildings and other disproportionate monuments to the new royalty in overalls and zoot-suits. The Long mob wiped out the unique economy which the city had long preserved and enjoyed. Human history has demonstrated that communities adapt their manners to the conduct of their masters. And those were now a coterie of drunken thieves, up from the backwoods and the gutters, who hated everything genteel and cried for the blood of the nobility as did the Jacobins.

Only by such violent overthrow could New Orleans, the unchangeable, be overturned.

The leisurely charm, the culture which can be maintained only by a secure upper class, the contentment of the well-fed poor who live cheerfully, and even gaily, under the benign indulgences of their betters, were all routed by the sudden clamor for an unrealistic equalization which was out of character above and below.

New Orleans owes its origin to its strategic position as a port, on the River and on the Gulf. From that grew its wealthy strata in its ship-owners, ware-housers, financiers, merchants and great land-owners, holders of many slaves to whom emancipation gave back their own bodies, but scarcely altered their existence. The riffraff of the Mississippi, the sailors from the swill of Europe, Cuba and South and Central America, and a wave of immigration from Italy, which formed the first Mafia on this continent, brought together three-quarters of a million of the low-bred and inter-bred scum of the world. As river traffic declined, railroading took its place and drew the dregs of Texas, Alabama, Arkansas and Tennessee, ruffians of similar enough propensities to be assimilated in the lower layers of brawling, boozing, fornicating laborers and loafers and illiterate Negroes, who flocked there for the fleshpots of the city, not for the hopes and aspirations of stolid North-European immigrants who set forth to the promised land of small farms, little stores and the dream of some day owning a cottage.

In such an environment as New Orleans afforded, with its lazy climate, its vested French and Spanish morals and its accepted imported barriers between the few elect and the many in hoi-polloi, there came about an esoteric product of rarefied civilization, serenely floating above the lowest conglomeration of all the races and of all the nations.

No place, including the New York tenderloin, could approach the obscene and lecherous extremes, the excesses of some sections of the old French Quarter; but within its confines were also the mansions of the finest families, behind high outer walls, with verdant hidden patios, where morality was sacrosanct and growing girls were chaperoned almost to the edge of the marriage bed; and here also was the French Opera House, subsidized by wealth for the highest in world artistry; and here, with proud, loving and dedicated hands the finest restaurants served the dishes which are still unknown and unequaled elsewhere on earth—at Antoine's, the Louisiane, Fabacher's, the old Monteleone, Gallatoi's and many small cafes which catered only to local gourmets.

Along the Shell Road, the beautiful drive to the water's edge favored by lovers in the dim of the moon, was the Half Way House.

Even Canal Street, the major avenue of commerce, was quaint and individual, and the merchants were reluctant to tear down the old bastard architecture to utilize the angular functional, chain-store, claptrap design for economy of floor-space and maximum of illuminated display. Even the early movie "palaces" followed in a measure the stately patterns born long before they were conceived. These may appear to be whimsical considerations in an age indoctrinated with the worship of peak production, intensive collectivism as against the workings of the human equation, extortion by taxation of the prosperous for largesse to the shiftless and shameless incompetentts and parasites. But it was such imponderables that combined to set New Orleans apart from all other cities, not only in the cold North but in the sunny South.

Long and his gang put everything that was rare and beautiful under the hammer as concessions, degraded it into a Coney Island with magnolias and a third-rate factory town. This sort of political seizure brings with it the need to pacify and hold the preponderant majority. And since this was state rule, in one of the most backward of states, it had to cater to Cajuns and others who hated the city and who set out to remold it by their own criteria, including their Sunday school standards, to which the godless bosses paid heed. And while Long and many of his cronies caroused with easy women, they fell in with the new rash for "reform."

Basin and Rampart Streets and some contiguous blocks on Dauphin, Royal, St. Louis and around the Vieux Carre were flagrantly and honestly given over to reasonably regulated and frankly tolerated houses of sin, from luxuriant and selective bordellos down to unspeakable cribs. And while these were sprawled about pretty widely, they were still segregated and policed. Though this may be deplorable, the district became a tourist attraction, advertised by libertines everywhere and by sailors who trumpeted its superior seductions around the globe. Now fewer tourists and salesmen and seamen come there, and what they spread could as well be told of the loathsome hookers of Baltimore, where, on The Hook, that generic word originated.

Vacationers stopped coming. Business was diverted elsewhere; to Houston and Miami. The scandals of the Long rough-riding antics scared off investments—nothing was safe, including newspapers. Even the perennial Mardi Gras lost its carnal carnival characteristics, for royalty was passé, though in motley.

Huey Long was assassinated. But his brother is now Governor and his son is a United States Senator. Neither is a wild firebrand like Huey; but Longism dominates almost all factions of the Democratic party (the only one) and all are crazy and crooked.

Nothing much goes in New Orleans without the nod of former Mayor Maestri, a spark-plug of the old Long machine. Mayor de Lesseps Morrison thinks he runs the town, but he doesn't. Morrison, young, social, ambitious and apparently clean, is one of the few reasonably successful "reform" city heads. He is in his second term. But there are things an unaffiliated Mayor can't do or doesn't know about. The mobsters are intrenched and their influence is higher up. So cops lock up strip-teasers, raid neighborhood poker clubs, after-hour joints and other such small-fry stuff, while politically immunized big boys operate, unafraid and unharassed.

Former Mayor Maestri is a multi-millionaire. He owned blocks of high income real estate in the red light district, which was recently condemned and torn down—and by coincidence, what do you think went up there? A public housing project. No one was surprised, because Maestri is the fair-haired boy in Washington. He and the late shipping magnate, William Helis, "The Golden Greek," were poker-playing cronies of General Harry Vaughan. Helis operated with Frank Costello. Maestri and Helis were partners in many deals.

Maestri owns New Orleans. Huey Long's son, Senator Russell Long, is a power in the state. He is tied up closely with Truman, though Louisiana voted Dixiecrat in 1948. Russell's candidate for Governor was young and debonair Congressman Hale Boggs, a joiner and a bleeding heart, nosed out in the primaries by Robert Kennan, a county judge and "poor man's" candidate who went into the run-off with the support of Senator Long, the left-wing *Item* and the back-parish sans culottes. He is the spokesman for the shipping interests.

Governor Long, who could not succeed himself under state law, is the head of another faction, which sometimes works with the Senator and sometimes against. He is closer to Allen Ellender, the senior Senator, a protégé of the late Huey, with everything that means. One of the times they worked together was when the Federal Housing Authority at first turned down the loan application of Claybourne Towers. This was a mistake. Its builder was boss Crump of Tennessee. So Ellender, of the Earl Long faction, and Boggs of the Russell Long faction, went to bat. The loan came through and the building is going up. The telegraph between Governor Long and Senator Ellender is Clem Sekit, an attorney, and, naturally, a popular one.

Being in good politically in Louisiana is most of the battle won. Take the case of State Senator LeBlanc, the fantastic Hadacol huckster. It seems he was in bad with Uncle Sam once before, when he was making a phony headache remedy. So Turney Gratz, the ex-RFC fixer, went on his payroll and Bill Boyle, his boss, called the Food and Drug Administration.

When the newspapers discovered that 4th Ward leader Henry Grelle, deputy Commissioner of Public Buildings, owned a lottery, his superior said, "Well, he's a sick man." That ended that.

To visitors, bald and syrupy-voiced Seymour Weiss, of the Roosevelt Hotel, is a combination Grover Whalen, Cesar Ritz and Sherman Billingsley. The swells, celebrities and top mobsters stay there. His Blue Room is New Orleans' leading night club, of the Copacabana grade. Weiss was high in Huey Long politics and was police commissioner of New Orleans until he went to the Federal pen on mail fraud charges in connection with the Long gang swindles. This was after Huey had broken with FDR. One who shared a cell with Seymour was fat Abe Shushan, immensely wealthy New Orleans furniture and department store owner, who also dabbled in Long politics at great profit to himself. After he got jugged it cost the municipality $35,000 to take the name "Shushan" off the municipal airport. Weiss and Shushan are thick socially and commercially and both are closely allied with many notorious leaders of the Unione Siciliano. Their close pal was the late Sam Maceo, of neighboring Galveston.

Shushan also supports a suite in New York, at the Waldorf. He is a flaming figure in cafe society, usually squiring flashy floozies.

The noted Seymour Weiss charm is about as bona fide as the smile of a hotel room clerk. But the real smoothie in New Orleans is Frank Costello's partner and most intimate friend, the man who is said to be the only non-Italian voting member of the Mafia— Dandy Phil Kastel.

Phil is a self-made gentleman. He was once in trouble in New

York on bucket shop charges. He could sell anything and the state said he did. Until the Senators meddled in New Orleans, Phil was operating the Beverly Club, just outside the city limits in Jefferson Parish. (Counties are parishes in Louisiana.) It was a genuine pleasure to lose your money at the Beverly, the most distinguished and distinctive gambling joint and cafe in the counttry. Kastel has the soul of an artist and he designed and decorated his salon as befit.

Pre-Kefauver Jefferson Parish was about as wide open as Nevada, with everything. When the whitewash got under way it was realized that a few of the publicized gamblers and racketeers would have to take the rap temporarily, so the public's attention would be focused away from the real evils and the real bosses. Jefferson Parish was blatant and it had to be hit. Furthermore, its sheriff was a pushover for probers, a public official whose only explanation for his bank account was that he always bet on the right horses.

Chumps who followed the committee hearings naturally believe that the plumed knights killed all the dragons; that Jefferson Parish is shuttered, the casinos are converted into churches and the gamblers have gone into monasteries. New Orleanians will tell you different.

Sheriff Clancy did put on a clamp—temporarily. None of the gay spots has been torn down; their owners are using the hiatus to paint and varnish and recarpet. They may be in action again before you read this.

Meanwhile, so as not to let the dice get cold, they moved their gambling equipment into St. Bernards Parish, on the other side of the city, and many so openly advertise in New Orleans.

The Club Forest, personnel and attractions, according to the ads, is "temporarily" at the Crescent and the Riverview Clubs.

Joe Brown runs the Jai Lai Club.

Terry and Judy operate the Araby.

The O'Dwyer (not our Ambassador) gang runs the Ritz.

All have slot-machines, gaming casinos and anything you want. Kastel is resting, recovering from a serious eye operation. And business is so depressing in Jefferson Parish since the emigration that a Protestant clergyman who yapped against Sheriff Clancy is now backing him.

The Kefauver investigation in New Orleans was streamlined and to the point, designed to hit the most front pages in the shortest time. And it succeeded. This took rehearsing, prompting and advance script writing. One committee investigator told a local newspaperman that stage-manager Halley had instructed the agents what and whom to pass by, all in the interest of justice and time-saving, of course.

These are some of the things that did not interest the stream-lined Kefauver Committee:

New Orleans, no longer the mighty catch-all seaport, is the country's chief gateway for the importation of illegally entered Sicilians, who are brought ashore in numbers as great as 10,000 a year, with connivance of local immigration authorities, under orders from the Department of Justice in Washington. These Sicilians are mostly law-breakers at home. They are joined with other criminals from the mainland and relocated from New Orleans by padrones to our leading big cities, where they are put to work as torpedoes, dope-pushers and other such menial under-world trainees.

Congressman James H. Morrison, no relative of the Mayor of New Orleans, is a Democrat from the Baton Rouge outposts. His ten years in the lower House have been distinguished chiefly by the large number of private bills entered by him to naturalize or grant permanent residence or halt deportation of undesirable aliens, almost all Sicilians and almost all ex-convicts either here or in Italy. Many have been naturalized under shady circumstances; oddly, our check showed only one resided in Morrison's own district. The rest were from other sections of Louisiana, mostly New Orleans, and at least one was a New Yorker closely affiliated with Frank Costello.

The Rumpus Room, on St. Charles Street, was not open yet when Kefauver was in town. This cocktail lounge is in a new apartment building constructed under the Federal Housing Administration. The lease for this desirable bar, a few feet from the swank Pontchartrain residential hotel, was mysteriously awarded to one John Vaccaro. Three weeks before the liquor license was issued, however, it came out that Vaccaro was an ex-dope-peddler, so the place opened with the name of Dorothy Grand on the license. But Vaccaro is on hand, entertaining tough-looking guests.

Gasper Gulotta is known affectionately as "The Little Mayor of the French Quarter." He is a brother of Pete Herman, the ex-pug. After a recent murder in the district, when a yahoo was killed with knockout drops, Gasper was named a member of the Mayor's vice committee. He owns Gasper's Bar, at 440 Bourbon Street, where a handbook was in operation when we were in New Orleans. His membership on the Mayor's vice committee is handy to clear the proper boys for below-town operations. Kefauver refused to allow testimony about Gulotta into the record.

The following is a list of some of the handbooks that were operating openly when we went through New Orleans, late in 1951: (After the enactment of the Federal tax law, they went underground a while, but at this writing most of them were again in operation, though less brazenly.)

Alphonse "Curly" Gagliano has a book at Curly's, on St. Charles Street, a block from City Hall. Jules Lopez runs a book in the bar-room at Poydras and St. Charles, across the street from Curly's. Sam Saia, pal of Gulotta and Pete Herman, has a string of books. The Two Jays Bar, at 1141 Decatur, in the French Quarter, is a betting place. So are Roses' Bar at 625 Poydras, run by F. Roses, and one at Clayton and Fernando, operated by J. Roses.

There's a handbook at Tranchina's, 729 Common. This runs with cops hanging around among the crowds coming into and out of the bar-room, in the heart of the business section.

To make it easy for the City Hall crowd one of the Marcello boys runs a book at St. Charles and Poydras, which can be seen from the Municipal Building. Maurice Washastrom has the 429 Bar and Poolroom, less than two blocks from City Hall.

One of the most powerful Italians, who throws his weight around politically, is Tony Cigali, owner of the Cigali Building, a noted lottery operator.

When charges were made to Kefauver that he was concentrating on Jefferson Parish to the exclusion of the city, he angrily brushed them aside, yet the minutes of his committee indicated that New Orleans gangsters and gamblers and their political stooges rated a preferential treatment. None of the above, which we found without trouble, was mentioned by the crusading candidate.

Carlos Marcello and Phil Kastel were too notorious to "bury" but the balance of the local Mafia council was conveniently forgotten. Among the important names given to him in executive session which he overlooked or flipped aside were:

Victor Trapani, Joe Poretto, Joe Barlotta, Sal Guerico, Philip Bonura and Luca Trombone. Nor did he seem to know that Frank Cappolla and Sam Carrolla, both of whom were "deported" to Tijuana, Mexico, are back at their familiar haunts in New Orleans.

He said not a word about the Mafia's ties to the top political mucky-mucks, blamed it all on a sheriff who was only a cog.

New Orleans was famed for its tail-for-sale. Now most of the demi-mondes are bar-room bawds up for grabs. Basin Street, which housed hussies of all nations, has been torn down and occupied by a housing project with little children's playgrounds where once the more mature frolicked. The only reminder of the glorious departed days is Lulu White's house, which still stands, shuttered and foreboding. This mulatto madame was famed for her gorgeous goods. Her house was patronized by the swells of the world. Now it is a landmark and mausoleum which cannot be torn down because most of Lulu's heirs are missing.

A few madames are operating, but quietly—little business in these days. Their main revenue comes from call-girl business.

Gertrude Yost, 935 Esplanade, phone FR 4814, is an agent who supplies party girls for conventions.

The famed Mme. Poursine is still running on Varone Street, but for chickenfeed take. Norma Wallace, who was married to Pete Herman, the little champ who went blind, is in the party-girl business at 1026 Conti Street, phone RA 1463.

The fabulous old French Quarter has gone rubberneck tourist. It's as bad as San Francisco's Barbary Coast and worse than Greenwich Village. New Orleans is washed up for spenders. Most of its dives are deadfalls. Only in one regard does the French Quarter hang on—retaining a half-dozen eating places still peerless. They line 'em up in front of Antoine's every night, with visitors from everywhere. The hicks have almost driven out the old New Orleanians, who were and still are connoisseurs of food. The sophisticated phone in advance and go in through the side door.

Now the typical FQ attraction is a place like Dan's International Settlement, where girls strip and do dirty dances. This tawdry cafe is noted for its dwarf waiters, chosen so they do not obstruct the patron's view of the stage.

But the faggot contingent, always large when such habits were not general, has multiplied. They hang out at Cafe Lafitte Uptown, which is not to be confused with the original Cafe Lafitte, 941 Bourbon Street, run by Tom Caplinger, a "character," one of the few genuine old Left-Bank atmosphere haunts left. Queers also patronize Tony Bacino's, 943 Charles, the Starlight Lounge and the My O My, in the West End.

Young Italian and Latin-American hoods roam the darker streets of the Quarter and rape and rob. But the toughest joints in town are on Decatur Street, infested with a pot pourri of waterfront rats, cheap chippies and stiletto-carrying Sicilians.

As Negro sections go, New Orleans is well behaved. The blacks have always been in a preferential position in this cosmopolitan and tolerant town. These were not plantation darkies, but superior and often educated house and body servants. Negroes vote, but they are no threat. Their ballots are bought and bagged in advance through "Beansy" Fauria. In the last gubernatorial election there was one Negro among the nine primary candidates for the top job. No lynching, race riots or hooded night-riders interfered with Negroes, to the chagrin of white and dark agitators and exaggerators who are running short of material.

One of these is carpetbagger David Stern, new publisher of the New Orleans *Daily Item*. Stern tried it in New York with the *Post*, which he lost, had to give up the *Philadelphia Record* and the Camden papers when the Newspaper Guild, a CIO union which he was the first to espouse, put him out of business with typical tactics—destroy your friends first, because they are the easiest. Stern thought New Orleans would be an ideal ground for FEPC preachments. He would show them. In this stronghold of one of the four states that voted Dixiecrat in 1948, he started plugging his causes. At once he instituted what so many Northern sheets still carrying the banner for an amplified Fourteenth Amendment do—he omitted identifying Negroes as such in police news.

Readers and advertisers tipped off David that Goliath didn't live there any more. So the paper quickly conformed. But business did not leap up so Stern started an anti-trust suit against the opposition, the beloved and solid *Times-Picayune*.

With all its vicissitudes, New Orleans is still way down deep. What Roosevelt and Long have done to it is irretrievable. But the boldest bosses must still allow for indigenous idiosyncracies which valiantly resist complete conquest. The rebel yell is still heard and cheered.

11. NEW ENGLAND CONFIDENTIAL

Codfish and Conmen

*I*T ALL began when the Pilgrims landed on Plymouth Rock; it seems now that maybe Plymouth Rock should have landed on the Pilgrims.

The *Mayflower* carried a band of religious extremists who

braved the stormy sea and a strange land of redskinned savages so that they could practice intolerance in their own ways, slaughter Indians and burn witches. Yet from this experiment in untrammeled barbarism developed the sources of our wealth, our culture, our conquest over hostile land and uncharted oceans, and our national independence.

The indomitable English peasants and city dissidents were grasping, individualistic, stubborn and indestructible. Their faith was in Bibles and blunderbusses, their objectives were material aggrandizement under rule of dogmatic Protestantism and higher learning. This combination grew great men, the like of which human history has seldom paralleled.

New England became the repository of our riches, our refinements and our temporal liberty. It incubated our most fiery patriots, our earliest poets and professors and scientists. It founded our financial power. It hazarded all its gains and its very lives in a precarious revolution for principles. The story of man has written no chapter more noble.

But now New England is provincial and off the beaten track. Progress passed it by and swept on elsewhere. Perhaps this is because of its geographical location, difficult of access to most of the newer states—especially since the Erie Canal and Hudson River water route brought products to New York instead of Portland and Boston. New England's retrogression began when its native sons, the smart, scheming, shrewd Yankees, headed west to relocate in Ohio, Illinois, Iowa and further, and their places were taken by waves of European immigration less endowed than the early ones.

Which is cause and which effect no longer matters; it isn't important whether the Irish, Italians and Poles drove the Yankees out or they came into a vacuum. Either way, today's New England is the result. Here is how it looks:

It is an anachronism, decadent and broke, the only important section of the country where the indices continually go down, not up.

The people reflect the atmosphere. They have sour pusses. You seldom see a smile break through their tight, thin lips. Whereas all the jaspers in the Midwest look like Truman, who is their reflection, and are grinning gladhanders, most New Englanders look like Cal Coolidge, their archetype.

When the Yankees moved out and the hordes of unwashed moved in, they failed in New England to bring the new cultures which they had transplanted with such marked success to New York, New Orleans and San Francisco. Few true Yankees remained behind, but those who did took over and conquered the newcomers, making them all into puritans—on the surface, you understand—so that even the Roman Catholics, usually tolerant of big-city license, are puritans here.

Assets are still enormous. The Boston banks are among the largest and strongest, but this is mostly inherited and invested wealth, dating back to early days.

But New England industries are in deplorable shape, squeezed dry by overunionization. For it is ironical that this former backbone of conservative Republicanism and protectionism should now be the nucleus of New Deal strength in the East. Its three most populous states now habitually vote Democratic nationally and frequently locally, while the other three continually send left-wing Republicans to Congress.

Many New England communities are practically ghost towns as industry moves to the South. Yet the unions refuse to face the situation and impose even more stringent handicaps on manufacturers, seeking to force the remaining factories to support the workers left behind by the factories which departed. Brockton, Fall River, Lowell, Manchester and Providence are among the nation's most critical unemployment areas. Relief rolls in Lawrence skyrocketed 500 per cent since last year. Thirty-seven woolen mills in New England have been liquidated since 1949. Other lines are as badly hit; not by factories that moved away, but by those that tore up their charters. Hundreds did move out.

The textile wage differential between North and South comes to forty cents an hour. In addition, the unions, with characteristic win-or-destroy bullheadedness, insist on a workload in Northern shops absurdly less than that which prevails in the South. Against such economic outrages, New England industry cannot survive. It finds that, in addition to being strangled by labor, it is also in the grip of a monstrous, evil machine—one of the keystones of the Mafia—tied up on every level with the unions and the politicians, regardless of party. As muddle-headed "progressivism" is nonpartisan in this area—where Tobey, a nominal Republican, votes more often as a Democrat—so is crime; and in almost all the six states the mobs flourish, regardless of which party sits in the state house.

The region once did not tolerate race-tracks, but now the operators of its major ones are so powerful that they often dominate their states, name Governors and Senators, and in one case nosed in an Attorney General of the United States.

Mobsters and ex-bookmakers, bootleggers and rum-runners own stock in Suffolk Downs, Narragansett, Rockingham and Lincoln Downs, in which J. Howard McGrath is also an important security holder.

For the purposes of this book we brush off Vermont with the observation that, once the most isolationist of states—it even refused to join the union—it has been seduced by the one-world crowd and is now proud of its ex-Senator Warren Austin, the impractical head of the American delegation to the UN.

Maine's other phenomenon is Margaret Chase Smith, sole female U.S. Senator. The last time we were in Washington she was making one of her typical boneheaded speeches. A Senate doorman couldn't stand it any longer. When she reached the high point of her peroration, he sniffed and remarked about the lone female, "There's too many women in the Senate!" She is a lesson in why women should not be in politics. When men argue matters of high policy they usually forget their grudges at the door. She takes every opposing speech as a personal affront and lies awake nights scheming how to "get even." She is sincere—but a dame— and she reacts to all situations as a woman scorned, not as a representative of the people. She is under the influence of the coterie of left-wing writers and reporters who dominate Washington and they praise her so assiduously she believes it.

Maggie is pals with Esther Brunauer and made a trip to Europe with her, fare paid by the State Department. Mrs. Brunauer is now under suspension from the department as a security risk. Her husband was suspended by the Navy on the same grounds. Maggie traveled with her after the original charges were presented to the Tydings whitewash committee.

A. Boston Baked Beans and B-Girls

Massachusetts is where publishers pay to get books banned. But little else is ever bothered.

Boston and environs boast dirty burlesque, indecent strippers, cut-rate whores. It is loaded with fairies, after-hour spots, gaming dens, bookmakers and the Chinese lottery which surpasses the gross take on most legitimate businesses in town. The state and the city are venal and corrupt—miniature Washingtons.

The day we hit the Hub, the archbishop said in other words what we stated above. The authorities promised immediate ac-

tion. The public assumed they meant it. Eight joints of about
eight hundred were raided. The papers were full of it. But when
hearings were held there were no complainants and all but one
reopened.

The Boston mentality, as befitting the birthplace of the intellectual cult in America, is blind to reality. It is as if the entire
population worked for the *New York Times,* a statement we will
try to explain. After last November's municipal elections, both
Boston and the *New York Times* gloated over the success of the
"reform movement," which was going to clean up the town. The
successful candidate for mayor in the New Boston Committee's
nonpartisan reform landslide was John B. Hynes. The *Times* described the victory as won by a "good-government organization."
But both Boston and the *Times* forgot to mention that the winner
who would rout municipal corruption happened to be the incumbent mayor!

None but Harvard graduates can yet figure out how Hynes's
re-election as chief executive of one of the most crooked municipalities in the country suddenly became a victory for good government, when, in fact, for two years he was the quarterback for
the boodle gang which the new party was supposed to have run
out.

Schizophrenia in Massachusetts is best exemplified at the state
political level. The Commonwealth's two sitting U.S. Senators are
Republicans, both scions of old families who talk only to themselves and to God, and both, in tune with the new Eastern fad
of class anarchy, untrue to their aristocratic forbears in their in-
fatuation with "new liberalism."

Lodge and Saltonstall dream of the White House. They would
take the Vice-Presidency. Both are intellectually dishonest, but
Lodge has a brilliant, scheming mind and an overweening ambition. He must be viewed by many with alarm. Saltonstall is a
typical rich man's son, a snob even while he attempts to reform
the world, and without enough brains to make him more than a
nuisance.

If Massachusetts shows off in Washington with GOP blue-
bloods, it turns another face at home, where Paul A. Dever, the
Governor, is not only a self-made man, but a Democrat. Dever—
they call him "Dever the Road Builder"—brags that, unique
among Democrats, he has no mob contacts. He claims the underworld does not support his campaigns. He doesn't need it. Building roads is just as good. The inside boys get the contracts and

they are the right inside boys—right with the Mafia! Dever has the unions as well, and Massachusetts unions are gangster-dominated, as they are all over the country. We mean those not Communist-owned; though some are both.

Dever is a "poor man." His Cape home cost $80,000. His brother has an important state job and Dever rewarded him with the largest pay raise given any public employe.

The secret boss of the State House, and this will come as a surprise to most Bay Staters, is Jimmy Roosevelt, who couldn't annex California. Jimmy (who got it in Boston) is close to the Governor and calls the shots. The actual capitol is not across from the Common, but at 108 Water Street, the home of Roosevelt & Sargent, Inc., the politically wired-in insurance firm that paid our Jimmy and his mom hundreds of thousands annually, and from which he still receives an income.

The perquisites of the Governor of Massachusetts include one gilt-edged pip possessed by few other chief executives. He names the top coppers in Boston and most of its metropolitan district. The municipalities have nothing to do with their police except to foot the bills. Thus all police graft in Massachusetts seeps upward to the commonwealth government. Even sheriffs have been deprived of their powers. The state police is another force under the Governor. Its head is Dan (known as "Dever's Dan") Murphy, who functions directly under the Governor's orders. There are no investigations of Democratic campaign contributors, which include these worthy gents:

Philip Buccola, sport and fight promoter who operates the Goodwin Athletic Club, Donati Miranda, 55 Endicott Street, Boston. Nichela Carumarata, Springfield, Frank Iacone, Worcester. Joe Purpura, Lawrence. And Joe Contesi, Angelo Isabella, Tony Indelacata, alias George Carney, and Henry Selvitella, alias Noyes.

Boston Police Commissioner Tom Sullivan can't do a thing even if he wants to. The Governor's men cannot be disciplined or even moved. Certain police captains have sinecures that they retain for life. The heads of vital squads are hand picked by the state administration, and woe to the commissioner who tries to transfer them.

The force, under Governor Dever, is so venal that after the city officials voted them a raise the cops had to kick back to their captains.

The two most powerful local Democrats on the national level are the handsome Secretary of Labor, Maurice Tobin, and Paul

Smith, an attorney of quiet and mysterious antecedents, who was a recent guest of President Truman at Key West.

Smith's Siamese twin is David Niles, also of Boston. Smith was one of the largest money raisers for the last Truman campaign. Bostonians with income tax trouble come to him—even now. He is seldom mentioned in connection with the cases, so gets no bad publicity when the lid blows off. Tobin got that way because he was one of the few in Massachusetts who stood by the boss in 1948. He is in alliance with New England's other publicized cabinet member (at this writing), Rhode Island's J. Howard McGrath. If you are willing to pay to run your competitor out of business you see someone in his office, for the Department of Labor is a pip for rackets and shakedowns.

Now to return to the New Boston Committee, which is shaping up as the single most powerful vote getting force in the state. This is the group whose victory was described by the lame brains as "a New Boston Tea Party."

Let's tell you about it. The Democrats are and for long have been strongly entrenched in Boston. Though elections are on a nonpartisan basis it usually happens that all the candidates are Democrats, though of different factions.

Mayor Curley controlled the city as his personal domain for years. The present executive, Mayor Hynes, was a Curley protégé, but broke with him when Curley was pardoned from the pen by Truman and returned to politics. Hynes thought the aging ex-convict should give some younger man a chance.

Hynes was elected Mayor two years ago by a bare twelve thousand plurality. Curley built up a strong organization to make a come-back, so the Hynes boys, who included most of the grafting contractors, the Mafia gangsters and the crooked unioneers who saw no reason to return to Curley whom they thought "too old," decided to pull a steal and seal their control of City Hall.

What happened a few months ago was one of the greatest political robberies in the history of the country. The city was turned over lock, stock and barrel by the votes of the gullible and support of the naïve, who didn't know what was happening.

The first step was to organize the Boston Committee, with all the platitudes about clean government. At its head is Jerome L. Rappaport, now only twenty-four years old. Rappaport, a carpetbagger from New York, got into the act while studying at Harvard Law School. While there he founded the Harvard Law

School Forum, a nauseous and noisy organ of professional do-gooders.

Then Rappaport married the daughter of the late Democratic state chairman and started going places. He was assistant secretary in Mayor Hynes's office two years ago when, at the age of twenty-two, he "founded" the new political party that captured the citizens' suffrage. This boy wonder is now Assistant Corporation Counsel.

In addition to electing five candidates in the new nine-member City Council, the Committee also elected four of the five School Committeemen. The New Boston Committee also slipped over a bill to double the length of the Mayor's term, freezing Hynes in for four years. He was re-elected this time by seventy-seven thousand votes.

Boy Scout Rappaport said there was "no question of dictation." He claimed they "had asked for no commitments and they (the candidates) made none." He "denied" that the Committee was primarily a Hynes organization.

But it is loaded with pinks, lefties, union overlords, and those who serve the underworld, including a prominent dope peddler.

This is what goes in Boston and environs—after two years of reform Governor Dever and two years of reform Mayor Hynes:

Liquor licenses cost anywhere from $10,000 to $50,000 under the table. The competition among licensing officials is so keen that local councils and state liquor bodies continually feud, each with their own approved applicants.

Meanwhile Mary E. Driscoll, chairman of the Boston Licensing Board, defends the terrible drunkenness in the Hub by blaming it on the "outrageous" cocktail parties in the private homes of citizens. They aren't licensed, she complains, dreaming of a new field for government enrichment and control.

A newspaper suggested she take a closer look at some of "the joints she has licensed." It mentioned "the dark, grubby, dirty, pick-up and sex-nasty places which have flourished under her regime for a long time without so much as a wrist slap from her licensing board . . . the joints which feature after-hour drinking, the serving of bum booze to minors and the swish form of so-called entertainment."

Sounds like Lait and Mortimer, so we went to see it. It's all there, exactly as described. So this is Boston Confidential:

The legal liquor closing is 1 A.M. on week-days and Sunday nights—midnight on Saturday. Some obey it. But we had no trouble finding several who don't, especially on Hanover Street.

Most obvious is the Copa on Tremont, next to the Shubert Theatre. It's owned by Sicilians who make their own law.

The Pioneer is a colored joint which never closes. Neither does the Stork, across the river in Charlestown. It should be borne in mind that unlike most other jurisdictions where the cheaters are unlicensed "bottle clubs," these and other all-night spots also hold permits to sell legally during regular business hours but they have no clocks so they don't know when to close.

It is true that Boston is a sleepy place after midnight, without too much action, but such places need little. Hustlers, gambling house steerers and junk pushers find prospects in them.

Staid old New England seems to have more than its share of the third sex. We asked a cab driver where the pick-up gals hang out. He said, "You used to be able to find them at the Silver Dollar chasing sailors; now the fags have chased the babes out and they're chasing the sailors."

Apparently puritanism backfired in reverse. A society that frowned on sex woke up to find that sex had gone underground. Massachusetts and Connecticut are the only two states where rubber contraceptives are forbidden by law, even on a doctor's prescription (though you can buy them everywhere in both). Apparently the law-abiding have decided the best way not to beget is to make love to their own sex.

Massachusetts is still the center of the academic world and it has been pointed out elsewhere in this treatise that the campuses are now prime breeding grounds for intermediates.

Harvard is so gay you can hear the swish across the River Charles. Girl queers breed at Wellesley and many of the fine finishing schools.

The nicest boys meet often at the gracious old Touraine bar.

From there they would flit to the College Inn, now the Mayfair Club, operated by Rocky Palladino, No. 1 Sicilian in the Boston hierarchy. Hoods are running gay spots all over the country because they know they're the only ones that constantly cash in; furthermore, queers are not only swell prospects for dope but are pips to put the blackmail bite on. They usually have money. Many ex-cons got to like it in jail. Palladino's associate is Max Chipman.

Another noted gay spot is Phil Harris' (no relative to the bandleader) which specializes in shows in drag with men made up as women. The Show Bar and Tic Toc also get their share.

Boston is noted for its cheap street tarts but they are being driven to the walls by the queers. Indeed, the historic Common, for so long the floozies' flirtation walk, has been invaded by hip-tossers.

Boston is nationally noted for its burlesque and its peelers, arts forbidden in wicked, worldly New York. The Old Howard theatre is the most famous burleycue on the continent. You get exotic dancers at the Rio Casino.

Scollay Square, long known as "No Man's Land," is one of the last of the old-time Bowerys still permitted to run, near the heart of the city, and quite as dirty as the Barbary Coast. Its stripteasers are the lowest, its whores the cheapest, its bars the lousiest, and its denizens the most degraded.

You can usually find some of the classiest girls at the bar of the swank Darbury Room, across the square from the Copley, a unique place. Its rear dining room is the ritziest in town with El Morocco pretensions and inflation prices; its cocktail lounge attracts the niftiest nifties.

With Rocky Palladino running the works for the Sicilians, the town is aware of a swarthy mystery man even above him, known only as Tony Canadian.

Boston's Chinatown is one of the oldest in the land, predating San Francisco's by half a century. The first Celestials came on the clipper ships; now they control hundreds of millions in wealth and property and monopolize certain forms of vice and crime.

Because of the piker nature of the town and the 1 A.M. liquor closing, Chinatown is the main drag for late night life. When everything else locks up, Bostonians flock to Tyler Street and environs, where there are more than a score of fine eating places. The best is the Cathay House where the show-crowd hangs out.

One of the most important figures in Boston's netherworld is a reporter on the staid old *Boston Post* who, unknown to his employers, throws so much weight around he is practically the arbiter and umpire of gangland. He is constantly seen in the company of big hoods.

Gambling is wide open now and always has been. Bookies frequent the Parker House and Bellevue Hotel areas, and still take bets openly, though not on the phone.

Floating crap games run all over town; the axis is in Chelsea.

Boston is slowly being strangled by its workers—who prefer not to work. The city's commerce had been badly damaged by the depression in the neighboring mill towns, but in order to kill Boston permanently the longshoremen's international got so rambunctious Boston is practically a closed port. Many big lines now refuse to enter the harbor and are taking their cargo to New York for rail transshipment.

Other unions are viciously Red and pink, and show it by taking it out on the FBI. One example will suffice. Members of Local 163 International Ladies Garment Workers Union were having a pre-Christmas party in Steuben's Vienna Room. At another table, girl employees of the local Federal Bureau of Investigation office—secretaries, stenos, file clerks and other unimportant personnel—were throwing a farewell to one of their number transferred to another location. When the unioneers heard the girls worked for J. Edgar Hoover, the Commies' pet hate, they began to boo and broke up the party.

Nice goings.

B. *What They Raise on Providence Plantations*

When the Attorney General's special grand juries get going, you can be sure they'll find little in Rhode Island.

Rhode Island is the smallest state in the union, but for its size it swings ponderous weight.

J. Howard McGrath, who at this writing is Attorney General of the United States, is the political key to New England, one of the most important men anywhere in the country, who will continue to be so even if he is retired, bounced, or laid low with Truman sickness. The reasons for the two foregoing factors, which are interlocking, will be confided in the proper sequence.

But first let us consider the city of Providence, capital of the state, and in colonial days one of the nation's chief seaports. One of the country's largest fishing fleets still operates from its environs, manned almost entirely by Portuguese, some in the fourth and fifth generations, who make up an important voting segment. Though fishing outfits are useful for smuggling all over the world and are one of the chief means of slipping illicit dope into the country, Providence does not have a regularly assigned agent of the U.S. Bureau of Narcotics, an oversight pleasing to the Sicilian mobsters who run the town. U.S. Customs agents it has, but apparently some have the blind staggers, because Providence is one of the main havens of entry for smuggled merchandise of all sorts as well as illegally entered aliens. But during the McGrath incumbency there were no prosecutions for such traffic.

Providence is dead and dismal. Rhode Island is so tiny no member of the legislature lives more than an hour from the State House. The result is the solons have no excuse to remain overnight and away from their wives during sessions. That means there are no high jinks, no parties paid for by lobbyists, no imported whores, no unrestrained guzzling. Furthermore, Providence is only forty-five minutes from Boston. Even its own residents do their hell-raising elsewhere. Boston's fleshpots are not exactly Lucullan, but they are several grades above what is offered locally.

Providence was once a good show-town. Even the muse passes it by now, because you can catch a pre-Broadway run in Boston and still be home in Providence by one o'clock. There's seldom vaudeville for the same reason, and even the hotels go in for only medium name bands or cocktail aggregations.

But there is the Celebrity Club—a miniature hot spot playing the most expensive Negro bands. How does it operate in this otherwise dreary amusement atmosphere? The mobsters have money. And we saw several well-known gambling steerers enjoying the hot licks. School-kids contact reefer peddlers outside its doors.

Providence is a bust in all ways—as a seaport, as a capital and as an old, civilized center of population. About all it has to offer is whores. They are undergrade, as the more choosy cheaters skip to Boston. The local prosties live almost entirely off the sailors who man the freighters and tankers which tie up there. They are in cahoots with cab-drivers, who work the docks at all hours. We saw seamen leaving an incoming ship at 3 A.M. The waterfront was crawling with hacks, which picked them up and hauled them back to Wickenden Street, where the lowest dives are located.

Providence's chief racial groups, in addition to Portuguese, are Poles who work the factories and Italians who own and control the town and state. Many French-Canadians live nearby, especially around Woonsocket, where they talk only patois. Their daughters drift into Providence, where many peddle their charms. The habitantes, prolific and sexually prolix, are highly esteemed for their skill if not for their looks or odors.

Most of the vice and crime is found in the smaller towns, all convenient to Providence. Johnson City, across the Providence line, is host to after-hour spots and cheap ginmills. The C-Note there does not get hot until the bars have closed in Providence at one o'clock.

Newport, once the unapproachable summer home of entrenched wealth, lost out to taxes, servant shortages, inheritance-dues and the corroding influences of the new socialism. A picked handful of the die-hards refuse to surrender, but nowadays Newport is better known as the home of one of our largest naval bases. That makes it a dilly. Everything rolls there, including slot-machines. There are so many wenches set up in rooms for the sailor trade that sometimes it looks more populous than Providence. Faggots also operate, of course, and you can buy anything, including liquor after hours, dope or gambling. The heat goes on only occasionally and soon everything is back to normal. All this proceeds under the eyes of the commandant and shore police.

Central Falls was and is one of the dirtiest towns in the state. Howard McGrath started his career there, as town solicitor. During his term, Central Falls was no cleaner than the United States was with him as Attorney General.

This state is the feudal domain of a handful of powerful men who wrested control from the original rich, who have been ground down by unionization, depression and immigration.

These are the chief proprietors under the new system:

U.S. Senator Theodore Francis Green is the titular boss, but because of his advancing age—he is in his deep eighties—he has surrendered control of the commonwealth and the Democratic Party to young and vigorous Howard McGrath, for fifteen years his law partner. McGrath is the wonder boy of New England. Though still in his forties, he is a self-made millionaire many times over. When McGrath sat in the Senate, it was one of the rare instances in our history when a pair of law partners both sat in the Senate at the same time.

McGrath won his skyrocket career as Senator, Democratic National Committee chairman and Attorney General by professing to be an ardent New Dealer and sworn enemy of capitalism. Yet he's a stockholder in a dozen dissimilar enterprises and in general the perfect picture of the movie capitalist, with a $20,000 beach cottage in which to put on his bathing suit, and three saddle-horses on which to caper.

McGrath's closest associate is Antoine Gazda—an Austrian inventor and munitions salesman who sneaked out of Germany in 1940 with a pocketful of patents on the famed Oerlikon 22mm antiaircraft gun. Clapped into custody on Ellis Island, Gazda's release was obtained by McGrath. He was arrested by special order of President Roosevelt a year and a half later—after receiving a Navy contract for $187,000,000 worth of the guns. But Gazda once more beat the undesirable alien rap and got out, with McGrath's assistance. For many years they shared the same residence and phone, at 715 Elmgrove Avenue.

Gazda isn't the only millionaire friend who has business dealings with McGrath. Sam Shore, big-time real estate man and supermarket operator in Providence, is said to be in lucrative partnership with him. There was Frank Crook, a highly successful automobile dealer and real estate developer, with whom McGrath was said to own one of the largest beach resorts in the country—Bonnet Shores, at Narragansett. Also with Crook, McGrath reputedly owned a big block of Lincoln Downs race-track and stock in Pawtucket radio station WFCI. Crook died, but J. Howard McGrath is his executor.

McGrath is said to be a stockholder in three outfits not mentioned in any previous stories about him—Kay's Newport shoe factory, the Otsby & Barton jewelry firm in Providence, and the Construction Equipment Company of Providence, which sells trucks, ploughs and other highway equipment to the state and to various municipalities.

Other McGrath activities were trusteeships in the Lonsdale and Textron corporations, organized as non-taxpaying "charities" under a corporate merger law in Rhode Island, put through by former Governor John Pastore—a McGrath handyman. Pastore put the "corporate merger law" through and appointed McGrath a trustee at a "high financial increment," because Pastore inherited the governorship when McGrath resigned the post. Another trusteeship McGrath held, and which is being attacked by Republicans, is in the Rhode Island Charities Trust, from which McGrath drew a "cigarette-money" salary of $5,000 a year. Former McGrath clients have had amazing good luck in litigation against the government.

Patriarch of the Italians is Raymond Patriarca, suitably named, probably the No. 1 Sicilian in all New England, which makes him the No. 1 citizen of New England. John Candelmo is close to him.

Ray is completely contemptuous of the law. His word is so feared that after he murdered a cop in Massachusetts and was convicted for it, the Bay State governor quickly pardoned him. He is in every illicit racket in the area and has close ties with New York. His Rhode Island mobsters harbor lamisters from Gotham. They freely circulate in Providence, yet the local police and state officials never turn them up nor does McGrath's Justice Department invoke the fugitive criminal law. Vital witnesses of the infamous Scottoreggio killing, eningeered in Marcantonio's hoodlum precinct, hid out safely in Providence for months.

Patriarca is also heavily immersed in legitimate businesses, owns hotels, New Hampshire summer resorts, race-tracks, real estate and laundries. But just to keep his hand in, he also runs float-ing crap-games in Providence. When the raiders come they are always a day late; the play has moved on to another location.

Rhode Island Italians vote as Patriarca suggests, and they swing a lot of votes. That was how Rhode Island became the first to send an Italian to the United States Senate—John Pastore, for-mer Governor, who got the seat vacated by McGrath when he entered the cabinet. Pastore was enthusiastically supported by Patriarca's Sicilian hoods, who raised potent campaign funds. Be-fore that they had supported McGrath.

Pastore votes the standard bleeding-heart, New Deal platform, and is assiduous in not fighting measures designed to help crooks. Under his tenure as Governor, and that of his predecessor, McGrath, Rhode Island was sold out to them.

Joe Morelli was the mob boss of Pawtucket, McGrath's home bailiwick, and owned the Rhode Island horse-wire, numbers and Narragansett track. Now a couple of his relatives are handling the affairs. They are closely allied with the East Harlem Italian mob of New York.

One of the great Italian monopolies is the construction and sand and gravel business. Many of these firms headquarter in Rhode Island, but procure public work throughout the six New England states. The Sicilians have set up a gravy kickback depart-ment which rewards contracting officers; and a blackmailing de-partment to make sure that the uncooperative change their ways.

Only one important non-Italian is still "operating" in the state. He is Carlton O'Brien, who runs "The Farm," with gambling, at Cranston and recently bought the Burns Restaurant on Broad Street, in downtown Providence.

Justice is proverbially blind; but Rhode Island Attorney General Powers is in fact sightless. His closest pal, associate and "seeing-eye dog" is Bob Connolly, Mayor of Central Falls, who earns an annual stipend of $2,500 but is now building a home to cost 60 Gs.

The few honest citizens left in the state think everything is under control because the "crusading" monopoly paper, the *Provi-dence Journal-Bulletin,* is supposed to be fighting crime. There are a lot of naïve youngsters on its staff who get themselves worked up over dice shooting or peanut hankypanky on tax rolls, but they turn the other way when unions or minorities are in-volved in payoffs. Nominally Republican, the paper is disgust-ingly left-wingish and do-gooder.

The Kefauver Committee did not visit any of the six New England states. Of course, Senator Tobey, from New England, was on the committee.

The next section will explain why the near-Rev. Charlie did not want the mud turned up in his backyard.

C. St. Tobey Confidential

The sanctimonious Charlie Tobey was too good to be true. Such things just did not exist off the stage, and we thought stock troupes were all washed up.

So we hopped a rattler to New Hampshire and did a little look-see. Mortimer published some of what we found in the *American Mercury*, but Charlie didn't let out a peep. He went about being just as righteous as ever. His latest sage suggestions were spiritual reawakening and the whipping-post for faithless government officials. Pray as ye flay the sinners—great TV stuff.

This is what his neighbors know about Charlie, but few people live in Temple, New Hampshire, and they aren't talking. We had to piece it together the hard way:

Those familiar with the career of Senator Charles W. Tobey were not surprised when he stole the Kefauver hearings with revival-rouser shouting and divine name-dropping. New Hampshire's aging junior senator has long been on terms of intimacy with the Lord. He was a lay preacher and a former president of his state's Baptist convention. For more than forty years he has led his neighbors in outdoor hymn jamborees while he pounded an upright piano in the middle of a hayfield. One al fresco religious rally at which he was the chief spellbinder was interrupted by a cloudburst. Charlie raised his hands high to heaven and called on his connections up there to stop the rain. It ceased immediately.

Tobey has been in public life for thirty-seven years, but until the Kefauver hearings he never had an opportunity to demonstrate his celestial drag to the country.

Nothing is more remarkable in the unique career of Charlie Tobey than that he found the Promised Land after he had passed the biblical allotment of three score and ten. By how much he has passed it is one of the major mysteries which confront the researcher. He failed to supply his birth-date to the editors of *Who's Who* and the *Congressional Directory*, though since he hit the bigtime with Kefauver in 1951, he tells the press he was born in 1880. But you can't blame a Messiah who forgets five years.

After graduating from the Roxbury, Massachusetts, Latin School, which isn't as imposing as it sounds, because "Latin School" was nineteenth century terminology for what we call high school, young Tobey went over the hill to New Hampshire, where he sold eggs, then real estate and insurance, finally graduating into the one calling for which he was so eminently suited. He became a stock salesman. There were no blue-sky laws then, no SEC. The fact that investors lost millions of dollars on some of the securities he peddled was not his fault, now was it?

Charlie got elected to the legislature in 1915, but that was no major ascension. New Hampshire's lower house is the largest in the land, with some four hundred members in a state which ranks forty-fourth of the forty-eight in population—about one member per five hundred voters. Even now the job only pays $100 a year.

In New Hampshire most solons use the legislature as an adjunct to their outside professions or businesses. Charlie found it valuable to his. He became president of the F. M. Hoyt Shoe Company, in which many of its employes bought stock on the assumption that a guy as friendly with the Lord as Tobey would protect their savings. They lost their all.

Charlie served several terms in both houses of the legislature, reaching the speakership and the presidency of the senate, which high posts, you may be sure, did not handicap the sale of securities.

During Prohibition Tobey was politically a dry. He says he lives that way, too. But we know he sniffs sherry. Because of its geographical location, New Hampshire was a key spot on the rum-running map. Its northern boundary borders on the Canadian province of Quebec. Its southern is the Massachusetts line—thirty miles from Boston. All booze destined for the sopping New England metropolis was run down through New Hampshire, much of it earmarked for New York and the rest of the East.

New Hampshire's short coastline was also ideal for smuggling. Portsmouth has a fine harbor. It is not now a port of any consequence, but during the mad 1920's its contraband tonnage quite often approached New York's legal clearances. This traffic in booze was carried on with the knowledge and connivance of New Hampshire authorities and police. A definite rate of bribes was set up, amounting to $5 off the top of every case, which was split down the line, with a final 50 cents on every case to the campaign funds of the then dominant faction of the Republican party.

In 1928 Tobey was rewarded with the governorship and elected with campaign funds sweetened liberally by the rum-runners. His years as chief executive were years of clover. Prohibition was at its most prodigal height. By this time the major liquor outfits were

organized. Men like Al Capone in Chicago and Dutch Schultz,
Owney Madden and Waxey Gordon in New York dominated the
trade. There was nothing on record to show that Governor Tobey
did anything except spout platitudes to cut off the arteries of the
scandalous traffic. He could have dried up New England. But dry-
ing up is not a Tobey habit. And those who were most benefited
were properly grateful—at election time.

A lot of the stock he had peddled began to go bad after his
term as Governor, during bleak 1931 and 1932. But even then
Charlie was a walking Bible concordance. He turned away wrath
with the inspired words of the Apostles—and sometimes he got
them right. He adopted the Townsend plan and promised those
who lost their socks on his shady stocks that, if he were elected to
Congress, Uncle Sam would make it all good. He got the nod in
1932—a Republican winning in the first Roosevelt landslide. The
bootleggers threw the bankroll into his campaign, because they
desperately needed professional dries to stem the wet tide and retain the Noble Experiment. Charlie was fighting the good fight.

New England was without horse-racing. Massachusetts, it was
believed, would never legalize it. New Hampshire is within commuting distance of Boston. As early as 1929, when Tobey was Governor, hoodlum racing interests cased the state. A drawback was
the king-sized legislature, which meant more votes to buy. But the
price is cheap in New Hampshire; as low as $100—a year's honest
wage—is the standard quotation. Deals were completed during
Tobey's last year as Governor. By 1932 Rockingham Park, in
Salem, New Hampshire, was open and in business a stone's throw
from the Massachusetts border.

This proud enterprise was financed by "Big Bill" Dwyer, known
as "King of the Bootleggers"—a likeable character genuinely ad-
mired by everyone in the underworld and half-world because he
had taken the rap for the top shots and done a Federal stretch
himself. After his return to circulation he owned the New York
Rangers hockey team and Tropical Park race-track in Miami.
Rockingham was to be the summer branch of Tropical, then one
of the crookedest tracks in the nation.

As front-man Bill Dwyer installed Bill Gallagher, president of
the Pennsylvania Exchange Bank, in New York, which was shown
in Kefauver Committee testimony to be tied up with the operations of Frank Costello and Frank Erickson.

Bill Dwyer transferred some of his stock to one Lou Smith, a
former bootlegger. In time Smith acquired Gallagher's interest

also, and now appears as majority stockholder in the Rockingham Park Corporation.

There is nothing on record to show that Charlie Tobey got righteously wrathful over the influx of shady money into his state or the shenanigans that took place after it arrived. That money was not "unclean." It helped elect him so he might continue his labors in the vineyard.

Bill Phinney, who was state chairman of Tobey's campaign committee in 1950, is chief counsel for the Rockingham track and is registered with the legislature as lobbyist for the New Hampshire Jockey Club, which controls racing in the state.

Kenneth Graf, a Manchester, New Hampshire, attorney, and one of Tobey's chief backers in the last Republican primary, is clerk of the Rockingham corporation.

It is, of course, needless to remark that Tobey did not question anyone in New Hampshire about racing, bookmaking or lay-offs. Smith controls the state. Rockingham often elects Governors and Senators. Smith is wealthy, with fingers in many pies. He was a $10,000 investor in the Steelco Drilling Company (oil wells), in which two Florida bookmakers are also listed as important stockholders. They are fronting for Murray Humphreys, Chicago vice overlord.

Deacon Tobey served three successful terms as a Congressman in Washington, then, in 1939, took his seat in the U.S. Senate. At the time he was politically an isolationist, which arose to plague him often and almost cost him re-election during the war, when he received hundreds of umbrellas by mail. But Charlie Tobey never let consistency or sincerity be a mote in his eye to disturb holy work, especially if there are loaves and fishes to be gained by a switch. So he coyly allowed himself to be seduced by the One Worlders in 1944, just in time to get himself re-elected.

Dave Niles, the Rasputin of the White House, was the snake in the garden who worked the transformation. The *quid pro quo* to make Tobey a New Dealer was that Charlie was to be appointed as an American delegate to the International Monetary Conference which, as a further *quid pro quo,* was to be held in Charlie's state, in Bretton Woods. Tobey thinks first of Heaven, then of New Hampshire, the next best thing.

The Senator's enemies keep charging that he is disloyal to his friends. They bring up one instance when his covert opposition killed the gubernatorial ambitions of a man who had endorsed his unsecured $10,000 note. But maybe that's how he saw his duty and did it. Otherwise Charlie Tobey keeps a watchful eye out for the interests of those close to him. Before it was publicly announced that the great international gathering was to be held in Bretton Woods, Charlie tipped off his pal, the late Dave Stoneman, of Boston. Like any shrewd businessman might, Stoneman acquired the Mt. Washington Hotel for a song. Tobey, representing the host state, recommended that inn. The government refurbished it, and it only cost the grateful taxpayers a few million.

After the conference the hotel reverted to the owners, who also got sixty extra complete bathrooms—strictly rationed for others—in addition to a full complement for every room in the hotel. The extras were kept under the verandas. This was in 1944. Greater love hath no man for a friend!

Bretton Woods is in New Hampshire's noted White Mountain resort center, where, the last time we looked, ninety-nine locations had paid the Federal license fee on gaming devices, such as one-armed bandits. Tobey didn't open his mealy mouth about that. The big hotels in this lovely region are held by absentee owners, few from Boston, many from New York. Some hotels have crap-tables, horse-rooms and bookmakers, and roulette wheels. There is gaming at such caravansaries as the Mount Washington, Gray's Inn and the Tarleton, when the heat is off. Uniformed guards at the gates keep the unidentified public as well as Confidential writers from the Mt. Washington. There is no discrimination.

The amount of play in the White Mountain region far exceeds the best years of Saratoga, which Charlie Tobey said "smelled to heaven." That is because the New Hampshire resort colony has more hotels and longer seasons.

The State Attorney General, Gordon M. Tiffany, is a tolerant man. He recently refused to prosecute Tobey for failing to report certain campaign funds, because "Charlie probably overlooked them."

That was for the 1950 primaries, which Charlie won against young Wesley Powell by only 1,300 votes. His opponents claim he wouldn't have made that if the Fair Deal and the CIO and some shady characters with only initials as first names, and no addresses, hadn't come in to help him. One contribution which Charlie the Cherub carelessly forgot to declare was a thousand bucks from a committee once headed by James (Jimmy Got It) Roosevelt, who at the same time was being licked in his try to be Governor of California. The fact that Democratic Prince Jimmy was once on the payroll of the company that made Frank Costello's slot-machines had no bearing; he just adores Republicans. And Charlie is a good Republican. Didn't his printed campaign material contain endorsements from a number of prominent GOP Senators? That many of them, including Leverett Saltonstall, later denied they had made the endorsements, is pure politics. With Tobey everything is pure. Amen.

Another ten grand came from a Wall Street house for which Charlie had formerly sold securities. Of course, when he sold them, he couldn't guarantee them to his customers, most of them millhands.

Henry J. Kaiser's attorney also came up with some powerful encouragement for Churchy Charlie. We want you to understand this was not a payoff to our hero after he headed the committee investigating the RFC and went blind when he came to the Kaiser transactions.

But he was stern when he pursued the Textron investigation, which resulted in New Hampshire's loss of a major industry. He gave his own begotten son a job on the government payroll as an investigator. Now the son is promoting a cancer cure and Charlie is eager to investigate the American Medical Association, which refuses to accept it.

Tobey fights Jehovah's battles against crime and corruption, but he follows the admonition to bear with the sinner. Several local New Hampshire bookmakers were frequent callers at Charlie's headquarters in Temple, especially during fund-raising time. When informed that heads of the Nashua gambling ring, and Manchester's three leading bookmakers, Roger Mara, 305 Myrtle Street; Ray Cameron, 106 Merrimack Street; and Maurice Scanlon, 336 Tarrytown Road, were spending money to get him re-elected, Tobey is reported to have advised his followers that the workings of Divine Providence are mysterious and not to be questioned by mortals.

Some of Tobey's critics try to make fun of him by pointing out that he frequently gets his quotations mixed up, attributing something by Longfellow to Whittier or Emerson. But that is unkind when you consider that he stayed up all the night before, boning up on the Bible and the New England poets. Anyone who has crammed for a school exam knows how easy it is to misquote in a showdown. The Senator is a keen student of the Good Book. He strives to follow its precepts. The fact that a piece of property he once had for sale carried a sign saying, "For Christians Only," is proof of his conviction this earth is not for heathens, atheists and nonbelievers.

But we think the classic story about Charlie's New Hampshire is the one about the three-day police chiefs' convention at the Balsams Hotel, in Dixville Notch. In view of the assembling of the visiting peace officers, someone sent out word to close the games and slot-machines until they had left. That made the transient coppers very unhappy. What do you think they had picked the place for in the first place?

D. Connecticut—New York in Pink Pajamas

It's funny about Connecticut: the rich advertising agency executives and the fairy dilettantes who moved up from New York think they took it over; but the big boss of the state is, as he has been for two decades, Homer S. Cummings, erstwhile Attorney General of the United States.

Cummings was a prime mover in the great turnover that gave us Harry Hopkins and Harold Ickes. So he was rewarded with the purple plum in the first Roosevelt administration, happily made available by the death of old, crusading Senator Walsh of Montana, who had collapsed after a few hours of his honeymoon with a young bride a few days before inauguration.

Cummings first emerged as a phenom while District Attorney of Fairfield County, when he was involved in a controversial case later made into a hit movie, "Boomerang." Fairfield, in Cummings' day, was the New England headquarters for the "Dutch" Schultz mob, and always wide open, even when the pressure was on elsewhere.

Cummings resigned as U.S. Attorney General after the big McKesson & Robbins scandal had rocked the nation in 1938. He was not only a lawyer for Donald Coster, who had robbed the respectable old corporation of millions, but was his intimate. Coster, real name Musica, was tied up with other Italian crooks, criminals and gangsters who worked with him to divert alcohol and narcotics from legitimate sources into underworld channels. Cummings left the government but he did not leave Washington, where he was so integral a part of the New Deal machine. He had exalted connections, so he stayed on to become one of the ace contact men of the country and one of the most important powers behind the scenes.

Cummings' boy was Brien McMahon, who served as his Assistant Attorney General in charge of the criminal division. While McMahon held that job, the underworld organized and flourished.

McMahon, who owes everything to this important behind-the-scenes power, now sits in the Senate, where he is the chairman of the vital Congressional Atomic Energy Committee. He appointed Gordon Dean, a former law partner, as chairman of the AEC. McMahon's law firm has defended many gangsters. Now Oak Ridge is loaded with them. McMahon was close friend and attorney of Serge Rubenstein, the convicted draft-dodger.

By a strange coincidence, Fairfield, third most populous of the state's eight counties, is the home of both its Democratic and Republican bosses, its two U.S. Senators and its Governor. The carpet-bag New York wealth is concentrated there and the huge Italian population in Bridgeport, its county seat, always votes en bloc and nonpartisan, according to instruction passed along the line.

One of the most curious political merry-go-rounds in the country revolves around Benton and Bowles, the millionaire happiness boys. As youngsters, in their twenties, they formed an advertising firm and mutually pledged each other to be millionaires before they were forty, famous before fifty, and presidents before sixty. The first two have been fulfilled. After amassing fortunes, they sold out their advertising agency and went into politics—New Deal, of course. Bowles started the ball rolling as OPA commissar during the war, when his policies played directly into the hands of the welfare-staters and black marketeers. With that background he got the nod and was elected Governor of Connecticut, whither he had recently moved among the dreamers and pansies.

The time came to do something for the other half of the team. Artistic Benton, who actually lived in New York, in an apartment with nude male murals, was, like Bowles, a part-time resident of Connecticut. Unfortunately the state was entitled to only one Governor and two Senators. McMahon wouldn't get out of the way for Benton. And the other Senator, Raymond Baldwin, a Republican, was a Connecticut tradition and could not be removed by means short of death. But the B & B boys figured out how to get around that one. Senator Baldwin's ambition had always been toward the bench. So Governor Bowles appointed him to the State Supreme Court and Baldwin accepted, throwing a panic into the Republicans by his "double-cross."

Whereupon Bowles appointed his business partner to the vacant Senatorial seat.

Benton's governmental experience consisted of a term as Assistant Secretary of State in charge of the cultural and international division of the State Department, in 1945 to 1947. During his administration of that desk it was publicly described in the Congressional Record as "a monstrosity conducted by a group of pro-Communists, fellow-travelers and muddleheads. They fill the ether and tons of paper with a combination of material favorable to the Soviet Union and the Communists, or just plain twaddle."

Benton's direct assistant was William Treadwell Stone. Stone has a long record of association with Communists and pro-Communists. He served on the editorial board of the notorious *Amerasia* magazine, associating with such "intellectuals" as Owen Lattimore, Frederick V. Field and Philip Jaffe, all of whom have been named under oath before the McCarran Committee as being "Communists." Stone, with Esther Brunauer, was one of the incorporators of the Institute of Pacific Relations. Mrs. Brunauer is currently under suspension from a high position with the State Department. Benton appeared as her character witness.

Benton's special assistant was Haldore E. Hanson, named under oath before the Tydings Committee as a member of the Communist party. In his own book, *Humane Endeavor,* Hanson wrote that he was trusted by the Communists and given official documents by them.

Strangely, Benton had earlier oozed isolationism and was proud to hang around Colonel Lindbergh and others he professes to abhor today. In his formative years, when he was still on the way up and handling the advertising of the capitalists against whom he now crusades, he even thought of running on the Republican ticket. He approached Carroll Reece, then GOP chairman, who turned him down, though Benton bragged that Colonel Bertie McCormick of Chicago had called him his friend. After that cold shoulder, he was taken over by the lefties, who promised him political preferment.

In the 1950 campaign in Connecticut, Bowles ran for re-election as Governor and Benton for the Senate seat to which he had been appointed. But the strangest thing happened. Former Congressman John Lodge, brother of the Massachusetts Senator and himself a glamour boy and ex-film actor, also had ambitions. He made a better connection. The surprising results put Lodge in as Governor by a small vote, but Benton, who had been appointed by the defeated Governor, was elected—by an even smaller vote. Truman took care of lame duck Bowles by sending him to India as ambassador. There he is assiduously scheming for recognition of Red China and playing handmaiden to all of Nehru's other dizzy, visionary, Socialist and un-American schemes. His pleadings just turned up a hefty gift for the America-hating Hindus, from the Mutual Security Agency, and he is trying to promote a billion hand-out from Congress.

Governor Lodge's connection, which turned out to be even more potent than that of Bowles', was Eddie Sandula, undercover Republican boss of Fairfield, where the respectable GOPers stay out of politics because of their disgust with what has happened to the state. Immediately after his election, the grateful Governor appointed Sandula Deputy Motor Vehicle Commissioner, which is one of the prize jobs in the state. Sandula doesn't even know how to drive a car. He does have this to recommend him: he is a saloon-keeper.

Though New Haven and Hartford are better known to the world, Bridgeport is the power house and industrial center as well as the metropolis of the rich New York homing pigeons. It reverberates with murder, rape and other violence. That is not according to the prescription, because Bridgeport has, and for many years has had, a Socialist Mayor, one of the few in the country over, outside Milwaukee. He bears the unbelievable name of Jasper McLevy. He is a parsimonious, narrow-minded Scotsman with a personal machine and a personal following that is unbeatable. He is courted by Democrats and Republicans alike, especially the latter, who have offered him the governorship or a seat in the Senate. He plays with both sides and in return he never has more than nominal opposition.

These are a few things you see in Socialist Bridgeport: Many of the bookies who left the Bronx are now operating without any restraint in front of the Savoy Hotel and all the diners around Congress and Main. Neither Feds nor locals bother them.

Bridgeport whores have a unique gimmick. They hang out in the lobby of the post office, where there are two public pay phone booths. Their regular customers, as well as bellboys and cab-drivers who are their agents, know the numbers, and call whenever there is action. Meanwhile, they can always be mailing a letter. They charge $5 to play post office.

Pick-up girls frequent all the better-class cocktail lounges, such as the Stratfield, Lavery, the Pink Elephant and Club Rio.

Bridgeport has a large fag population, which is understandable because of the many artistic colonies in the Fairfield County villages, but they seem out of place in this hard-boiled, dingy, and dirty factory town. New York's notorious 181 Club opened a branch at the Cross Road, in nearby Westport, where it transported an entire show. Business was bad, so they moved the production and the swishes into the Club Rio in Bridgeport. It became such a fad that all the pansies in Connecticut flocked around until the cops closed it a few months ago. Now some fairies seek company at the Esquire bar in the St. George Hotel.

Per population, Bridgeport has almost as many Puerto Ricans as New York. They are one of the city's most serious problems, sleeping thirty to forty in a single room, around the clock. They were flown in during the war to work in defense plants. Now they have taken over State Street, with their whores and reefers and knifings, but they are not molested. They vote for McLevy.

The city also has a swollen colored population, centered around South Main Street, where you can buy marijuana or policy slips without trouble. Bridgeport is one of the few cities in the country that has escaped publicity on teenage narcotics, but that doesn't mean the kids don't use it. They do. It's as bad or worse there, but the local administration doesn't talk about it. A reefer scandal at Bassick High School, the town's best, was hushed up. So parents don't know that at least half the kids in the school are on the weed.

Incidentally, the public schools are terrible. Many are firetraps. The juves take advantage of that by burning them up. Mayor McLevy refuses to waste money on schools. Having quit his studies himself at the age of nine, he doesn't believe in education. He also refuses to wear a tuxedo. But his thriftiness is not directed only at the school system. He won't clean up the snow, either. He says it will go away by itself.

The Mayor has been in office so long, he must know about his crooked police force. However, you can't blame the cops, who are denied raises. The last time, they emulated the policemen of Yonkers by getting tough with traffic tickets, but when they tagged some of the favorite Marxists they were quickly slapped down by the Socialist Mayor. To make up for the stinginess of the taxpayers the coppers have several good sidelines. One is a tie-up with two garages, Mucci's and Mason's, to which they send all accident repair cases. All smash-ups reported over the police switchboards are automatically referred to one or the other of them and they then send out the tow-cars.

After-hour spots are everywhere. They take care of the beat man. The money isn't big enough to justify gambling upstairs.

The kids have a picnic in Bridgeport. P. T. Barnum, who came from there, donated Seaside Park to the city. Harry Neigher, the brilliant columnist of the *Bridgeport Herald,* dubbed it "The Boulevard of Broken Dreams and Muffled Screams." Many a University of Bridgeport co-ed learned about life there. Though the sale of rubber goods is illegal in Connecticut, the clean-up crew sweeps out grosses every morning. The come-on is to invite a girl to Seaside Park for a "shore dinner," which turns up as a Coke and a hot dog. Another nesting-place for young love is the Ritz Ball Room, on the outskirts, where ga-ga babes come to listen to name bands. They are pushovers for a shiny convertible.

The undisputed boss of Bridgeport's Little Italy is Louis Richards, a Sicilian undertaker. He sponsored and supported Clare Luce when she ran for Congress, though she was certainly no stiff.

As powerful as the Italians are in Bridgeport, they throw even more weight around in Hartford and New Haven, which have not been subject to the infiltration of wealthy New Yorkers. The late Tony "Z" was the most powerful Italian in the state. Now his brothers are pulling the strings. Another potent Hartford Italian is Rocco Di Palloti, deputy motor vehicle commissioner under former Governor Bowles. He relinquished his job to a Republican Italian when Lodge came in. This is one of the juiciest gravy pitchers in the state and is a perquisite of Sicilians.

New Haven is wide open, with numbers, policy, reefers and hookers. Its Italian Mayor, William C. Celentino, is on close terms with all the big Sicilians. He, too, is an undertaker. His coppers lay off everything, including the abortion racket of the late Dr. Savorese who made millions at $350 a throw. Since his death his clientele has been taken over by another Italian doctor and several Italian midwives. Tony Maresco, recently nabbed by Feds, had half the police on his payroll.

The state is loaded with after-hour spots and cathouses from end to end, all running with connivance of local police. In Stratford, the cops protect the gamblers against the state troopers. On one recent occasion, when the outside cossacks came in to make a raid, they had the forethought to lock up the local police station and shut off the switchboard so no city police could get out to warn the gamblers.

The big graft in Connecticut is in the small towns. There are hundreds, many with biblical names, and the more holy their nomenclature the more crooked they are. The graft works through justices of the peace and local officials, who have a price for everything.

If you still remember the Kefauver hearings, you may wonder

why the chairman stopped his investigations at the New York state line. Connecticut would have made knockout television sequences. But Estes, avid showman that he is, ducked it. Matty Brescia, a newscaster who went from Bridgeport to Memphis to do publicity for the Kefauver senatorial campaign in 1948, had nothing to do with it. Matty took on running the Kefauver-for-President Club, when not functioning as liaison man between the minor league baseball teams and radio.

Crusading brings rich rewards if it doesn't jump barriers.

12. NORTHWEST CONFIDENTIAL

THE BROAD prairies, the rugged mountains, the heroic scenery and the hardy pioneers of the Northwest have not often been the subject of folk-songs. We can't recall "Sweet Ruth from Duluth" or "My Heart's Tonight in South Dakota." Some cowpoke movies have been made about them, but the law and lore and literature, except for historic documentation, is thin. The rest of the country has no visible sentimental feeling for this section. And when we came out of it we had none either.

If outsiders think of our empire west of the Mississippi and north of California at all they are inclined to regard it as a chastity belt two thousand miles long. And this superficial impression has survived because no one thinks to go there and find out. So we did. Not on snowshoes or burro-back, but via fast planes. We found it a region of political anomaly; and where there is political unorthodoxy there is deviation in public and private morality. Nowhere is it more flagrant than it is out in the tall wheat. From the turbulent Mississippi headwaters to the calm Pacific we found variegated skulduggery common to the rest of the country, though tinted with the marked idiosyncrasies of the climate and the isolated detachment from major centers of population.

We found a rampant radicalism, a wild-jackassism permeating both old-line parties plus Farmer-Laborism, nonpartisanism, Progressivism and other splinterisms which would be at home in East Harlem, though its people would be outlandish there, for this is pretty sturdy native stock with a sprinkling of Oriental infiltration.

For purposes of this chapter we include Minnesota, the Dakotas, Montana, Washington, Oregon and Idaho, sometimes thrown in with the mountain states. It isn't one, but it deserves to be.

The manifestations of "political independence," though they seem incurable, play directly into the hands of the professionals and are utterly ineffective against concentrated bossism which can always call the turn and deliver the pluralities. The Northwest is misgoverned, mismanaged, graft-rotten and as corrupt as Chicago, Baltimore or Brooklyn. But its people, whether used as bait by Communists, Socialists or crooks with more conventional labels, are happy. They are holier than thou—and dumber. The more political mavericks, the more organized and more important the crime; and the more hypocritical assumption (except in Butte) of clean living.

South Dakota is the most conservative of the group in its relation to national political ties. It is usually organization Republican, and every four years it solemnly invites the GOP to hold its national convention there—which would about double its population for a week. But Sioux Falls, the largest of the three one-jeep cities, is a prime example of left-wing administration in the rawest Democratic tradition. Mayor H. B. Saure was elected by the Non-partisan League. Soon after the latest municipal results were in the bag, Police Department Memorandum No. 24 was issued, setting out the official—but confidential—orders on gambling, liquor violations and other infractions for privileged clubs, of which the following is the text. *

> 1. Effective this date until further notice the City Commissioners direct that officers take no official public action in any of the following clubs and organizations:
> Forty et Eight, 212 West 10th
> Veterans of Foreign Wars, 210 West 10th
> American Legion, 300 West 10th
> Labor Hall, 312½ West 9th
> Moose Lodge, 121 South Main
> Knights of Columbus, 315 North Summit
> Elks Club, 128 West 9th
> Le Elbon Club, Cataract Hotel
> Country Club, West 22nd Street
> Town Club, 228 So. Phillips
> 2. Commanding officers shall notify all officers assigned to their command of the provisions of this directive.

* The above is an exact transcript of the report. We know that the VFW and the Legion are on 9th and that the country club is the Minnehaha.

Tammany Hall in its ripest days never dared put anything like that on paper.

North Dakota, equally small, equally rural, and equally isolated, has a powerful statewide Non-partisan League. Trace-jumping Republican Senator Bill Langer was elected with its support. He cast the deciding vote that vetoed the full-dress investigation of the Kansas City vote-frauds in which the late Binaggio's Mafia organization stole thousands of votes for Harry Truman's hand-picked Congressional candidate. The state capital, Bismarck, a community of picayune proportions, is wide open during and between legislative sessions. Prostitutes are imported from Minneapolis for the Non-partisan farmer legislators, who guzzle in the Grand Pacific and Patterson Hotels, thick with railroad lobbyists. Votes in Bill Langer's state are so cheap, they don't bother paying off with money.

There are a million square miles in the Northwest with only two great population centers—the Twin Cities and the Seattle-Portland metropolitan groups. Spokane is a solitary outpost in between.

On the surface, the states included in this survey have nothing in common at election time. Two usually vote GOP, two Democratic, one splits, and one flirts with the Non-partisans. This is only an illusion. With the possible exception of South Dakota and parts of Montana they usually plump left-wing in Congress and crooked at home. What more perfect example of this party-be-damned spirit could you want than Bill Stern, Fargo, North Dakota, banker. He is Republican boss of the state. He also is Warren G. Magnuson's foster-father. Maggy is the state of Washington's U.S. Senator, a hair-shirt New Deal Democrat. Immensely wealthy Republican Stern supports his Socialist adopted son in lavish luxury. Between them they split up patronage, power and perquisites of the great Northwest Empire.

A. Carry Me Back to Old Minnesota

While Governor Luther Youngdahl was bragging to the Kefauver Committee that crime, vice and corruption had been driven out of Minnesota under his administration, whores and pimps were working overtime on Minneapolis' broad Hennepin Avenue; relievers of the state's liberal "ham-and-eggs" pension system were being robbed by dive operators on Washington Street; and out-of-town hoodlums were toasting each other in wine at the flashy Flame Club to celebrate their take-over of the city.

Youngdahl's testimony was about as accurate as most of the drivel before that probe; however, it provided a peg for Truman to appoint him, a Republican, to a high Federal judgeship. The Hon. Luther's defection caused cries of anguish at home, where the local GOP smelled a sell-out. The worker of this political legerdemain was young, good-looking Hubert Humphrey, former boy Mayor of Minneapolis. This was not Hubert's first miracle. He had pulled himself out of a hat as a pharmacist to State Director of War Production before his thirty-first birthday. Two years later, he was assistant director of the potent War Manpower Commission. He was elected chief executive of Minneapolis when a lad of thirty-four.

As a U.S. Senator, Hubert is a noisy and annoying New Deal cheer-leader. His forte is equal rights and fair employment practices. Minnesota, until recently lily-white, is swarming with tens of thousands of more recently arrived darkish emigrés from the deep South, who now can vote and, under Hubert's tutelage, vote right and often.

Pungent-tongued Senator Byrd described Humphrey as "constipated of brain with diarrhea of mouth."

Minnesota has long been thought of as the habitation of peaceful, home-loving Svenskas whose only vices were Saturday night binges on 100-proof aquavit and a yen for their neighbors' wives, mostly gaunt Anna Christies. To picture this as a commonwealth where organized hoodlumism thrives under the protection of a bi-partisan political alliance takes imagination—or deep digging.

This is the confidential lowdown, from gutter to State House, with Minneapolis the chief guinea pig, because it is the state's largest city; however, some of our observations are about St. Paul and surrounding areas.

Sexual lawlessness begins early here, contradicting the thesis that females mature later in the North. Girls of fourteen are habitual patrons of taverns on Hennepin Avenue. They are driving professional prostitutes out of town, which is why the Minneapolis arrest rate for whores is lower than that of many cites of similar size. Hennepin Avenue is the tender-age tenderloin.

On one Saturday night we saw girl teensters picked up or attempting to be in the Frolics, Smitty's, Brady's and the Playland Arcade, all on Hennepin. Proprietors are helpless. The youngsters take up every available inch in the taverns, especially on Saturdays. Still younger kids hang out at the hot dog stands, known in this part of the country as "Coney Islands," though in Coney

Island they are called hot dog stands. The girls seek the older trade. We saw many with men in their thirties and forties.

Those who prefer experienced, sophisticated hags, say of eighteen, often find them at the bar of the Andrews Hotel and at the Flame night club. These are not B girls. They are not employed by the house. They come in as customers. Older girls hang out in the back room of Eddie Holman's Saddle Bar. Most of them live and operate in the Loring district, which resembles Chicago's Rush Street, with cheap hotels patronized by hookers.

Minneapolis has some of the worst dives in the nation along its multiple skidrows. There is a huge population of transients—railroad workers, migratory farm hands and roughneck woodsmen from the Northwest and Canada, as well as drifting hoboes. Sooner or later they gravitate to Minneapolis.

Crackpots, aided and abetted by shrewd and conscienceless political machines, have burdened the state with a Townsend Plan old-age pension. When the checks arrive on the first and fifteenth, every skidrow joint is packed with elderly drunks, who end up in the sewers, broke and sick. Next to the saloons on S. Washington are stores which cater to those on the dole with signs in their windows such as "Relief prescriptions for pensioners filled here." That includes hangover remedies.

The main skidrow is on Washington Avenue, terrible. Another is Cedar Avenue. The Nicollet Hotel, the city's finest, is surrounded by dumps. One of the most degrading places we have ever seen is a hell-hole called the Nicollet Inn, across the street from the swank hotel. We have seen all the dives in the land, and few are quite as bad as the Chez Paree, the Bowery, the 114, the Persian Palms and the Arabian Nights, all of which cater to the lowest winos and the blowziest hags. A sign over the Hotel Bar proclaims, "Rooms 50¢." No questions asked, either.

A principal crime problem is spawned by a small but active Mexican colony, strangely out of place so far from the Rio Grande. They come seasonally as railroad and farm workers, then gravitate to the city to spend their savings. They congregate at Little Tampico, the Bridge Square and South of the Border, patronized also by Negroes. We were accosted in both the latter by pimps. In front we saw Mexicans pushing narcotics.

Sexual deviates patronize Curley's, in the Loop, as Minneapolis' business district is called. Here are gay shows with entertainers working in drag. We bought drinks after hours from bottle-peddlers outside the Market Barbecue and the 1400 Club.

Bingo, even for money, is not considered gambling. Sixth Street, between Hennepin and Nicollet, is Bingo Row. The places advertise the game openly. You can place a bet on a horse in almost any cigar store, despite the new tax act. We saw a bookmaker operating in front of the cigar store at 4th and Hennepin.

Negroes pour in on every train and bus. Few tarry around the Loop, and most townfolk do not realize how many new neighbors are strictly from Dixie. Olson Highway, fittingly named after a former left-wing Governor, is almost completely black and tan. Colored influxers have also taken over at 38th and 4th, in the south part of town. Anything goes in the Negro neighborhoods, including all-night liquor sale, reefers and gambling. The cops are under orders not to disturb the new voters.

Minneapolis, St. Paul and the entire state are ruled by a tight little concentration of sordid figures, with Minneapolis the new bourse, clearing-house and communications center for illegitimate deals consummated far away. Senator Humphrey's local Democratic machine is on the receiving end with political contributions. The active head of the local underworld is Kid Cann, square monicker Isidore Blumenfeld, who got his unique name because of his many trips to the penitentiary. The Kid now claims to be a legitimate operator and, to prove it, he and his pals recently took over the Twin City Transit System. But when they put slot-machines in the carbarns there was indignation in the local press. Kept confidential, however, was the important news that Joe Massei, of Detroit's Purple Gang, with a bundle of Mafia cash, was in on the deal.

Kid Cann and Tommy Banks, another Minneapolis character, are now operating the poker-games in Gardena, California. Cann secretly bought into a Honolulu hotel. He is active in Democratic politics, enthusiastically supported Humphrey's Senatorial campaign by importing expensive floor shows from New York to play at his Carnival night club, then sent them to Humphrey rallies instead. This handsome, costly contribution to the campaign was not recorded.

It isn't healthy to annoy Kid Cann. Some years ago a man named Liggett, who ran a weekly paper, accused Cann and the police department of being in cahoots, and threatened to expose their gambling tie-ups. His wife soon was a widow.

The Cann touch was magic even in the days when Humphrey ran for Mayor. Ed Ryan, now Hennepin County sheriff, was only a detective. But he knew the Kid. Hubert appointed him police chief. Under Humphrey the town was wide open. Cann claims he's moving to Florida. Flippy Sherer, an associate, went to Los Angeles, where he sells Dad's Root Beer.

Cann is notorious. But the undercover power is Tommy Banks, owner of five liquor stores, the man who can put over anything. Banks's protégés are Eddie and Fred Gates.

Much of the slot and gambling profits is funneled into Democratic campaign coffers—the figure at the time of Humphrey's Senatorial campaign was said to be a million bucks. Humphrey and his secretary, both reputed to be poor, bought lavish homes in Washington after his election to the Senate.

One of Tommy Banks's closest friends is Charley Ward, millionaire calendar publisher. Ward, while serving a ten-year term at Leavenworth for selling narcotics, became friendly with H. H. Bigelow, an owner of Brown and Bigelow, who was sojourning in the penitentiary on a tax charge. After Ward got out, he went to work for him. About three years later the benefactor and his Indian guide did not return from a fishing trip. The will left one-third of his estate to Charley, and he became president of the firm.

Ex-con Ward now befriends other ex-cons. Several hundred work for him, and there is a body of former jailbirds in Minneapolis, brought together through this spirit of brotherhood. Mugs and thugs from all over the nation feel at home in the Twin Cities and many are at home there. Other ex-cons travel as salesmen for the company.

Ward is one of the most powerful men in the state and swings plenty of weight nationside, too. He was a personal and political friend of Floyd Olson, the late wild-jackass Governor of the Commonwealth, and he has not since permitted his important contacts to grow rusty.

Anna Roosevelt borrowed $200,000 from the ex-junk pusher to finance her short-lived daily newspaper in Phoenix, Arizona, stiffing him with a one-cent on the dollar pay-off (standard Roosevelt terms) when the paper soured.

Ward and his pals also contributed a recorded $20,000 (and about $100,000 not reported) as one of the lonesome group that supported Harry Truman in 1948. The Chief Executive has been properly grateful and answers the phone personally when the former narcotics-peddler calls.

But Ward shows no favoritism with his largesse. He turned over two cashiers' checks totaling $105,000 to the late Bugsy Siegel, infamous East Side murder chief. When questioned, the Minnesota millionaire said it was a loan to aid Bugsy in a business deal "to purchase a dog track or something."

Minneapolis has a small but potent Italian population, but the Italian king of all he surveys is one of the big three who run the state, Ward and Tommy Banks being the others, and by us is believed to be the top kingpin of all.

He is Fred A. Ossanna, a criminal attorney and the real boss of both the Democratic and Farmer-Labor parties, with Humphrey and all others merely puppets. Ossanna is the smart boy who dreamed up the mob take-over of the transit system and guided its destinies while the stock was in the name of Banks and Kid Cann. Twice decorated by the King of Italy, czar Ossanna was once indicted for forgery in a bank swindle, but when his fellow defendants pleaded guilty and took the rap, the charges against him were dismissed.

The policy wheel is run by Chinese, the former boss of which was the rich man named Wong, who shot and killed a U.S. narcotics agent during a recent raid. There are two colored policy wheels operating in the Olson-Lindale neighborhood. The boss of Little Harlem is a liquor dealer named Cassius.

Minneapolis is now the focal point for the lay-off of football bets throughout the country, as well as the operating headquarters for football parlay-cards, which channel through Billy Hecht.

Among the busiest numbers on the Minneapolis phone exchange, with toll calls constantly flowing in from all parts of the nation, are Lincoln 5656, Lincoln 8924, Geneva 2727, and Geneva 3137. Four men work in the organization—Leo Hirschfield, 635 Second Avenue North; Harry Schuman, 815 Newton Avenue, North; Max Stein, 3145 Girard Avenue, South, and Girard Blat, 3852 Grand Avenue, South. The company engages in two lines of endeavor. First, compiling sports data in booklet form. There are several of these pamphlets; for example, the baseball form and rating of pitchers in all major baseball clubs; basketball record and schedule book; pitching record book; football schedules; weekly basketball record, and the Gridiron Weekly. Second, and more pertinent, handicapping or odds-setting on all athletic contests played anywhere in the United States. These ratings are sold to individual gamblers and bookies all over the country. Their business is conducted by Western Union and long-distance telephone as a daily service.

The employes must keep abreast of all circumstances that would cause the odds on any given team to change. They sub-

scribe to and read the sports pages of every leading city and college newspaper in the country and correspond with team managers
and college athletic directors relative to team schedules and
scores, and handle extensive mailing lists for the pamphlets. Four
years ago, this company applied to the Post Office for a mail machine to eliminate the use of stamps. The postal authorities investigated all their publications and found nothing that could not
be sent through the mail.

Geneva 2727 and Geneva 3137 are listed to the Gopher Cigar
Stand, 1319 Nicollet Ave. It was a telephone booking operation,
run by a man named Litwin.

These two Minneapolis enterprises are constantly in communication with Harry Corbett, in Kansas City, Missouri. Corbett operates the Pennant Cigar Store, 1109 East 12th Street, phone numbers Grand 1516 and Harrison 9756. Through him contact is made
with the outside world.

St. Paul is the older of the two cities. It is inhabited by the conservative rich, the builders who hewed the Northwest out of virgin forest. Minneapolis is the home of the new rich, the traders
with fat, loud wives who sport mink coats at Charlie's Cafe Ex-
ceptionale, which tries to make with the swank like Chicago's
Pump Room and is just as corny. Personally, we prefer Augie
Rattner's Theatre Lounge on Hennepin.

Minneapolis has a yen for culture with a rash of symphony or-
chestras, little drama groups, etc., but it ends up with the only
first-rate operettas in the state in a gin-mill called Schiek's, on
3rd Street, where the college kids hang out.

St. Paul is the state capital. Like most such it is quiet between
sessions but loaded for bear when the hick legislators are in. Then
the lobbyists rent suites at the St. Paul and treat rural solons to
free liquor and free gals. Little money changes hands. The legislature belongs to the railroad lobby, though the breweries are
powerful. Most of the latter have been taken over by the underworld.

St. Paul's Italian boss and king of the town and state is Billy
"The Wop" Romano. His word is final. He is a friend of Frank
Mondike, head of St. Paul's morals squad. Frank also buddied
with the Chinese who killed the narcotics agent. Mondike is a
close friend and supporter of Humphrey. This cozy little group
also includes St. Paul's Mayor and police chief, both of whom
were at various times yachting guests of Wong.

Its leading underworld figures, according to the Internal Revenue Bureau, are Thomas Filbin, Alexander Glickman, Maurice Roisner and Samuel Harry Taren.

On the surface, St. Paul and its county territory are fairly clean, perhaps because of its sheriff, Tommy Gibbons, onetime fight champ.

Incidental observation—We never saw so many dames who wear glasses as we did in Minneapolis. All, including society broads in evening gowns, high-class predators in the better hotel lobbies, skidrow slobs, bobby-soxers and barmaids, seem to wear them. Why, we wouldn't know. There is nothing much to see.

B. Seattle—Skidrow on the Sound

Seattle likes to think of itself as a miniature San Francisco. But it smells of fish. More of it is packed there than in any other port. It is a hundred years old, a world gate to the Pacific, with a cosmopolitan population. Its women are good dressers compared to most other hick towns, but still in the second division of the Pacific Coast league. Orientals slink (they have always slunk since Bret Harte discovered that) in Frisco fashion. The dusk is murky with mist. Ships' whistles and the bellowings of drunken servicemen rend the nights. There the similarity ends.

Long before Seattle had reached any degree of industrialization it had become the nation's most notorious battleground of union agitation and violence. The Knights of Labor, trying to drive out the coolies, brought in to build the Northern Pacific, gave way to the Wobblies, who tied up everything in a general strike and left behind a community conditioned to what it has become—a regimented and restricted town owned by the multi-millionaire mikado of the AFL Teamsters, fifty-eight-year-old Dave Beck. Everything happens when he shakes his head up and down; when he shakes it side to side nothing happens.

The union dictatorship is firm and cruel and complete, except for the mechanics at Boeing Aircraft, where the astonished tyrant lost one of the few skirmishes that bloodied his nose in his long and insatiable career. Imported thugs with Mafia training, whose padrones are in close alliance with the labor bosses and the politicians, enforce the iron rule.

The payoff to the absentee connections comes from a sort of holding company, a laundry union, operated as a racket which penetrates into almost every business and building. Its funds buy the votes and the beatings and the killings. Without its ukase no bar or grill or card-room or cafe can open its doors. It is more than a source of revenue; it is a system of tight central control. Beck runs it and Italians in New York, Chicago and Detroit own it.

Beck's unions have their heavy fingers around the throats of organized labor, decent and nefarious; the cab-drivers who bootleg and pimp; the bartenders who sell after hours and book bets; the barmaids and waitresses who cadge drinks as long as they can stand up and then make what they can lying down. No wheel can move under anything that rolls, not only in Seattle, but anywhere in the nation, if Dave Beck wants it tied up. He has more voice in international headquarters in Indianapolis than the aging Dan Tobin, Franklin D. Roosevelt's pal. He muscled in on the locals accredited to the huge plane factories which mushroomed in the Northwest for the needs of World War II and are again working full blast. His setback at Boeing has left him plenty of power even there.

The Mafia penetration is exemplified by a Sicilian foreman in a Boeing finishing shop, who has the bookmaking monopoly and on paydays ends up with a fat share of the wages of thousands of workers in all branches. He did not buy a government tax stamp. He does not declare his gross business on his revenue return. T-Men don't tangle with entrenched unioneers. The gigantic gambling profits are funneled back to the Syndicate, less a liberal cut at the source for the protected privileges of operating. If the management should interfere, there would be "labor trouble."

When the Department of Defense wanted to move the Boeing plant to the Midwest for security reasons, because Seattle is only a few hours by air from Russian territory, both of Beck's messenger boys in the capital, Senator Warren Magnuson and former Governor Mon Wallgren, yelled murder in Washington. They wailed, "Too many Democratic voters would be moved out of town. Anyway, Dave wouldn't like it."

The Northwest wants to think of itself as rugged territory where virile men make their own laws. That is true here as to gambling. No one pays much attention to Uncle Sam and the cops don't pay any attention to anyone who pays off.

Floating crap and poker games run most nights in the Waldorf and Knickerbocker hotels, operated by guests—not the management. We saw servicemen shooting dice in the Caballero, on Pike near 8th. The Mecca, nearby, has a sign in the window, "Card Room." In a joint called Carlo's, at 2nd and Washington, we saw cops lounging while card games were running. There was an announcement of a lottery in the window. A store in the Grand Union Hotel also carried a window sign, "Card Room." Bookies who claim they are only taking "sociable" bets hang out on the sidewalk in front of Head's, Green's and the Stadium cigar stores.

Seattle is a major port of embarkation and debarkation for Korean expeditionary forces; therefore the ancient trades are profitable. The Rivoli Burlesque is usually the only place in town where chorus girls play in the flesh, and the majority of them have plenty of it. Most of them are bags. Those who want the best send for call-girls, provided by almost every cab-driver and bell-hop. The best are expensive, from those metered at $20 an hour to $100 for the night, and the best are scarce. But streetwalkers fall all over you, so many and so common and so lousy, some have to turn a trick for a meal and a room. The favorite gathering, drinking and dining place for the hustlers, where they meet to discuss trade affairs, is the Totem Pole, on Skidrow.

Many whores work in restaurants, ostensibly as waitresses and barmaids—which means they are members of Beck's unions. The chain of payoff is a surefire pip, set up this way: All restaurant employes must be tested by the public health department for t.b., syphilis, etc. Tarts who work restaurants kick in for health cards, even those who come up negative and clean. No payoff, no health card, which means the cops run 'em in even if they give it away.

The cops dig deep to pinch streetwalkers without union cards or health cards. They use teen-age servicemen as decoys, boys picked up for slight infractions, usually imaginary, with threats they'll be turned over to the MP's if they don't cooperate. Negro soldiers with marked $5 bills are sent out to pick up white girls, and vice versa. The Mayor, chief of police and prosecutor were at this writing not disposed to stop the practice, condemned by the Bar Association. Everyone knows the police are shaking down the jezebels, but some of the money is finding its way back to higher ranks—and into Democratic campaign funds.

Seattle has one of the nation's largest Japanese colonies. But its Chinatown is more to the point, being the drop for prostitutes, dope-peddlers, after-hour liquor and gambling. Seattle tongs are not related to other American tongs. Seattle's Chinese came largely from Canada, most of them illegally. There are two associations, the Hop Sing and the Ping Kong. Danny Wu is the boss of Chinatown and the owner of the new Chinatown bottle-club where you can get a drink after 1 A.M. or on Sunday if you know the right approach.

For white men who desire a whiff of the poppy there are four opium dens on King Street, in Chinatown, near the Coast Hotel. The Chinese gamblers and dope-pushers are closely allied with the national crime Syndicate. They act as local agents for many forms of organized vice and crime. There are few Italians and fewer Sicilians in Seattle. The Chinese have taken over many functions performed by them in eastern cities.

The biggest gambler at the Boeing No. 2 plant is Chinese. He pays no taxes. Who can read a Chinaman's books? Anyway he is a friend of the sheriff's office, which has great political power. There are slots in the China Pheasant, next door.

Seattle has not escaped the blight of narcotics; in fact dope is one of the city's chief problems, due to the ease with which it may be smuggled in over the Canadian border, in planes from the Orient and on the trans-Pacific and coastwise ships. Most of the major junk shipments are landed at Piers No. 39 and 54, in Bremerton, then ferried across Puget Sound.

Many youngsters have been hooked. In some of the better high schools, like the Queen Anne and Roosevelt, as many as 90 per cent of all the kids in certain classrooms are reefer users. Wealthy youngsters from Seward Park inhale reefers like you use cigarettes. While under the influence, they engage in sexual orgies in the Golden Gardens lovers' lane.

Dope addiction is already in its third and fourth high-school generation. The number of users at the University of Washington is far above the national average. Many students at this institution of higher learning have graduated from muggles to hard stuff. Many girls come to class with their arms scarred, punctures from "mainliners"—underworld jargon for hypodermic incisions into arteries.

This university is noteworthy also for its extremes of homosexualism among undergraduates, often a manifestation of left-wing and outright Communist alignments, which obtain among students and faculty. In so many instances that it cannot be coincidence, all these traits are perceptible in the same individual.

The limited Italian population is disproportionately powerful. The king of Little Italy is Frank Calcuccio. He operates in close alliance with Frank Di Caro, Italian boss of Riverton, in the county, outside the city limits, where dames openly solicit at your table. Slot-machines whirl twenty-four hours a day when the heat isn't on.

With a companion we visited the Union Social Club, on the Empire Highway, in Riverton. We were served drinks after hours.

Women hustled us. There were slot-machines on which the Federal tax of $150 had been paid and duly registered in the collector's office. The one-arm bandits at the Union Social Club ranged from five to fifty cents, but there was little business. Things were so bad, one disconsolate hooker, seeing she could do no business with us, offered to stand us a round of drinks just for company.

Two slot-machine czars who recently pleaded guilty to an $800,000 tax fraud after their case had been sidetracked for years on orders from D.C. had as their attorney Joseph Burns who shares an office and a phone in Washington—NA 2560—with Rudy Halley!

Anything can be fixed in the state of Washington for a price, and the price is usually low. Speed and parking tickets are squared through a cab-driver in a Green Top cab who parks daily in front of certain hotels, the location changed from day to day. This driver is a member of the Beck union. The ice finds its way upward.

There is, in fact, hardly a dividing line in the state of Washington between unions, the left-wing Democratic party, and the criminal combines. This close tie is constantly demonstrated. An instance was a private bill introduced by Senator Magnuson, to permit the Nazi husband of Virginia Hill, the underworld's kept glamor-gal, to remain in the country and become a citizen.

Magnuson is the gay blade of the U. S. Senate. According to himself he is a bachelor, though film starlet Toni Seven claims they are secretly wed. Magnuson consistently votes New Deal, left-wing and pro-crackpot, which crowns him the powerhouse and patronage dispenser for the state of Washington.

The other member of the inseparable political twins, Mon Wallgren, is Harry Truman's poker-playing and bourbon-boozing crony. At this writing he is out of office, but still one of the most powerful men in the Northwest. He served with Truman in the Senate, then returned to his state as its New Deal Governor, transferring much state manipulating from Olympia to New York's swank El Morocco night club, where he conducted official business surrounded by gals and hooch supplied without limit by Howard Hughes' fat check picker-upper, Johnny Meyer. This squared accounts for Wallgren's correct attitude when he sat on the Truman Committee investigating Hughes' dealings with Uncle Sam.

After the voters of Washington retired Mon, Truman appointed him to a vital security post, for which the Senate did not find him fit, so the President tossed him another.

A state character is Nick Bez, who met Harry through mutual

pal Mon and soon bought a fleet of government surplus fishery
boats at ten cents on the dollar after the war, making him a
millionaire. And the RFC, which lent him the $750,000 of govern-
ment money to buy the boats from the government, is now out
that sum. The fishing deal went sour. At the same time, Uncle
Sam gave away millions in fishery rights to deserving Democrats.

Nick also tried to buy UNNRA's fleet for two cents on the
dollar but lost out on that to the Chinese Reds who were given
it gratis. That was Nick's sole failure since meeting Harry. Congressman Henry Jackson, of Everett, is Nick's leg-man in Washington, running errands between the Seattle gang and the White
House.

Dave Beck's representative in Congress is Hugh Mitchell who
frankly acknowledges that the teamsters' union has the bit in his
mouth. Mitchell is the gent who walked out on General Mac-
Arthur because he didn't want to hear "a political speech." He re-
paired to a corner bar where he heard him on the radio and got
so mad he started screaming, "It's a lie," and lost his balance, falling on his face and busting his arm.

This thing of being hand-holder of a presidential hand-holder
means money. Take the case of Jack O. Gorrie, Assistant Governor
while Mon was the nominal chief executive. He ran the state
while Mon was playing New York, and that was most of the time.
Gorrie served as president of a "club" made up of state employes.
The dues of $1 a month went into a special fund, "used to pay
entertainment expenses when the Governor was host to high visiting officials."

When Wallgren was nominated to be chairman of the National
Security Resources Board, Gorrie got a job as consultant at $50
a day, "to help Wallgren learn the ropes." Gorrie stayed on at
the NSRB, though Wallgren was not confirmed, rising rapidly
under Dr. John L. Steelman, acting chairman. When W. Stuart
Symington came along as the permanent chairman, Gorrie was in
No. 2 spot. When Symington left to head the RFC, he recom-
mended Gorrie as his successor to the job for which the Senate
had turned Wallgren down.

The most amazing of Northwest cities is Spokane, proudly calling itself the capital of the inland empire. You figure Spokane
for a center of farmers and yokels, perfumed with the odor of
dung and alfalfa. So you are surprised to find this rube burg a
mobster concentration point, patronized by hoodlums on the lam.
The local population is usually generously amplified with im-

portant Italians from Chicago, Kansas City, Denver and Los Angeles.

By no whim did Virginia Hill pick it for the place to live. "Hot" visitors made it a point of contact with the outside world, kept in touch through her message bureau. The police chief does not discourage such conditions. The town welcomes the outside trade. If anyone cares to deny that, we would call attention to a club known as the Brotherhood of Friends, with 5,000 members, which at this writing had hundreds of one-armed bandits working. Many bottle-clubs run openly after hours. One is the Early Bird's Breakfast Club, the swankiest joint in town, started in 1937 primarily as a blind pig and turned into a late spot after the repeal of the state's tough liquor law. The Cougar Club is second rate. B. Kaufman, of the Sellman Hotel, is the pooh-bah of the cafes and restaurants. None run without his nod. He is an owner of the race track.

OBSERVATION: Vice is unionized in the state of Washington. How about an NLRB election for call-girls?

C. From Portland, Maine, to—Portland, Ore.

Portland, Oregon, is every kind of a dirty town with a spotless record. Its public reports are censored by the Mayor of the City of Roses, prissy, practical, ambitious and voluble Mrs. Dorothy McCullough Lee, whose nickname among coppers and reporters is "Mrs. Airwick." She is fifty-two, married to a minor Standard Oil executive, and a living monument to the folly of electing women to public office. She will probably pop up soon as a Congresswoman in Washington, the natural abode of monuments.

Portland always was rich pickings for the smart guys. It is the leading logging port of the world, and lumberjacks, flush with money, are sports, suckers for a broad or a hot deck of cards.

Oregon was off the beaten track, its underworld disorganized, a haven for free enterprisers who vied with each other for the woodsmen's shekels. Competition forced inducements at lower prices, not easily available in other, more civilized communities.

When the Eastern gamblers decided to take over, they figured Dorothy Lee would work out fine. They supported her, possibly without her knowledge, under the assumption she'd close up the independents, after which they'd move in. That worked out swell. As soon as the final vote was counted, Mrs. Lee sent her cossacks out to raid the unorganized bookie-joints, drove the non-paying madames out of town, and got tough with the retail bootleggers.

The wise boys moved in quietly and did a job of it. Meanwhile, Dorothy was bitten by the bug, and decided she wanted to go to Congress. She is a shrewd dame—while these words were being written she ordered the town cleaned up again. Then her friends sent word through the back door that she is willing to vacate the Mayor's office if they'll send her to Washington. The boys listened to reason. She is promised the next nomination. After which Portland will return to its manly pastimes—it hopes.

Oregon is a dizzy state. Its metropolis is a dizzy town. You don't hear much about it elsewhere, because the natives are shy, not given to publicity. When it loses population the Chamber of Commerce gloats.

Oregon was founded by exiles from New England. They tossed a coin to decide whether to name their town Portland or Boston. Portland won, and ever since the state has been the Maine of the Pacific Coast, a backwash, happy in its isolation, not envious of its expanding neighbors, not inclined to emulate California or Washington.

Like Maine, Oregon always votes Republican; but like Maine's new Republicanism, which gives the U.S. Senate a left-wing apologist in Margaret Chase Smith, the Oregon G.O.P. elected Wayne Morse, who new-deals left-handed. Because the Democratic party is weak in Oregon, Republican Morse is the actual handler of D.C. patronage in the state. This sets up the comic opera picture of Monroe Sweetland, Democratic National Committeeman, and William L. "Pinky" Josslyn, former state chairman, on their knees to a Republican for patronage from a Democratic President. Morse welcomes campaign money from any source and votes from remnants of the I.W.W., Reds, and the other intransigents that flourish with the Pacific breezes.

Portland has a large Chinatown. Its tong leaders are tied up with Italians in most of the rackets and work with Chinese Reds, under duress, who ship narcotics in from behind the Iron Curtain through the Northwest. Many have tried to explain Senator Morse's almost pathological hatred for Chiang Kai-shek. The answer may be Red-controlled Portland tongs, whose campaign coins have no holes in them.

Morse, and his opposite number among Marxist apologists on the East Coast, Senator McMahon, of Connecticut, shrieked for a measure to investigate the so-called China Lobby, the group backing the Nationalist cause. Yet Morse, himself, is a vociferous lobbyist—for Red China. In October, 1950, four months after

the beginning of the Korean "police action," Morse was quoted
by the Oregon *Journal* as follows:

"Seating of Communist China (in the UN) will speed along the
'divorce' of that nation from Russia. The average Chinese citizen
eventually will demand that China live up to its commitments in
order to obtain American recognition. If China does, Russia will
be alienated."

The chief powers in the Portland political set-up are six:

Lonnie Logdson, vending-machine king of Clackamas county.

Al Winter, who runs the horse wire when it operates.

Tommy Luke, florist and fancier of flowers, as well as the fair
sex. He can square anything.

Lai Sun, spokesman for Chinatown.

Earl Riley, ex-Mayor, now a Packard dealer. Lots of people
die and leave him money.

But the most powerful is Mike di Cicco, cousin of Hollywood
glamor-boy, Pat. He is high in national Italian circles. Like Pat,
he likes dames. He is a fixer for everything, including Republican
Wayne Morse, though he himself was once the Democratic State
Treasurer.

This is what we found running in Portland when we were there
briefly before the Federal tax law—despite the lady Mayor's publicized clean-up:

Horse rooms at Oak Street and Park Avenue; SW 4th Street
near Washington; NW Court near Everett.

Fifth Avenue Smoke Shop. Bookies out in front. Punch boards
and scratch sheets inside, as well as a type of machine ruled by
the U.S. Treasury to be a gambling device and on which a $150
tax was paid.

Bookies operating openly in front of the 4th Avenue Smoke
Shop, 4th and Morrison. When this appears in print, the boys
may have changed their addresses because of the new gambling
tax law. But card games and craps are not yet taxed by Uncle
Sam. Nor does Portland's lady Mayor consider such to be gambling. This is an abbreviated list of some of the card-playing
rooms running openly, and publicly so advertising:

Lotus Cafe and Card Room, 932 SW 3

Marinis Cafenion, 210 SW 6

Moonlite Inn, 503 W. Burnside

O'Connor's Restaurant and Card Room, 415 SW Washington

Oregon is partially dry. Only beer may be sold for on-premises
consumption. All hard liquor must be purchased in bottle stores.

If you have any trouble getting liquor after hours or on Sundays, phone a cab dispatcher and he sends a well-stocked driver.

Oregon is kept that way by the brewery lobby, which in this part of the country is dominated by Emil Sick, of Seattle, another crony of Truman's.

A legislative majority is purchasable at $100 per man.

Many joints openly sell liquor and do not bother to take out any kind of license. These usually have photos of cops and reporters on the walls, so they'll be known if they come snooping. We expect ours to join the galleries.

The lady Mayor may believe her town is free of whores since the army closed thirty-seven houses. Call-girls did increase. But there is a parlor house in a cheap hotel on 5th Street, a few doors from the Benson.

We saw working chippies hanging around the Saranac, the Lynn and the Canadian.

Portland has four skidrows. Each is worse than the other. But they all have one thing in common—trollops. Northwest 3rd Street is not considered a skidrow—it is Tart's Row.

Northwest 10th Avenue, West Burnside Street, Northwest Glisan Street, and the Willamette River front are the principal Bowerys. The corner of 3rd and Burnside, according to local boosters, is the "toughest in the world." The Lumberman Club there is the toughest of the toughest. Only beer is sold legally, but everything goes in this joint, next to the Star Burlesque Theatre.

Loggers go to the north end taverns. When well-heeled, at the end of a season, they pay as much as $10 for girls, otherwise worth $2. Call girls are high—$20 to $100.

The town's two better night clubs, the Clover and Amatos, occasionally import name acts from outside. They are the places where the smart money boys and the big underworld operators gather for relaxation.

Those in search of strong narcotics find plenty in Chinatown on NW 4th. You can buy anything you want at the corner of 4th and Davis. Reefers are openly peddled in the colored sections, and by that we mean all of Portland, because the colored brethren have increased by over 1,000 per cent since 1940, with more than 50,000 Negroes picking their own spots.

Like many other well-to-do cities, and Portland is strictly upper bracket, a major problem, completely unpublicized, is juvenile delinquency. Its focal point is in the schools attended by the wealthiest kids, with Lincoln on the rich West Side, and Grant on the good East Side, hotbeds of drinking, doping and sexing.

You'd hardly expect it in this supposed-to-be land of hairy chests, but Portland has a considerable homosexual population. Many aren't mincing effeminates, either, as you soon realize when you see rugged loggers who prefer boys. There is a fairy club in Lincoln High School, but most of Portland's queers hang out in Lownsdale Square, or meet each other around the Circle Theatre.

While this is being written, Portland is going through soul-searching about an abortion racket. The city is the Western lying-out HQ. Customers come from as far away as Seattle and northern California. Many prominent doctors were raided. The real bosses will never be apprehended, because the abortion racket has become Mafia-controlled. It is operated for the West Coast out of a female physician's office in San Francisco.

You will not learn these things in Portland, because the lady Mayor has set up a local censorship, and when that doesn't work she talks you deaf. On the Federal level, U.S. Judge James Alger Fee is also a leading exponent of censorship of the press. He has on more than one occasion attempted to muzzle the newspapers. That's why we must tell you these things confidentially.

OBSERVATION: Women in politics are no worse than men. They only talk more and tell less.

13. INDIANA — POLITICS ON THE PRAIRIE

*T*HIS IS the Hoosier home, birthplace of John Dillinger, a century of literary prodigies, the apex of the Ku Klux Klan, the puritan President Benjamin Harrison, the playground of Belle Gunness, our foremost mass murderer of her sex, and heterogeneous manifestations including great artists, dramatic stars, historic confidence men and Paul V. McNutt.

It is an axiom in the underworld that strange thieves avoid Indiana for fear that they will be skinned there. They say that is where Diogenes quit hunting for an honest man because somebody swiped his lantern.

We little foresaw that this inbred interior flatland would ever make good turf-turning for a confidential treatise.

Then Frank McKinney of Indiana was made chairman of the Democratic National Committee. Ex-Judge Joseph Howard of

Indiana was his right bower. So we thought we ought to dig a little and we went and dug.

We had been there many times before, in pursuit of various newspaper researches, almost always in connection with murder. But we always got out as soon as possible. Few who don't have to have lingered there. To the average traveler rushing by road or rail to and from Chicago, it is a blur through a window. More Americans are more familiar with Liverpool or Marseilles than with Indianapolis.

Indiana has a legend of typical Americanism. In the days of the Midwest's literary and cultural ascendancy it produced such as Tarkington, George Ade, James Whitcomb Riley and Paul Dresser, composer of the deathless "On the Banks of the Wabash."

But Indiana's undying fame came from a crack uttered by a distinguished native son, Vice-President Tom Marshall, who said, "What the country needs is a good five-cent cigar." During the eight years he served under Wilson, he said nothing else. (What we need now is a good five-cent nickel.)

Indiana has a quaint custom of mixing politics with business. The late Tom Taggart, Democratic national committeeman, also owned French Lick Springs, with its gambling establishment. There converged political leaders who held powwows while restoring their health with Pluto water.

Frank McHale, the present Democratic national committeeman, is Chairman McKinney's political godfather. But McHale has been tied up for a decade in one of the capital's most unsavory cases involving influence peddling—the Empire Ordnance Company, a munitions corporation investigated and excoriated for dealings during the late war. McKinney made a $60,000 profit on a $1,000 investment in this company.

In Indianapolis everyone said, "Nothing goes unless you talk to Joe." They meant Joe Howard, then a Municipal Court judge. It wasn't this minor post which made him powerful. He was and is the poobah. And he was before he became the assistant big Democratic cheese in Washington. In Indianapolis he secretly supported the Republican candidate for Mayor, another judge, who like him knew the right people. Joe, a Democratic county committeeman, did not endorse the Democrat. Well, what do you think happened? The Republican won. This was mighty embarrassing, because in the same week Bill Boyle resigned with Truman poisoning, and these two staunch Democrats went to Washington though they lost their home town.

In purest friendship, McKinney had given a $1,000 contribution to Joe Howard's Republican friend. When the news that put Indianapolis on the map broke, the Grand was returned, to save McKinney's face. But the election of the new Republican Mayor tightened Democrat Howard's already strangling grip on the city and the state. The gamblers, gangsters, whores and their kept lovers are happy.

Governor Henry F. Schricker, left-wing Democrat from the lunatic fringe, does not believe in invading local rights—surely not where the locals vote for and contribute to Harry and the burglarbund in Washington.

That is Indianapolis. That is why it was so signally honored, to provide the man to conduct the 1952 political squirmings and squarings of Harry S. Truman.

Personally, McKinney is a swell guy who jumped from a $50-a-week job to become the richest man in town. Though he was trying to procure a government priority for 100,000 tons of scarce steel for his United States Pipeline Company when he was called to Washington, he is considered a man of probity by his neighbors, who say Joe Howard will be his General Vaughan and will measure up to it.

For the benefit of those who have not been to Indianapolis recently, which is most of the population of the United States, we take you to the home city of the new Democratic boss as it existed under the benign overseership of his new chief assistant.

There are three or four liquor stores in every active block. Illinois Street, into the main shopping center, is one of the most wretched skidrows in the world, worse than Baltimore's "Block." The Illinois Street levee is so loaded with streetwalkers, you have to fight them off. Almost every store is a dive, an assignation hotel, a hole featuring switch-blade knives and rubber goods in the windows, or a burlesque theatre or a handout station for dope. And you can't walk three blocks in any direction without running into another bums' bedbug row.

The Three Pigs, on Virginia Avenue, is aptly named, though females who hawk fornication around there are nearer 300. We don't know where the customers come from to patronize these swine. Some servicemen drift around, but most of the farmers prefer the pork in smaller Indiana towns. The legislature is in session infrequently. Yet Indianapolis is flooded with girls for sale. Most come from Louisville. They are all kinds, ages, and prices. The streets crawl with hookers; cab-drivers carry them; they work the bars and hotels; you can find them around dumps like the Atlas, Kirkwood, Stone and St. Zita. The latter is a half-block from the court house. Price five bucks. Tramps hang out and work the Greyhound bus terminal and the lobby of the Fox Burlesque. They take their customers to the Colonial, Morton and Grand hotels, among others. There's another burlesque theatre in the Earle Hotel, where pick-ups are easy. The New Occidental Theatre, on Illinois Street, shows dirty movies.

You can buy spring knives at No. 50 South Illinois.

In our travels, certain things stood out in certain towns. Of Indianapolis our recollection is a blur of trollops. They are not confined to skidrows and the dives, but invade the better places, like the tavern of the Claypool Hotel. Nor do they work only one part of town. They infest all sections. They paw you in the Meridian Cafe on S. Meridian. The B & M Tavern nearby runs stag parties with nude girls in the back room. Coppers come over while off duty to watch the show.

The horsemen hang out at Berki's Bar and the Paddock. The gals hang out there to get the horsemen.

When Governor Schricker doesn't pull his shades down he can see the Danube Cafe, across the street from the State House, and the broads and bookies operating there. Bookies foregather at the No. 39 Bar and the Ohio Hotel, on W. Ohio. When we were there, we saw a horse-room operating next to the West Point Hotel, in back of a cigar store with one box of cigars. There was another horse-room at 215 N. Illinois. Bookies hang out also at the Colonial Hotel and the Silver Moon Bar, on Illinois.

Indianapolis is the center of the baseball, basketball and football pool business. Tickets for the entire United States are printed in the Wilson Building, at New Jersey and Wabash. Until recently the racket was locally owned and conducted. It had no connection with the outside mob. The widow of the founder is still trying to run, but is being driven to the wall by the Syndicate. Two newcomers, one named Slim Stallings and the other Brooks, are putting Mrs. Emil Rahke out of business. The interlopers are tied up with the Chicago and Cleveland boys, which are moving the operation of the nationwide pool to Minneapolis.

The pool business has become one of the largest gambling enterprises in the nation, far surpassing the take from numbers and policy. The new tax on bookmaking, which drove much of that underground, also technically applies to ball pools, but cannot be enforced against them because the salesmen are small independent operators who handle them as a sideline to their jobs in factories, offices and stores.

The pools, not the bookmakers, are responsible for the big fixes in basketball and football. The change of one point on a game may mean millions of dollars to the operators. At times it may be necessary to change the score in a small fresh-water college on which the bookmakers don't even take bets.

The Chicago mob is operating here through absentee ownership. When visitors come down from Chicago they hang out at the Milano Inn or Iaria's, on S. Noble, where you get swell spaghetti.

The Indianapolis police are laughable. We saw a traffic cop smoking on duty at the corner of Illinois and Ohio, in the heart of town, in midday. Squad cars go around to make the collections for the higher-ups. The money is apportioned in the right percentages to the right officers—city officials, judges and Democratic middlemen.

East Washington, between Noble and Alabama, is the toughest stretch in town. It is off limits for servicemen. Yet it is only a half-block from police headquarters. All the high brass have to pass through it. But the most dangerous part of town is Ohio Street, where the uncouth from Kentucky and Tennessee revel. They fight with knives and the police shrink from them.

Though the most prominent man in town is Dr. Kinsey, we found few fairies and fewer fairy joints. All whorehouse coppers know the good doctor. He is always around—on business, of course. He was caught in a raid on Capitol Avenue. The dicks let him go when he explained who he was. One of the biggest treats is to be allowed to view his exhibit of pornographic books and articles, said to be among the most comprehensive in the world.

But there's plenty of juvenile delinquency, especially around Short Ridge and Broadripple High Schools, where the rich kids go. The Showboat on N. Keystone, is frequently cautioned for selling liquor to kids but was going full steam when we were there.

Indianapolis is the big sparkler on the Democratic diadem because of its large Negro population. In that respect it antedated most other northern cities. More recent migration from the South vastly swelled the colored proportion. Their section runs to one block from the shopping center, at Ohio and Illinois, on Indiana Avenue.

There are said to be 100,000 Negroes. They all vote as Judge Howard directs. The line of contact is through Joey Mitchell, a white man, whose brother "Toughie" Mitchell is locally famous because he gets around with a blonde on each arm. At the top of the colored heap is Big Perk, the king of Indiana Avenue, who owns a food market, a liquor store and a lot of other property.

Indiana Avenue runs around the clock. Even phonograph record shops there are always open. For they sell pool tickets, reefers and liquor after hours, too. The black-and-tan Cotton Club runs all night, for white girls with Negro men. The colored citizens are breaking out all over town. They have penetrated as far north as 38th Street, where they buy swank homes that cost up to $50,-000. The boondogglers in Washington built them Lockefield Gardens, a chichi Federal project. To get in requires the right connections. Many dusky prostitutes, gamblers and dope-peddlers had them.

What goes for Indianapolis applies to most other parts of the state, often double in spades. Some farmer trading centers run wild. There is little law in Indianapolis, and the farther away you go there is less. The Emerson Club, outside the city limits, runs all night when there are customers. Nearby New Castle, where Chrysler built a big plant, has everything. Muncie, supposed to be the typical American town, is the hideout for dangerous criminals, protected by the city administration.

The organized underworld is investing important dough in Indiana industries, many in vital war production. They had such connections during World War II and robbed the government with special top prices for inferior products through payoffs. That is happening again. Mobsters have made deals with many men close to McHale. Military brass is being bribed.

Indianapolis business is vulnerable to gangster infiltration because the AFL unions are so powerful there. Many AFL locals are fronts for racketeering. Indianapolis is the headquarters of the Teamsters Union president, Dan Tobin, a Democrat, and the Carpenters Union chief, Bill Hutcheson, a Republican, who recently retired and handed the presidency to his son in truly regal fashion. Between them the AFL can knock down or crack down on anything. Crooks and thugs take over individual enterprises through unions; if the present owners don't declare them in, they call a strike.

Governor Schricker does not dare expose or contest these conditions. He is pro-union. In Indiana that often means pro-gangster. The drab, amoebic Hoosiers are particularly susceptible to this national epidemic.

14. CALIFORNIA CONFIDENTIAL

THIS IS the blessed state which has everything. And everything is on a vast scale. But its boosters and braggers project all its wonders on gigantic screens far beyond life size. Nowhere except in Texas is there such a constant and deafening tom-tom of egotistical exploitation.

California is inordinately swell-headed over its history, which is picturesque and worthy of worship. But it sticks out its jaw as aggressively over its freak religions, its twisted politics, its herb-healing, Upton Sinclair, Jimmy Roosevelt, the aristocratic descendants of the Harvey girls, its saintly nomenclatures, its rugged mountains, its valleys and its vineyards, Joe DiMaggio, the Warren daughters, the San Francisco waterfront, and, of course, Hollywood.

The loudest ballyhooers and the most insufferable snobs are the carpetbaggers who have washed in on land waves for new gold strikes. The grandsons of the native sons have been largely swallowed up by the eastern subdividers, movie immigrants and mid-Western pensioners.

Iowa would be a great state were it not for Los Angeles, Long Beach and San Diego. Wilson Mizner, who expressed his impression of the southern California mentality when he built a restaurant in the shape of a brown derby, quipped that the Iowans came there with one lung and one dollar, determined to keep both.

California is really two states, really two worlds, each with its own radically different climate, scenery, people, habits, viewpoints, dress and traditions. The dividing line is Tehachapi—not a sneeze, but a town and a mountain range—the site of the women's penitentiary. That is symbolic—the fraction line separating about all that both ends have in common—wicked women—from the blowzy flops of the Barbary Coast to the casting couches of Beverly Hills.

Around all this is an incalculably rich and strong web of honest and progressive commerce, sparsely press-agented, though it accounts for most of the great horde of increased population. But the Yankee traders and the millions of conventional workers have failed to level off most of the weird growths implanted by the earlier avalanche of settlers who discovered California at about the turn of the century. That leaves California with three major heterogeneous strata: the pioneers and their breed, the Iowans, and the factory-workers and migrant farmers from everywhere.

Governor Warren, the GOP strong man, got that way with Democratic support. So he can't be independent even with what would be the opposition cause or organization. Warren, with boundless political ambition, plays with both sides. He is for socialized medicine and other sophistries. The Democrats were not hit as hard as the 1950 election results might indicate. In addition to Federal patronage, doled out through moneybags Ed Pauley, Red-fawning Helen Gahagan Douglas, and Truman's pal, George Luckey of Imperial Valley, Warren deals out with both hands.

Jimmy Roosevelt, deflated candidate for Governor, is quiet now, mending fences. A lot of dough has come into California from Chicago and some of it is earmarked to give Jimmy another crack, in memory of old times when he was associated with one of Frank Costello's slot-machine manufacturing companies in juke-box movie production. The word went out that Jimmy had promised to open the state to gambling if elected. He was secretly taking support from a group of political brigands, tied up with the organized underworld and the left-wing lunatic fringe, who were planning to annex the state with a campaign fund sweetened with gangster money, ladled out by Art Samish, overpublicized Sacramento lobbyist.

On the ballot with him was a constitutional amendment not only to legalize all forms of gambling in California, but to appoint—by name—a five-man commission with czarist powers over wagering. Jimmy did not disown it too loudly. His workers were told to go along. These final arbiters of the works, whose names and dictatorial powers were to be frozen into the California constitution, are the same bunch of professionals who sponsored the malodorous "Ham and Eggs" scheme of the 1930's. They disguised their proposed gambling amendment as a "welfare and pension" law, but its text belied that. The amendment required the state to pony up $6,000,000 to start the racket, with the further unbelievable proviso that thereafter the five czars who wrote themselves into office would have a blank check on the California treasury, which would be required to honor all warrants of any nature; and if there were not enough money in the gambling-pension fund, it "shall be paid out of the general fund in the state treasury, and such amounts are hereby appropriated."

The commission was to have the final word as to what forms of gambling were to be permitted, how much the cut, and who could get licenses. The commission could suspend or revoke any license for any reason.

But Section 11, the joker, stated that "the commission may, at its discretion, operate . . . gaming, lotteries, raffles and machines." That says the five commissioners could run their own gambling spots, set up a gambling monopoly, pocket the profits.

Let's see how it got on the ballot. Where did the moolah for the publicity and organization work come from? Who sent more than a million bucks into California to slip this unbelievable piece of legal legerdemain over on a gullible public? Boys, it came from coin-machine manufacturers of Chicago. They are still sweetening the kitty to keep it alive. Under the sponsorship of the Tax Payers' Research, secretly backed by bookies, it goes on the ballot again this year. In view of other silly laws adopted by California, this could be put over.

California's fertile soil raises more than oranges and grapes of wrath: crime blooms and blossoms here and is one of the state's lushest crops.

Conditions were so impossible that Governor Warren was forced to disown Fred Hauser, his Republican Attorney General at the last election, resulting in a victory for the Democrat under whom the organized underworld is no worse off. Wiley Caddel, co-ordinator for law enforcement for Hauser, was convicted of attempting to bribe the Sheriff of Mendocino County. Caddel was tied up with the Georgetti mob and Bob Chang, Forest Hills gambler.

State enforcement agencies are corrupted, not only to overlook prosecutions but to tip off crooks before raids. After a leak in Sacramento the government's chief witness in a narcotics' conspiracy round-up was tracked to his hiding place and slain, forcing a nolle prosse.

When Warren Olney III, a crusading San Francisco attorney, turned the State's Special Crime Study Commission into something more than a Kefauver whitewash, the whole organized force of the state government impeded him and it.

Next to Hollywood and oranges, Samish is California's biggest crop for export. Bright-eyed national magazine editors fall for press-agent garbage which makes him king of California. *Collier's* did, recently. (So did Kefauver.) But Samish is only head errand-and-contact boy for the real state bosses. Like lobbyists we described in *Washington Confidential*, Samish devours the planted puffs, takes advantage of such fame by claiming credit when the Legislature votes his way. When the bill goes against his clients he complains they did not provide enough sugar. Samish has his uses—he can fix liquor raps.

When Kefauver asked for his canceled checks, Art said, "I threw them in the waste-basket." And that was that. But when he was questioned by Treasury agents he added, "And the waste-basket is in my safe."

California is one of the toprunners in unemployment. But the figures are misleading. There is no lack of jobs or opportunities, but many won't work while easy relief pays so well. A million Californians are on the dole. Yet the state is forced to import labor. No reliefer has to toil. Not if he votes.

Alien Filipinos from Hawaii are being brought in under bond to work the farms. During their stopover in Hawaii they are organized by Harry Bridges. In California they do not work at wages under the prevailing scale. They are not undercutting native labor, which largely scorns to work at all.

This meddling with natural laws by the planned economists brought about a curious situation. Relief payments moved most of the Americans off the farm labor rolls. And left-wingers are making it impossible for farmers and ranchers to import migratory Mexican hands, so priceless crops rot, unpicked, while the world clamors for food. Some scent a designed plan to weaken the Western world when it needs all its strength.

The professional socializers see nothing wrong with this. Eleanor writes vapid columns about the plight of the Mexicans. Alice-in-Wonderland newspapers like the *New York Times* fall for the manufactured propaganda and grieve for the poor, downtrodden "wet-backs." The agitation guns are fired by Phil Luciano, of the Civil Rights Congress, and Ralph Freedman, southpaw organizer. They worked this fraud up and apparently got away with it. The truth is, Mexican peasants are so anxious to work for the acknowledged low wages, they swim across the rivers at night to enter the U.S. That is why they are called wet-backs. They are fine workers, thrifty and decent. They save their money and send it home to Mexico, where it is a small fortune. Many employers have taken advantage of their eagerness to work. Even the packed Supreme Court cannot repeal the law of supply and demand.

Luciano and Freedman work an ambivalent routine. They needle Mexicans in Mexico with the old song of racial inferiority, to turn them against their northern neighbors and point out they are banned here. The wet-backs in the states are harangued by Phil Usquiana, noisiest of the Civil Rights Congress breast-thumpers, who tells them American bosses are victimizing them. And get this—his meetings are held in public school rooms furnished by the taxpayers of California. At this point the Russia-loving Agricultural Workers Alliance steps in to secure legislation to deport the wet-backs. So the innocent peons are kicked around by dangerous, designing schemers whose chief purpose is to instigate unrest on both sides of the border.

But don't get us wrong. We love California. Why even when you die there you look nice—brown but nice.

A. San Francisco—Bridgeport on the Golden Gate

Duty too often betrays sentiment. We love the Bay City. Almost everyone whose interests are scattered learns which are his lucky spots. San Francisco has been kind to us, has treated us handsomely, has paid us generously. But those who undertake to compile reports like these have to be as clinical as surgeons, who must operate though they hate to hurt.

This flavorous and fascinating city, which has evoked the hyperbole of poets, wits and entranced historians for more than a century, is no longer a lady; it is a slattern in slacks.

Until World War II this was our well-beloved, a city of spirit, romance and memories, the lone pearl of the Pacific Coast, created as nature and man had never found and polished a duplicate.

It fashioned its aristocracy from the hardy, adventurous stock that defied fire and flood, lynched its bounders, made its brave freebooters millionaires, idolized its women and built a self-contained metropolis in magnificent isolation.

But mass-production defense factories and shipyards, which brought in the riffraff which characterizes the jobless, about doubled the metropolitan population and reduced this cultured, cosmopolitan, well-mannered and smartly clad community to the common denominator of our sweaty Midwest conglomerations.

Those who take a pride in San Francisco, which is too deeply rooted to be exterminated in a generation, cling to the fond illusion that it is still what it was; that the broad-shouldered ghosts of the forty-niners still hover over *sui generis* San Fran, which they fashioned from their own blueprints for social and physical architecture. Instead, it is haunted by go-getters who visualize only the vulgar and the functional. And it is in the slimy hands of racketeers, not the brawny fists of its progenitors.

So San Francisco covers up with the fierce local pride of the frustrated and dispossessed. It is a personal insult to any citizen to call the city "Frisco." But we have irritated bigger places and lived, so from time to time we will use the contraction as a patriotic paper-saving device.

Frisco's traditional tourist frumperies are Chinatown and the old Barbary Coast, neither of which now exists in its pristine form. Both have been re-created as stage sets to catch the traveler's dollar.

The Barbary Coast is now called the International Settlement, we will have you know. An illuminated sign across Pacific Street so proclaims it. The short block is a sightseers' trap, like New York's Greenwich Village or 52nd Street, lined with dumps and dives which promise plenty but give out with little.

A strange quirk in the municipal laws prohibits public dancing in this block, though stage entertainers, third rate, may hoof and writhe. The idea in the minds of the city fathers forty years ago, when they passed the ordinance, was that if they shut off dancing in the Barbary Coast it would end sin. But dancing was allowed on all other streets—where sin didn't count, no doubt. Dancing or no, you can walk out with a broad in the Pago Pago, the Conga, the House of Blue Light, the Gay 'n Frisky, and the Arabian Nights. So many reefer-peddlers work the block, the Army declared it out of bounds.

The town's rawest burlesque house, the President, is nearby. So is the heart of San Francisco's new and sprawling Negro section, one of the largest, dingiest and most lawless in the land. The recently arrived southern immigrants—150,000 of them— took over what was known as Japtown before the Nipponese were confined to relocation centers.

Frisco's tenderloin is the most active on the continent. It is bounded by Polk and Powell, Turk and Bush, with hundreds of assignation hotels, cocktail lounges and cheap night clubs.

A complete catalogue would be as dull as the phone book. They won't ask questions if you check into one of the following hostelries with a female bag your only baggage:

The Clark, Roosevelt, Padre, President, Dalt, Oxford, Governor.

If you don't carry your own, you can usually find some at the Silver Rail Bar or the Tin Pan Alley, with B-girls, or Rafael's 150 Club, which specializes in strippers.

Kearney Street, a block from Grant Avenue, the main kick of Chinatown, and parallel to it, is Little Manila. Filipinos get away with everything and anything. The Hall of Justice and Police Headquarters are here, maybe too close to see what's going on.

Here's a quickie rundown—only a fraction:

Sam Piquita Cafe, white gals picking up Filipinos.

Palm Hotel, next to Hall of Justice. Filipino men and blondes. Don't come if both are white.

International Hotel, ditto.

Bataan Cafe, blondes stalking Filipinos. Hotel Squire, ditto. New P. I. Cafe, ditto. Oh well, you get the idea.

Price $5 to $10 depending on weight. The fatter the blonde, the more she gets.

There are so many sex markets in Frisco, even our hardened stomachs weaken. We'll brush this off in a few paragraphs.

For girls: Almost any massage parlor. Mrs. Dorothy Albrecht, wife of a cop, operates on Sutter Street. She gets pinched, but continues to run.

Winsome winnies hang out at the 288 Club. Annex Hotel, on Fillmore, caters to whites, Chinese and Filipinos—no baggage, no questions. Golden Gate Hotel, on Kearney, specialty colored gents with white gals, no questions.

Middle-bracket bimbos—$10 to $20—hang out at La Palermo, Bingo's, 49ers and the Sevilla Club, also work Stockton Street and North Beach. Some frequent the Sarong, on Geary.

Quickies are available at Josephine's cigar stand, Jackson and California. You pay your fiver at the counter, get a key for a room upstairs, go blind and take what you can get. What you get is pretty lousy.

Best stuff for sale is provided by bell hops at the best hotels. They phone Sally Stanford, who is to San Francisco what Polly Adler was to New York. Sally announced her retirement from the field when she married an heir to the Gump department store fortune. He knew who she was, having met her on business. When a national picture magazine publicized the marriage, he couldn't stand the kidding. Sally is back in the racket, dealing through a front at Valhalla in Sausalito.

Bobby-soxers and victory girls pick up servicemen at Mason, from Market to Geary. Many stores in the neighborhood stay open at night to rent civilian shirts and trousers to GIs at $1, so they can go out of bounds.

San Francisco says it has no juvenile delinquency problem. Crime and vice, yes; they've always gone with the Spanish-pioneer-native son progression. "But we're adult," they say. "Our kids don't beat the barrier." Oh, don't they? The last count on reefer sales at Lowell High School was 1,000 sticks a week, average price fifty cents each. There's no heroin there yet.

Queers are now so common that queers consider normal people queer. In the old days, before people whispered about them, San Francisco was lousy with nature's misfires.

The nation's No. 1 exhibition spot for fags was founded here in a barn-like second-floor saloon known as Finocchio's. Elaborate shows are presented in drag, engaged in by nances clad in expensive gowns, who look more feminine than most of the dames in the audience. But it's for tourists.

The local gay set prefers the Chi Chi, the Black Cat, the Iron Pot, Tommy's 299, and the Echo. Lady queers frequent Mona's and the Echo. The sad conclusion after a trip through Frisco is that the ginmills doing the best business are those which cater to the intermediate sex.

In some cities narcotics is mainly a neighborhood problem, confined to Negro, Puerto Rican or Mexican sections. Frisco has always been a main stop on the dope gravy-train. Long ago the Chinese seduced the whole town, then most of the Celestials stopped using it themselves. Dope costs less here than elsewhere. At this writing opium is down to $5 a bindle—50 per cent off the usual—because the city is being flooded with poppy from Red China, imported to raise cash for Chinese Communists. A little pinkish group in the Federal Building is helping.

For only a short time there was a shortage of opium. Many Chinese elders were forced to go on white stuff temporarily. The opium drought occurred after the FBI broke up a unique racket. A high official in the Frisco Customs House resold seized opium shipments back to the same Chinese importers who were caught with the contraband in the first place. That's how he got his cut.

He was nailed on other charges and suspended, awaiting trial. The clean-up threatened to starve Frisco hop-heads, but now larger quantities than ever are coming in again, easily available in Chinatown. And the routine is the same.

Heroin, morphine and reefers are sold in colored and Mexican neighborhoods. Cocaine is sold on almost every corner in the white tenderloin. General trade practice is to make the contact, inside a bar or at a cigar counter, then go outside for delivery. For instance:

T-men and cops make frequent pinches in front of the Tia Juana Cantina, on Broadway. Other fertile fields for collars are in front of Jack's, on Sutter, a hot Negro joint, and in front of the Flamingo, on Fillmore. The same goes for the vicinity of the Little Harlem Cafe, on Folsom, and the New Orleans Swing

Club, on Post. The corner of Geary and Webster is the social hangout of Frisco's poppy-puffers.

Much has been written about San Francisco's Chinatown. And most of it is pure malarkey.

In the old days it was something, but like everything else in the nation, Chinatown is enervated, commercialized and straitened. The rubberneck who walks up Grant Avenue sees a layout for tourists, with street lamps and municipal paving—Oriental in design to conform with the illegitimate décor. He never gets a peep at what goes on in the side streets, where Filipino and Negro pimps travel from tenement to tenement, supplying Mexican hookers to lonely Chinese men.

Many of the big tongs are in close alliance with the Italian Mafia to control dope and gambling. Both these standard spines of underworld profits are close to Chinese hearts. They have been playing with them for thousands of years—some more of their original inventions.

The Chinee is unsurpassable in gambling. Wherever the heat is on, Chinese take over. No convictions on possession of a Chinese lottery slip—it's a laundry ticket. And try to unravel a Chinaman's books.

The Chinese tong set-up is used by the Mafia to transmit narcotics and other contraband; such things as laundry bales, cases of Chinese vegetables and packages of tea are blinds.

Chinatown has been dulled by the Reds. The neon signs are still as bright, but the spirit is gone, the gaiety is restrained. Even the colored lithographs of pretty Chinese girls in the raw which used to adorn most of the shop windows are out. Now they show dressed-up young women, usually wearing glasses and engaged in some serious pursuit like reading or sewing or raising kids. The Commies are against all frivolity. Most of the local Chinese are furiously anti-Red, but are forced into line through threats against their relatives in the old country. They are bled white in shakedowns. There is a wave of suicides.

Many Chinese become local characters and are courted as celebrities by whites. Charlie Low, of the Forbidden City, is a noted horseman on his chop suey earnings. Andy Wong, of the Chinese Sky Room, goes in for artistic white shows elsewhere. Dr. Margaret Chung, a physician, mixes in rarefied circles with the queerest people you ever saw. During the war she was known as the stepmother of the Flying Tigers, which gave her the opportunity to meet white lads and girls half her age. She is a close friend of

Virginia Hill. We frequently saw her night-clubbing in Hollywood with Virginia and the late Bugsy Siegel.

Chinatown's most exciting character is a middle-aged grandfather. His name was almost never mentioned in print. We have never seen it published and we scrupulously refrained from mentioning him, though he was "copy" often, during all the time we have known him, most of the thirty years of his amazing record as an ace special agent for the U.S. Bureau of Narcotics. He has just retired, so we feel free to discuss Gon Sam Mue, whose anglified monicker is Sam Gon. He is in San Francisco, where he ended his service. An American-born college and law-school graduate, he speaks English with no accent, but is fluent in Chinese with all the regional variations. He is short, neither fat nor lean, always dresses inconspicuously but not shabbily.

You would think a full-blooded Chinaman—one of the few law-enforcement officers of his origin on the U.S. mainland—would be disqualified; that his decidedly Oriental appearance would attract attention. The exact reverse happened. Chinese are, by common consent, regarded as "harmless." No one thinks to fear them. Therefore this tough, shrewd, daring dope-foe entered unnoticed and faded out almost unseen as he destroyed some of the biggest narcotics gangs in New York, Chicago, California, Hawaii, and points between.

Suppose you took a trip through Chinatown—not on a suckers' bus—but with a guy like Sam as your guide. These are some of the things you'd see:

A social gathering of white hustlers in front of Li Po, on Grant Avenue.

The On On Pharmacy (means twenty-four hours) and that's how long it's open. Joe Yuey, its boss, publishes the New Dealish *Chinese World*. He's very friendly with big Chinese gamblers, many of whom hang around his store.

At the intersection of Grant Avenue and Bush Street—dividing line between the swank shops and Chinatown—dope-peddlers and bookies, on the northeast corner, and white whores who wait for the Chinese trade on the southwest corner.

Chinese bobby-soxers frequent the Jade Palace on Grant Avenue.

All is not quiet on Grant Avenue these days. Most of the trouble, as elsewhere, is charged to youth. Until recently, there was never a record of a Chinese arrest for juvenile delinquency. Now there are gang wars on the side streets of Chinatown almost every night. Some are between different factions of Chinese kids. But more are fought by Chinese and outside gangs, Italians, Negroes, Mexicans.

The dominant San Francisco tong is the Bing Kong, with headquarters in Sacramento, the site being there so its books and membership lists were not easily available to the San Francisco cops in the days of the big tong wars. Many Bing Kong members are professional gamblers. The control of the profitable San Francisco opium trade is held by Bing Kong members.

The most powerful man in San Francisco's Chinatown is Tommy Tong, whose contacts with Mayor Robinson are his brother-in-law, Stanley Chin, and Dr. James Hall. Despite his huge financial support from the Chinese gamblers, and the Chinatown vote, Robinson barely won re-election last November.

The Chinese rackets and perquisites are not merely neighborhood stuff, but run into big business. Every Chinese community depends on lotteries for fluent funds and recreation. Local Chinese gamblers pay $5,000,000 a year protection money. This goes to cops. Some trickles to Sacramento, on both sides of the fence. The executive headquarters of the Chinese lottery are in Oakland. Every major city in the state has one or more Chinese wheels. Lottery tickets are on sale in most Chinese grocery stores, where they hang in the window alongside strings of garlic.

The size of the Chinese take is illustrated by a Federal tax lien recently filed on Chin Bok Hing, one of the heads of the Chinese mob, of about $250,000.

In the organized underworld, San Francisco is an independent principality, owing some allegiance to the powerhouse in New York and Chicago. It is completely independent of, though in frequent communication with, the Southern California mobs.

San Francisco's Black Hand is hoary with age. Italians were among the first settlers in this part of the country, the slur "wop" being an abbreviation of Western Pacific, which brought Sicilian immigrants over to lay rails. Other tens of thousands headed for farms and vineyards, which reminded them so much of their native Italy. With every Italian colony travels the inevitable Black Hand. When the Cammora and related secret terroristic societies were organized and amplified into the worldwide Mafia, or criminal syndicate, the San Francisco branch was already old, rich and deep. Among its members were contractors, truckers, politicians, bankers, wine-growers and olive oil merchants.

There is a little Italian restaurant at 957 Columbus, known as

La Rocca. Expensive convertibles draw up in front of it and discharge important underworld leaders who like the little restaurant's food. They also find it a convenient place in which to meet friends and business associates. Some of its more important customers are Pop Vincenzzo, perhaps the most exalted Sicilian in the city; Joe Aliota, Sam Lima of Sacramento and the feared La Rocca brothers.

Frisco's hierarchy also consists of these gents—most of whom were unmentioned by Kefauver and none bothered, though listed in a secret document, supplied by the U.S. Bureau of Narcotics to the Kefauver Committee, which burned fingers. It was pigeonholed:

Michale Abati
John (alias Alessi) Alicata, 49 Water Street
Antonio Campagna, 13151 San Fernando Road
James Franzone, Frisco and Chicago
Frank Garafolo, Palace Hotel
Philip Maita, 98 Curtis
Sam Ricotta, 322 S. 26th Street
Peter Scambellone, 1644 Grant
Frank Scappatura, 2069-A Mission Street
Epifano Trafficante

San Francisco controls the northwest coast into Canada from Vancouver on the north to Fresno and Bakersfield. Its influence reaches into Reno, neutral territory divided among several mobs.

Just as the Arkies have driven most of the socialites from Nob Hill to the suburbs, many of San Francisco's top gangsters moved outside the city, to Alameda and Marin counties and the Peninsula. One of the most powerful is Mario "Crip" Balestrere, of San Jose. Sebastian Nanni, 1577 McKendrie Drive, San Mateo, is the big tree in Redwood City.

Italians are not at all active at the retail level, using others as front men. The local king of gambling, under Mafia direction, was Bones Remmer. Unfavorable publicity and a tax rap removed Bones from active command, but his bar, Bones' Corner, at Taylor and Eddy, was rolling when we entered it. It was not too difficult to get a bet down, despite the tax sleuths.

The bookies still congregate in front of Honest John's Cigar store, on Fillmore Street. Colored bookies hang around the R & R smoke shop, 600 Turk Street.

The most powerful Frisco Negro is mystery-man Shirley Cattrell. You can bet nothing goes in the colored section without his knowledge. He is wooed by politicians of both parties. He can deliver the Negro vote.

Police find it difficult to close dives patronized by whores, gamblers or dope-peddlers, even after arrests and convictions. When they try to pull licenses, George Reilly, local member of the Board of Equalization, refuses to go along, saying, "How do we know the owner of the place knew about it?" Reilly is a friend of lobbyist Art Samish, the string-puller for the California liquor industry.

Most nightlife is gingerbread, set up for the gawkers who come in bus loads on an all-inclusive ticket. The only big-time club running is Bimbo's 365, same caliber as Chicago's Chez Paree.

You can still get plenty of booze after 2 A.M., but you won't like the surroundings. There's a dive called the Pup, at the notorious and bloody Seven Points, which will serve you if you're not too particular. Other after-hour spots dealing under the guise of bottle clubs are the Plantation, the Kublai Khan and the Long Bar.

The smart crowd, including politicians, visiting show people and the Lindy set, patronize the Papagayo Room, run by genial Al Williams in the basement of the gracious old Fairmont Hotel, on Nob Hill, or Tommy's Joynt, near the Civic Center, a favorite of officials and Frisco's top criminal lawyer, Jake Ehrlich.

San Francisco was as noted as New Orleans for good food. Only old spots left are John's Rendezvous and Jack's. The Omar Khayyam, highly publicized, is strictly for ga-ga tourists. Mardikian, its owner, is a pal of the proper politicians. He pulled a wire during the late war for a world-girdling appointment as consultant to army chefs. That fits. To us, his food tastes like mess rations.

Brainy lawyers worked out a surefire way for San Francisco gangsters to escape the death penalty. From twenty to thirty are released each year under Section 1026 of the penal code. Not only murderers, but well-fixed hoodlums convicted of any other offense, are so accommodated. The defendant pleads not guilty by reason of insanity. Then he is adjudged not guilty because he was insane at the time of the crime and is committed to a state bughouse, with the right of a sanity test at the end of a year. Most of them go to Mendocino, a country club. As many as seven or eight sanity hearings are held each week and the judges must rely on the testimony of staff psychiatrists from the state hospitals. Invariably these testify the prisoner is now sane. Under California law he must be discharged.

While "confined," the prisoners or patients live the life of Riley in private rooms with specially prepared meals. Even those who have been adjudged homicidal insane are—if they have the proper connections—permitted off the grounds and in some instances are sent out of the institution on errands by the authorities.

A half-hearted investigation by army authorities, quickly turned off, indicated that employes and members of the staff of Letterman Army Hospital were selling marijuana and other narcotics to patients in the hospital. Two patients and a staff man were temporarily held, but eight other Army personnel were only investigated, then forgotten. The quietus was put on the probe because revelations were too startling to publicize. We are telling you a ring exists at Letterman which brings marijuana from the outside to sell it to patients and hospital personnel. It also robs the hospital's drug supplies of hundreds of thousands dollars' worth of narcotics.

More than 50 per cent of the residents of the metropolitan district on both sides of the Bay and the Golden Gate live outside the city limits. The county line is coextensive with the city limits. Is has no county territory of its own. The area outside the city borders is strictly independent. On the tastes, habits, traditions and social standings of the residents of the suburbs and municipalities depends how wide open they are.

When the heat is off, Alameda County is usually jumping with gambling casinos, cat-houses and the rest of the galaxy.

Directly south of San Francisco is San Mateo County, which runs the gamut of extremes from the factories of South San Francisco to the swank millionaires' retreats of Hillsboro and Las Altos. It is the policy of authorities to stay open regardless of investigations or clean-ups elsewhere in the state. Bosses of the county, who are powerful right up to the top in the national Mafia, are the Georgettis. Emilio "Gambi" Georgetti is on visiting terms with former Sheriff McGrath. Al Granatti is first lieutenant and operating head for the Georgettis.

One of the most famous gambling casinos in the Frisco area—protected by the Georgettis—is the Cabbage Patch, in south San Francisco. Any time it isn't running is brief and unusual.

Monkey business in San Mateo is not strictly underworld stuff. This is a rich county. Last year it was discovered that San Mateo High School students had been given a sex education course of such unreserved nature that it not only described completely "an ideal physical love relationship" and the physical and emotional sensations involved in such an episode, but it suggested a manner for performances which would not grow monotonous. "The possibilities are so various that no two experiences should be exactly the same," this section concluded. The syllabus contained descriptions and diagrams, interpreting in minute detail the nature, appearance and functions of anatomy involved. It discussed various aberrations and certain practices of abnormal individuals as well as furnishing a good deal of general information of the type commonly found in biology books.

After the usual uproar, in which the state board of education hemmed and hawed and said parents weren't fit to educate their children about sex, the offending cracks were toned down. But those responsible for them were not fired. Meanwhile, such instruction is being given in San Mateo in a round-about fashion. Many members of the faculty, in off-the-record-talks, recommend to teen-agers that they do homework in these subjects. A few of the teachers are even willing to give up their free hours to help. There are, at this writing, at least two teen-age sex clubs at San Mateo and one youthful group of homosexuals, in which a teacher is involved. Reefers have been introduced at the meetings, plus a generous infiltration of Red ideas.

All of this is training for students who plan to continue their education at the University of California, in Berkeley. They will not feel out of place there, because the U of C is a bed of sexual perversion, left-wing teaching and narcotic addiction, with plain old-fashioned love-making regarded as corny.

But so is Frisco. It is manacled as a port by Harry Bridges and his Communists and what shattered sea traffic remains annually sifts in thousands of Sicilian stowaways, smuggled by Black Hand padrones and concentrated in Italian jungles in Alameda county and up and down the Bay. They and the newly-arrived Negroes and the reefered Pachucos have loosened a crime wave on this city dwarfing any in its robust lawless history.

B. City of Lost Angels

Our fourth biggest congregation has had a million times as much publicity as Paris, London or New York, because, tucked into one of its back pockets, is Hollywood. That was a natural habitat for the world's factory of fiction. For Los Angeles was a phony before the first stunters ever faked for stars. And the emphasis on making and passing counterfeit currency has grown with its expansion.

Los Angeles is a misbegotten mistake, a misnomer and a profile set staged for synthetic effect, from its non-indigenous palms to its "smoggy" climate, to its seaport, which is twenty-four miles away. Its people dress and live like Grapes of Wrath, like beach-combers—or maharajahs.

What background it had has been blotted out by a preponderance of aliens who swamped it with oblique causes, wild politics, distorted morals and grotesque murders. Its aristocracy is graced with semi-literate movie tycoons, oil and aircraft profiteers and dispossessed Eastern gangsters.

It is the hokum-happy haven for psychopaths and confidence-workers of every stripe and degree; self-made messiahs, superficial intellectual world-savers, pinks, fellow-travelers, rabid Reds and many others who invent and pursue their own cults for saving the world; for racketeers who sell miracles with herb-healing, laying on of hands, naturopathic therapy, palmistry, numerology, elec-trology and many other contrived mystic commercialized practices which flourish openly. In addition there are dark conspiratorial cells dedicated to secret worship and to secret vice. Here the warped misfits gravitate and find others even more unorthodox and unnatural. Here come the young with preposterous hopes and the old with one frantic foot in some mail-order preacher's para-dise. Suckers prey on other suckers and sharpshooters take them all.

Its most elaborate commercial structures are mortuaries. Its chief tourist attraction is Forest Lawn Cemetery.

Los Angeles' "eternal" sun shines at intervals. The "pleasant" winters are sometimes frostbitten and the "dry" summers are ac-companied by cloudbursts. A low-hanging, evil-smelling smog hides the advertised mountain view.

One of your authors is a property-owner there, but, honest re-porter that he is, he confesses these facts with a full realization of what might happen to real estate values.

Residents of other cities are often willing to, and frequently eager to, admit their shortcomings, so something can be done about them. But the native Angeleno, who qualifies for such after a six-month residence, is a superior braggart, annoyingly boastful over what turns out nonexistent.

In size, L.A. is large. But its area includes some hundreds of square miles of completely rural farming area. In population it did not quite make 2,000,000 for the last census, couldn't pass stodgy Philadelphia, while boosters were talking as if they had already outrun Chicago and were hot on New York's neck. So they drag out the county, with 4,000,000—with territory larger than many an Eastern state—and the No. 1 farm producer of the state. You can travel all day and still be in Los Angeles County.

The city has a good Mayor, and, on the whole, honest and efficient cops. But it is hamstrung by geography, by an unrealistic political system and by skulduggery at county and state levels. Mayor Bowron is one of the few men of probity in a city hall anywhere. The underworld continually harasses him with recall elections, which he wins hands down. The municipal government is set up on a nonpartisan framework, but Bowron is personally a Republican.

The local Democratic big shot is Michael Fanning, the postmaster, whose phone calls go to the President direct. He is not snubbed in Sacramento, either, by a Republican Governor who depends on Democratic votes. Fanning, unknown five years ago, wants to be, and probably will be, L.A.'s next Mayor. To achieve that his boys are colonizing Negroes from the deep South, instructed to vote Democratic and New Deal. They are overrunning the town in such droves, it is impossible to keep track of them. The Federal census admitted almost 400,000 came to California since 1940. Local police estimates put the colored population much higher, at 750,000. Newcomers arrive at the rate of 3,000 a week, driving whites beyond the city limits and leaving the municipality wide open for a major political steal. The first sections so block-busted are in Congressional or legislative districts usually represented by Republicans.

The boys are also working on Bowron's known weakness for the bench, hoping to pull a Luther Youngdahl deal. They've offered him a Federal judgeship. If he resigns to accept that, as some of his friends say he will, Fanning can't be beaten for Mayor.

The first thing on the Dems' agenda is to wreck coppers. All ranks, up to and including the chief, are civil service. But the commissioners, appointed by the Mayor, can bedevil and force out higher officers.

Bill Parker, present chief, is a serious student who follows in the footsteps of General Worton, a retired Marine officer who cleaned up the department. The bull's-eye target of the Fanning crowd is the police department's intelligence unit. This is the only outfit of its kind in the country, organized with the knowl-

edge that crime is no longer local, but syndicated; that it cannot
be effectively fought on the precinct level. The intelligence unit
knows more about high-powered criminals across the nation than
does any other local police force anywhere.

It had set up an agenda for the Kefauver Committee, which
blew into L.A. for a two-day stay, but left without touching anything of importance. A $50,000 slush fund was raised by the movie
industry and was passed to one of the committee's aids. We know
who passed it and who got it.

The city police are good. The sheriff and his cops are something else. Glamor-boy Eugene Biscailuz thrives on perpetual
publicity that plays him up like a star in a hoss opera. He and his
posse appear in rodeos on blooded palominos, saddled with
silver trappings. He has an air posse. He grants enameled deputy-
sheriff badges to newspapermen and others of the useful and
faithful, including cons and criminals, entitling them to carry
guns. So he is re-elected forever. The area he patrols is more
populous than many big cities. He employs 1,800 coppers, the
largest sheriff's staff in the country. Most of the copy that makes
front pages originates in his bailiwick—such as fights in the movie-
star hangouts and mob operations. The datelines read Los Angeles
or Hollywood. The city cops get the mud. But when they are
fired they often go to work as deputies for Biscailuz. The Los
Angeles police take the rap for shortcomings of officers in nearby
independent municipalities, too. With the exception of Beverly
Hills, most others have crude and often crooked forces.

One of the most powerful men in Los Angeles is William Bonnelli, local member of the State Board of Equalization, which controls liquor licensing. Bonnelli is now very well fixed. His wealth
increased recently when he sold a ranch to the city, to be used as
a drunk farm. The police commission and city council had decided on the purchase of a jail farm. Three or four sites were offered. One was owned by Bonnelli. City prisoners are never
sentenced to more than six months, with one-third off for good
behavior, and most sentences run one to two months, so the development for a jail farm could be considered a whimsy in luxury.
However, the city council insisted and the police commission
voted it in, four to one. And it was decided to purchase the Bonnelli ranch, the most expensive one explored. But Bonnelli retained the mineral rights. Mineral rights in Southern California
means oil. Again the police commission voted four to one for the
buy on those terms. As soon as the deal was consummated, Bon-

nelli petitioned for the right to drill for oil. The whole affair smelled fishy and rotten.

Former Police Chief Worton, serving as a nonpaid commissioner, who alone had stood out against all that raw monkey business, resigned.

Like his opposite number in San Francisco, Bonnelli is friendly with Artie Samish, fixer for the liquor industry. When L.A. cops make a pinch on the most scandalous practice in town—B-girls in downtown cafes—Bonnelli refuses to revoke any licenses. He uses the same sickly alibi we heard in Frisco: "How do we know the proprietor knew they were B-girls?" (They wouldn't. Many are absentee owners under phony names.) It costs 5 Gs under the table to the right parties for a new license.

Liquor board raps are a cinch to fix. Los Angeles police tell us $500 judiciously spent with the right board agent can take care of almost anything. If it's too foul, a temporary suspension is imposed, until it's forgotten.

Another power is a bail-bond broker named Izzy Glasser. He does a lot of business with the Italian boys when they get in trouble.

It is a part of American folklore that there are no native Angelenos. The city is supposed to be populated by old folk from Iowa and young Arkies and Okies. It is as true that L.A. now has no native underworld. The old-time badmen were unhorsed when the out-of-town hoods took over. When the boys got rich or hot elsewhere they headed for Southern California's salubrious climate. The town's leading Sicilian is an emigré from Chicago, Momo Adamo.

Mickey Cohen, a peewee character, became an eminent citizen after his arrival with Benny "Bugsy" Siegel, who moved to California for his health when Brooklyn became too small to hold him and his sawed-off shotguns. After Benny was rubbed out, Mickey, who had no weight and no protection, was a clay pigeon until he became a stooge of Sammy Rummel, underworld lawyer. Rummel was murdered last year. But Mickey always was a ham. He craved the limelight. For a while the big boys were glad to let him have it, because he monopolized the headlines. The Kefauver Committee fell for it, of course, as it fell for everything set up, and concentrated its California inquiries on Cohen, while shying from and end-running around the important Italians.

When Rummel was riddled, Mickey's fix died with him. The boys decided if anyone had to be the goat, he would wear the

horns. Mickey was harassed by cops and indicted and sentenced
by T-men. Though he threatened to blow the whistle, no one
cared or was scared or threw in with him. A nationally "notorious" Page 1 figure faded out fast.

The mobsters are withdrawing from city gambling, spreading
their bucks into big business and union rackets.

The brother of the convicted dope chief, Happy Meltzer, was
business manager of the local Cleaners and Dyers Union. Johnny
Roselli is a pal of studio VIP's and is a producer of one. He was in
a Federal penitentiary until some important producers interceded
for him and Postmaster Fanning signed references for him. Johnny
is back as the mob contact between crooked union officials and the
movie industry. That's what he had gone to jail for the last time.

Many hoods are moving into the San Fernando Valley, taking
over cocktail lounges, night clubs, whoring and motels thriving as
assignation houses.

The top thugs travel in the most elite social circles. They hang
around the elaborate restaurants and hotels. One of their favorite
gathering places is the Venetian Athletic Club, downtown. They
like to dine at Sherry's Restaurant, in Hollywood, where the
high-class girls make rendezvous. Sherry, a brother Italian, had a
branch on the Sunset Strip a couple of years ago, operated for him
by Barney Ruditsky, a former New York police detective who
came to California as one of Bugsy Siegel's handymen. Mickey
Cohen was once shot at there. Another favorite haunt is the Country Club Hotel, on Rossmore near Vine. You see some of the
flashiest bims in town there.

The king of Little Sicily is Tom Dragna. His brother Jack is
merely the front. Jimmy (the Weasel) Fratiano is the new enforcer.

One of the most important Sicilians in the area is Frank Milano,
who owns a mansion at the beginning of Beverly Hills, where the
Strip becomes a bridle path. Milano is one of the elder statesmen
from Cleveland's infamous Mayfield Road Gang. He has been
absent from Ohio for ten years, spending most of his time in
Mexico. He defied Beverly Hills authorities to eject him on the
ground that not he, but his family, lives on the estate; he visits
them only occasionally.

Another important Sicilian family is the Siccas. Joe is the head.
When no one is watching, some Siccas make book at the California Hotel. They also hang out at the Formosa Restaurant, on
Santa Monica Boulevard. It runs after hours when there is no big
beef.

Frank Desemones, prominent attorney, frequently represents the Dragnas, Roselli and their pals. He is good. Joe Farro is the habeas corpus expert, bargain prices, $25 up.

One of the minor Italian tough boys is handsome Johnny Stampanato, who was general stooge and bodyguard for Mickey Cohen, introducer of gals for visiting mobsters and dancing escort to the stars and would-be's. The last time we heard of him, Chief Anderson of Beverly Hills had escorted him to the city limits and booted him over into Bel Aire, where the local cops are keeping an eye on him. Johnny had been entertaining a lady at the smart, quiet Beverly Hills Hotel cocktail lounge. The management didn't like it. They phoned the station. The chief, himself, came. He ordered Johnny to leave, but the guy tried to impress the dame by being tough and stood on his constitutional rights. He was removed through the service entrance to city hall and was about to be booked on a disorderly conduct charge. His mouthpiece advised him to apologize and then shut up. He is not expected back.

Another Siegel associate is Allen Smiley, the Bug's first lieutenant. Smiley sat alone beside Siegel when the elegant mobster was knocked off in Virginia Hill's home. Al stated he had asked Benny to sit next to him on a love seat. A minute later a man concealed in the shrubbery shot Siegel with a police carbine. The seat Smiley had ushered his boss to was the only one visible through the drapes, which seemed to have been precisely parted for just such a job.

After Benny cashed in, Smiley married Lucille Casey, a lovely starlet. The newspapers were told by Feds that he had been deported, but he was living in a palatial suite in the Shamrock Hotel, in Houston. After your confidential reporters wrote that Smiley was holding mob conferences with New York and Louisiana gangsters there, the G-boys picked him up. His new attorney, Maury Hughes, of Dallas, a lifelong buddy of Supreme Court Justice Tom Clark, got him no deportation and a light sentence which he served standing on his head in a Federal country club, with the privileges of the house, such as entertaining friends; and frequent leaves to the great, free outside. He is now back in Houston, one of its more prominent Shamrock residents.

The few big books still operating in Los Angeles are run by the Sicca mob. Many gamblers get their calls on Webster 11531, the "Your Exchange Service," at 643 Vista which doesn't know what its lines are being used for. We called a bookmaker there. We

were asked to leave a name and number. We got a call-back in
fifteen minutes.

You ask yourself how crazy can people be when you realize
there is a small area surrounded completely by Los Angeles where
gambling is clothed in the veil of legality. Everything else goes
there too, by local sanction. It is the sovereign and independent
city of Gardena, hemmed in on all four sides by impotent Los
Angeles. Some geniuses discovered a joker in the statutes. Each
game had been specified by name in the state anti-gambling code.
Through an oversight, draw poker was not included. The dizzy
courts decided poker is a game of skill; but pinball is a crime.
Games of skill are permissible by local option. And the town of
Gardena voted them in, the only community in the metropolitan
area which permits the racket. And with good reason—the legal
cut to Gardena pays its entire budget. And the undercover payoff
keeps local authorities in Cadillacs. The town's few hundred
voters were easily seduced on the proposition. All employes of
the resorts must reside and vote in town. The gambling clubs made
a deal with the city to build a youth center. It is understood that
if gambling is shut off before the expiration of five years, the city
must reimburse the gamblers. The wise boy who figured this out
was the late Sammy Rummel, criminal mouthpiece. As Ernie
Primm's lawyer, Rummel took his fees from the Gardena boss in
shares in the gambling casinos. When we were there we saw six
running.

Even Sammy's connections couldn't keep the Mafia out. The
Syndicate delegated the Minneapolis mob to take over. Kid Cann
and Tommy Banks moved in, opening the splendiferous Horse
Shoe Club. Rummel was murdered. Then the word got out that
the owners of all six clubs were in splendid agreement; no more
bloodshed—it hurts business.

The houses operate through a kitty system which runs into
tens of thousands of dollars a week. Most of them slice 25 per
cent off the top, which never appears on the books. On the surface
these games are supposed to be honest. House-sharks usually sit
in. If a customer still manages to win too much, he may be followed home and relieved in his car. Casino operators sent a
$250,000 fund to Sacramento to kill the anti-poker law in Senate
committee.

Gardena, a minor league Las Vegas surrounded by the big
city, is tolerant all around. The Casino Club sold liquor after

hours. The Colony Club, at 149th and Western, presents burlesque. It isn't too hard to buy reefers in the vicinity.

Dope is one of Los Angeles' most serious problems. The evil there far exceeds in intensity that in most other centers, because of the example set by the movie colony and the glorification of such law-breakers as Bob Mitchum. Barbara Payton, who made the alibi for a suspect in the Davidian killing when the government's chief witness against the dope-ring was murdered, becomes a sought-after glamor gal, though the day after her marriage to Franchot Tone she was called back to tell the grand jury how come she swore so positively when subsequent events evidenced the wanted man wasn't anywhere near her neighborhood.

The Los Angeles' junk squad has the names of scores of addicts who cannot be touched because they are valuable cinematic properties and the studios are too powerful to buck.

Pinched Negro pushers' address books contain the unlisted phone numbers of dozens of stars, among them one whose marriage to a hopped-up singer was big news.

Narcotics are plentiful here. The overflowing Negro colony provides the background for a huge trade. Mexicans form a firm nucleus of addicts and traders. Los Angeles is close to the Mexican border, easy of access at San Diego. Despite the huge incidence of addiction, the U.S. Bureau of Narcotics is down to three men for the entire area and never more than eight. So the city police are burdened with maintaining one of the largest municipal junk squads in the country—and good. There are 38 in it, but 3,800 wouldn't be enough.

For years, in the courts of Southern California, Federal and state, judges with left-wing leanings and underworld sympathies have presided. Judge Yankwich is conspicuous for radical rulings. Only rarely will a jurist convict a Negro or a law-breaker with New Deal drag. This is an example of what happens frequently:

Milton Schaeffer was a professional bondsman. He got involved with Feds on a narcotics charge. The Federal judge let him off with a fine and a term of probation. He then was pinched by city cops on a new narcotics charge and tried under state law. He was found guilty. The judge handed out a jail sentence, then suddenly and in chambers changed it to a fine and probation. The Federal authorities refused to take up his parole. He is now in the contracting business, but was still selling bail-bonds at 5th and Stanford while out on appeal. He lives with a Negro wench whom he took away from a colored dope-peddler—a reverse switch.

Dope is so easy to get in Los Angeles that prisoners called up for sentence and brought in irons from the county jail are often high in court-rooms. Two deputy sheriffs on the jail staff have the concession.

You can buy almost any kind you crave on any corner in the colored confines, which is beginning to mean almost all Los Angeles. The infiltration surpasses anything we saw in Chicago or Washington. The Central Avenue Black Belt, traditional Los Angeles Harlem, now extends fourteen miles on a band several miles deep. But the immigrants from the Southland are in every section, from Boyle Heights to Western Avenue, near Hollywood, where they have taken over another twenty or thirty square miles.

Before the war there were few dark-skinned folk in Los Angeles, most of them gentle and law-abiding, with respect for the community. During the war hundreds of thousands of them, as unskilled workers, were needed in the mushrooming defense plants. The CIO took them off plantations, prison farms and chain-gangs. Los Angeles was the green pastures. They remained, then sent for relatives, who were financed by the NAACP, pinkish Democrats, confessed Reds, and Jimmy Roosevelt promoters, all for purposes of their own.

Many hit it rich as their women went whoring while they peddled dope. Now you see more Cadillac convertibles on the "Avenue" than you do in restricted studio lots.

The center of Negro social life is the Elks Club. This is pretty classy, far more so than most other colored spots in any city. For instance, the Domino Room, on 12th near Central, operated by the Smith Brothers, is known as the "Gas Chamber." It has frequently been raided for selling liquor after two, and for gambling. The cases died. The Bird in Basket, on Central Avenue, is a jive hangout. Bootleggers and dope-merchants are busy near here. Colored queers hang out at the Chatter Box. The Oasis, on Western, is a de luxe dump with black and tan name bands. It is where the musicians go. White gals meet colored sports here.

Graham at 102nd is one of the hottest narcotics bazaars anywhere. Cops have made scores of pinches at its hot dog stand. The Watts section, nine miles from city hall, is all black and Mexican, in proportions of two to one. If you want to see something, stick your beak into the Iris Cafe, in Watts, where young white gals hang out with black peddlers of everything. A stranger takes his life in his hands here. Part of the way, Central Avenue is the dividing line between city and county. In the two blocks between

6800 and 7000 Central Avenue, there are 100 bookmakers on the county side, all paying off to deputy sheriffs.

Negroes are Los Angeles' chief crime problem. They commit two-thirds of its felonies. Mexicans form the next largest criminal segment. Unlike the Negroes, they aren't coddled. Comparatively few are citizens and voters.

As soon as a Negro is arrested for anything from speeding to murder, the Communists and their outer fringe yell "race prejudice." Judges choose to believe prisoners instead of policemen. The actionists for protection work through the NAACP, which delivers votes in blocks to Fair Deal candidates. Jimmy Roosevelt made one of his few campaign speeches on Central Avenue. Chrispus Wright and Walter Gordon, NAACP lawyers, are powers. When they take a case, cops, judges and the Sacramento hierarchs quake.

Caucasians are moving out of Los Angeles, into the Valley, as are many respectable colored folk of the earlier generation, who are shocked and frightened by the vice, criminality and effrontery of levee and plantation barbarians. When they move it is too late. Their children have been contaminated by the licentiousness and lawlessness impregnated in the reckless desperation to clinch California for office-hungry upstarts such as Helen Gahagan Douglas and Jimmy "Got It" Roosevelt.

A mass operation is being carried out with that noble-sounding ward-heeler legerdemain, public housing—which shifts Negroes and others of the overcrowded slums in droves to heretofore Republican neighborhoods, where they swing the balance to "civil rights" and political lefts.

A $100,000,000 Los Angeles project financed by Federal funds will force 30,000 families out of their homes and make them virtually displaced persons, while screened Democrats take over. For one of the eleven Los Angeles housing developments, in the Rose Hill area, the city's home-owners and other taxpayers will be stuck for $1,500,000 for streets and sewers. This process is being repeated all over the state.

The toughest Filipinos are around Temple and Figueroa. If you want to buy a Mexican lass look in at the Carioca. If you're afraid of infection, you won't. Mexican zoot-suiters, known as pachucos, are tough hombres handy with knives, slick-haired pimps and dope-passers.

Los Angeles' Filipinos work hard in restaurants or are employed as houseboys. They save their money to buy dope for fat blonde sweethearts, whom they keep cooperatively, along with a Buick convertible, with six other boys.

Los Angeles is generously endowed with skidrows, many dating back to early days when the town was inundated with hoboes, cheap bums on the lam and cowboys in for a toot. The winos hang out on 5th Street, from San Pedro to Main. They sell their blood to get booze money. They sleep in all-night movies, of which there are plenty, a hangover from defense factories which worked around the clock. You can buy a floozy or a reefer or a policy slip in front of the cigar store at 5th and Gladys.

Main Street is the principal skidrow, loaded with raw burlesque houses and burlesque bars. There is nothing furtive about burley-cue here. Kleig lights and stationary soundtrucks in the street act as barkers to pull in the derelicts and trailer tourists. The chief police problem is B-girls and waitresses in the Main Street dives. Raids and pinches get convictions of girls, but never of managers or proprietors. Their defense is that the girls were customers, stepped out of line on their own. Arrests of girls in or near such places as the Follies Village, the Theatre Cafe, the Gay Way and the Waldorf Cellar are habitual. But Bonnelli refuses to lift licenses.

While we were there, a judge handed down a presentment listing the above-mentioned places as the most nefarious. But the vice squad is stymied. We made the rounds with a police officer and saw B-girls in each of these places—necking or worse in corners with servicemen and civilian drunks. The armed services refuse to put them out of bounds, though police frequently request help to delouse the area. It hurts us to disclose that some MPs and SPs are on the take. In typical police fashion, the money finds its way up to Army, Navy and Air Force brass.

The girls claim they are not B-girls. They say they do not solicit drinks or men, but wait to be asked. If the proposition is right, they take the dates to handy assignation hotels in the block.

Lonesome men also play the taxi-dance halls. Roseland is the biggest, but the girls are more accommodating at Dreamland.

Most wenching is done by semi-pros who work neighborhood bars, where bartenders pimp and take phone calls. In Hollywood it's different. Major movie studios have young good-lookers on hand, signed as bit players, who listen to reason. Important visiting exhibitors, home office officials, angels and government big shots go back home and hate their wives.

Cecilia Potts, 1454 Havenhurst, is the official madame for the studios. They use her to get gals for VIPs. Another purveyor is

Billie Bennett. She had a fine stable of working-girls who went to hotel rooms for fifty bucks a throw.

New York's scarlet Polly Adler barged into Hollywood after being exiled from Gotham. She operated a high-class service discreetly for old Broadway customers, now big shots, including famed screen Casanovas, in the movie industry. Now she is out of the racket, retired and wealthy and living on "royalties" of her unwritten memoirs, which she announces for publication every year, then suddenly calls off when old patrons beg her to observe the ethics of whore-house honor. She still occasionally turns a trick for an old friend by acting as the ambassador on a particularly difficult negotiation, such as a recent deal when a busty blonde box-office draw got 20,000 oil dollars for a night with a Texan who had always yenned for her. The fanclub fave needed the money to pay her income tax.

Los Angeles is oversexed. Tens of thousands of pretty girls flock in to run Betty Grable back to St. Louis and end up as waitresses, salesgirls and car-hops. They are still hoping, need money and are plain lonely. Girls mature younger here. Many fifteen-year-olds look like twenty and act like thirty. With this female oversupply, Los Angeles wholesales girls for the entire state. They work out to Bakersfield and Fresno to service farmers and miners, and are sent to San Francisco for turnover in the hotels, booked by Los Angeles agencies or freelanced by truck-drivers who transport them, deliver them to madames or macks along the route, in return for fun on the cuff and ten bucks.

Other girls support themselves by posing nude in what purport to be art classes, advertise so as to indicate they will come to your home and pose naked. There is a place at 5066 West Pico Boulevard (Phone YO 8888) which has nude groups afternoon and evening, featuring Raven!!!—who "brings Paris to Los Angeles, the most exciting new model you've ever dreamed of."

Nancy, at DU 8-7104, charges $2 for the private phone numbers of fifty models, together with their undraped photos. Paulette poses undraped "a la Paree" at 7511 Santa Monica Boulevard. Faye Sandra, 6911 Lexington, sells obscene films.

Los Angeles is Elysian fields for lonely-heart and introduction clubs, many palpable call services. Some advertise in the personal notices with ads that can be taken either way, such as "Romance by Phone. Girls Free to 35, immediate dates. Call AX 2-5769." But Ann O'Neil advertises she will be out of town until the 25th. Her phone number is DU 9-3544.

The personal columns of the tabloid *Los Angeles Mirror* are clearing houses for men and women in search of matrimony, companionship or just plain sleeping accommodations. Most of the masseurs who advertise are blinds for you-name-it.

But in the homosexual department Los Angeles really specializes. Our first great wave of fairies and Lesbians originated in or was drawn to Hollywood, but the impressionable youth of both sexes there, which reflects the manners and mores of the movie colony, was quick to take up such filth as a fad. Now it is a habit and they like it. Homosexualism runs through every race and class of society of California, including husky cowpunchers, rugged U.S.C. football stars, middle-class home-owners and voters, Negroes, Mexicans, Chinese and Japanese. The high schools are hotbeds of the unspeakable. Many important politicians, several leading industrialists, and an incredible segment of the movie personnel and associated fields are perverted. This seems to run hand in hand with the nutty religions and twisted "modern" political philosophy that permeates the area. Many exotic cults encourage strange eroticisms.

Homosexualism cannot in the main be controlled by police. They make arrests in the parks and other public places. That is about as far as it goes. Yet there is a lucrative field for shakedowns. Some who slip find themselves in hock for life to blackmailers. Many Los Angeles attorneys specialize in defending sex-offenders. Gladys Root is the most active. Her usual fee is what she can get. Business must be good, because she wears a new Adrian gown about every day. The fine for a first fall is $200.

According to records of the Los Angeles police department, homos frequent the Maxwell Cafe on 3rd Street. The Hollywood bunch goes to the Flamingo, at 1027 La Brea. Favorite hangout of the Hollywood Lesbians is the If Club, 8th and Vermont. Negro homos meet white friends at Daisy's, 5th and San Pedro.

Sex per se is passé in Los Angeles. Sex and non-virgin clubs, startling in other towns, are old hat here. Every high school is infected, but in some ways Hollywood High is the worst. Not only has it a full quota of homos and dope-addicts, but ever since Lana Turner was discovered by a talent-scout in the soda fountain on Highland Avenue, across from the school, most of the girls come to classes in full make-up. Many develop round heels for anyone with the remotest "in" in a studio.

After the success of our other Confidential books, floods of well-wishing fans suggested "Hollywood Confidential" as our next. We had signed a contract to write it. We bought it back. We reneged because we felt there was no book in Hollywood. In fact, there is practically no Hollywood. The public's impression of the place does not square with the facts. Instead of dominating Los Angeles, the film colony is a peanut therein, supporting no more than 50,000 people. They are cut off socially, geographically and in spirit from the metropolis. A book about Hollywood would merely be a repetition of gossip in fan magazines and movie columns, chiefly about personalities, trade stuff and who shacks up with whom at the moment of publication.

The movie business has been much maligned in some directions. In others it has been absurdly overrated and overemphasized. The fabulous wealth that poured through its coffers for thirty years caused those in the colony to think of themselves as superhuman. Their roots were on farms and in ghettos, but they thought they were a race apart. Handsome louts who couldn't earn an honest living driving an ice-wagon suddenly became experts on world affairs. Former dress-manufacturers who signed their names with crosses pontificated about taste, culture and manners. Elevated trollops were telling Americans how to dress, what to smoke, how to vote and how to live.

Hollywood has not been cleaned up. But it is frightened by a depression which pinches the pocket, cutting $15,000-a-week producers to $10,000. So it pretends goodness and cries "persecution" if you mention what happened two years ago. A whitewasher is hired to "clear" the pictures of suspected Reds. He is an ex-movie writer of little talent, Art Arthur, who was identified with ultra "liberal" movements not long ago.

One reason for the present sorry plight of the movies is that some who manufacture them have contempt for the bread-and-butter customers who make it all possible at the box-office. There are wild-eyed zealots who believe the function of the cinema is to make people socially conscious. These are aided and prodded by hard, cold, professional Communists, who still try (and often succeed) to slip subtle left-wing doctrine over, diaphanously disguised as entertainment. The gangs of pinkos that infiltrated into every level of photoplay production have not departed or changed.

Two predominant types are gangster-lovers and Red apologists. We are not surprised when we discover the two blending in one individual. Maybe the psychiatrists can explain this affinity.

Many theatrical personalities are courted by left-wing outfits and organized gangs for the same purpose—to make the outlaws respectable. Many are on both lists. A chump is a chump, no matter how many paid idolators he has, and flattery is his meat. Shrewd people know suckers. They know how to butter up a million-dollar-a-year ham who has a feeling of inferiority because deep down in his soul he knows he is temporary, accidental and insecure. Many actors got tied up with hoods in their early days, when they worked ginmills owned by the sporting fraternity. And when they got rich and famous, they tried to compensate with social consciousness.

But the love affair between the mobsters and the Commie-lovers is even more passionate than that. Throughout the country you will find many of the same mouthpieces who defend Reds advising and representing the organized underworld. An example is former Judge Isaac Pacht, a shining light of the Communist-shaded National Lawyers' Guild and a loud and fervent pleader for left-wing causes. But Judge Pacht's law firm also acted for Bugsy Siegel and the Flamingo Hotel. A member of the firm was an officer of the Flamingo Corporation when Benny was alive.

Hollywood is frightened, too afraid to fight back. It tolerates anyone who crashes in and pushes it around.

One who discovered this was Jimmie Tarantino, a mean little character from Jersey. Through $12,000 obtained from Frank Sinatra, Tarantino and Sinatra's manager, Hank Sanicola, operated a scandal-mongering pressure sheet which Tarantino, practically illiterate, edited. Sanicola's name appeared for some time as publisher. Soon Tarantino had the entire film colony eating out of his hand so he wouldn't print his irresponsible libels. Only tough newsgal Florabel Muir had the guts to try to stop him, but the judge ruled that calling her "a Yucca Street panderer" was not criminal libel. The studios and big and powerful men pretend he doesn't exist. But he hurts, and plenty. He branched out with his *Hollywood Life* to include the entire state, especially Frisco, now his most important revenue-raiser.

Artie Samish came to the rescue of the rag with liquor advertising. It is now pushing a bill to permit sales to minors. Meanwhile it plugs those who turn handsprings for the underworld. We know this Tarantino of old. We owe him nothing, though as recently as last June, when it served some purpose we did not fathom to do so, he gave kudos to our "smart reporting."

Jimmie was a lead dime as far back as 1933, when he drove a hack in Orange, N. J. He painted it yellow to resemble the local "Yellows" and called it the "Mellow Cab Co." His chief source of revenue was loading up with prospects for the traveling crap games. His associates were other punks who ran errands for such Jersey mobsters as Joe Adonis, Willie Moretti and Joe de Carlo.

Here is a quick rundown on some of the independent territory in the Los Angeles area:

The famed Sunset Boulevard Strip, a mile of unincorporated county land between Los Angeles and Beverly Hills. No law except the sheriff. This is where bookmakers operate, madames get their calls and after-hour joints run. It is also the site of Hollywood's two most famous night clubs, Ciro's and Mocambo. Mickey Cohen's haberdashery store was in the middle of it until he went to jail.

Beverly Hills, with a population around 40,000, is America's richest community for its size. It is one of the few cities in the world without slums, Negro quarters, depressed people or reliefers. All its residents live in expensive restricted homes or luxury apartments. Servants and clerks commute. With so much wealth to protect, the Beverly Hills taxpayers support a swell police department. Chief Clinton H. Anderson has made it the best policed community on earth. You can't stop your auto five minutes after midnight without being quizzed from a prowl car. But this has disadvantages, too. Gangsters and gamblers move in, figuring they'll be protected from other gangsters. There's nothing Anderson can do about that. Though he doesn't let them operate in town, he can't keep or drive them out, for they buy gold-plated legal advice and are hot hell for their constitutional rights.

Beverly Hills also has Mike Romanoff. The three most prominent citizens and social arbiters of Hollywood are restaurant men:

Herman Hover, boss of Ciro's, was an Earl Carroll chorus boy in New York.

Charlie Morrison, of Mocambo, was a booking agent, son of a family of showmen. He began professional life as an usher at the famous old Palace on Broadway.

Romanoff's is the creation of a former Brooklyn pants-presser born Harry Gerguson. He pretended he was Russian royalty. Run out of New York by creditors and bailiffs, Mike went to Hollywood, where fake royalty is as good as any other. He became one of the town's leading chop house impresarios. An amusing impostor with an Oxford accent, he was financed by the late Mark Hellinger and others for laughs. But he made good in a big, smart way and is a citizen of substance who can now be a snob. When he built his new place, among those who helped him were Vanderbilts and Rockefellers. They like him. So do we.

These three control the social destinies of the colony. If you are barred from their restaurants you are a leper. If you get a good table, you are a prince.

Swank, aristocratic Pasadena, at the other end of the county, has a Negro revolution. The colored brethren flocked in so fast, the local administration has to play ball with them or else. North Fair Oaks now looks like Harlem with palms. Burbank is home-base for most of the area hoods. The Sicca family holds out there in splendor and controls the hand-book in the studios and plane plants. It is the cesspool of Southern California.

Long Beach solved its Negro problem by segregation in reverse. Negroes are permitted anywhere. Whites are not tolerated in colored neighborhoods, bars, restaurants or pool rooms. The result is that while the Negroes run wide open, whites are cut off from their sources of supply of dope, policy and late liquor. Long Beach has more Iowans than Des Moines. It is quiet on the surface, like a typical Midwest Bible Belt town, but it is duck-soup for sailors, where young victory girls flock in volume and open their arms, etc., to anything in blues.

Politically, Long Beach stinks. The public is interested only in keeping tax rates down, and if they can the voters don't care what the cops or officials do, out loud or on the side. So gambling joints run openly across the street from the police station, except for temporary closedowns, such as when word got out that we were in town. Long Beach has an organized underworld run by members of the Bagliazzio family, which moved there from New York's East Harlem. You see Bagliazzios behind the cash register at the Melody Cafe in Pedro and the Lux Club, in Wilmington. The family is on intimate terms with East Harlem's left-wing boss, ex-Representative Vito Marcantonio, and through him made contacts with Harry Bridges' Communists.

Manhattan Beach is another looloo. Since the days when Bugsy Siegel and Tony Carnero ran its tango parlors, it has been wide open and crooked. When publisher Haynes of the South Bay *Daily Breeze* tried to clean up the town he was shot at.

The town's ace madame attends every council meeting in her sable-dyed gopher and empties seats around her with her aroma. "Madame Fifi" swings a big stick, is a power in the town.

Palm Springs is a hundred miles away, in the desert. For all practical purposes, it's a suburb. That's where film notables do their playing. When the town is open it is prepared to offer anything you want. When it isn't things hum across the border in

Cathedral City. The bosses of the area are Bobbie Garcia and George Zouganites. The Werthheimer gambling emporium, in the 139 Club in Cathedral City, is operated by members of the famous family, tied up with Detroit's Purple Gang and Reno interests. Nearby San Bernardino is a sink-hole of vice and violence, a fief of the Russo family and Caspar Rotundo. His assistant is dour Joe Basquez. Joseph D'Ipollito and Mimi Li Mandri throw plenty of weight.

That gives you the City of the Angels and its celestial environs —confidential.

C. San Diego—Springboard to Mexico

The fairy fleet has landed and taken over the nation's most important naval base.

We are hard characters, shocked by nothing; but what we saw in San Diego frightened us. Picture a sailor burg, plentifully supplied with bars, cocktail lounges and strip-joints, all equipped with B-girls and other hussies, and yet the sea-dogs seldom come. The lonesome broads sit by themselves, moodily getting drunk alone, while the fairy dives roll merrily.

There are dozens—packed every night. Young sailors queue up in the street—waiting their turn to get in. There is nothing anywhere as disgusting as the Cinnabar, in the 800 block on 5th Avenue. Its waiters are prancing misfits in peekaboo blouses, with marcelled hair and rouged faces. They flirt and make love with sailors, competing with the B-boys, a switch on an old institution. These sit at the bar, solicit drinks, kiss and pet customers. At the Cinnabar, dates are made for assignations elsewhere. For those in a hurry jobs are performed in the men's rooms and telephone booths. Even one bouncer, a six-foot 200-pound giant, looks queer.

San Diego, off the beaten track, a sleepy quasi-Mexican town with a gracious central plaza and wide palm shaded streets, is one of the Italian underworld's most important locations, fifteen miles from the Mexican border, where the immigration and customs set-ups are a joke. Anything can be and is smuggled, including dope, diamonds, taxless liquor and cigarettes and aliens into the United States, and stolen cars and hot money out of it. High powered crooks on the lam, or those who don't want to answer subpoenas flit across. Deportees from the United States sneak back.

It's only a half hour from San Diego to Caesar's restaurant and hotel in Tijuana. This is the hole-up place for American mob boys. Important international underworld conferences are frequently held in Caesar's back room. When Binaggio was killed, a dozen hoodlums were staying there to provide alibis.

Mexican police and officials, so corrupt they make Chicago coppers look like honest men, protect them. There is a price for everything in Mexico. That goes even when American authorities try to extradite fugitives. Mexican cops insist on a gratuity from American officials before they turn the prisoner over. If he bids more, you can bet he is going to stay.

One of the most profitable trades across the border is the smuggling of phenobarbital sleeping pills, bought in wholesale lots in Mexico for a cent and a half each and sold in Los Angeles without prescription for 25 cents. American automobiles bring great premiums, so stolen cars are headed that way and smuggled into Mexico at the point where the famed Lopez Ranch meets the border.

American dope peddlers pick up supplies outside the Jockey Club, in Agua Caliente, where heroin is sold in vacuum-sealed tins made up and trademarked like well-known brands of coffee and tomatoes.

The Mafia headquarters and assembly point is in an auto court along the road to Caliente.

Tony and Frank Bompensiero are the Sicilian bosses of San Diego. Other powers are Tony Mirabile, alias "Rizzo," and Momo Adamo. Sicilians operate the Roma Inn, and the Gay Paree, with B-girls. The Vitello brothers, formerly of 8011 Madison Avenue, Cleveland, run the gambling in Ocean Side, near San Diego. When the Sheriff planned a raid on the Vitello establishment— he notified the State Board of Equalization in routine manner— whereupon an employe of the board tipped off the Vitellos so there was no gambling that night.

San Diego is a switch. The Sheriff does a good job, but the city set-up is dumb. Sheriff Bert Strand doesn't have enough deputies to move into the city limits—but keeps the county as clean as possible, considering the terrific Big Mob money and influence there, protected right down from Sacramento.

He is trying to hold them in bounds with a county intelligence unit—presided over by bright Bob Newsom, a six-foot-six deputy who is an entire posse by himself. Newsom also handles Communist problems, very hot here because of Mexicans and the Navy.

Mirabile runs most of the joints, including the Panama, on 4th Street. Mucio's High Life is owned by an associate of Mirabile.

Sam Bompensiero "sold" the swank Colony Club, a gambling joint at Coronado, to other Italians from L. A. The Bompensieros also operate the Gold Rail on 3rd Ave., in San Diego, where the Dragnas have an interest in the hustling and bookmaking. A minimum of thirty-eight liquor licenses are held by mobsters with the knowledge of the state beverage authorities.

The town is loaded with card rooms, all owned by Mirabile, such as the Lucky Spot and the Bomber on 4th Avenue. The Mirabile influence extends to the bartenders' union.

Sanford Adler's Del Mar Hotel, in the county, is a playground for rich gangsters. It is one of the Fischetti brothers' favorite spots. Adler runs gambling at Cal-Neva. He horned in on the management of the Flamingo in Las Vegas the day after Bugsy Siegel was killed. After a squabble about a division of the profits the boys ran him out so fast he never came back to pick up his clothes.

For a while he was on the spot. He shivered and sulked in his luxurious Beverly Hills home—while Chief Anderson tried to make it uncomfortable for him by establishing a roadblock at either end of the street. All who left Adler's house were stopped and questioned in an attempt to embarrass his socially-minded wife. But Sanford made his peace with the boys and he is again in their good graces, providing he stays out of Vegas.

Did you ask us where to get reefers and wenches in San Diego? Why, in the Frontier Housing, a government project for Mexicans and Negroes.

Go no further.

15. DETROIT CONFIDENTIAL: CRIME ON THE ASSEMBLY LINE

*M*ICHIGAN hatched whole nests of millionaires who changed the ways of the world with inventive mechanical miracles such as only titans could bring forth amid free American enterprise. And it became the first state to surrender to a Socialist Labor form of government. Its Democratic reign stinks with all the preposterous maladjustments of the British Labour Party, allied with two perpetuated powers: felonious unions and rapacious racketeers. Nowhere else has this combination, which is steadily taking the country as Hitler overpowered Germany with hollow panaceas and loaded guns, reached the impregnable extremes developed in Michigan.

Detroit was a sanguinary spawning-ground for homicidal criminals before its phenomenal industrial mushrooming; its Purple Gang rented out killers to the rising mobs in other cities off assembly lines that antedated Henry Ford, and they still do. Today the goons are virtually official arms of the government, as they "protect the rights of labor," and protected labor rules Michigan.

Governor Gerhardt Mennen (Soapy) Williams is a captive stooge. Both the CIO and the AFL have "bugs" on his telephone wires to see that he stays in line.

The state first fell to the unions during the administration of the late Frank Murphy, who was hand picked for bigger and better things in Washington by Eleanor Roosevelt. When rioting labor thugs took over Lansing during the motor sit-down strikes, first to use that technique, Murphy stood on the steps of the capitol, his mouth foaming, his eyes rolling, his body palpitating in orgastic ecstasy as he shouted to the mob, "The town is yours!" It has been ever since. So has the state.

Murders over so-called union activities are not even filed against John Doe. Before the Detroit newspapers knock our brains out for such a statement, we suggest they consult their records. Last September they referred to the mayhem and manslaughter accompanying the restaurant strikes as "Anarchy Unlimited."

Weak-kneed, vacillating officials do nothing. They smile and smirk and mumble platitudes about the sacred right to organize, and they toady to killers and despoilers.

Murphy, a redhead radical, was Mayor of Detroit, Governor of Michigan, then U.S. Attorney General before he disgraced the United States Supreme Court. At home Murphy gave the green light to the underworld to syndicate and ex-bootleggers from his backyard came in for a big cut in the Crime Cartel.

Malcolm Bingay, the Detroit sage, greeted the Supreme Court appointment by observing that Murphy wasn't sure whether Blackstone was a cigar or a hotel.

The crosscurrents in Detroit and the state are so complex, you can't wrap the picture up in one bright paragraph. Nothing that happens is what it seems.

For instance, Walter Reuther, boss of the CIO United Auto Workers, gets shot up. The newspapers beatify him as a crusader against Reds and gamblers. They say he risked his life to clean up his union. The union appropriates thousands, collected from its stiffs, to solve the "crime." But Reuther was no martyr to the cause of the honest bread-winner.

Spoils from protected gambling in factories subject to the UAW run to half a billion dollars a year. A big chunk funnels back to secret funds and into pockets of those close to the sainted Ruether.

The gambling monopoly is assigned by some UAW officials. Management has no control over it. The organized underworld splits fifty-fifty. The attempt on Reuther's life was not made because he refused to permit gambling, but because another union faction wanted to take it away. Reuther is still president and gambling is still running in every plant, despite the Federal tax law.

Any union member who complains gets slugged or loses his ticket—then he can't work.

If an employer squawks, a strike is called—any kind of strike—which ties him up.

The driver who took us from the airport to town said he gave up a better-paying job in a motor plant. "I kept losing my wages before I could draw them," he said. "Even girls are cheaper."

Employers resent gambling. Not only does it interfere with morale, but—insult to injury—they must pay the salaries of the betting commissioners, who do little work beyond collecting and paying off. In war-production plants those salaries are passed on to Uncle Sam, on a cost-plus basis. Meanwhile efficiency languishes while skilled workmen waste much time doping form and getting results after each race.

The set-up in most factories shapes about like this: There are twenty-five bookies and numbers operators for every thousand employes. The runner makes the rounds in the morning to pick up bets and pays off in the afternoon. He holds out 10 per cent. The average worker bets $8 a day and wins some back. The average loss is $4 a day. Multiply this by the number of employes in the motor industry—more than a million. No tax collector dares bother union tycoons. And anything turned over to the treasuries of the local is exempt.

Next to assembly-line gambling, absenteeism is the major problem. Workers go on week-end sprees, fail to report on Mondays and often on Tuesdays. Employers are powerless to discipline. The Reds are delighted with any defections that cut down the defense effort. Many UAW locals are preponderantly Communist.

Pleasure cars were rolling off as usual, but plants converted to war products were turning out little of anything when we were in Michigan.

Suckers who followed the Kefauver comic opera got the impression that Detroit mobs are employed as strike-breakers. That came from a twenty-year-old record of days when hoods were imported by Ford and is now as old as the Tin Lizzie gags. They stayed on, moved into and took over the unions. And that's how it is today. A few isolated cases where gangster-owned enterprises fought labor were turned up, but generally speaking, in Michigan they are partners.

Unions enforce orders with threats of violence against families of employes and employers alike. They use Polish and Negro sluggers and killers, recruited by the local branch of the Mafia.

The authorities sworn to uphold the law turn their faces against the helpless public. These are some:

Governor Williams, unaffectionately called "Soapy" because he comes from the shaving cream clan, is a flat tire—a society lad nominated for his looks, connections and bankroll. He campaigned in an ancient jalopy as a pauper, now admits he's a millionaire.

Soapy is a Phi Beta Kappa from Princeton. He was a protégé of Red-loving, gangster-affiliated Frank Murphy. He served as OPA enforcement attorney and sat on the liquor commission as the champion of private clubs that got in trouble. He is remembered for his proposed "Operation Epicure," to improve public taste in liquors.

Williams takes orders from Gus Scholle, CIO head, who delivers them through Paul Weber, the Governor's press secretary and former firebrand in the American Newspaper Guild. Weber is the brains of the executive mansion. Williams' other puppet masters are Reuther and Emil Mazey, another CIO top dog. Mazey will be recalled as the agitator in Manila who started the movement "to bring the boys home." Jimmy Hoffa, of the AFL teamsters union, splits power with his CIO opposites.

Democratic Williams was elected by an extremely close vote in a Republican year, because Michigan GOPers are split between conservatives and supporters of the eastern liberals. The latter secretly made a deal with the union mobsters; in return the Republican nonpartisan Mayor of industrial Detroit was re-elected a year later.

To succeed the late Senator Vandenberg, Williams appointed

Blair Moody, Washington correspondent for a Detroit paper. Blair is a darling of the Commies. He is the author of a left-wing tract, *"Boom or Bust."* As soon as he was sworn in, he aligned himself with the pink boodle wing of the Democratic party. One of his first actions was to recommend seventy-six postal positions. And soon charges were heard in the Senate that Michigan postal employes were shaken down for Democratic campaign purposes. After Republicans demanded an investigation, the new solon jumped in with a request for his own. That made it a stand-off and nothing developed.

The pinkish complexion is just as pronounced on the county level, where Gerald K. O'Brien, a typical bleeding-heart, is prosecuting attorney. He seldom prosecutes criminals; almost never if they belong to unions or the Mafia.

George Edwards, onetime CIO choice for Mayor, scrapped for the nonpartisan Republican, was rewarded by Governor Williams with a probate judgeship, cream of the certified milk.

Frank Picard, who sits on the Federal bench, is a voluble crusader for radical causes.

Such conditions hang over Detroit, where customers who cross picket-lines are slugged and sometimes killed while unarmed cops cringe and make no report.

The UAW is not anti-gangster. Neither is it anti-Red. Ford Local 600 is violently and viciously pro-Red and anti-American. Reuther, who claims to represent the moderates, hangs onto his job with covert Communist support. The rank and file are not pro-Soviet, but they do as they are told, otherwise Mafia goons show them who is the boss.

The metropolitan press, usually retching to paint a halo over the oily UAW president, buried the story of what happened in Grand Rapids when the Hayes Manufacturing Company tried to fire an employe who had visited Russia as a guest of the Soviet Trade Unions. The UAW forced the manufacturer to take him back, though fellow employes working on torpedo parts for the Navy refused to work with him.

Detroit has been plagued by crooked, impractical or inefficient city governments for years. Mayor Cobo is good, but he is hamstrung by a machine, by a system, and by political backers who are forced to play with the underworld and with the unions. One of Detroit's worst problems is the streetcar system which the city acquired when a former mayor, James Couzens, a dreamer, tried to turn Detroit Socialist. He was a Ford partner, bought out for

$30,000,000, the interest of which he used to promote the welfare state—tax exempt, of course.

The trolley line is financially as badly off as municipally-owned projects elsewhere. But Detroit has an extra special gimmick. Executives of the line are forced to apologize to workers whom they reprimand. And that includes bookmakers and policy-slip sellers who operate in the carbarns through union concessions.

Cobo, a Pole, is also handcuffed because he owes his election to the huge Slavic vote. No laws can be enforced where they live. And civil service personnel cannot be penalized or sacked because two of Detroit's four Civil Service Commissioners are union officials.

The Citizens' Research Council of Michigan, a little Hoover Committee, sounds the cry, but its battling directors, Floyd Miller and Dick Ware, can't count on the support of the better people who finance it. Even such citizens have about given up the battle in Michigan.

Detroit has always spawned and attracted criminals. Its geographic position, with Canada across the river, incubated smugglers. Prohibition and the swelling dope markets enlisted all the supporting undesirables. Rivalries led to slaughter, which brought on organization. When the infamous old Purple Gang was absorbed by the Sicilians, the world-wide Mafia organization of today was formed.

Allen B. Crow, hard-hitting and far-seeing president of the Economic Club of Detroit, submitted a confidential questionnaire to important Detroiters in all walks. One question he propounded was:

"To what extent do you think organized criminals are now operating in Michigan?"

The consensus was: Serious, 32 per cent; average, 32 per cent; below average, 36 per cent. More people thought there was little organized crime in Michigan than saw it as an important danger.

The most potent Sicilian is Joe Zerilli, of Lafayette Motors, Inc. This man, who was charged with being in the numbers racket, is the undercover king of the big Italian vote. All candidates must be cleared through him.

The executive end of the Sicilian machine is dominated by Joe "Scarface" Bommarito, a pal of radio star Arthur Godfrey. "Scarface" backed the inflammable "nylon" sweater racket that recently made front pages. Pete Corrado, his enforcer, handles police affairs. Payoffs take place two blocks from police headquarters.

Louis Ricordi, who used to swagger about when he was one of Detroit's tough guys, is now prominent in the wholesale linen business. You take your towels and napkins from him or you don't operate a restaurant, bar or hotel.

Joe Massei handles the roving business for the Detroit Sicilians, in charge of investments in transportation companies as well as Florida real estate. The boys meet socially at 1003 Anthony Street. Their headquarters was behind a clothing store on the Circus, recently closed to avoid some unpleasantness. They eat only the best, so you can find them at Mario's, on 2nd, or Berman's, the local Lindy's.

The Michigan hierarchy, as outlined in secret testimony before the Kefauver Committee, but dropped like poison, follows:

Pete Licavoli, 1154 Balfour Ave., Grosse Pointe. Angelo Meli, 1060 Devonshire Rd., Grosse Pointe. Filippe Abate, 2154 Sheridan, Detroit. Santo Agrusa, 8902 Bassemore, Detroit. Antonio Baggerello, 3321 Jefferson, Mt. Clemens. Mike Bartello, 1068 Bedford, Grosse Pointe. Domenick Bominto, Detroit. Danny Bruno, 1068 Bedford, Grosse Pointe. Joseph Bulgarella, 3526 Graland, Detroit. Joe Cantalanotte, Detroit. Frank Cassese, 295 Martinique, Detroit. James (Sparky) Corrado, 3900 Three Mile (cousin of Pete). Lawrence Corrado, 3022 Springle (cousin of Pete). Pete Corrado, 765 Middlesex, Grosse Pointe.

Giuseppe Cusimano, 978 Woodbridge, Detroit. Frank Gambino, 4826 Lenox, Detroit. Tony Giacalone (address unknown). Vito (Bill) Giacalone (brother of Tony, address unknown). Vito and William Iocco, 781 Middlesex, Grosse Pointe. Giuseppe Leviqui, 1976 Catherine, Detroit. John Lombardo, Detroit. Pete Lombardo, 11497 Stanford, Detroit. Salvatore Levola, Detroit. Sam Lucido, 1507 Sunningdale, Grosse Pointe. Joe Massei, Detroit and Miami. Frank Metranga, 2170 Lakewood, Detroit. Rosario Milazzo, 2511 LaMay, Detroit. Dominick Miteo, Detroit. Bruno Monti, Detroit. Antonio Munaco, 3226 East Fort, Detroit. Frank Munaco, 1917 McDougall, Detroit. George (Moses) Nassu, Seward Hotel, Detroit. Sam Orlando, 5191 LaMay, Detroit. Rosario Palarmo, 10937 Shoemaker, Detroit.

Sam Palazzalo, Detroit. Anthony Piazzo, 5702 LaMay, Detroit. Antonio Pipitone, 428 Gray, Louisville, Ky., also Detroit. John Priziola, 1349 Devonshire, Grosse Pointe. James Randazzo, Detroit. Jasper Randazzo, Detroit. Mike Runino, 1068 Bedford, Detroit. John Ruggieri, Detroit. Vincenzo Seta, 1935 Fort, Detroit. Gus Spacca, Detroit. Roy Spada, Detroit. John Tagliavia, Detroit. Anthony (Black Tony) Teramine, 12349 Corbett. Joe Titta, Detroit. Nick Titta, Detroit. Joseph Tocco, Detroit. Anthony Tuzza, 957 Lincoln, Grosse Pointe. Tony Venuto, Detroit.

It is a pleasure for a gangster to do business in Detroit. He moves his family into Grosse Pointe, where he rubs shoulders with motor magnates and plays golf in their clubs. He is practically immune from arrest because of the convenience of operating on an international border. Windsor is across the river, a few pennies by bus. It is as simple to travel between Detroit and Windsor as between New York and Jersey City. Windsor's municipal government is one of the most corrupt on the continent. Local officials, as well as territorial and Dominion officers, are in cahoots

with gangsters, a Canadian tradition predating American Prohibition.

Canada is and always was a place of refuge for American crooks,
at a price. American peace officers tell us it is easier to extradite
fugitives from Mexico than from Canada, which throws all kinds
of roadblocks in their way. Canadian courts usually insist on what
is practically a full trial before surrendering an alien, which is
contrary to the spirit of mutual comity and treaties covering it.
If the wanted man has good connections, or enough dough, it is
practically impossible to bring him back.

Many American rackets are operated from the Canadian side,
such as fake stock selling, smuggling of contraband and unquali-
fied foreigners and laying off of bets. Gangsters who operate in
Canada cross with utter impunity. If they are arrested here on
anything serious they make bail, then return to Canada before
the trial.

Gambling is usually wide open in Windsor, operated by the
Detroit mob through Pete Licavoli, rackets head for the entire
province of Ontario. Several drops are maintained around Windsor, where Americans on the lam are sheltered.

Detroit's big gamblers and numbers wheels keep their books in
Canada and thumb their noses at American authorities. Detroit
gangsters are not worried by the new Federal tax. Their runners
gather bets and phone them, "as friends of the bettors," to
Windsor. The new tax law is a godsend for Canada, in need of
American dollars and with no illicit booze to run out. The gambling headquarters for the entire country is being moved to
Windsor. All important bets from out of town will be phoned
there, to be handled by the Detroit mob. Much of the gravy will
remain on the Canadian side, in banks or invested in Canadian
industry so Uncle Sam can't grab it. Plenty goes in bribes to
Canadian officials.

In Detroit there is a quota on liquor licenses. Wherever such
is the case it's a gold mine for the right people. It costs 25 Gs to
buy a $500 license.

The local liquor board man is Johnny Kozarin of Hamtramck,
an independent municipality surrounded on all sides by Detroit,
like Beverly Hills is encircled by Los Angeles. But Hamtramck is
no Beverly Hills. Its almost total Slav population supports a dirty
political machine which allows everything. Commissioner Kozarin
was Governor Williams' first appointee. He is the guy with plenty
of political influence.

the legislature meets. But Lansing holds some records. There are a hundred more lobbyists than members. Among the leaders of their profession who throw the most sought-after entertainment are Bill Doyle, for the chain stores, and Big John Lovett, representing the Michigan Manufacturers Association. But alongside the CIO's Gus Scholle they are small stuff. He reserves a fulltime desk in the Governor's office. The little he misses is covered by Tom Downs, chairman of the Michigan Employment Security Commission, who is a paid CIO lobbyist.

In the state penitentiary, at Jackson, gangster "concessionaires" supply dames, dope and booze. "Leaves" are available for a fee. Killers are rented out from the Big House for torpedo jobs not only in Michigan, but all over the country, especially in Chicago. They have perfect alibis—they're doing time.

The prison is governed by a "model correction law," slipped over by hare-brained do-gooders.

The visionaries have not neglected the schools, which are bubbling over with the same social ferment. In many, teachers are afraid to go to work. In Cleveland Intermediate, instructors and students are kept away by knives and other gang activities. In some elementary schools, pupils beat up the teachers. Some tough kids come to classes carrying blackjacks in their pencil boxes.

Juve gangs are widespread. Members wear identifications when going into action. One group raped several teachers. Some who complained to school authorities were fired—charged with impairing the morals of minors!

16. THE LOST FRONTIER

A. Denver—Mile-High Monkey Business

*D*ENVER is the perfect example of what happens when a young socialite goes into politics on a reform ticket. Its Mayor is the Honorable James Quigg Newton, Jr., Yale Law '36, who has served as chief executive since 1947, when he was elected at the age of thirty-eight.

Quigg comes from a "17th St. family" which, if you know your Denver, is a breath above even the city's mile-high rarefied atmosphere. He is technically a Democrat, but was covertly supported by the Republican Governor.

His trainers are scheming his next stop at the Senate and are dreaming of the White House. In accordance with that goal of every red-blooded American youth, Quigg is now playing for the mass audience, a panty-waist who speaks liberal and bends left. He is a professional crusader and a thorough-going pain in the neck.

In February, 1950, the Honorable Quigg was chosen by that sterling upholder of public morality, J. Howard McGrath, to act as temporary chairman of the Attorney General's Crime Conference, which was supposed to wipe out all lawlessness in a one-day session. Newton's keynote address was the typical nauseous tripe about how easy it is to clean up a city—just look at Denver. Well, let's look at Denver.

On the surface, the town is fairly clean and quiet, nothing like Denver's lusty days when the red lights blinked brightly on old Holladay Street.

Street vice and gambling are only peanuts these days to the organized underworld. If they run—swell; the boys toss it out as cigarette money. But they won't put up a fight to keep the wheels moving one minute. They'd rather have a deal, like the pretty little one worked out in Denver, which permits them to do their power house operations there without hindrance. The complaisant city administration which shelters them points with pride that nary a harridan haunts the highways.

Here, in the capital of the great Rocky Mountain Empire, is one of the strongest and most powerful Mafia machines in the country, with ties into every form of villainy throughout the world; itself tied up with all the major gangs of hoodlums. Its special location makes it ideal for conferences and the relaying of communications; it is a grand hide-out for hot Blackhanders, and its transportation facilities afford cheap and easy access for contraband to the major markets of the western half of the nation.

There is nothing undercover about this huge Sicilian concentration in Colorado. It just seems immune to the laws, investigations and clean-ups which are directed against other citizens.

When Virgil Peterson, brilliant managing director of the Chicago Crime Commission, told the Kefauver Committee under oath that dozens of the most important criminals in the nation make their headquarters in Denver—and named them—most of the Senators walked out.

When Gene Lowall, fearless fighting crime reporter of the *Denver Post,* got too close to the main spring he was quietly called off and given other assignments, until he quit his job in disgust.

There have been Sicilians in Colorado in great numbers for more than sixty years. Many of the hoodlums of that nationality are already in the third generation. Rockfeller interests colonized Sicilians to work Colorado Fuel and Iron Company mines during a bloody strike in which both sides were responsible for more deaths than all the gangster killings since. Each Sicilian group had its own boss, a Black Hand padrone, who dealt directly with the employers.

Sixty thousand Italians live in North Denver's Little Palermo. Sicilians are spread throughout the state as well, one of its largest voting blocs.

It has been testified that Charles Blanda, 1104 Carteret Street, Pueblo, Colorado, is the leader of the state's underworld. He is associated with "Whiskers" Incerto. Other important Sicilians are Carl Cascio, 506 East Evans Avenue, Pueblo, Colorado, phone 6462, and Turk and Scotty Spinuzzi, who have been accused under oath of being Blanda's enforcers.

Clyde and Eugene Smaldone are in control of the north Colorado branch of the gang. The principal enforcer is Frank "Blackie" Mazza, the slot-machine man. Joe Salardino, 725 Greenward, Canon City, Colorado, and Gus Salardino are big-shot gamblers tied up with Clyde Smaldone.

James Spinelli, 921 18th Street, is the titular head of the Mafia in Denver, while John Dricco, of Trinidad, is the leader of the Sicilian society for the entire state.

Immensely important is the little town of Trinidad, a short stop on the Santa Fe railroad. Through-travelers may have noticed the Colorado Cheese Company. There Trinidad, once a coal mining town—a little Herrin, Illinois—has, since the troubled days of the 1890's, been completely Italian. During the 1920's it was the alki manufacturing center of the old Carlino mob.

The Colorado Cheese outfit was organized with these officers: Paul Surace, of New York, president; Nick Bisulco, a clerk of the county court at Trinidad, vice-president; Frank H. Hall, local attorney, secretary-treasurer; Chris Blondi, manager, and A. J. Sardello, a cashier of the Trinidad National Bank, and one Salemoni as directors.

It has been testified to under oath that Joe Bonnano, of 114 Jefferson Street, Brooklyn, alias Joe Bananas, controls Colorado

Cheese. He is on the Mafia Grand Council. Joe spends his winters in Tucson, Arizona, where he lives in a comfortably handsome house at 3814 East Fourth Street, phone 54986.

Other important Sicilian leaders are Robert Victor Dionisio, Trinidad; Frank Mortellero, Denver, and Joe Salardino.

Clyde and Checkers Smaldone, the actual operating heads of Denver's northside, also control its huge Italian vote. Clyde is a miser who likes the feel of money. He always carries a stack of 500 G notes which he fondles as he talks.

5401 North Federal, two blocks out of the city limits, is the Smaldone mob clearing house, now running under wraps. At this writing, three long distance trunk lines and five local lines were connected to the premises.

Visiting mobsters constantly come to Denver as well as to other Italian dominated towns in the state. Rockvale, Colorado, where boss Joe "Ram" Salardino lives, boasts only a couple of dozen families, mostly Sicilians. When conferences are held there, sometimes there are as many as 100 Cadillacs and Lincolns with out-of-state licenses parked on its unpaved roads.

Once, when we went through Denver, Jimmy "The Weasel" Fratiano, Los Angeles enforcer, was checked in mysteriously at the Brown Palace with Steve Sambor. Virginia Hill, the nerve center of the underworld, frequently stays at the historic hotel, once registered in a party with "E. Costello, of New York."

All Italians and mobsters as well like to eat well, and as a result Denver has some excellent restaurants which they patronize, notably Boggio's and Gaetano's. The Trent Cafe is where the Mafia boys drop in to meet each other when they don't go to the Manhattan of nostalgic memory.

When things get hot they have worked out a cute gimmick to hide out or supply themselves with alibis. They are temporarily jailed with forged and phony writs of capits.

On the other hand, one of the boys doing life, John J. "Pocky" Routa, is a paretic with softening of the brain. He is beginning to babble and talk about the old days. A rump court passed a death sentence to be carried out by another prisoner in Canon City; but he may still be alive when this reaches print. Anything can happen in this Canon City pen, including a warden who didn't keep books for twenty years and sold prison-made merchandise to private retailers who resold it to the state, and still kept his job after the exposure.

There's a price for everything in Denver. For instance, liquor licenses are issued under a home rule system and the undercover price is $2500 and up, depending on the location. Then after you get the license, the Italian mob exacts $5000 for so-called "key money," which means that you can't open the door of your premises until that's paid.

The Denver police force is shot to hell though the cops profit very little. Payoffs are made directly to city councilmen, therefore all the gumshoe can expect is an occasional tip.

The power-house for city affairs is Ralph Radetsky, executive assistant to the Mayor. On the state level you consult the firm of Morrissey, Dickerson & Zarlengo, which includes among its partners a lawyer who is a former U.S. attorney.

The Washington wireless is handled by Maple T. Harl, director of the Federal Deposit Insurance Company. The labor and minority string-puller is attorney Sam Mennen. Palmer Hoyt, dilletante editor of the *Denver Post* and pal of Red-loving U.S. Supreme Court Justice Bill Douglas, is pally with pink Washington bureaucracy.

Among most important powers are Mike Pomponio, Democratic boss of Little Italy and brother of the Postmaster, and Dominic Lapore, a bail bondsman. They have everything tied up.

The town's chief crime problem is Mexicans. The Mexican population comprises the largest single foreign element—with 15 per cent responsible for 60 per cent of the crime. Mexicans vote Democratic and for Mayor Newton, which gives them special privileges not accorded others. King of Little Mexico is Councilman James Fresques.

Their main drag is Curtis Street, typical with whores, reefer pushers, and knifings. Mexican kids are tough little hombres and they have organized scores of armed gangs. The most feared are the Heads, the Dukes and the Lefties.

Generally speaking, Denver's Negroes are better behaved than the Mexicans, though the Five Points is wide open, an area the Mayor ordered the police to leave alone. Irene Barbee, a bail-bonder, is the protector of the colored settlement. They come to her for everything from speeding tickets to house-breaking.

The most active rabble-rouser is Art Bary. Professional Reds and pinks came in from the East to establish a beach head on the new atomic energy plant ear-marked for Denver. The word is out you can't get a job from certain contractors unless you've been cleared by the proper unions.

The following is a rundown on how surface shenanigans shape

up in Denver, once the bawdiest town in America. It's pretty anemic, a commentary on a blood-thin age.

No open whore houses running. Streetwalkers solicit at the northwest corner of the state capital. You can usually pick up a lonesome lass at the Embassy, Algeria or Chez Paree. Cheapest bums work the Larimer Street skidrow, patronized by seasonal workers and cross-country road stiffs.

Bell boys and cab-drivers supply call dames as usual, most in demand during sessions of the legislature. Lobbyists make their headquarters at the Shirley-Savoy Hotel.

Sex has a lavender hue here. Shades of the rugged prospectors! East High School is tainted with young faggots. The older queens gather around the Civic Center at the outdoor Greek Theatre.

Denver's gamblers no longer admit they are. If you want to find out what's running where, phone the Jack Rabbit Delivery Service. At this writing the phone number is Dex 4559. Unless you know the ever-shifting code, you get no service. It is run by Miles Klein. When the cubes are rolling in the county area the most popular places are Wolhurst, once the home of Senator Walsh, and the Stockade run by Smiling Charley Stevens.

A scandal will yet break at Fitzsimons Army Hospital, where whores, dope and gambling are supplied to patients, certainly with the knowledge, if not the connivance, of some of the high brass.

Nearby Denver is the "disaster" Fort Knox, where fifty car loads of assorted narcotics have been assembled by the Department of Defense, to be used only in the extremest emergency. The Bureau of Narcotics will deny this, but we have knowledge that T-men are feverishly working on leads that tons of this precious dope have been funneled out, through tie-ups made in Washington and have gone into underground and illegal channels. (After reading about the larceny of grain from government warehouses in the South, one also wonders whether all the gold is still in Fort Knox.)

The Washington bubblehead and boodle crowd, as represented by the Department of Indian Affairs, has its sticky fingers in the $6,000,000 bankroll ear-marked for ninety-six Ute Indian families. Financial agents are already dreaming of new Cadillacs.

Colorado Springs has an active artistic colony with what always goes with it, a harem of homosexuals. Among the local patrons of the arts and the artists is Blevins Davis, long-time friend of the Truman family and frequent escort of Margaret Truman. Davis, who had nothing until he married a widow many years older

than himself and inherited her fortune when she died, now owns
the lovely and beautiful old Baldwin estate near the Broadmoor
Hotel in the shadow of Cheyenne Mountain. It is so breath-taking
the natives call it "Fairyland," and not because Davis loves to
entertain the local artists.

B. Nevada—Punks' Paradise

Nevada—there she stands—around a craps table. In the twenty
years since it became the only state in the union to legalize gambling, its population increased roughly 100 per cent and its net
wealth 1,000 per cent.

After two decades of experiment, the nation's most sparsely
populated state is held up as an example—by both sides—of what
happens after gambling is legalized.

Technically, any citizen of good repute who pays the license fee
may operate any kind of gambling device from a jitney one-armed
bandit up to a roulette wheel in a gilded gaming casino.

That was the theory behind the law, which was designed to
drive the underworld out of gambling by making it open, legal
and a source of revenue to the state and local communities.

But don't be naïve enough to think you or your neighbor can
go to Reno or Las Vegas and open up. The state is controlled by
a monopoly every bit as tight as the netherworld groups in non-
legal jurisdictions, and allied, just as they are, with the national
crime syndicate.

Within one year after the galloping dominoes and whirring
slot-machines were invested with official approval, Nevada was
taken over by the side-of-mouth-talking fraternity. The reason
was simple; there were few honest people who knew how to operate the suddenly legalized age-old swindles.

The same went for entrepreneurs. Honest men did not know
how to figure odds, were not inclined to invest in such enterprises. On the other hand, legalization came at about the time of
Repeal, which found a whole segment of the community looking
to place their bloated bootleg profits and divert their experience
and skill in devious channels.

Reno was taken over first, by San Francisco's and remnants of
Detroit's Purple Mob. When Las Vegas, the dream city in the
desert, was built, the Chicago, New York and New England hoodlums were ready to move in.

Nevada authorities apparently welcomed this influx of fresh
money, because the laws were soon interpreted to read that a man

with a record out of state had none in Nevada—unless he was convicted there. Peace officers, district attorneys and even state-side law enforcement officers went on mob payrolls under liberal provisions of the law which permitted them "outside practice" while still in office.

Meanwhile, through an agreement by the factions, violence was kept to a minimum in Nevada, so as not to scare tourists away.

Whenever executions were necessary, they were carried out far, far away, as in the case of Flamingo Hotel owner Bugsy Siegel, who was rubbed out in Virginia Hill's Beverly Hills mansion.

The shot that put Siegel out of business was fired by an expert who knew how to use a carbine. The gun came out of the Las Vegas police arsenal.

Thirty minutes before Siegel was killed, the late Moe Sedway, who had constantly been bickering with Bugsy, walked into the Flamingo and announced he was in charge. Mind you, Siegel was still alive in Beverly Hills.

Also moving in with Sedway were the following: Morris Rosen of New York; Jack Durant, alias Allen, from Phoenix, with a long record as a pimp and a gambler, and Gus Greenbaum, Phoenix gambling boss. Sedway, a former New York mobster with a long criminal record, left Gotham by request some years ago. In Las Vegas he ran for City Councilman but was defeated.

The Siegel murder weapon was a 30/30 carbine. The executioner was a Las Vegas policeman or deputy sheriff. When the West Coast end of Murder, Inc., blew up, many Los Angeles cops quit or were bounced from the force. They went to Las Vegas where they were taken care of by the boys. City policemen and county sheriffs are hired by gambling establishments to work as guards in full and official uniform. As many as fifty Los Angeles law-enforcement officers ended up in Vegas.

Immediately upon taking over in the name of the real owners, Frank Costello, et al., the Eastern hoods put one Sanford Adler in charge of the Flamingo. Adler, originally from Providence, with a record back to 1926, moved to Detroit, where he was a rum-runner during Prohibition for the Purple Gang. He's a smooth character and was chosen to act as front man for the Detroit end of the syndicate to invest their money in hotels and manage same. He currently owns hotels in Delmar, Los Angeles, Reno and the Cal-Neva Lodge in Lake Tahoe.

When Adler went in as dummy head at the Flamingo he manipulated the stock and ended up with 51 per cent for himself. The boys didn't like this. They had had to kill Siegel to get the hotel. Now they found themselves about to be squeezed out again.

Adler got in a fist fight with Rosen, Greenbaum and Durant. That night to save his life he hurried out of Las Vegas and fled to his palatial home at 608 Trenton Drive in Beverly Hills. The boys got him on the phone, told him to make over the stock to them or else. He made it over. Now he's O.K.

The eventual complete syndication of the underworld wiped out the danger of mob warfare, except in the case of individual soreheads or executions of trace-skippers. So now Nevada is a "paradise"—for criminals on the lam, for sports, playboys and ladies of easy virtue, and, of course, any of the rest of us who want to gamble or play where things run all night and the out-of-towner is greeted, feted and fleeced.

The Mafia controls all of Las Vegas, which is divided among four groups of non-Italian figureheads, with each group permitted a major operation downtown and one in the County Strip, where the swell hotels are located.

The Flamingo—New York and Chicago mob.

Desert Inn—Cleveland and Detroit mob, fronted by Wilbur Clark, fabulous Southern California host.

Thunderbird—Missouri and Kansas money.

Rancho Vegas and Last Frontier—Local interests.

The locals were unaffiliated Los Angeles gamblers, driven from California when Italians took over. They came to Vegas in the early thirties and built the unique desert resort.

They include the Kattleman family, Guy McAfee, a former Los Angeles policeman, and Tutor Sherer, one of the most colorful of the old school gamblers. Farmer Paige is the "arbitrator."

When the Big Mob moved into Vegas a treaty of non-aggression was signed, but no one is insuring it.

These locals were permitted to keep Rancho Vegas. They have since purchased the Last Frontier from the Texas boys who are building the Sands. Benny Binion, Dallas underworld king, wanted by Texas coppers, just got a license to run the Horseshoe.

All the syndicates are backing Sherer's new project, the luxurious ten-story Caribbean Hotel on Highway 91 Strip, which is going up at a cost of $9,000,000. New York money is voted by Mack Kupperman.

Though scarce steel is forbidden for all civilian use, including public schools and hospitals, the Las Vegas mob got the necessary nod from Washington late last fall to permit construction to proceed.

The record shows that fully 50 per cent of those in the state make their livelihood directly or indirectly from bouncing cubes and associated snares. The Nevada government is supported by out-of-state suckers. The profits go to carpetbaggers and out-of-state racketeers.

Pete Licavoli and the Detroit Purple Gang have the Nevada Club in Reno, and shot up locals to get it. The old Shelton Mob is operating in Reno, too, where the new Mapes Hotel, the state's largest building, was built on an RFC financed loan which covered the construction of the gambling casino as well as the sleeping rooms. Now the RFC is also stuck on a guaranteed $350,000 bank loan made so Charlie Binaggio could build the Tahoe-Biltmore. It's been a white elephant since his murder. Anyone want the country's biggest gambling joint for a song? Apply to the Reconstruction Finance Corporation. San Francisco gamblers are interested in the Golden Hotel.

Nevada, a large state with small population, must live on the leavings of visitors. Easy divorce was the first lure. It still provides much revenue. When neighboring states adopted stringent marriage laws, Nevada jumped in with Gretna Greens. The extent of this business is so large Reno ministers are sore because judges are performing marriages "illegally." They say JPs come in from the sticks to cash in. The loss in marriage "tips" to Reno clergymen alone is said to be $150,000 a year. Vegas, nearer Los Angeles, does thrice that business.

Nevada permitted red-light stockades by local option. Las Vegas and Reno legalized them until the crime syndicate came in. The Eastern lads, with millions invested in ornate gaming casinos like the Flamingo, did not want $5 competition, so they knocked the option out in both cities. A few of the mining towns still allow it.

But not all is peaceful in Paradise. There's a feeling here that instead of curing the evil by taking gambling out of the grasping hands of the underworld, Nevada has been turned over to the criminals with small return to the taxpayers.

Government projects like Boulder Dam, the atomic tests and Air Force bases bring industrialization to the desert. Along with it come sober householders who do not want their children raised in such an atmosphere.

There always has been a powerful minority against the sin-bund, mainly Mormon emigres from Utah. Mormons are the largest single religious group in Nevada. These are prim conservatives who neither smoke, drink nor gamble.

An indication of how the wind is blowing is the startling success of a new newspaper, the *Las Vegas Morning Sun,* which after only a year and a half is running neck-and-neck with the established monopoly journal.

The *Sun* fights hoodlums in this hoodlum-owned town. Nine times it lost its advertising; the public forced it back. Editor Hank Greenspun, erstwhile Bugsy Siegel press-agent, knows what he's talking about when he demands the exile of "foreign" mobsters or an end to gambling.

17. THE LONELY STAR: TEXAS CONFIDENTIAL

ON THE surface Texas is one big joke. But don't ever underestimate it. Hiding behind the hoss-opera makeup of pearl handled guns, diamond stick pins, $100 Stetsons and fourteen-karat spurs and saddle trappings, is as brazen a bunch of freebooters as ever rustled a steer.

Texans, who profess to be he-men, are thin skinned and touchy when in the presence of "foreigners," which includes all unlucky enough to reside elsewhere than in the Lone Star State. They are insatiable for special privilege, greedy for prerogatives denied other Americans, riddled with inferiority complexes, jealous, surly, poor drinkers and comical as lovers.

Whatever else you've heard about Texas happens to be true. As for instance:

A banker, a businessman and an editor were reviewing Texas' accomplishments.

Said the editor, "We have the largest area, the prettiest girls, the strongest and bravest men, the biggest fortunes, the most oil and the best cattle. Is there anything we don't have?"

"Yes," answered the banker. "Culture."

"Well, let's buy some," said the businessman.

Texas believes it's an independent republic that could exist without the other forty-seven states. American Airlines southbound passengers hear over the loudspeaker: "You are now crossing the Red River from the United States to Texas." Amon Carter, Fort Worth tycoon, is a big stockholder in American.

Texas' superiority is dinned into our ears so much, Yankees believe the drivel.

Instead of supermen, most Texans are merely uncouth and vulgar money-flashers and impossible poseurs. Many great ranch fortunes were started by outlaws who stole the land from the Mexicans and the cattle from each other. Now they are little Hitlers, living like kings on huge estates with thousands of Mexicans working for pennies and keep, which often consists of horsemeat. Texans vote Democratic by tradition and New Deal, which they detest, because laws are rigged by both to give them special exemptions and easier taxes.

Money talks. Texas has money. That's why it gets favorable laws, such as the joker in the income tax which allows oil speculators to take 27½ per cent off the top of their income for depletion, plus permitting them to charge off about 90 per cent of the cost of sinking the well against current operating expenses if it hits, and deducting all if it doesn't.

That is why so much loose money floats around the fantastic desert empire. Many of the newly rich distrust banks. They buy diamonds by the bushel, bracelets for their women and jeweled trouser belts for themselves costing $100,000 or more.

They erect huge mansions and mausoleums and you can't tell which is which, dress their fat farm wives in minks and sables, cover their floors with rare Persian rugs and their walls with Aubusson—then spit into solid gold cuspidors.

In its earlier days Texas prided itself on being rip-roaring and rowdy. Now ladies who run culture clubs tell you there is little crime in Texas. The reason is that very little counts as a crime.

They tell you never to resent a remark or get into an argument because the other guy will blow your head off and the coroner will put it down as self-defense. If not the only state in the Union, Texas is one of the few where bail is made for first degree murder as a matter of right and law. We know of many instances of individuals arrested for first degree murder, out on $1,000 bail and never brought to trial. Through another gimmick in the Texas law a murderer can inherit from his victim. Wives kill their husbands, sell the property to pay the lawyer, then go free because the gallant authorities don't like to try or convict women.

The most serious offense in Texas is raising the price of tarts.

Northerners have been killed for giving whores $10, breaking the market. Possibly only one offense is more turpitudinous: sexual intercourse between a black man and a white woman. We asked a local newspaperman what happens if a white adult rapes a ten-year-old colored girl. He replied, "Those lousy nigger parents got no right to let a young girl out on the street. We'd stick them in jail for breaking the curfew."

The only reason Texas is not a divorce paradise like Nevada is that its residential requirements are tougher. But for residents of the state it's a pip. Grounds are mental cruelty which is anything, including burping at the breakfast table. An uncontested divorce costs only $35 and Texas law does not recognize alimony.

The municipalities in this overblown state are rotten at the core. There is a payoff for everything. Franchises are given and contracts are let at meetings held secretly, sometimes in the dead of night, without notification to minority party members.

Most of Texas is dry by local option and hard shell Baptist by birth. In these counties bootlegging and moonshining are more profitable than cattle rustling. The balance of the state permits the sale of beer and light wines for on-premise consumption, but you must buy your hard hooch in bottle stores and carry it with you.

Cafes are permitted to sell set-ups. Imbibers carry their own whenever they go out. They get drunk as a lord because no one wants to leave anything in a quart bottle. Bars close at twelve, and after that they can't even sell you a Coca-Cola because you might pour rum into it. Of course, many not only sell Cokes but cheat with mixed drinks at all times.

The state is owned by the beer lobby and the biggest brewer in the state is Howard Hughes, whose income from suds is perhaps even larger than his return from the fabulous Hughes Tool Company. The beer lobby is instrumental in keeping hard liquor from the bars. Emmet Morse is the brewers' lobbyist in Austin. Ironically he also handles legislative affairs for the wholesale liquor dealers. He explained it to them this way: if Texas were permitted to open wide there would be a reaction and a return to complete prohibition. As evidence he showed what happened after the race tracks were abused. Pari-mutuel racing was outlawed. Morse serves his clients well, indeed. He got through a bill requiring all retailers and bars to pay cash for beer. This saved the big breweries millions a year in bookkeeping, credit and bad accounts.

The Texas Rangers, famed in movie, TV, song and story, is a

comic opera outfit living off its history and handouts. The once great organization is now the shakedown crew for the state administration. They handle the payoffs and conduct the raids which follow failure to pay. On the other hand, they frequently pull phony raids as a white-wash, but tip off the raidees in advance so gaming tables and dice can be hidden, as they are in the fabulous gambling joint in Midland run by a guy by the name of Harvey, who presses an electronic button, after which the whole shebang disappears into the floor of a concrete garage. This was one of Mickey Cohen's hide-outs.

When the Rangers are hell bent on a raid they come in full regalia, with ten gallon hats, trick cowboy shirts and two pearl-handled guns in their holsters. The newspapers are advised and photographers are on hand. Meanwhile the miscreants have vanished, except for the one guy left behind who is supposed to take the rap.

Another typical Texas brag is that the big mob from Chicago and New York does not operate here. Texans say, "We are too tough for the Ginzos and they know it. We ain't afraid of their guns so they keep away from our gamblers." The example they give you is the late Herbert Noble, who defied a dozen assaults on his life before they got him. Texans will tell you he was killed by another local gambler. But we know better.

As for the crime syndicate being out of Texas, that is just so much soap suds. The Mafia made one of its first major inroads in the United States in Galveston half a century ago and has since extended its sway across the state from Texarkana to El Paso. This is fertile land—a lawless community with fast, loose money.

The underworld has a tight monopoly which overlooks nothing, from the 50 per cent commission on the earnings of a $2 whore in Galveston to the fixing of the biggest college football events in the state. It is in this field that the big blowoff which will rock Texas to the foundations of its spurious civilization will come when the lowdown on the fixing of college football coaches to insure point spreads comes out. College football is the biggest thing in this big state. Games draw by the hundreds of thousands. Important ones are as big as a Mardi Gras. Texas is nuts about its colleges which have been turned into huge learning factories by benefactions from rugged prospectors who sign their names with X's.

Texas also has Sam Rayburn, bachelor Speaker of the House, who spews his hatred for Truman over his bourbon but pulls all his vocal stops shouting his praises publicly.

It also has old Tom Connally, chairman of the powerful Senate Foreign Relations Committee, a fixture in Texas politics, now frightened for the first time over a bad attack of Acheson-Hiss acid.

A. Dallas—Culture and Fairies

Dallas is a pushover—with its aspirations to culture, pretensions to style and heartburn for civilization.

Newly rich wives and daughters whose millionaire husbands and fathers shoveled cow dung for a living a few years ago earnestly join book-discussion groups and jabber about Plato, Aristotle, Montaigne and Adam Smith. They aren't up to James Joyce yet.

Guys who were day laborers on wildcat oil wells now cannot do without crepes suzette, which they import by airmail from the Vendome, on Madison Avenue, in New York, where such goo is dished up only as a come-on for tourists.

Dallas has a symphony, a week of the Metropolitan Opera, and a civic music season, all underwritten by local department stores as a shill to sell evening gowns. Neiman-Marcus sponsors the first, A. Harris the second, and Sanger Brothers the last. Sixty-year-old dowagers, some of whom slung hash in a Harvey restaurant in their youth, patronize these affairs in expensive décolleté designed for debutantes, with unwilling husbands who'd feel more comfortable in cowboy chaps or levis.

There are two subjects you must speak of with proper respect —the local girls, who are supposed to be the most beautiful in the world, and the Neiman-Marcus store.

One night we made fun of both. We said we had seen no pretty girls in Dallas, because all the local lookers had gone to New York. That's not too wild. Half of Gotham's glamor girls come from Texas. We also inferred there were stores in New York considerably better and more exclusive than Neiman-Marcus. We said we had stores like that on side streets in Manhattan. We almost got our heads knocked off by a couple of Dallas citizens. This was high treason. One character pulled out a pencil and began figuring on the back of an envelope the number of mink coats Neiman's sells in a day. "Does any New York store sell that many?" he shrieked.

Nouveau riche come from all over Texas to buy at this emporium. Dried-up farm women who never owned anything better than a $2.98 Sears-Roebuck dress until oil pushed through the back yard, shop six fur coats at one sitting. Neiman boasts of the pick of all Paris and New York designers. It splurges with fan-

tastically priced merchandise that a smart New York woman would
not wear for fear of being mistaken for a Christmas tree, or a Texan.

The Neiman store also designed the Hereford cattle exhibit at
the State Fair. Stanley Marcus is one of the most important men
in Dallas, honored and courted; the center of the town's flashy,
wealthy, "intellectual" and "cultural" set.

He may not know that some Neiman models are call girls—the
top babes in town. The guy who escorts one feels in the same
league with the playboys who took out Ziegfeld's glorified. Price,
a hundred bucks a night.

The salesgirls are good, too—pretty, and often much cheaper—
twenty bucks on the average. They're more fun, too, not as snooty
as the models. We got this confidential, from a Dallas wolf.

Neiman-Marcus also contributes to the improvement of the
local breed when it imports New York models to make a flash at
style shows. These girls are the cream of the crop. Oil millionaires
toss around thousand-dollar bills for a chance to take them out.

Neiman's was a women's specialty shop until the old biddies
who patronized it decided their husbands should get class, too.
So Neiman's put in a men's store. Well, you should see what happened. You wonder how all the faggots got to the wild and
woolly. You thought those with talent ended up in New York and
Hollywood and the plodders got government jobs in Washington.
Then you learn the nucleus of the Dallas fairy colony is composed
of many Neiman dress and millinery designers, imported from
New York and Paris, who sent for their boy friends when the men's
store expanded. Now most of the sales staff are fairies, too.

The Dallas rich are crazy about modern décor. Scores of in-
terior-decorator shops have sprung up in the Cedar Springs section. Probably no city in the country, including New York, has
as many expensive and elaborate home-furnishing shops on one
street. They stretch out for blocks, most of them owned and operated by queers.

So Dallas boasts more "gay" joints than any town in the country, including Frisco, where they are a tourist attraction. Even
many that are actually straight are set up to appear queer.

The Flamingo, on McKinney Street, is the best-known queen
hangout in Dallas, because it's the worst. The Reno Lounge, at
Ervay and Wood, is obvious. The Mona Lisa and the Blue Bonnet
are quieter. The Diamond Horseshoe attracts the middle-class
deviates. Many fairies hang out at the Fox Burlesque Theatre.

The streetwalkers in trousers pick each other up in front of the Rock Island offices, at Commerce and Field.

Dallas snoots Houston, the lusty newcomer. Dallas sniffs at Houston as commonplace and commercial, though it's bigger and richer. It sneers at it about the way San Francisco holds its nose at Los Angeles. But Dallas will never be what San Francisco was.

Dallas has a "cafe society" which in reality is only a beer tavern society, but it supports one of the better night-life columnists, Virgil Miers, of the *Times-Herald.*

Dallas talks of its large local "aristocracy" and snubs towns like Fort Worth and Houston, which are one-man affairs. But this is what Dallas has:

H. L. Hunt, a story-book millionaire whose income from oil leases is said to be a million dollars a day, was once a professional gambler in El Dorado, Arkansas. Now, as a hobby, he maintains his own private racing-wire, which runs into New Jersey, where he often bets from $40,000 to $150,000 on ponies.

The children are raised by Dallas standards. For instance, a gang of two hundred young hoodlums was organized in which no kid could belong unless his old man was worth $5,000,000. They call themselves the "Lakewood Rats." These young thugs preyed on local merchants, forcing the shopkeepers to hire sluggers of their own to protect their windows. They also fought other rich young gangs, especially from wealthy Highland Park. The cops tell you loudly the "Lakewood Rats" are disbanded. We tell you confidentially they are not.

The Dallas police force is a Keystone outfit. The town's big shots run it. Coppers get fired for ticketing the "wrong" parked cars. Mustn't arrest the son of a millionaire. The Mayor, a businessman's choice, attends to that.

The real boss of the city hall gang is Wallace Savage, ex-Mayor. The boys let the incumbent, a banker, think he is running the works and let him have fun squaring tickets.

The contact situation is simple and easy. There are so few people you have to see, depending on what you want. U.S. Supreme Court Justice Tom Clark, former Attorney General, is THE man. You cannot go to him directly, so you see his pal, Maury Hughes, of the law firm of Hughes & Monroe. Tom's brother, Bob, is also his go-between. Tom introduced him as "my brother, who also practices law." Through Bob Clark, a firm known as Nichols Brothers grabbed the taxicab monopoly for the city. They operate fleets under different names, which makes

the stranger think there is competition. Bob Clark was instrumental in discouraging veterans who wanted to run cabs. The
trust runs lousy, ancient equipment, into which they crowd six
strangers. Many of the cabs are driven by old women.

While heading the Department of Justice, Clark took two trips
in the private plane of a man with tax troubles. He appointed
the unhappy Theron Lamar Caudle as head of the department's
tax division in the face of a negative report from the FBI.

Such charges roll off Tom Clark's back like a duck sheds water.
He is used to them. In 1937, after Clark's law partner, William
McGraw, became Texas Attorney General, an investigating committee reported that the future Justice of the U.S. Supreme Court
experienced "a tremendous and startling increase in earnings."
The upholder of the Constitution was then censured for not being
"willing and eager to make a full disclosure of his financial
affairs." But he was not held in contempt like others unfortunate
enough not to know Tom Connally.

For in the very same year he left his $70,000 law practice to be-
come a special assistant to U.S. Attorney General Homer Cummings, the first step on his upward climb to the august bench
which, before becoming ridiculous, was once graced by such sublime names as John Marshall, Oliver Wendell Holmes and
Charles Evans Hughes.

At the other end, the Federal contact is Perry Rice, a Dallas
lawyer whose wires also extend to Senator Connally. Rice takes
care of the utilities, pipeline and natural gas boys. At this writing, Connally, who has been forced to go along with the Administration in the whitewash of the State Department, is on thin ice.

Dallas may be a center of cosmopolitan life, but if so it is the
only one in the world where the biggest event in the year is the
State Fair. This municipal orgy runs for two weeks, plays to
millions from all over the state. With it come a couple of Broadway musicals, the big football game of the year and confidence
men and strip-teasers who work the carnival circuit. During Fair
time, gambling is wide open in town as well as on the Midway,
and the hinterlanders who flock in from the Texas wilds are
properly titillated as well as cleaned.

Then you see strange characters you didn't know existed outside silent movies.

Dallas skidrows are unique in their habits, vices, get-up, breeding and background. They have fairy bars here, at Ervay and
Jackson, and barber shops with "lady" barbers so ancient they

sit down while they cut your hair. The winos drink bay rum and spend the day between periods of unconsciousness playing checkers in barbecue joints. There's another skidrow called Deep Elm, which the locals all pronounce "Elum."

South Akard Street is the tenderloin, with dozens of assignation hotels. Cab drivers call it "Whore House Road." The hotels have small red neon signs in front. No questions are asked at the Melba, the Modern and the Oriental. Instead of a room clerk, an ancient Negro sits in a rickety chair at the top of the staircase. You pay him a dollar for the key. No tip necessary. Many Akard Street hotels also supply call-girls. The price is $5 regular, $10 French, $15 combination. The connoisseurs prefer Mexican girls. But only a lazy man bothers to send for them. Stand at the corner of Akard and Commerce or Akard and Main and just wait for a broad to come by. If she doesn't pick you up first, whistle or mumble. Many bims on the make drive around in open convertibles.

Because of the liquor laws there are no cocktail lounges, so you do your bidding at drugstore soda fountains. Ask any girl. She won't get sore. She will or she won't, and either way she's used to the blunt approach. Lots of friendly girls hang around the Pirate's Cave, a beer tavern and juke joint. There are a slew of beer bars with broads on the Fort Worth Pike, and cheap motels to take them to.

The Dallas whoring industry is the best organized in Texas. Many call services work out of so-called "massage parlors."

The Dallas phone book lists some thirty or more massage parlors under the headings of massage treatment and baths. Those that advertise they are open until 10 P.M. are good prospects. When in doubt you say, "Do you think we can get something else besides a massage?" If the answer is, "Well, we think you can," you're set.

A lot of the boys call the Belle Fille Baths, which means "pretty girl" baths. May Hoskins is the manager and Carleen Ovelby is the assistant. The ad is illustrated with a cut of a busty damsel massaging the back of an undraped man. Phone number, Union 6075; if busy call Tenison 9133.

Nina's Health Institute, which illustrates its ads with a picture of a nude woman, is popular, and open on Sundays. Phone Randolph 2592.

The standard parlor price is $2 for a rub; $5 for extra "attention."

The motel and tourist court situation is a dilly. All motels have two rates, one for genuine tourists and one for quickies. Most of those which specialize in the latter are on the Fort Worth Pike and Harry Hines Boulevard. Some are legitimate, but most aren't. One sure way to tell is by the presence of a colored porter in front, playing a portable radio. That means more goes on than slumber. Courts that supply call gals charge $6 extra.

The largest tourist courts in town are the Blue Top chain, three of them, one on each side of town. Each does a turnover of a thousand customers every Saturday. A check for Southern Methodist University as a thesis found this outfit catered only to cars with local county licenses, which meant the occupants weren't planning to stay all night. Travelers with foreign licenses were told, "No vacancies."

A motel on Davis Street frankly advertises, "$4, two hours."

Twenty-one is supposed to be the legal age for beer and indoor necking, but local racketeers sell forged birth certificates for $5 and $10 to youngsters. Lou Ann's Dance Hall is where the bobby-soxers and college kids hang out. Sex is natural in this primitive land. It is not unknown to see SMU students letting nature take its full course in the back of automobiles, in daylight, on the college campus.

Abortions are reasonable—$35 each.

This is the organized underworld situation here: Vice on the street level is operated by locals, who pay off to the Syndicate, which declared itself in. Those that don't pay off get the lethal treatment of the lately deceased Herbert Noble. The outside Italian boys came in here to invest some of their boodle in oil, beef and zooming real estate. At the same time they made connections to affiliate the local crime with their own nationwide organization. The late Charlie Fischetti was a big property-owner in Dallas. His last acquisition before his death was in the 6300 block of North Gaston.

Charley Blanda, of Denver and Kansas City, is in charge of local operations, working through a Sicilian named Colletti. The Real Juice Company, 2201 Leonard, is the local distributor for the Capone beer, out of Chicago. It will be remembered that the underworld took Kansas City first through Tony Gizzo, distributor of that beer there.

Other important Italians operating in Dallas are the Grandenetti Brothers of the Casino Lounge, 2403 North Henderson. A lot of the paisans hang out at the Bohemian Cocktail Lounge, 1705 North Carroll, where only beer, ostensibly, is sold.

When you first ask, the local citizens insist there are no Sicilian operations of any nature. The following names, culled from official but confidential government files, say otherwise:

Joseph Piranio, 1427 S. Ewing St.

Joseph, Leon and Sam Civello.

Victor Trepani.

Nick Cascio.

Joe De Luca, of Kansas City, the direct tie to the Mafia.

Here's the local set-up of actual operators who pay off above: Ivy Miller and Mack Willy, gambling. Benny Binion, now in exile in Nevada, still in control of numbers. Jim Carroll, operating as "Carroll Oil Co.," who lays off track money through Fritz Rechenburg, a bookmaker with contacts in Louisiana.

Charley Stevens represents the Tulsa interests. Augrie Abay, a man with a long record and now supposedly retired, is the contact man for narcotics. The so-called Deloise Green Mob of Dallas supplies torpedoes and killers all over the country. Buddy Malone, an associate of Binion, is his wire. Binion, incidentally, has been at many social gatherings with Mayor J. B. Adone.

Ben Whittaker, horseman and bigtime gambler, is close to the boys. He owns the Whitmore Hotel, sporting men's hangout, which serves the best food in town.

Which reminds us. If there's no sin, how come the citizens had to found a crime commission? Unfortunately Alphonse Ragland Jr. and Dan Reynolds have no dough or staff, so this is to tip them off. The fast money crowd and the bookmakers gather socially at the Royal Grill, where there is no gambling. The Bachelor's Club, a so-called private bottle set-up, gives race information but won't itemize your check, and if you insist you're asking for a clip on the jaw. The Top-of-the-Hill Terrace is a swank after-hours gambling bottle club, supposed to be private, but the card of admission is a $10 bill. The Cipango is an expensive after-hour club, with gambling when the heat is off.

The Big Mob is sending millions into Texas to invest in wildcat oil leases. The Fletcher Brothers are often brokers in such speculative holdings.

This is the heart of the cow empire, but restaurants advertise Kansas City beef and many sell horsemeat instead.

B. Houston—Hustleton on the Canal

The home of fellow-author Jesse Jones, Houston is big, loud and proud. It appears to be the product of a mesalliance in the sagebrush between a Texas dance-hall girl and a high-pressure Chicago traveling man.

It is the biggest, the fastest-growing and the richest spot in the whole god-damned state of Texas, which is the god-damnedest state in the world. You can hear the horn-blowing from both borders, which, according to local surveys, are something like 100,000 miles apart.

This is the port and capital of the oilgolconda.

It claims more millionaires to the square foot than Wall Street ever had, and there is some basis for the boast. We will not get statistical. What's the use, when we tell you that one Houstonian of whom you never heard has given $70,000,000 to Christian causes and meanwhile got richer than ever? Those who haven't got millions owe millions; that is almost an equal mark of distinction. The skyscrapers form a view like Newark, if not like New York, yet down below are the garish fronts of markets with marquees and chain stores with names like U-Totem and Pick 'n Go, reminiscent of Los Angeles, while in the distance is the gingerbread Shamrock Hotel, which could have been the drunken dream of a dozen delirious architects, conceived by Glenn McCarthy, the village bad boy who was early infected with publicity poison, and the condition became chronic and incurable.

Almost as prominent and even more symbolic is Doug Prince, who parlayed a gob of brown beef on a bun into a fortune as the Hamburger King of Houston, and who slathers money around as though it were mustard.

Of course, there is an element of dignified men who financed and managed the enormous substantial growth of Houston, which boomed past New Orleans in proportions and importance and population, and who have become weighty national figures in the mahogany offices which still manipulate what is left after taxes—which are lower for Texans than the rest of us.

But most of the ear-puncturing bellows come from the strident Northerners, who swam in on the high tides of the new bonanza burg, and whose nasal shrieks have contaminated the unique Texas drawl which Hollywood cowboys still simulate.

Those who haven't seen McCarthy's hotel imagine it a combination Taj Mahal and Palace of Versailles. Actually, it is a gaunt and ungainly square box, half a dozen miles from downtown. Its décor is shoddy and gaudy. The furniture in our suite was wearing out, though the hotel has been open less than three years. The place is a wildcatter's free-hand version of the Waldorf seen through a hangover.

McCarthy, hot-shot oil speculator, is a product of gushers of publicity. Now he believes it himself. He is not as rich as the Sunday supplements tell you. (Neither are some others whom local boosters blow up.)

McCarthy hangs around with a sporty crowd and is a wild man. His behavior when he drinks is notorious. He has had to pony up dough to square mayhem. To protect himself against himself, McCarthy, a nice guy when sober, travels with a bodyguard. He is also almost always accompanied by a psychiatrist, who gives him advice as they go along.

McCarthy's fabulous rise was accompanied by a similar growth in the size of his head. Jesse Jones hurt Glenn's ego. There wasn't much he could do about it, because Jesse is the wealthiest man in town. He owns or has the lease-hold on almost every foot of downtown business property. He owns the rich and powerful *Houston Chronicle*. So McCarthy wanted a paper. He merged a group of shoppers into a chain of neighborhood weeklies. Jones owns the Rice Hotel, the town's best. Glenn wanted a hotel, too. He couldn't get downtown frontage. Jones vetoed it there. McCarthy decided to develop his own section. He was going to move Houston's business district miles out to the flatlands. The Shamrock was to be a beginning. Around it would grow a huge development.

McCarthy has many playboy friends. He built his hotel with them in mind. There are several secret ways of getting into and out of the hotel, without going through the lobby. That was designed for routing girls in and out, but it accidentally turned out to be even a bigger asset. Mobsters and others who don't want to be seen find it convenient.

The Shamrock got off big. It was the most flamboyant thing Houston had ever seen. The sports had to support it. McCarthy built a private bottle club on the ground floor, the Cork Club. Its purpose was to circumvent the local midnight closing law and the ban on mixed drinks, and 750 members paid $1,000 each to join, plus $180 a year dues. Most of that goes to the hotel for rent. The $750,000 saved the hotel.

Its other business was not up to expectations. McCarthy tried to borrow $40,000,000 from the RFC, but was turned down. New York and Chicago Sicilians came down to look it over and would have signed a deal, but Mortimer broke an inside Mafia story in the *New York Daily Mirror*, which scared them off. It also impressed the Hilton hotel chain, though McCarthy is now on intimate terms with the Hiltons and there is a rumor they are operating it; the take-over might be announced before this reaches print. McCarthy finally obtained $45,000,000 from The Equitable Life in a deal now being scrutinized by the New York State Insurance Department. Thereupon the operation of the hotel was revamped, with new managers, staffs and crews, McCarthy remaining chiefly as a figurehead for his publicity value. And the life-size painting of him in the lobby is still up.

McCarthy did create what palpably passes as cafe society, anemic and ridiculous by civilized standards, but so enthusiastic that all Houston papers put in local gossip columnists whereas pre-Shamrock Bill Roberts, the *Houston Press* chronicler, was the only one. Now he has vigorous competition from George Fuermann, Charlie Evans and Jerry Doyle.

Near the Shamrock, in this stark, flat expanse, the Prudential Life is building a skyscraper office-building. Houstonians, puzzled by this development in what is practically desert, say the insurance people are trying to bail out McCarthy by getting some population around him.

The hotel caters to free-spending ranchers and oilmen, who seem out of place walking in $500 cowboy shirts through the plush green lobby where tea is served every afternoon at five.

Glenn is looking for new worlds to conquer and the tiny banana republic of Guatemala doesn't know what's in store for it, now that it has come under his restless eye.

Glenn flew there with a couple of companions and announced he was going to create the Monte Carlo of America there at an investment of $20,000,000. He didn't say where the dough was coming from and the Guatemalans were too polite to ask about the forty-five million he owes the insurance companies.

One of his associates on the trip was Frank Casone, a Memphis gambler. The other was Howard McCormick, listed as an Oklahoma City truck line operator with a long police record on minor gambling charges.

Howard Hughes is so seldom regarded as a Houstonian that even a good newspaperman like our friend George Fuermann almost overlooked him completely in his book, *Houston: Land of the Big Rich*. Yet the eccentric Hughes is possibly even a greater power in Houston than Jesse Jones. One reason is that Mayor Oscar Holcombe was on the Hughes Tool Company payroll at $25,000 a year. Texas law permits the Mayor to accept outside employment. Though Hughes gets most of his clippings on his "eccentricities" from New York and Hollywood, he is still and has always been a legal resident of Texas, which has no personal income tax, unlike California's stiff bite. Howard's parent holding company is the Hughes Tool outfit in Houston, which he inherited from his father. Hughes' friends laughingly say he doesn't own a suit of clothes himself—all his private belongings are supposed to be in the name of the tool company, and so he has no property in California. This is probably apocryphal, but with Hughes' thrifty disposition anything is possible. Though worth uncounted millions, Howard never carries money in his pockets. If you go out with him where he is unknown and cannot sign a check and charge it to the Hughes Tool Company, you pay the bill. If he wants to make a phone call, you lend him the coin.

He was once barred from New York's hoity-toity 21 Club by a doorman who thought the man in the unpressed suit, grimy shirt and tennis sneakers, with a week's beard, was a hobo. His friends say he buys one low-priced shirt at a time, wears it until it's disgraceful, then throws it away. When he moved from the Town House in Los Angeles he owned no suitcase, so he carried his few belongings in a bureau-drawer wrapped in newspapers.

Howard is in many respects a loveable guy, unspoiled by being a rich man's son. He has increased his fortune many times. His company is said to receive a royalty from every gallon of oil surfaced anywhere in the world.

Mayor Holcombe has other profitable business connections. A screaming New Dealer, he knows the proper people in Washington. At home he is in the building business. That doesn't hurt either, because, by coincidence, he just happens to know in advance when new roads are about to be laid. One of these was a superfluous boulevard and freeway in front of his home, named after himself.

Another local power is Charles Francis, a lawyer with strong ties to Washington through Senator Lyndon Johnson, who is usually found in the Truman camp. Johnson and Francis have a strange political alliance with Leverett Saltonstall, aristocratic, impractical and "liberal" Republican Senator from Massachusetts.

One of Francis' clients is the gigantic contracting firm of Brown and Root. They have received hundreds of millions of dollars' worth of construction work from Uncle Sam, to build defense and other installations in Guam and Alaska. They also get most of the government work in Texas, where, on their private jobs, they never use union labor if they can help it. They built the 70,000-seat Rice University stadium in six months with all non-union hands, while their labor-loving friends in Washington kept on handing them more government work elsewhere.

The lobby and soda-fountain of the Esperson Building is the Houston bourse, where the biggest oil deals in the land are kicked back and forth, then made legal in one of the numerous lawyers' offices upstairs. Most effective of the town's young attorneys is Seymour Lieberman.

This is also a swell place to make a pick-up. Wise Houstonians operate on the law of averages. (If you sit next to enough girls one is bound to move closer.)

On the local political level, the most powerful man in town is Sewall Myer, AFL lawyer and former city attorney. He is also the Mayor's personal attorney, and while so acting he represented as well the local phone company and got a rate raise from the city council. The top contact man under Myer is Joe Steel. George Woods, an insurance man, also has a lot of influence with His Honor.

The county boss is ex-Sheriff Neal Polk, who suddenly retired and bought a ranch. Polk was the typical wild-west movie-type ten-gallon-hat and side-arms sheriff. He is a tall, handsome, weather-beaten character and attracts stares from the dolls at the Shamrock, where he is now chief of the house-dicks. His political errand boy is Jack Halphen.

Herman Wright and his pal Arthur Mandell, shrill left-winger and CIO attorney, also throw a lot of weight around. Herman Williams, who spends most of his time now in a $150,000 Arizona mansion, is strangely potent when it comes to the Texas Rangers.

Generally speaking, Houston has been closed on the street level for years, through one of the strangest deals ever set up anywhere in the country. The Maceo mob in Galveston, fifty miles away, pays off Houston coppers to keep their town "clean"—so gamblers and pleasure-seekers will have to come to Galveston!

The Mafia has other large interests in Houston, running some things which do not provide competition for glamorous open casinos in Galveston.

The Big Mob's interest in Houston is mainly in real estate, oil leases and narcotics. The top Italians all over the country are investing their loot in oil. They have rigged up a surefire way so they can't lose. If the well comes in, it belongs to them. If it doesn't, they sell the rights to crooked executives of large corporations, who invest corporate funds in the properties, then get a cutback.

Local newspapermen, cops and others, while admitting Houston has a large underworld, insist it has no connection with the Mafia. They say the only important Sicilian in town is Biaggio Angelica, who took a ten-year rap for the late Sam Maceo in a Federal narcotics case. Biaggio's headquarters are in the Italian Village, a little bar and restaurant in the 3300 block of Milam. This is the clearing-house for the entire Texas Sicilian colony. Important members of it, who live in Houston, are Isadore Caberetta, 1122 West Bell Street, Luke Saporita, 2122 North Main Street, and Don Vincenzo Zallone. Frank Redisi and Jack Passerella, of Chicago, have established headquarters to represent their organization.

When the heat is off, there are eight numbers wheels operating, all syndicated. Instead of competing, the eight share rent on a premise, with paymasters lined up in booths, as in a bank.

Local gambling and other vice are operated by non-Italians who pay off to the Sicilians. Ed Payne, who ran the defunct Southern Dinner Club, is one of the more important gamblers, though temporarily inactive. Shelby Williams is still operating. The payoff to cops runs high, crap games being taxed at $800 a week.

Jakie Freedman, undercover bookmaker, openly ran a swank gambling joint in the outskirts until recently—so brazenly, coppers had to close him. His place was called Domain Privee. The biggest people in town came to splurge. Glenn McCarthy was a frequent visitor. He escorted Mrs. Georgia Neese Clark, Treasurer of the United States, whose name is signed on all currency.

In his book, Fuermann tried to do a "Confidential" by telling, almost out loud, the names and addresses of two madames. They are Addie Sasser, 208 Bastrop Street, and Lucile Laporte, 2719 Capitol Avenue. But he didn't seem to remember their phone numbers. We are helping him out. Addie, a Negro who specializes in white girls, can be reached at FA-0833. Lucile, who runs a white house in the Negro district, answers her calls at FA-7590. George failed to mention Lou Ayres, whose Ayres Hotel in the 400 block of San Jacinto gets raided regularly, but is never closed; or Gussie Stanford, of the Wyndham Hotel; or Thelma Denton, 3333 Scott Street, the ritziest assignation madame in town. She discreetly supplies girls for big boys like bankers, industrialists and rich gangsters.

Far and away the best known of Houston's call house numbers is LI-3800 (the LI for Linden). It has been since about 1947 or

1948 and is definitely such today. It is owned by a madame named Helen and it is also the number most peddled at the Shamrock.

Why Houston needs madames is conjectural. The run-of-the-mill girls are so amiable. You can pick them up almost anywhere, then take them to a tourist court, which will have swimming pools if you prefer to high dive.

Houston is faced with a serious homosexual problem. It is not as evident as Dallas', because there are no expensive imported faggots in town like those in the Neiman-Marcus set. Houston's are schoolboys, college kids and lonesome servicemen. The gathering places are the Pink Elephant, La Tonga and the Gingham. The high schools and colleges are burdened with queer teachers, who initiate their young charges into daisy chain social circles.

Juvenile delinquency is serious. Rich teen-age gangs wage pitched battles in drive-ins and juke-box joints. The South End Gang, with two hundred boys, is the most feared of the four young mobs in town. Worried parents in swank River Oaks hire special policemen to back up their knife-carrying juniors when they get into gang wars with kids from the bloody 5th Ward.

Houston is on the shank end of the Bible Belt. Its blacks and whites go for the old-time religion. Hugh Bimbo, a former prize-fight promoter, who now sells wild-cat oil leases, quotes the Bible with each sale so successfully, it's a one-two to the glass chin of the prospect.

Anyone can get into the racket. Take handsome, six-foot-four Dale Richardson. He was a constable of Laporte, Texas, a small, wide-open hick town. Someone told him that under state law he could exercise his law-enforcement authority in Houston. So he invaded the city in full regalia, with pick-axes and two guns, and smashed up half the gambling joints in town. Every time he returned he called the dailies first. They covered this one-man cyclone with pictures and front-page tales. It was a lot of fun, but it irked the boys.

So one day they got him into a cab and talked to him. They had a wire-recording machine in the vehicle. When the grand jury heard the record, it indicted Constable Richardson on a shakedown charge, but he was acquitted. He resigned, however. While these words were being typed he was studying to become an evangelist. We understand he expects to do better with the collection-basket than he did with the pick-axe.

C. Where the West Begins
Fort Worth

Dallas tries to be Boston. Houston, with shipping from all the seas, frenetic building and a mania for expansion does an imitation of an oil-dripping New York. Fort Worth is where the West begins. On your map Dallas-Fort Worth looks like Minneapolis-St. Paul, San Francisco-Oakland or Seattle-Tacoma. Don't let it fool you. They despise each other, and the thirty miles between them span a transformation such as no short distance parallels in the land.

Forth Worth, center of the cattle industry which is the rich, bloody heritage of Texas, glories in its affectionate nickname, Cow Town. It is woolly and individual and about the only burg of proportions where there are no fairies. Four of these were murdered there and the other handful wafted off for Dallas.

Cow Town has to pay some tribute to the hard-shell Christians who can dominate the state which made Pa and Ma Ferguson governors. There was a surface clean-up in Forth Worth when we went through. But the locals were muttering. They wanted it wide open, with the money flowing free. When the lid is on, the rich ranchers stay home or go to their county seats, which they tell where to get off at, and where theirs is the last word.

Except for oustide pressures which cannot always be resisted, the city openly doesn't give a damn. Its grand juries bring in presentments on pay-offs by criminals to grafters, but seldom name names and rarely indict. When Cow Town is its own homey, normal self, the gravy greases so many hands that the overhead breaks the crooks. It is parceled out to squad-car boys, captains, the inspector's office, the chief's office, the constable's office, the district attorney's office and the sheriff's office. If the ice hasn't all melted away, it goes through the hot palms of Texas Rangers.

When the big gamblers have any jack left, they hang around the Court Hotel. Right now, most of the action is scattered. Tiffen Hall, which is not a square monicker, owns two joints called the Mexican Inn No. 1 and No. 2. Here is the Sicilian territorial clearing-house for Dallas and Forth Worth. The Mafia has huge ranch holdings, putting beef into the black market. Fort Worth is a stop on the dope-run to Mexico.

Cow Town is Western and honkytonk. Main Street is alive and lousy with shooting galleries, ambulating hookers and dollar hotels. The swell Hotel Texas is the borderline between the good and bad parts of town.

You see city cops smoking pipes on duty. The Downtown Club operates openly with cards. They sell reefers in the night clubs on East Lancaster, where colored bands play. The Sundown, on Jacksboro Highway, across the county line, is an after-hour spot. The Western Hills motel, ten miles out, is a junior Shamrock, gaudy, elaborate and set up for rich guys and gals on the loose. The prettiest in town are the models in the Fair Store. Some are on call at fifty bucks a throw. You can't rent a room at the Yale or Regal Hotels unless you also take the girl who goes with it.

If you want to see the West at its wildest, visit the stockyards any Saturday night, when the cockeyed toughs fight with brass knuckles, knives, guns and teeth. Exchange Avenue is the worst. The whole police force couldn't civilize it.

He-man among he-men of this town is Amon Carter, king of all he surveys, one of the richest men anywhere, who owns Fort Worth's hotels, principal newspapers, and about anything else you can mention. A hearty, loveable rancher, fabulous host, he is an old giant who typifies Texas at its romantic best.

San Antone

When you get to San Antonio, you are in Mexico. It has two industries: the Alamo and catering to GIs. One of our largest concentrations of soldiers and airmen is at its permanent and temporary bases. During periods of international calm, business is somnolent. Army payday is the last day of the month. Then the broads are $10 and up. By the middle of the month, the price goes down to $3, including room. San Antonio has the prettiest girls in the state, probably because so many are the perfect Mexican types. Dallas, which brags about its girls, doesn't come close.

Mexican votes run the town. Nobody bothers Mexicans. Their section not only resembles Mexico, but is for all practical purposes outside the confines of the United States. American law has no standing there.

Monterey Street is a typical Latin-American alley, with girls soliciting from cribs on both sides of the street. Another such thoroughfare is Matamores Street, where the price is $5 to $10. A trip through the west side takes you to as foreign a land as a journey abroad. Dumps like Rosita's and Cinco de Mayo, on Concho Street, abound with tough hombres and muchachos. Other typical Mexican places are the Twilight, the 211, the 3 Sisters, El Reno,

the 400 Club and the San Antone, which employs a Negro orches-
tra and thirty white and Mexican B girls. The gals at La Mucira
and the Washington Square Bar dance with you for two bits per—
about thirty seconds. Then they make dates for later.

All these tamales have Mexican pimps. They usually roll customers. Reefers are sold everywhere. The lovers, being Latin gentlemen, do no work, but sit around and drink tequilla while the
girls are earning enough to enable them to train and fight blooded
cocks.

All regular Army men know Snake Hill. Generations of whores
have lived there off generations of soldiers. Most of the gals hang
out in the Avenue Inn, the Long Horn Bar, and the Victory Bar.
They register as man and wife at Hal's Courts motel—price $3.50.

There are so many girls here and they are so easy to get, it
comes as a shock to discover that this part of the tough Southwest
is loaded with homosexuals. They prey on servicemen. Places like
the Circle B Bar, where GIs used to hang out, are empty these
days. But the young men in uniform pack the Circus Club, with
a fag show, the Spot, and the Navarre. Many of the queers live at
the Havana Hotel.

Meanwhile, the MPs are making it difficult for GIs who like
their fun straight. There's a campaign on to pick up unaccompa-
nied women in bars. This has caused a terrific local furore, because
some of the females arrested by Army coppers—without the slightest guise of legality—were respectable women waiting for their
husbands. The upper-crust trollops drive around in Cadillac convertibles and charge 20 bucks up, including the ride. The more expensive call girls operate out of massage parlors. You can phone
almost any in the classified book and click. Bakers' Clinic is an
elaborate set-up that never closes. After a heavy night of drinking,
visiting ranch-men like it for a rub down and what goes with it.

The prettiest pick-ups hang around the Travelers Hotel and
the Oyster Bar. The Sfair brothers, Syrians, operate the San Antonio, Merry-Go-Round and Showtime bars, with waitresses working as B-girls. These are the only girls in town making real
money. The Showtime goes in for dirty acts, but strips are banned.
Another place which employs B-gals is the C & M Bar.

The Texas law, with its midnight closing and no-hard-liquor
on premises, has raised a race of beer topers. People sit at bars for
eight hours at a stretch, drinking as many as a dozen bottles of
beer an hour.

San Antonio is full of so-called bottle clubs, which operate after hours and usually sell hard liquor. The Kopy Kat publicly advertises, "Open from noon until ———."

In back of the Rocket Club is an all-night bar, supposed to be private. The beautiful 400 Club is private—to anyone with less than $5. So is the Oasis Club.

Bookies hang out at the Playmore poolroom and at the Turf Bar, across the street from the Court House, where gambling runs upstairs when let alone. Horse-betting finds few takers. The Federal tax law didn't bother the boys at all. The big thing is football pool tickets. These are sold by individuals who keep no books. A half-million a week changes hands on these cards in this comparatively small town.

The sporty and hot-money crowd hangs out in the Gunter Hotel lobby, but the St. Anthony is the best hotel in town. Mayor Jack White, a former bellhop, is now manager of the White Plaza Hotel. He became pious when he was elected, but he knows all the angles, because about everything goes in hotels, including his own.

When we were there, the town was partly under wraps because the new city administration had not yet found out where the body was buried. Anyway, it was getting tough as a prelude to new shakedowns which should be working as these words are being typed.

San Antonio is strategically located as a hide-out for important fugitive criminals. It is near the Mexican border. Velirio's restaurant and Yuse's, which specialize in spaghetti, welcome visiting Sicilians.

San Antonio is Maury Maverick's town. He and other left-wingers work on soldiers, Mexicans and Negroes. That makes Maverick a power. Nothing goes unless he gives the word. Plenty goes.

The churches compete valiantly with sin. Every church advertises with neon signs. But the Lord seems to be losing out.

San Diego, Texas, one hundred miles south of San Antonio, is owned by the wealthy Parr family. Its Mexican population votes unanimous under direction. So does the county. The result is, there is no law to speak of. During a recent investigation there to find out why New Deal Senator Lyndon Johnson got all the votes, against none for his opponent in some precincts, a janitor accidentally burned the ballots. Apparently Kansas City Harry is operating a correspondence course.

D. Galveston—the Free State

A sub-tropical toy land of fifty square miles, its shores caressed by the warm waves of the Gulf of Mexico, embraces America's liveliest, naughtiest, least-inhibited city.

Galveston is connected with the United States and Texas by two causeways and by nothing else, tangible, spiritual or spiritous. The inhabitants, 80,000 they claim, like to talk of it as the Free State of Galveston. They do not regard it as part of Texas, which willingly disowns it as the bad boy of a good family.

Two-thirds of the vast Lone Star State is hard-shell Baptist, dry by local option, and where alcoholic beverages are tolerated they may not be above beer or wine proof in public places; strict closing time is midnight. But Galveston, the detached domain, deals all night, gambles gauche and unafraid, sells with no gesture of camouflage across its bars—anything you call for.

Downtown, on Post Office Street, unblinking red lights burn outside in the ancient tenderloin tradition, an anachronism in American advertising, not to be confused with the Russian Embassy.

In this one-time harbor of pirates the innocents no longer walk the plank, but out-of-town suckers are clipped with off-true wheels, educated dice and tougher odds than you buck in Las Vegas or Tijuana.

All this is possible on Pleasure Island because of a unique merger of powerful old plantation paternalism and powerful modern benevolent gangsterism. Everybody prospers. Nobody objects. Taxes are modest. There isn't one citizen, white, black or yellow, on relief.

Galveston is a resort burg related to growing, industrial, hustling Houston somewhat as Atlantic City is to Philadelphia. It's an hour's drive over perfect highways. It's away from home. It's wealthy. And it's terrific. Galveston is visited by thousands of tourists from distant parts, too. It's a seaport where freighters of the whole world dock, their sailors fat with accumulated pay and famished for the fleshpots. They couldn't get shore leave in a happier town. They get deliriously drunk and usually wake up rolled but otherwise unharmed.

The municipal setup is a ball-bearing, copper-riveted dilly. The only thing closed in Galveston is its tight four-family power. And that sways its industry, jurisprudence, journalism, underworld, finance, society, electorate and civic conscience. A benign despotism it is. There is almost no violent crime. There are stick-men but no stick-up men. The liquor is excellent and not costly—50 and 60 cents at contraband bars. The locals are steered away from the rigged boobytraps set for "foreigners." You could not fancy a more pleasant Shangri-la for more contented citizens.

As in Hawaii, where everything that amounts to anything is owned by the "Big Five" clans, here the strategic interests belong to the Big Three—who look aloof at a Fourth, which operates all the enterprises which laugh at the law—conducts, owns, leases and otherwise skims the milk and lops up the cream of protected gambling, vice, and other violations of drastic state statutes and city ordinances, solemnly passed and kept on the books for the purpose of barring outsiders from enjoying the privileges and the profits.

The three are:

W. L. Moody, Jr., who at the age of eighty-six at this writing, is still active as the head of his tribe and is the over-all boss of Galveston. He owns the principal hotels and both newspapers, the *News* and the *Tribune;* he is the leading banker, holds sway over untold insurance, realty and cotton interests. He is probably one of the ten richest men in America. He could bang the shutters tight on anything in Galveston at any time by a loud sneeze.

Ex-Mayor Isaac H. Kempner, patriarch, seventy-two. The Kempners are Jewish, which is no handicap in this liberal province. They are in finance, cotton, sugar refining, railroads and real estate.

The Seelys, too, are in the major industries, indigenous and developed, on this garden spot of transient fun and dead-end traffic.

The present picture is drawn with the lights and shadows of this oligarchy. Galveston was once the largest city in Texas. But the Big Three drove out any intruders who tried to invade the important sources of income and influence. So the prospectors went to Houston, and in time made it the largest city in the South, the second port of the United States.

The ancient architecture, the wide streets blazing with lush foliage, the built-in shades over the hot walks are in the pattern of a century ago and attest the closely-knit aristocracy and complete feudal dominance of a few men determined to keep out an onrush of middle-class strangers with their chain-store notions and their go-getting proclivities. "Self-made men" rarely flourish here. The sin and disregard for law are in keeping with the ways of the Spanish dons, who built missions and said their masses, who raised walls around their mansions, but opened their gates to Lafitte and other big buccaneers, to do handsomely from them as well as by them.

Sam and Rosario (known as Rose) Maceo were the Fourth; the comparative newcomers tolerated within the golden circle, though denied membership in the snobbish country club. They hogged the concessions in practices and trades which the owners and overseers refused to touch with their bare hands. The saga of the Maceos is a colorful success story—a gangster tale almost without gunplay, an example of what ambitious immigrant boys can achieve if they know the right percentages of wrong craps, blackjack and roulette.

Rose, the older, was the brainier. Sam, in his early fifties, was well dressed, well built, swarthy but presentable, a suave frontman in the grand manner. He came from Italy by way of New Orleans, practiced as a barber, then took off on his first flight to fortune as a one-bottle bootlegger in early Prohibition days. Rose harvested the hay while the Volstead moon shone, invested in property and business, guided his younger brother and numerous nephews and cousins, who came on, into the small and easy ways of the insider on local politics.

National repeal was no disaster, it was a bonanza, for the state obligingly cracked down with tough rules. Galveston took full advantage of no interference from Washington and too much from Austin, quietly seceded and set up the one oasis in the colossal Texas desert. The populace did as it was told. Its officials were elected by default, named not in smoke-filled rooms, but in the most luxurious baronial castles. There is seldom a ripple on the smooth surface of the monotonous city elections. But once, when a trouble spot developed, enough scarlet sisters found it advisable to stop playing post office on Post Office Street long enough to sweeten the count in a ward where ballots were needed.

Sam Maceo died in a hospital last summer. He was scheduled to talk to the Kefauver Committee. He had long been ailing. But Charlie Fischetti, his opposite number in Chicago, also wanted by the committee, died the same week, also from "natural causes." The missing body of Phil Mangano, of Brooklyn, was found in an empty Flatbush lot two days later. To some sophisticated Federal agents all this seemed an unrealistic coincidence.

After Sam's death, mourned by Galvestonians as a public catastrophe, it was announced all Maceo gambling enterprises "are closed." The Balinese Room indeed was—for a month. Friendly newspapers were tipped off that Rosario had returned to his native Italy to live in retirement. That was a bald lie. He is still in Galveston, directing his clan's manifold enterprises.

The front men are Vic and Anthony Fertitta, Maceo nephews.

Thirteen other partners are members of the closely held firm. They are Frank Maceo, A. J. Adams, O. E. Voight, Sam Serio and nine little Maceos and Fertittas. They handle all details of maintaining the political status quo. There is no need for terrorism or flophouse colonizing. Where the men who run the politics also dominate virtually every business, and therefore the sources of employment, licenses, sites, private and public concessions, there is no incentive for a two-party system.

The Maceos, though they are unsubtly tied up with the big underworld national combination, are not strutting hoodlums with their well-tailored jackets bulging over holsters. They are generous, affable, civic-minded. They love the place and the place loves them. They are in on every charitable and every church drive, every movement for improved conditions, every booster promotion and every plan to enrich the good life. They are in legitimate enterprises, too; patrons of Rotary and the Lions.

Once when an indignant bloc in the state capital sought an investigation of the Maceos and the notorious law-flouting in Galveston, fifty of its ministers in a body converged on Austin to protest and to defend.

In a town that lives largely off strangers, every stranger is suspect. There is an underground intelligence system which tips off any visitor who seems or acts suspicious. Even the Texas Rangers do nothing. They visit thrice a week on a regular "milk-man's run" and their approach is telephoned from the mainland, which gives fifteen minutes' notice—and that unnecessary. When they visit the spots nothing runs until they leave. Thus they may report "No action." But the dice roll before their self-starters do. Whether the island cops are honest or not is of little importance. They know there is no point in arresting anyone connected with the approved underworld. The force has little to do except lock up a few sailors after a rumpus or help home an occasional drunk.

The Maceos have as their principal attorneys Charles Dibrell, Jr., and Emmett Magee. Dibrell is the son of Judge Charles Dibrell, of the 56th Texas District, for twenty-five years on the bench which has jurisdiction over criminal cases. Magee is the brother of Raymond E. Magee, the county (district) attorney, and is the city's foremost criminal lawyer. Thus the bosses of the underworld engage as their two lawyers the son of the judge and the brother of the prosecutor!

That crusader for the people, the press, not only makes no demand to "run the rascals out," but if anyone appealed to the courts or the city council against the vested ins the local press wouldn't even publish it. When, once in a blue moon, the Houston dailies raise a flurry, the copies are bought up before they cross the county limits. The odds are heavy this book will never rest on a counter in Galveston.

The pride of Galveston is its beaches. Some of the better drinking, dicing, dining and dancing rendezvous were installed on beautiful piers extending over the Gulf of Mexico. How, no one can explain. Texas law requires such protrusions be authorized by state legislation. There is no record in Austin of such sanction or even application. But Maceo occupied the best wharf and no one arose to question that. There he built a tremendous enclosure called the Balinese Room, the highest-grade retreat in the resort. It is supposedly a private club, but the Maceos run it for their own profit. When you enter the covered pier you are screened by a man and woman, who phone back to the office. If you get the nod you are admitted through a locked door. You walk two hundred feet out over the Gulf, scrutinized by husky, tuxedoed guards, strung out like policemen in the Holland Tunnel. The main dining room, in Balinese décor, is slightly more gorgeous than a gala Hollywood chop suey restaurant. Here foremost name bands and top entertainers appear. The atmosphere attempts to be extremely El Morocco but comes up extremely rococo. There is a cocktail lounge and bar at which hard liquor is sold. This would be a violation even in a genuine club. Back of the bar is a small and well-decorated complete gambling casino.

This is only one of three piers occupied by the Maceos over public water for which no payment is made to any governing authority. The Supreme Court of Texas has ruled that the waterfront must be unrestricted; that no exclusive franchises may be given. Yet the Maceos "own" every wharf in Galveston except a municipal auditorium and pier, and that they operate with W. C. Moody, Jr., through a public company for the city, and nobody can cut in on it.

Most mysterious of the Maceo units is one with its doors as wide open to anyone at any hour as the police station. It's the Beach Club, on the boardwalk, across the street from Moody's Buccaneer Hotel. You step into a barroom with subdued lights and fairly urbane trimmings. You see young and pretty girls, most of them unescorted. They loiter about, awaiting phone calls, which come to the Negro bartender. This is the communications

HQ for the semi-pros. They get calls individually by name, or a man may phone in for just "a girl."

The red light stockade on Post Office Street is smack downtown. The houses are of two and three stories, wooden cottages, all with the bulbs hanging over the doors or windows. Most visitors are delivered by cab-drivers who get commissions out of the fees, which range from $3 to $5. In the days before all such things were taken over into a narrow channel of control, this restricted area was under the dual regency of Margaret Sossman and Mary Russell. This became centralized as the duchy of one Jessie Elliot, who is spoken of as The Duchess. She was the toast of the oilmen in Corpus Christi before she was brought in to take over by the Maceo set-up. Mmes. Sossman and Russell were permitted to retain management of one house each and pay off to The Duchess. She kicks in to Joe Laviana, imported from Chicago.

The Maceos also own the Sportsmen's Club, hangout for visiting mobsters who spend much time there. A principal interest is in the dope traffic, which flows in and out with the aid of one of Galveston's all-year-round callings, shrimp fishery. Hundreds of small boats sail daily into the Gulf. Out of sight of shore these fast small craft are met by similar boats from the Mexican coast. The crude narcotics are hidden under the day's haul, concealed beyond the possibility of discovery by the few government agents assigned to Galveston, where there is no patrol along twenty miles of beaches.

Sam Maceo and thirty-two alleged conspirators were tried some years ago by Uncle Sam. Another Italian took the rap, most of the co-defendants went to jail, but Sam was ordered acquitted.

The Galveston temperature is uniformly mild all year. The summer or bathing season starts in April and goes through October. But the other attractions and numerous conventions keep it lively enough at all times to support ten gambling houses, one hundred illegal bars and two thousand call girls, despite a state crime investigation which purportedly "closed it down," a comic opera wave of indictments and a stage-set raid on the Balinese which netted a couple of Councilmen, but nothing else. The local police asked us to deny that Galveston is shuttered. The rumor is hurting business.

Around Galveston the breeze wafts gently and the breakers woosh softly. No one works very hard. There is little labor trouble. There is no unemployment. There are no Communists. Gaiety echoes in the balmy air even during droughts. The good life pervades this island of iconoclastic isolation, as it always has, under six flags—not including the skull and crossbones.

18. PENNSYLVANIA CONFIDENTIAL — THE CAPTIVE KEYSTONE

*P*ENNSYLVANIA IS and always has been the great captive commonwealth, always owned by "vested interests."

Before the Roosevelt upheaval the proprietors were mine owners, industrialists and railroad kings. These were superseded by John L. Lewis and czars of other unions who stole the state with the aid of the underworld and the predatory poor, with an assist from the anemic scions of the original robber barons.

While these words are being typed another vested interest, more powerful than both its predecessors, is moving in. These new lords are the Mafia.

From time immemorial, Pennsylvania had voted GOP and conservative. Labor agitators and organizers were escorted across state lines by Pinkertons and Coal & Iron Police.

Then came the New Deal. The orders from Washington were to destroy the Republican monopoly. Hundreds of millions were poured in, disguised as PWA, WPA, relief, and other giveaways. The NRA, the Wagner Act and the NLRB were big sticks wielded by ruthless politicians and unioneers to beat the daylights out of the old ruling caste.

Pennsylvania finally got its Democratic Governor, George Earle, impractical as are most society snobs turned visionary and reformer.

The New Dealer-gangster alliance tried to operate the same way the GOP had done under Grundy and Pew. It was not so successful. The Republicans came back with a man who was "right" —and by that we don't mean right-wing.

Governor Duff chose our dear friend, Charlie Margiotti, noted Pittsburgh lawyer as his chief law enforcement officer. Margiotti, a registered and practicing Democrat, had served as Attorney General under Democratic Governor Earle, before GOP Duff reappointed him to the same job. Duff's administration resem-

bled the nonpartisan New Deal brand of Republicanism practiced by nominal GOPers in New York, California and New
England.

Under Pennsylvania statutes the Attorney General of the state
may retain his law practice. Now Margiotti, no longer in office,
numbers among his numerous and profitable clients some of Pittsburgh's leading bookmakers. We do not say this in disparagement,
because all men are entitled to counsel. Furthermore, Margiotti is
one of the most delightful people we know, having spent many
pleasant hours with him in the William Penn Hotel. He and Duff,
now U.S. Senator, were the organizers of the Eisenhower for President boom in Pennsylvania. Many of its preliminary expenses
were contributed by bookmakers, bootleggers and bipartisan Bill
Lias, West Virginia gambler.

When Duff went to the Senate he chose Governor Fine to succeed him. After he took the oath, Fine decided he was Governor,
not Duff. The Senator's calls from Washington are not being answered. Though the choice of the left-wing cell of the Pennsylvania GOP, Fine "double-crossed" those who put him in office
and swung conservative. But the underworld, which has neither
politics nor emotions, is now tied up with both sides and both
parties.

Pennsylvania is vitally important to the Mafia. Much of the
legitimate business they are taking over is located there. A list of
their blue chip holdings would show the Mafia to be the largest
single financial power in the state, wealthier than the Philadelphia bankers, the Pittsburgh iron masters and the Wall Street
absentee owners.

A curious thing about the Kefauver Committee is that when
it went into Pennsylvania, it only touched Philadelphia, while
the nearest it got to Pittsburgh was Steubenville, Ohio.

That is because Philadelphia, alone of major American cities,
had a Republican political machine, whereas Pittsburgh is operated by a Truman New Deal Democrat.

The braintrusters in Washington figured they could take the
heat off Democrat exposures by torpedoing the dishonest Republicans in the nation's third largest city. That was easy. But while
doing it, they kept away from Sicilians as they did elsewhere, con-
fining all the questions and accusations to non-Italians like Nig
Rosen.

A. Philadelphia Confidential

The Senatorial hearings in Philadelphia were timed to coincide with the approaching municipal elections. Incumbent Republicans got panicky and threw their Mayor overboard, nominating a clergyman to run in 1951. Reverend Daniel A. Poling took a licking.

Prior to election, the GOP began a house-cleaning which made Philadelphia look like its reputation—a cemetery with lights. Instead of being the sleepiest burg in the country before, there were few more wide-open. Hundreds of speakeasies served liquor after hours and on Sunday. Bookmakers were so thick you had to fight them off. Gambling joints ran unrestrained. Gals were so easy, New Yorkers came down for a good time.

Then one of the strangest political campaigns in history went into high. Opposed to Poling was Joseph S. Clark, Jr., a Chestnut Hill socialite and Harvard alumnus, typically impractical and completely unknown. Clark was sponsored by the powerful *Inquirer* and its brilliant publisher, Walter Annenberg, a Republican. Ironically, Annenberg, whose horse-wire fortune bought the paper, attacked Poling as a candidate of the bookmakers. Annenberg still owns the *Morning Telegraph* and *Racing Form,* high class scratch sheets.

When Kefauver quizzed Philadelphia gangsters, Chief Counsel Halley courteously ambled out so that Alfred Klein, a junior counsel, could take a bow in his home town. Klein, a former Philadelphia court house hanger-on and newspaperman of no distinction, was a political hack. His conduct of the Philadelphia session was planned in advance to generate campaign material; he turned considerable delicate material over to the Democrats for use last fall. After the right triumphed, Annenberg rewarded Klein with a sweet job at a hefty salary to write for and edit a true crime magazine.

In this treatise we are not going to bother with the names and addresses of street vice because, as we said, the desperate Republicans closed everything down before election and these words were being typed before the boys had a chance to find out who got the Democratic lagniappe.

We looked with amazement through the record of the Kefauver hearings to find something about Sicilian operations in the Philadelphia area. Whenever such names were mentioned accidentally in unsolicited testimony, they were dropped like hot potatoes. Narcotics Commissioner Anslinger and Virgil Peterson of the Chicago Crime Commission turned over impressive lists and documents which were buried. We searched in vain for enlightenment about these characters who dominate the Philadelphia-Camden Little Italy:

Nick Amato, Camden. Felix Buccichio, Camden and Philadelphia. John Di Tullio, Camden. Pat Massi, 1420 Park, Camden. Nino Calio, Philadelphia. Pete Cassella, Philadelphia. Casmo Demail, Philadelphia. Filippo Pollina, Philadelphia. Frank Serno, Philadelphia. Marco Reginelli, Philadelphia.

The Philadelphia-Camden axis extends to Atlantic City and the south Jersey vineyards and wineries.

For many years Atlantic City was the personal property of Enoch "Nocky" Johnson, Republican Party boss. Under him Atlantic City was neutral territory where out-of-town gangsters checked their guns before playing or conferring.

After Repeal the Italians bounced Johnson from his kingship when they prevailed on Brien McMahon, then high in the Department of Justice, to nail Nocky on Federal charges. While he did his fall, they moved in and took over.

The D'Agostino family, an aristocratic old South Jersey and Philadelphia bootleg clan, extended its sway to the boardwalk under the late Johnny D'Agostino. He operated Atlantic City night clubs, was a stockholder in Renault wine and backed Frank Palumbo, Philadelphia glamor-boy, about whom more later.

During the excitement preceding the resignation of T. Lamar Caudle as Assistant U.S. Attorney General in charge of tax fraud prosecutions, it was noted he took a trip to Italy to settle a currency problem for the D'Agostino wine family. Newspapers failed to tell who the D'Agostinos really were.

Frank Palumbo tried to be a Philadelphia Sherman Billingsley. He hired a New York press agent to get him a lot of publicity as a fabulous host. He topped Billingsley's gifts of $15 ties and champagne by giving Cadillac convertibles to columnists. We didn't get one.

At one time he owned or operated most of Philadelphia's important night clubs and cafes. One, the C-R, was an all-night joint where everyone went after the two o'clock closing. We spent many an evening there. But it was no Stork Club. No imported champagne, only Renault.

It was later testified under oath that the C-R was the official meeting place for policy operators. The managers of fifty wheels gathered there every week to transact business. During the recent clean-up, the C-R was annoyed least of all. It is again running after hours.

Palumbo married movie starlet Kippy Velez, and branched out to become a Ford distributor, with money said to be lent him by the D'Agostinos. At this writing he was on the lam in Mexico from a grand jury which wanted to question him about Blinky Palermo, the fight manager, and some taxes.

But Philadelphia does have suave Jack Lynch, of the Zodiac Room, one of America's great hosts.

We made one last quickie trip to Philly to check up on the new City Hall gang. Apparently they've found the cash register.

Under the new administration, jobs are for sale. Price one grand up. Salesroom in a Ritz suite. Dope, dame and booze concession in city lock-ups and institutions are auctioned off to the highest bidders.

Limousines to the crap games leave from the corner of 15th and Market. Bookmakers are coming out of limbo, operating in the Widener Arcade, in front of Lew Tendler's, around the Warwick, and in corner candy stores. Policy sellers, never underground in South Philadelphia, are back all over town—with a new gimmick: they call on customers but once a week, and limit them to the same number for all six days.

Dave Glass, Cappy Hoffman and Bill Weisberg send out the "word" when the heat is off. The cost of "ice" is up 250 per cent, cops rightfully pointing out that under the new set-up they've got to take out "insurance."

Bootleg whiskey is a new source of profit for the local hoods, sold in legitimate refills. Dope is obtainable on every corner of South Street from 8th to 12th, and practically every other crossing in town. Lieutenant Leinhauser of the municipal junk squad echoed other officials and said the town is clean—there's no dope in the schools. The following week thirty-five kids at Olney were pinched. And that's how it is in most of them.

Hookers solicit in and out of every block between Market and Pine, and 12th and 16th, with the cream of the broads parading Broad Street. The most expensive congregate at the Embassy. Faggots make their dates at the Parkway Free Library.

The new Mayor already has four press agents—all on the city payroll at $9600 a year each, and they're turning out copy on an assembly line basis to prove there's no crime in Philly—look, there are no arrests.

That's right—no one is pushed around, especially in the Negro and Italian areas of South Philadelphia.

Everyone loves everyone else like a brother—or sister!

B. Pittsburgh—Steel and Steal

The giants are long gone. The air is purged of smoke. The great mills are supine under unionism. The rowdy vigor that marked its growing pains has disappeared, along with the individuality that once made Pittsburgh a unique American phenomenon.

Fairies prance along avenues which once resounded to fancy Hunkie profanity and drunken Saturday night brawls. The city administration is no longer Republican. Mellons are merely tolerated by the new hydraheaded municipal magnates, the twin bosses of labor and the underworld.

Kefauver, who found so little in Philadelphia, might have found plenty in Pittsburgh. But it already had a Democratic Mayor.

New Dealers took over by organizing the unskilled Negro mill hands. The CIO assisted the Reds to line up immigrants. Mayor Lawrence is a loud supporter of accused Communist sympathizers. He turns City Hall over to vocal pinks. He is a defender of Socialists and socialism, but he didn't let that interfere with duty when it came to slipping the city's $6,000,000 public parking garage to a private company operated by one John T. Stabile.

Pittsburgh is in a pip of a position with Federal patronage. John Kane, chairman of County Commissioners, nominated Truman first. You know what kind of entree to the White House that gives him. Together with Mayor Lawrence, an unbossed chief magistrate because he himself is the city boss, these two birds run everything in town and county.

The police superintendent is appointed by Lawrence.

It costs a grand to get on the force. There are under-table dealings on everything. Most of the District Attorney's county detectives are crookeder, which is why no one gets nabbed.

State Senator Joe Barr is Mayor Lawrence's hearing-aid. He hears mostly what Sicilians tell him. Frank Amato, of Braddock, is the boss of Little Italy. Vincent Cappizi also is important. He lives at 706 Fulton. Other Italians reside in East Liberty, the Northside, and the Hill district. The numbers bosses are Sam Grosso and Frank Balente.

Many prominent emigrés from Palermo congregate at Unione Fratellanza Siciliano, 1854 Forbes, phone Court 1-1181.

Rackets are on a ward basis. There are thirty-two but some are quiet and residential. Each has a local racket boss who does business through the official Democratic ward leader, who sends the word downtown through police inspectors. More important matters are taken to the Court House or City Hall directly.

The area of greatest Democratic strength is in the first five wards including the Hill (Negro and Italian), the Golden Triangle and the downtown hotel and shopping district, with the skidrows and tenderloin. These five wards together resemble Chicago's famous old First Ward in the days of the Levee.

The Pittsburgh ward set-up is the most typical in the country and is offered here as an example to show how all deals begin on the street level, protected and encouraged there, before they work up to interstate and international syndication.

FIRST WARD: Jake Lerner, from the Second where he controls the produce yards, recently moved in alongside Frank Grosso, who runs policy in the downtown office buildings.

THIRD WARD: The bulk of the business in the Third is handled by Tony Grosso, Frank's brother. Others are a man named Gillotti and Fran Prezioso, alias Frank Christy. Christy was the biggest numbers writer in Pittsburgh. He suffered heavily because of a series of raids by the State Police, and for a long time dropped out of sight, but recently made a come-back. James Spinkard, the Democratic chairman, is the political power in this ward.

FIFTH WARD: Jakie Daurora is the new czar.

SIXTH WARD: Must see Tut Taylor, Stanley Plucinski or Slicker Chalmers. Judge Fiorucci, Mayor Lawrence's boy, is the big political cheese.

SEVENTH WARD: There is only one big racketeer in the Seventh Ward. He is Frank Cardone, in partnership with his brother Joe. Brother Jimmy operates independently. They are tough hombres. Jimmy fled to Florida to evade service before the special state grand jury. He lost $200,000 there in a beer distributorship. His numbers operation is being handled by his partner, Lou Thomas, from jail.

EAST LIBERTY: Jimmy Pella is the boss because Ralph "Foots" Arcadia made the mistake of falling out with Mayor Lawrence.

EIGHTH WARD: Operated by John Collinger, whose family

runs a saloon, a beer business, a fur business and has one member on the county payroll.

THIRTEENTH WARD: The chief operators are Bernard Kelly and George Messer.

FOURTEENTH WARD: Squirrel Hill, a fine residential section largely populated by Jews. The chief operators here are Joe, Frank and Jim Cardone.

SOUTH SIDE: The South Side Wards (Slav town) are divided among Chester Stupak, "Yee" Terleski, Walter "Rocky" Twardy, Peter Stathis, Joseph "Moon" Miller, and Walter Rosenberg.

NORTH SIDE: Czars are the Cangeliers, Phil Lange, Pete "the Greek" Moshas and Art Rooney. Rooney owns the Pittsburgh Steelers, professional football team. His front men are John Laughlin, his brother-in-law, who owns the Shamrock Room, a popular restaurant and night club, and John "Harp" Vaughn, former Pitt football player and local Republican politician.

WEST END: Tony Grosso and Refal Pace.

Negroes are in every ward. They make up an independent entity not subject to local leadership. Others must pay for non-aggression by the police. Negroes are immune, gratis. Colored people vote for money and whiskey and then are taken back and voted again. The protector and patron of the colored is "Pappy" Williams, a Negro whom Mayor Lawrence appointed as Police Magistrate.

County territory outside the city limits is set up pretty much like Pittsburgh wards with each village or township standing in the same position as a city ward.

Some of the big boys are:

Dominick Bernardino, of Penn Township; Joe Roppo, Ambridge; Jimmy Cardone, McKeesport; Charles Jamal, a Turk who runs the swank Ankara night club in Clairton, where Frank Orsini also throws much weight, and Tony Ripepi, Washington County.

Local hoods had hysterics when Dominick Anzalone showed up as the villain of a piece in *Collier's* purporting to give the low-down on the western Pennsylvania rackets. Instead of being the boss of Westmoreland County, he has a piker interest in one gambling joint only, Donners in Monesson. The big bosses of Westmoreland are the Mannerinos.

There are vital Mafia concentrations in other parts of the state. They got here when Sicilian sluggers were imported by the mine and mill owners to break the unions. They remained and took over the unions and through them got control of the local county and city machines. John L. Lewis' United Mine Workers is no longer his, though they let him think so.

The Mannerino gang, which goes for whores, gambling and numbers in New Kensington, supplies votes and campaign funds for left-wing Democratic Congressman Kelley.

Nick Stirone, boss of the Common Laborers Unions, runs the rackets in Johnstown.

West Virginia is a colony of Pittsburgh. Its Republican state committeeman, Walter Hallanan, a millionaire but an obnoxious tippler, operates his domain from the William Penn Hotel in Pittsburgh. West Virginia goes Democratic these days because of the close tie between Hallanan and his Democratic opposite numbers.

Wheeling is Pittsburgh's escape town. Bill Lias, owner of Wheeling Downs, is tied up with Pittsburgh and Detroit mobs. He was referred to on the floor of the U.S. Senate as a dictator of rackets in West Virginia and southern Ohio. The Internal Revenue allowed him to owe more than $2,000,000 in back taxes and penalties without placing a lien on his property.

Lias, like all top racketeers, is nonpartisan politically. He contributes equally to the Duff Republicans in Pennsylvania through Hallanan and to the Fair Deal Democrats through the Pittsburgh mobsters and Mayor Lawrence.

The fairy situation hereabouts is pretty bad, encouraged by dreamy "intellectual" partisans of Mayor Lawrence. Many half men thrill to the virility of mine and mill workers and stalk their drinking places, hoping to make liaisons when the sweaty Slovenes are plastered. This is the nucleus of a large colony. They like to gather at the Monte Carlo, in town, and the Jewel Box in Pleasant Hill on the road to the airport.

Those old-fashioned enough to prefer females will find the prettiest in the cocktail lounges of the Roosevelt, Fort Pitt, Pittsburgh and William Penn. Others work the bars on E. Liberty, ask $20, take $10.

Lyiola Belle offers "friendship contacts" at 6124 Centre Ave., Phone HI 1-3908. If you're still lonely, try the stage door of the Casino Burlesk.

19. MILWAUKEE AND WHAT NEVER MADE IT FAMOUS

IN CHICAGO CONFIDENTIAL we made passing reference to a burg only a few minutes' flight away, which had no resident agent of the Bureau of Narcotics. So Milwaukee, we said, had become a storage point and drop for Chicago wholesalers of dope and a safe and handy jaunt for junkies. This we noted as an adjunct to the Chicago scene.

That factual observation raised more hell than the exhaustive major operation we committed on Chicago, which never offered an official protest or denial, but absorbed all we disclosed like the big tough champ who knows he must take some on the chin, shakes them off and goes right back punching.

But Milwaukee, the lightweight busher, screamed.

Police Chief Polcyn said we were liars. The foreman of the grand jury demanded that we come to Milwaukee to prove what we had said or confess that we were "irresponsible." Virtuous citizens proclaimed that if anyone had enjoyed poppy dreams in Milwaukee, it must have been Lait and Mortimer.

We are not in the business of purifying cities or prosecuting malefactors. We dish it out, dare local officials to act on our statements, and go on to the next book.

But we became immediate best-sellers in Milwaukee, because it is an obscure and neglected point off almost all the main lines, unaccustomed to attention from national reporters. So this time we descended on the sensitive city which beer and socialism had made famous, and this time we took a deep, sharp look. We were never more surprised.

We found this supposedly homey and largely homogeneous lake port for cheese and suds a polyglot hive of the lowest elements of our national life, saturated in sin, infested with Mafia gorillas tied in with the Chicago power-house, in control of everything that can turn a crooked buck.

We knew what we were talking about in the Chicago book, and we knew the Milwaukee cops knew. We could have testified then, and do now, to the jury of our readers, that the police had

raided the second floor of 317 West State Street, almost next door
to the building of perhaps America's richest paper, the *Milwaukee
Journal,* and found large supplies of opium.

Chinese from Chicago and Waukegan were found at 943 N.
4th Street, 1206 N. 27th Street, and on the second floor of a structure one block east of the Federal Building. Those arrested told
cops they and others had been coming up from Chicago for years
to buy and smoke opium. Could the chief have been unaware of
these facts when he publicly denied them? He knows opium seiz-
ures in Milwaukee far exceed those in Chicago, a city many times
as large.

And we know white girls and Negro youths are engaging in
wild sex and marijuana parties in the city schools. Lincoln High,
with a large colored attendance, is an explosive problem. And
the wealthier kids in swanky suburban Shorewood High are just
as bad.

The files of the police department are overflowing with reports
on cases in which gangs of Negro boys, white girls and older men
take part in sex and dope parties. For every case disclosed by the
coppers, twenty are kept confidential.

When you think of Milwaukee, you think of the untranslatable
German word *gemutlich.* It has a calm connotation of comfort
and innocuous innocence. You think of fat *hausfrauen* and portly
descendants of '48ers who fled to escape Prussianism. You do not
envision, as we did not, that Milwaukee has as brazen and brutish
private sin and organized traffic in lawlessness as the Hoboken
waterfront.

In the old days, Milwaukee was an overnight trip from Chicago
on the Lake boats, where fellows took their gals to cheat out of
sight and those who had none came up to get some. Milwaukee
was never prudish. But the big changes came with new ownership.

For the benefit of the nearsighted chief, who was praised by the
Kefauver Committee, and the grand jury men, we submit herewith Milwaukee's Sicilian Social Register, together with a partial
rundown of what was going while we were in town:

Sam Farara is the Italian boss.

The Maniachia family are the Sicilian aristocrats. One member
is on the Mafia Grand Council.

Frank Balestrere, nephew of the Kansas City power, is Frankie
Carbo's local prize-fight representative.

An old Capone man is a power in the Cooks and Waiters Union.
Ralph Capone is the statewide boss.

Little Italy is in the 3rd Ward, where votes are sold and bartered for protection. The boys like to do business with Socialist Mayor Zeidler, a practical idealist.

Unafraid of the police, the hoods strut and throw their weight around. Most of the Italians dress like George Raft, try to act like tough guys. At the Tic Toc, the town's version of New York's Copacabana, the audience looked like the cast in a film gangster thriller, as hard a set of characters as we've seen anywhere.

The standard bribe for a liquor license is $250. This is a piker town, where you can buy a judge for $200 and an alderman for $50. Socialists take at standard prices.

Liquor trucks passing through town or county are hijacked unless the mob payroll is met. Those okayed are convoyed by cops.

Louis Simon, wire layoff man and big bookmaker, is running what's going. Lonnie Minor bosses policy.

Sidney Brodson, pilloried before the Kefauver Committee, took the rap for the Italians. He's Jewish.

Ray Ryan, Hollywood oil wild-catter, used to be a 5th Street bookie. He won a well in a crap game, became a big-time operator and friend of movie stars, whom he declares in as partners. After a burst of publicity last year, he returned to Milwaukee and looked up his old pals in the Plankinton Arcade and Antlers Hotel poolrooms. As he knew they would, they begged to be taken in on his next well. Five came in dry. He dented the Milwaukee books worse than did Kefauver.

Milwaukee's rep in the Middle West is that it's friendlier and cheaper than Chicago. Thousands of servicemen from Great Lakes Naval Station and Fort Sheridan head for it instead of the bigger town below.

Rich dairy farmers and their hired hands come to Milwaukee, too, to play, afraid of Chicago, which is too big and confusing for them. So Milwaukee is loaded with dead-falls, joints, clip-dives and carnival midway attractions, cheap, corny and crummy.

The night we were at the Terris Club we saw a pretty low strip-tease exhibition—dirty and disgusting. The blue material of a fat female emcee was what farmhands repeat behind the silo. The Milwaukee Night Club also goes in for unveiled nymphs.

We were solicited at the Casino Tavern. The price is low because of amateur competition. Sailors say this is the best pick-up burg in the nation. Easy to make contact at the Highlife Spa. One of the most amazing joints we ever saw is Lakota's, a big, bare barn where Great Lakes gobs pick up bobby-soxers. The room was packed with sailors—not a soldier in sight. They dance with their hats on. Babes—just that—thirteen and fourteen—pile into the place. Harry Lakota is a friend of Police Chief Polcyn.

And they say hunting is still good on the night boat to Muskegon.

Late at night the hoods, hookers and gamblers gather at the Belmont Hotel coffee shop for breakfast and social chats. If they want to drink after hours, many all-night speaks run in the lower East Side.

Milwaukee's great black-and-tan section in the 6th Ward is growing fast, with labor imported for the stockyards. Negroes vote Socialist at home and New Deal nationally. Former Congressman Biex Miller is the Washington contact boy who is able to pull the strings.

Milwaukee is old-fashioned in many respects. White men still "deal in coal." Those who want to change their luck with a wench wait at Vliet and 7th. White gals with black men can be seen at the Stage Door and Eagles' Dance Hall.

The town's seven policy wheels are Negro-operated but Sicilian-owned. Policy kings frequent Smokey's Candy Store and the May Tavern, on N. 6th.

King of Little Harlem is Smokey Goode, a police informer. You've got to get his nod to operate, otherwise he turns you in.

Queers, and there are plenty, congregate at Dante's Inferno regardless of color. We walked into the White Horse Inn, on N. 11th, in Little Harlem, where twenty men, black and white, were drinking at the bar. Some were made up. Others had arms around each other. A colored barmaid saw we were strangers. She said, "You won't find women here, just fags."

The best-mannered café in town, with the best show and the best-dressed patrons, is a black-and-tan club called the Flame, owned by Derby Thomas.

New Deal, Socialist Milwaukee and the pinkish campus in left-wing Madison prove that with deviation in politics you get corruption in government, apathy to crime and experimentation in sex.

The University of Wisconsin, alma mater of so many Reds, is now lavender, where swishes of both sexes stop lolligagging for their other pet pastime—getting up petitions against Joe McCarthy.

20. MISSOURI — STATE
OF TRUMANKIND

W*E LEFT* Kansas City by car. The sun was high. We were off on a brief ride to Independence, once the starting-point of covered-wagon caravans, now the humdrum hamlet which might have become a Mount Vernon, a Monticello, a Hermitage, or, Lord save us, a Hyde Park. For here had been cradled a son of Destiny.

The President was not in residence. One Secret Service man, grim and uncommunicative, sat on the front porch of the high-fenced, lawn-surrounded home. Neighbors came and went, not even turning their eyes toward the house which history might have hallowed. We drove on, "downtown," past shaded dwellings, well kept, not baronial, but comfortable and respectable. We saw the usual headquarters of fraternal and veterans' organizations, the chain-stores and the post office. We were unrecognized and we did not register at any hotel. Several people were expecting us and they admitted us.

We drove back in the dusk, along Truman Boulevard. We had listened to men and women who had known the man, for whom the broad avenue was named, since childhood. We had found them voluble, neither bitter nor tongue-tied by the exalted position of their townie who had made it. Oceans of ink had spread the story of Harry S. Truman over the surface of the globe. Casual and definitive biographies had been composed about him. But no reporters had questioned the frank folk who spoke to us of the famous, if not favorite, son of Independence.

Harry's mother had said of him, "He ploughed the straightest furrow in Jackson County." It was to take a long time until he again traversed the shortest distance between two points.

As you pass along through Kansas City and Independence you see many who look like Truman—smalltown-bred Midwesterners with seamed, weather-lined faces and the hardened hands that turned the turf in their youth. With them are plump, frumpy women who seem to carry themselves with character and the remnants of dignity; for here, in the Midwest, on the borders of the old frontier, their ancestors were the adventurous advance settlers whose wives defended barricades against Indians and bore and raised big broods. As civilization made such regions pallid, the best of the sons, with the blood of battlers in them, went elsewhere, to the markets and the centers where wealth and success beckoned. The daughters married what was left, for the era of female competition in the trades and professions was yet unknown.

Into such a lopsided society came Harry Truman, one son of a doughty mother who was the matriarch of a mortgage-ridden farm. When the time came for him to take over the management of the homestead, he was a failure; when, as a man, he undertook a modest business, he was again a failure. Then he won and married Bess Wallace. That was an alliance far above his worth and station. For the Wallaces were an old, comparatively rich clan, and Bess was a belle. The Wallaces were high church Episcopalian; the Trumans worshipped at a bare and humble Baptist tabernacle.

Her family opposed the match. Her classmates and neighbors shook their heads. Harry Truman was regarded as not much shucks. He had become a sort of professional Legionnaire after his return from militia captain's service in World War I, was frittering with profitless peanut politics, hounded by creditors. But Bess stood staunchly by him. He couldn't support her. He lived in her house and the town laughed behind his back. He looked to her as his mentor, his manager. She scanned his hazy horizon and saw on it only one ray, and a dim one—a handout from the kitchen table of the Democratic oligarchy which he had served in outer-fringe capacities.

When Harry Truman came, hat in hand, into the office of Tom Pendergast, a gangster chieftain who in his den above a bawdy Kansas City slum groggery was enthroned as the czar of Jackson County, there was something about the hen-pecked, harried little middle-aged mendicant that struck a chord somewhere inside the behemoth body of the infamous thief; it wasn't sympathy, for he had none. The imperious tyrant saw a cartoonists' symbol of the man in the crowd, thwarted by his own lack-luster mediocrity, who would take orders unquestioningly and follow them with servility. Pendergast began throwing him a few crumbs, the largesse of a bandit baron to a rear-rank vassal.

Truman advanced none in the esteem of his neighbors and the Wallaces. The merchants and practitioners of Independence knew what it took to feed at the trough of Pendergast's preserve. And as he crept upward he disclosed no flashes of congenial leadership; he was still a hack, a machine part replaceable at will or whim on a word from that iniquitous robbers' roost over the barrel-house.

The story of how Pendergast decided to send this flunky—who had never made more than $5,000 a year—to Washington has been told so often it is no longer confidential.

Harry was saddled on the most exclusive club in the world by fraud, perjury, murder and stolen ballots. He and Bess were in their forties. Margaret was a teen-ager when he became a U.S. Senator. A political reliefer does not become a statesman overnight and he didn't. Bess never let him out of her sight. She became his official secretary. They needed the extra income. She did the thinking and ran the office. Harry never protested against this usurpation.

His womenfolk still cannot visualize him as President. His neighbors still think of him as Harry, the piano-playing Legion Hall lounger, the bankrupt counter-jumper who went broke because they went by.

So the President of the United States gets his revenge by taking it out on others. He toes the line at home, but outside it he is a cocky little guy to those who can't answer back. He plays Boss Pendergast reincarnated when Bess isn't there to make him remember what Independence can't forget. But she gives him hell when he writes those letters. Then he locks himself in his room and pouts or calls up the boys for a card game and conviviality. It was charged on the floor of the Senate that Harry was "full of brandy and benedictine" when he ordered the Korean "police action."

Over the years, Harry has nurtured an abiding hatred against snooty Independence, against Kansas City and Jackson County—against those who kicked him around when he was nobody. Now that he's on top, he'll show 'em. And he does. It's an old gag that you have to be from Missouri to get a job in Washington. But most of Harry's appointments do not come from Kansas City. He is starving Jackson County out. He took care of a few old cronies, but brushed off the rest of his home community. In pique and bitterness he gives his Missouri appointments to the other end of the state—St. Louis.

The Homeric hatred engendered by the frustrations of his earlier years is the *deus ex machina* behind his every action. It is expressed every time he flaunts his contempt for other Americans —by whitewashing Communists with a "red herring" fillip or keeping Harry Vaughan or Donald Dawson on the White House staff, or firing MacArthur. As Vice-President he flew to Pender-gast's funeral. As President he threw out the prosecutor who con-victed that greedy grafter. Some call that "loyalty." We call it bile boiling over.

As will be seen in the succeeding pages, Kansas City has changed little from the days when Harry was an official garbage-collector for Pendergast, who shook down madames, gamblers and killers. Now Harry is the boss. He could clean the foul heap up with one grunt. But he doesn't. The decent citizens never did a thing for him. His mental processes work this way: So they never thought I'd amount to anything, eh? It serves the s.o.b.'s right. Now they're going to have what I say they'll get—and like it. I wish Tom could see me now. How he would laugh!

A. Kansas City—Suburb of Independence

Word got out via the grapevine that we were in Kansas City to do a job on Harry's town. We hadn't been at the Hotel Muehlebach more than a couple of hours when we got a call from "June." She insisted we had phoned and asked her to our rooms. But we already had guests. One was Arlon Wilson, a former FBI agent, who is making a record for himself as the managing director of the Kansas City Crime Commission. The other two were key Federal sleuths. This was too good. We told June to come on up.

She turned out to be a slender blonde in her late thirties, still good-looking. Right off the bat she told us she was on call. She couldn't explain how it happened that there was a message wait-ing for her to see us, professionally. She didn't know our business. And she certainly didn't know our friends.

After a few drinks we gave her $20 (not deductible) for her lost time and sent her home. We swear we did. Then we did some gumshoeing. The facts gradually unfolded. Word had gone out from Washington to "get" those bastards—Lait and Mortimer. The Balestrere criminal organization set it up and they were going to crash the room with cops. The extra guests stymied the play. Their spy saw us come in with our friends, but it was too late to head June off. We have her last name and phone number; but we won't rat on someone who drank with us. But a subpoena would find her and we have witnesses.

If it did nothing else, the mystery-shrouded assassination of Charlie Binaggio cleared the atmosphere. There is no longer any doubt as to who is the boss of Jackson County. It is Harry S.

Truman. Tom Pendergast's nephew, Jim, became "leader" after Binaggio got his. He is a dummy and on the way out. Because of Truman's loyalty to old Tom, Jim will keep the title, but his powers are gradually being assumed by Henry McKissick, a beer salesman and tavern-owner, once characterized before a Congressional committee as "a well-dressed fat slob." Pendergast doesn't know the skids have been greased. This will be news to him.

After old Tom got washed up, the Chicago hoodlums, who own the town, decided to come down and run it themselves. They sent in Tony Gizzo, ostensibly a salesman for Capone's beer. He dug up ratlike Charlie Binaggio and educated him in the ways of operating a crooked political machine. Truman was President, but he was too well disciplined in the ways of party to make an open break with the Sicilian to whose Democratic Club Truman belonged as "an honored dues-paying member." This was just one more frustration for Harry, who despised the punk but wasn't man enough to disown him. The boys had long suspected Binaggio of diverting slush funds to his own bank account. They said his wife was getting "ritzy" and wanted him out of the racket. They accused him of pocketing payoffs which they said were earmarked for state and Federal figures.

The execution was performed by killers sent up from Tijuana. They were deportees from the United States to Italy who had come to Mexico with "student permits" to study farming—a type of passport easy to obtain in Italy for a fee to the right official. Their kind wait in Mexico for the right opportunity to slip back into the U.S. under assumed names.

The following "students" disappeared from Mexico at around that time: Ralph Calico, John Vitale and Tony Giardana.

After Binaggio was removed, an entente cordiale was reached between the White House gang and the Mafia, with Harry Vaughan and Bill Boyle acting as intermediaries. The functions of Jackson County Democracy were cut in two. Surface politics would henceforth be operated in the orthodox way by the remnants of the Pendergast machine, which Harry now owned. The Mafia would handle the underground and split the take.

This is the sort of arrangement with which Harry is thoroughly familiar. When he was County Commissioner—they called him "Judge"—Johnny Lazia, the Black Hand boss, handled all the obviously illegal activities like bootlegging and women, while the so-called legitimate spoils from contracting, insurance, etc., went through Pendergast directly.

During Harry's terms as county judge, he spent more than $60,-000,000 of public funds, sound money then. He showed early that he had no respect for the taxpayers' dough. Most of it went into projects which Pendergast or his flunkies handled. Pendergast was in the construction and concrete business, so Harry spent $20,000,-000 for highways now held up as a monument to him. But it happened many of these roads were "dead-enders" running into the hills of Jackson County, where Lazia had his moonshine stills. Deputy sheriffs on motorcycles escorted Lazia's rum-running trucks.

Chain gangs from the county jail were used to quarry and crush rock to surface the roads that County Judge Truman built to the still sites. When Treasury agents raided one in 1932, they found county construction equipment, loaned by County Judge Truman, on the raided premises. It was seized as contraband and sold by the government, according to law.

In other crooked communities they built double lines of sewers, but Harry did one better. He built two courthouses, one at the traditional county-seat of Independence and the other in Kansas City. The concrete came from Pendergast.

Harry was a willing errand-boy those days. In addition to sponsoring building projects for the boss, he took care of faithful Democratic workers, even when there were no jobs for them. In 1930 he appointed two hacks as justices of the peace for Kaw township, though these jobs had been abolished by state law. In a spirit that would reverberate twenty years later, Truman first denied all knowledge of the appointments, but, after talking to Pendergast, he accepted the rap. He had no explanation to offer. The *Kansas City Star* said at the time, "The general belief was that the Democratic organization to which he was responsible cracked the whip and he performed."

Lazia broke into town in 1928, in a fashion reflected by Tony Gizzo's later conquest, selling a soft drink called Golden Mist. He smashed into the congested Sicilian north side—10 per cent of K.C. is Italian—and told Pendergast he was a partner. Dealers who bought Golden Mist were not bothered. Others were pinched, bombed or stuck up. At the ball park only Golden Mist and Tom Pendergast's beer were sold.

Tom never had occasion to regret taking Lazia and the Italians into the organization. He was a cagey conniver who knew tricks even Tom didn't know about stealing elections.

When Harry ran for the Senate in 1934, his opponent led to

the Jackson County line with a 95,000 plurality. Harry appeared licked. Not even the most sanguine figured Truman could cut such a lead, especially since the same candidate had drawn more than 92,000 votes in Jackson County in the previous election. Tom waited until all the votes were cast in all the other counties, then brought in the Jackson County vote: 137,529 for Truman, 1,525 for the opponent—in all of Kansas City.

Two years later, while Truman was a Senator, Kansas City registration lists were purged during a temporary clean-up. And 85,000 names were dropped. In the First Ward, 21,671 had been registered against a census of only 19,923 past the age of twenty-one. That was one example. The entire Kansas City registration, 252,000, compared with the census of 280,000 over twenty-one.

In the First Ward Truman had tallied 17,485 votes against less than 1,200 for three opposition candidates combined.

When Truman became Pendergast's boy in Washington, Tom expanded the racket into a national shakedown. Missouri was always a doubtful state. New Dealers needed Uncle Tom Pendergast, so Harry Hopkins turned the WPA over to him, giving him a national outlet for his contracting and concrete businesses. Harry got government appointments for Tom's boys. Many were ex-convicts. No one bothered to check. The record is easy to alter in Kansas City.

Those whom he had helped were grateful. When the time came to build up the new American myth which presents Harry S. Truman as a self-educated modern version of Honest Abe, it was deemed necessary to cover up the sad fact that Harry had never taken up his early notes and indebtednesses in Kansas City. So some hard individuals advised the holders of these debts that "you been paid in full, bud, see?" and Harry was pictured to the world as a paragon of honor who had slaved to pay off 100 per cent. *American Mercury* editor Bill Huie called him a "dead beat." He didn't even get a profane letter.

The present set-up in Kansas City is this: the county is Democratic, controlled by the Pendergast machine. The big loot is there. The courthouse is crooked. Fixes and light sentences are easy. Crimes are down-graded. Even murder can be bought off. The Mayor is nominally independent and anti-Pendergast; but strange alliances have been made between the mob boys and the reform administration.

A big scandal may break after a tragic fire; for a handout you can forget the regulations.

The police commissioners are appointed by the Governor, a machine Democrat. If cops don't obey orders they are exiled to a colored neighborhood.

While Jim Pendergast ostensibly runs the courthouse, the most important men in town are Jim Balestrere and Peter Di Giovanni.

James Balestrere and his son, Samuel, conduct the National Tobacco and Liquor store, 1124 East 18th Street, in the heart of the Negro section. Prior to 1933, James owned the Northside Motors, 431 East 6th Street, and was associated with Charles Binaggio in the Kansas City Syrup Company, whose most lucrative outlet was the sale of sugar for bootlegging. He is rich. His name is seldom mentioned in public and he ostensibly leads a quiet family life. But he is recognized in Italian circles as the arbiter of all disputes among and affecting the Italian element in the north end of Kansas City.

Peter Di Giovanni was born in Italy on June 29, 1886. He has been arrested in Kansas City in a murder investigation, but was never tried. He and his brother, Joe, were long in the liquor business, bootlegging before Repeal and since in the Midwest Distributors, wholesalers of Seagram's products in the area. Midwest's liquor license was recently revoked because of their connection with it. But a new one was immediately issued to this concern, in the name of Paul and Sam Di Giovanni, sons of Peter and Joe, respectively.

The operating head of the local Mafia is "Machine Gun" Joe Lascoula. Nick Civella is the new "enforcer." Only recently he told the town the mob was taking over the parlay cards. And it did.

Two absentee owners of great power are Lacoco and Carolla, sojourning in nearby Leavenworth, where they get the honored guest treatment. The boys frequently visit them there for conferences. Another important figure is Vincent Chiappetti. Joe and Willie Cummings—real name Cammisino—have an interest in the policy wheel and run the Patio Bar, at 8th and Charlotte, open all night though the legal closing hour is 1 A.M. They are in-laws of Balestrere. One of Balestrere's sons owns the Retail Clerks' Union.

Back of all this is Tony Gizzo, the powerhouse and communications center between Kansas City and the Chicago mob. Tony spends most of his afternoons at Pusateri's New Yorker Bar. We stood next to him while he was putting in a phone call to Chicago.

We checked the number. It was the Fischetti penthouse. During the evening the mobsters hang out in Sammy Goldberg's Delicatessen. Goldberg is doing a stretch, so Binaggio's widow is running it for him. This is an old underworld practice, to arrange for the support of a victim's widow and family.

While the Italians control everything, a few non-Italians such as Maxie Jaben, Tim Moran, Louis Schaeffer and Izzie Brenner also operate, with cuts going upstairs to Gizzo.

Having succeeded to all the emoluments of Tom Pendergast as Democratic boss of the town, Harry appointed his brother, Vivian, as Federal Housing Administrator in Kansas City. This job handles millions of government money.

Harry's friend, Enos Axtell, was nominated to purge a Congressman whom Harry hated, in a primary election. The ballot-box stuffing would have gladdened the heart of old Tom. The day before the grand jury was to begin its investigation, the boxes were stolen from the courthouse built by Harry fourteen years earlier, and unveiled by him with these words:

"I dedicate this courthouse to virtue and ethical conduct.

"I dedicate this courthouse to honor and good government.

"I dedicate this courthouse to law and justice."

Axtell was beaten in the general election. He now handles legal work for the Truman family, including the purchase and management of real estate. Some of that is 394 acres near Grand View, Mo. (pop. 1,556), and four lots in the town. A recent military construction bill included an appropriation of $12,800,000 as improvements for an airport at Grand View which is to be the headquarters of the air defense command for the entire country. Congressman Gross of Iowa called it "a Truman land boom." He said the President's brother is prepared to grant FHA loans for housing in the locality. The Democratic majority railroaded the appropriation through. But there have been no handouts to his in-laws, no "pork" for Independence.

Vivian is quite a little Caesar around Jackson County and throws a lot of weight all over the country. When the Senate District Committee recently probed Harry Truman's nomination of Wayne Beck as Recorder of Deeds for the District of Columbia, the sixty-one-year-old Kansas City Negro said he couldn't recall how he got the important job. After some urging he suddenly "recalled" that brother Vivian had arranged matters.

Opposition to Beck centered around charges that during the fifteen years he was superintendent of the Jackson County Home for Negro Boys and Girls he fed the youngsters sub-standard diets and punished them too severely and continued doing so until anti-Pendergast forces brought public pressure to bear.

Truman finally has a Congressman of his own choosing representing his home district—Leonard Irving, a professional unioneer. He was under indictment on misuse of the funds of the AFL union which he heads. The D.A. charged he used them for campaign expenses. A Democratic Federal judge invalidated seven counts without hearing defense testimony and took the rest under advisement. Thereupon he was quickly acquitted.

We do not know what the President intends to do in the future. But we know what he had hoped.

The Muehlebach Hotel, Kansas City's best and one of the country's finest, is constructing a new wing. Barney Allis, its owner, is a pal of the President. The new wing will have an elaborate presidential suite. Harry Truman is the only President who is expected to visit Kansas City. If he is no longer President after the suite is opened, it will be a waste. He will be back living in Independence. Harry is loyal to his friends. He would not knowingly make Barney Allis lose money. So we assume he was planning another four years as chief executive. QED.

We can't blame him if he wants to be only a visitor in Kansas City. This is a quick rundown of the town his boys sold out—today, not when Tom Pendergast was alive:

MOB: The Mafia controls the town. Nothing moves there, including Harry, without an OK. The Kansas City branch of the Syndicate runs the entire U.S. Southwest. K.C. is a haven for criminals on the lam, openly protected and entertained by local Mafistas, some so important they sit on the dais when Harry is dined at the Muehlebach.

THE BAR: Attorney Al Osborne was on trial, charged with jury fixing, after a Negro juror told the judge she had been approached by Matt Jones, a colored courthouse janitor, to sell her vote. Jones, who promised to turn state's evidence, suddenly clammed up. Then he changed his mind, explained his previous silence to the judge in a statement that said James "Pop" Balestrere had threatened him if he talked. The threats were backed up by a Negro hoodlum appropriately named Seldom Seen. But before he got the chance to testify, Jones's body was found in the Missouri River, chained to a concrete block.

COURTHOUSE: Jackson County Sheriff Eugene Purdome is an old Truman crony. He and a son of slain mobster Wolf Riman

own an auto-track in Platt County, where they're angling to put
in trotters. After Riman was killed, Sheriff Purdome divorced his
wife and married the gangster's widow.

COUNTY TERRITORY: Route 40, dives open all night. No
law. Johnny Molle owns the old Del Mar Club, usually open with
gambling. El Capitan, tourist court near Highway 66, but off the
main road, is for lovebirds. Mrs. Sollares owns it. Olympic Auto
Track, with stock-car races, belongs to Sicilians; Tommy Simone
manages it during the absence of John Mangansino.

NEARBY: The Playhouse, in Blue Ridge, Missouri, serves
liquor after hours, goes in big for strippers. No rules, no repressions. Mike Manzella runs it. Gambling open in Green Hills,
eight miles from Kansas City.

MADAME: Opal Davis, Montague Hotel.

COMPANY GIRLS: Read the personals in the *Kansas City
Star*. Almost any masseur's ad will do. Or try answering this one-
line ad: "Date?—VI-4799."

GAMBLING: Pennant Pen and Cigar store, where there is
little tobacco. Gold Tooth Maxie operates at Pusateri's New
Yorker. Traveling crap games at the La Salle, Aladdin and the
Robert E. Lee.

CAFE SOCIETY: Jungle Club, run by Bully Rich and Tom
Marcello, where out-of-town thugs hang out, making contacts at
the bar or in a corner of the dark room. Eddie Spitz's Latin
Quarter is one of the better places; Gargotta and Binaggio had
a cut. The Ship's Bar is a rendezvous for interstate robbers. Hula
Hut has the lewdest strippers. The fags hang out at the Jungle
Club. Eddie's Restaurant, pretty good; knocked off by burglars
who stole $65,000 worth of mob money, hidden in the safe; man-
agement couldn't report this to the cops, said only $10,000 was
missing; word went out through the underworld to get the money
back at once. The out-of-towners who had pulled the heist returned it hastily.

PICK-UPS, BETTER CLASS: Pusateri's New Yorker, El Ca-
bana, Philips Hotel and Town Royal. Gus Pusateri's Kansas
Cityan had the cream of the crop, but between our first and second visits it was taken over as a Christian Science reading-room.

PICK-UPS, CHEAP: Vicinity of 12th and Broadway, around
the Hollywood Café and Laurel Buffet. Take customers to cheap
assignation hotels.

PIMPS: Frequent the La Salle Hotel lobby.

SKIDROW: Twelfth Street, Wyandotte to Broadway. Immortalized by the "Twelfth Street Blues." Whores, reefer peddlers and stick-up men, winos, servicemen, farmers rub shoulders at the Gay Nineties, Stardust Lounge, Ball's Bar, Professional Club, Barrel House, Missouri Buffet and the Follies Burlesque.

JUNK: Pushers on 12th between Holmes and Charlotte. Reefers at 18th and Vine and Little Harlem.

AFRO-AMERICANS: Many, powerful, never touched by authorities. Everything runs on Vine, from 12th to 18th. Colored boss is Felix Payne, who turns in 10 per cent of the votes in town.

B. Don't Meet Me in St. Louis

Not that it hasn't a lot of charm. But if you want to do anything or see anyone you've got to talk to Morris Shenker. And he has no charm.

According to Leonard MacBain, the elegant social arbiter of New York's snooty El Morocco, Mrs. Adolphus Busch is St. Louis' richest and most aristocratic. J. G. Taylor Spink, of the *Sporting News,* is its most popular citizen. But Shenker is the boss—undisputed, confirmed in Washington after a battle to a decision. Shenker is unprepossessing, with a Brooklyn accent. He ran his ability to keep gangsters out of jail into the political dictatorship of the nation's eighth largest city. He nominated and elected his man, Tom Hennings, to the U.S. Senate, over the opposition of National Committeeman John Nangle and St. Louis Postmaster Barney Dickman.

Washington recognized the coup by choosing Shenker finance chairman of the Democratic National Committee—while he was appearing as counsel for gamblers quizzed by the Kefauver Committee. We exposed that and he lasted in the post two days. But the fix was in, and, despite much wind-jamming by Kefauver, Tobey and Halley, no harm came to Shenker clients. His touch was so magic, hoodlums from as far away as Rome, New York, retained him to sit at their sides when they were called before the committee. No harm came to them, either. Shenker has covertly promised to support Kefauver for Veep, which is all he's shooting for. His man Hennings is a pink of the Kefauver shade.

The further you get from Jackson County, the less pollution there is in the atmosphere. St. Louis, at the eastern end of the state, is clean on the surface, compared to the President's back yard, though in big money vice and corruption and political steals and highway robbery it is far up near the top, if not leading the parade. That is because Harry gave most of the Missouri handouts to political pals from St. Louis, instead of taking care of his neighbors, whom he detests.

St. Louis has less lowdown vice than Kansas City because East St. Louis, Illinois, is just across the bridge. Anyone looking for fun would be a chump to stay on the Missouri side when he could visit this cesspool across the Mississippi. The dumps there pay St. Louis cab-drivers well to steer customers. Gambling-houses pay $15. Whore-houses cut 20 per cent of the take back to the driver. After-hour saloons come up with a dollar a head. So it is obvious why conventioneers who flag hacks in St. Louis don't stay there long. The natives already know about it. (See Chapter 27A.)

The St. Louis police force is rated pretty high, as such things go. While much runs that is not tolerated even in New York, it is comparatively clean, considering the city's background and surrounding areas. But promotions are for sale—cheap.

The Kefauver Committee wasted a lot of time and money in St. Louis, but turned up nothing the local cops didn't know. Pasquale Miceli, undertaker, the most powerful Sicilian thereabouts, wasn't annoyed. Another important Italian is Lou Marcodia, who tosses a lot of votes and weight around. You can usually find the big boys at Ruggere's restaurant. They like to eat well, so they hang out also at Biggie's, in which Stan Musial is a partner. Other big Italians are Ralph Calico, Frank Natalie, Frank Pisciotta, John Vitale and one Calcitero who holds much stock in the Steelco Drilling Company, an oil-producing firm.

The mob is investing its money in hotels, trucking lines and real estate, keeping far away from street-level action. But the Italian crap-games run out west on Page, in the 5700 block.

Gangsters are active in unions. The brother of the Democratic sheriff is a business agent for a hoodlum union—the Steamfitters. Sheriff Callanan is the top boy. He joined with Shenker, the official mouthpiece, in supporting Hennings. The influence boys now go through Callanan and Shenker or get nothing.

Front page revelations about St. Louis' Democrats are as nothing to the unexposed dirt. Any Federal rap can be squared via pigeon-holing for the statute of limitations.

City Clerk Jimmy McAteer owned a bar on 12th Street, a block from City Hall, which was a hangout for visiting Kansas City hot shots. Fat Fahey has a bar on Locust Street, where they do business with local politicians who sell municipal contracts by the square foot. The Victory Bar on Market, near 16th, is another where high level fixes are made. You can square a murder or buy off your state tax here.

High-class hoods are seen with their high-class broads at the Hotel Kingsway. The Giordano mob frequents the 519 Club and arranges sanctuary for fugitive out-of-state hoods. St. Louis has one of the toughest skidrows anywhere in the nation, around 6th, Olive and Market. Bar-girls and B-girls work every bar.

You can buy reefers and heroin and waiting or walking dames without a seeing-eye dog. Strip-teasers work until the vice squad cracks down, then they call the girls "exotic dancers," and they shake, grind and bump with a few rags on.

B-girls hustled us for drinks at the Silver Queen, the Coconut Grove and the Bucket of Blood. We got out of the State Bar and the Grand Central before they had a chance to tell us the tale.

There's cheap stock burlesque at the Grand Opera House, where girls get $35 a week. Some double days as dressmakers and nights as hookers.

St. Louis has a unique section which Okies and Hoosiers frequent. They pick up broads on Broadway, go to cheap beer-dives where they get loaded on needled brew, then get rolled. The entertainment is hillbilly songs, accompanied by banjoes. There are nightly free-for-alls with knives, fists and feet. The dames join in. The most popular joints are Russo's and U and I Bar. The 1106 Club swarms with dames looking for dates. The cheap Wagner Hotel is upstairs and convenient. There are countless dives on Market Street, near the depot.

St. Louis is the most important point on interstate trucking routes. Hundreds of motorized mastodons lay over every night in huge lots around 6th and Hickory. Most of these giant carriers have sleeping quarters aboard for drivers. Many pick up farm girls or waitresses in hash-houses along the road and bring them to St. Louis for "a good time." In the city they take them to the dives for drinks, spend the night with them in the truck, then strand them, whereupon they join the overpopulated harlot population.

Local lovers go out to such tourist courts as the Catalina, the Autocourt and the Wayside. One of our informers was charged $3.50 an hour, and there was a knock on his door when the time was up.

A lot of call-girls moved into the new Ford Apartments, only a 35-cent cab fare from the downtown hotels.

St. Louis has a large Negro section and an overwhelming Negro problem. Though the state is Southern in tradition and sympathy, colored people vote, which makes them immune to white men's laws. Following the pattern in all Northern cities, they have cut across the main white residential sections, though their wenches still whore for $2 on the waterfront and along Convent Street, nearby, where stand some of the dingiest and most dilapidated Negro cribs we have ever seen.

Many colored cab-drivers carry their wives, daughters or lovers in the front seat. These will go into the back and turn a trick with the passenger, while the hack keeps rolling.

The Treasury is making no attempt to enforce tax laws on colored numbers operators, so they are thriving at Compton and Pine and at the southeast corner of Shanning and West Pine. You can get dope there, too, and on West Bell and at Eastern and Biddle. Junk is peddled in every local hoose-gow.

St. Louis has a high homosexual population. Faggots hang out at Grand and Olive and at Vandeventer and Washington. They meet each other in front of Gus the Fruiter—appropriately enough —and pause for refreshments at the Dixie Hamburger. They have their drags in the basement of an old college fraternity house near Vandeventer and West Pine, where they kneel for the queen. We were solicited by gay boys around Henry's, also Erv's, on Pine, and saw swishing at Uncle John's and the Entre Nous.

On summer nights, the excursion boat Admiral is popular for meeting girls, boys, and in-betweens.

If you were wondering how a nice girl can work her way through the University of Missouri, many earn their spending money by going on call, especially when the legislature meets in Jefferson City, forty miles away. A bellhop in the Missouri Hotel is the contact, through a student leader on the campus.

21. DEAR ALBEN'S
OLD KENTUCKY HOME

IF THERE is one state enshrined in our national lore, genuine and mythical, this is the one. Its thoroughbreds, its beautiful women, its bourbon mint juleps, its devoted darkies, its Virginia stock, its brave and bloody conquest, have all mingled in the sublime and stirring legends of our land. Our hearts bounded as we crossed from weedy, plebeian Indiana into this realm of poesy and history.

We had been there before, but scarcely wandered beyond the hotel and Churchill Downs. Now we were Confidential commissioners, dedicated to a diagnosis of Kentucky, not as its laureates sang of it, but as the stethoscope, the thermometer and the cardiograph would write its chart as of 1952, long after the iridescent days of its grandeur and its glorification.

We found the femme pulchritude above average. Racing wasn't in season. The first barkeep we asked for juleps snapped at us to stop kidding, what did we want to drink? The Negroes were not singing—they were shooting craps. The people spoke with stronger Dixie intonations than we had heard further south, but otherwise they dressed and acted like so many inhabitants of Pittsburgh.

We found the principal industry was neither whiskey, horse-breeding, tobacco nor cotton. It is politics. Democratic politics mainly, and that the private, personal domain of Alben W. Barkley, Vice-President of the United States, who owns the party there in fee simple.

This alone would make Barkley a weighty boss. But he also controls the patronage pickings of the U.S. Senate, of which he is president, working through Les Biffle, Secretary of the Senate.

In our *Washington Confidential* we said that Barkley is a distant in-law of Frank Erickson, jailed as Gotham's principal handbook operator. A man is not responsible for his relations, but we said Barkley and Erickson were on close and intimate calling terms and Erickson's grandchildren called the Veep "Daddy Long Legs." "Daddy Long Legs" is a well-known code in Kentucky, used to conceal the Veep's name.

The man next in mortal succession to the highest office in the world increased his large land holdings in Paducah shortly before the Senate voted $800,000,000 for an atomic energy plant there.

Political morality in Kentucky mirrors that in Washington. Barkley's son, David, had a $10,000-a-year do-nothing job with the notorious Garsson Brothers, in a Danville, Illinois, munitions plant, while his father was the majority leader of the Senate.

Barkley named the five members of the Kefauver Committee. It was the only time in history that the Vice-President, instead of the minority leader, chose the minority members. Though Kentucky is one of the most notorious criminally controlled states in the Union, the committee laid off Kentucky until after Estes and Rudy quit to cash in elsewhere. Cincinnati newspapers shrieked about conditions in nearby Kentucky, so Chairman O'Conor and Counsel Downey Rice held two days' perfunctory hearings. Not one suspected law-breaker or gambling casino operator appeared before the committee. The only witnesses heard were local office-holders, such as mayors, judges, prosecutors and police chiefs, all of whom were permitted to read statements into the record, wherein they alibied themselves and minimized the extent of the flimflam. No effort was made to show a tie-up between Kentucky gamblers and big Democrats in the Vice-President's home state.

This is a boodle state from top to bottom. Kentucky colonelcies are for sale to anyone who will buy a $100 ticket to a Democratic campaign-fund dinner. State income tax can be evaded for a fee through a fixer.

The big influence and friend of Barkley is W. S. Heidenberg, attorney. The Democrats in Louisville are Johnny Crimmins and Miss Lennie McLaughlin, now fat and forty, rumored to have been once strikingly beautiful, with a whispered glamorous past. Republicans are tied up with the Democrats and split the patronage. Occasional Republican state victories—there have been three or four since 1790—are arranged when it appears citizens can no longer stomach the stench.

U.S. Senator Earle Clements is the active Louisville boss. Governor Lawrence Wetherby, recently re-elected, is his stand-in. Fat and chubby Doc Beauchamp (pronounced Beecham) is the undercover boy who pulls the state switches. He wears a five-gallon hat. Wetherby says crime is for local enforcement, not his concern.

Louisville has a left-wing Mayor, Charles Peasley Farnsley, who wears a black string tie. He was a blender of bourbon and tried to patent the trade name "Damned Yankee," but was turned down for bad taste—not in the bourbon. So he labeled his products "Rebel Yell" and "Copperhead."

Another important Louisville Democracy power is State Senator C. W. A. McCann. He is in the soap business and sells it to the jails.

Under the set-up of the professional Southerner, "goodwill" Mayor and the Sheriff, who runs the county cops, everything in and outside Louisville spins.

The city has a monopoly newspaper ownership, a Fair Deal Democratic organ with a fighting past, which now apologizes for Truman, Acheson, Hiss, *et al.* Its view is so rarefied, it seldom sees what goes on at home. Radio station WAVE does the local big-time crusading. Three members of its newsroom, Les Gaddie, James Caldwell and George Morrison, are active, courageous and wise.

A sworn list of gambling joints was recently presented to former Commonwealth Attorney Frank Popke. With a great flourish, he announced a clean-up. He called the photographers and raided two on the list; those two and all the others were still running when we went through town.

Some of the joints on the affidavit are appended:

New York Bar (upstairs, second floor), Broadway and Armory Place. McCowan, owner of building and business. Cripple. Hustler. Greedy.

White Horse Cafe, Center and Broadway. John Acy runs the book. He is former newspaper salesman.

Famous Cafe, Broadway between 4th and 5th. Hyman Morguelan. Enter front or back.

Whiskey store at 608 S. 5th, formerly at Colonial Hotel until owner Eli Brown made it move.

Post Cafe, 400 block S. 5th. Bets taken at counter or walk into rear.

Hollywood Barber Shop, 200 block east Jefferson. Book in rear.

Bosco's Barber Shop, 2nd between Jefferson and Market. Book in rear run by Joe Polio.

C. L. Nolan's, 528 Jefferson, near 5th. Poker in rear, book upstairs, reach from outside. Mostly owned by James Humphries, close friend of A. J. Bartholomew. Humphries is silent partner of Nolan.

We were in a bookie joint at 530 Jefferson Street, directly across from the Mayor's window. Fletcher's, across the street from police headquarters, makes it easy for flatfoots to place their bets.

After the Federal tax law went into effect the curtains were drawn at some of these joints. Many are beginning to reopen.

We rolled dice for money at the Trianon and Arch Club. We saw judges and lawyers doing same at the Bridle Bit.

Almost every store has a one-ball pin game, or a race-horse machine which pays off.

The local liquor licensee arrangement is a prize-winner. It seems nothing can be done against operators unless they have five raps against them in any one calendar year, then the authorities can get an injunction to close the building. So all licensees are careful to limit their arrests to no more than four in one year. The Kentucky Tavern was selling to kids until they had too many complaints. Now the youngsters go to the Air Devils. The Nu-Mill, in the county, sells liquor after hours.

The expensive dames hang out at Gordon's, Baron's and the

Silver Mirror, as well as the Seelbach Hotel bar. Hot shots dine their expensive kepties at Lavisi's. Two bars near the University of Louisville sell after hours.

Five-dollar streetwalkers parade Jefferson, Market and Main. The skidrow is under the bridge and at the 7th Street station.

Queers hang out at Gordon's and Penguins Club, and at the Farthest West, on Main Street, in Jeffersonville, on the Indiana side, where we saw violet bartenders mixing drinks.

Louisville's large Negro population always votes "white," ringmastered by Ollie "The Goat" Ware, Mark Anthony and Titus Erwin, an investigator for the liquor board. Colored joints on Walnut are never bothered.

Nowhere has Federally-fed relief been milked as it has been in this once haughty and self-sufficient state. Negroes not only ran for it, they were dragged into it. Former Congressman May (who did a stretch in the stir, but not for this) had jammed more people in his home town onto the dole rolls than its entire population— men, women, children, white and otherwise. As a government inquiry loomed, his adherents burned down the courthouse, reducing the records to ashes. That is the classic, to date, of political grand larceny through relief padding for political purposes.

As for Cincinnati's Kentucky suburbs:

Shortly after the Senate Crime Committee held its abortive hearings, Governor Wetherby, running for re-election, advertised a raid a few days before the primaries. He sent forty-one state troopers to close up the Latin Quarter, in Covington, with proper publicity. The world was advised that the lid was on in Covington and Newport. We went through a few weeks later, while Kentucky officials were still insisting the area was locked up. This is what we discovered:

In this pre-election raid, only independent joints were sloughed. Syndicate operations were bypassed. Dives owned by the Cleveland mob have a line into the Democratic Party. They contribute when Barkley needs campaign cash.

We discovered that, in Newport and Covington, "closed" means only the door is closed. Anyone can enter. When they aren't "closed," you see slot-machines and gaming tables from the street. Now the machines have been taken out of the foyers and whirl in the casinos.

Since the independents were put out of business, mob-owned places no longer have to offer inducements to get business. Now they give only single odds with a limit down to $200. Previously, to attract good customers, they had to make special rules, with the always possible danger that a lucky run of the dice might clean out the house.

Newport and adjoining Covington are part of the Cincinnati metropolitan area, though in different Kentucky counties, making it easier to shift operations back and forth when there are local situations.

Pcte Schmidt built the beautiful Beverly Hills, but was forced out by the mob, which plays expensive floorshows imported from New York. The same boys run the Lookout. All Kentucky shows are booked by Frank Sennes, of Cleveland, who also books the Desert Inn, Las Vegas.

Pete Schmidt then built Glen's Rendezvous, but the Italian boys ran him out of that, too. It is now a mob hangout, sells booze until 8 A.M., and has slot-machines in the back rooms. A hotel, in connection, has girls.

Schmidt's son Glen tried for the third time, with a $650,000 room. But, as they are independents, he can run only on the sneak, occasionally.

The Hide-Ho, in Newport, is a bust-out joint, with whores and gambling. The Club Alexandria deals late and has blackjack. The 627 Club, in Covington, and the Yorkshire, in Newport, have action when there is business. The Turf Club, in Covington, is owned by Leonard J. Conner, sergeant at arms of the Kentucky Senate.

The Kentucky sides of the bridges from Cincinnati are lined with mediums and palmists, who get a good play from superstitious gamblers looking for numbers.

The Jefferson County area outside Louisville is as wide open. Colonel James Scully of the Commonwealth Attorney's office, ex-state policeman who couldn't get back in that small but high-calibre outfit, a political misfit, does as he is told. Gambling flourishes under either party.

Handbooks and card games, sometimes dice games, can be found in clubs along Seventh Street Road. Among them are the Arch Club and the Old Colony. The Mansion was the toughest. Had a shooting there a couple of months ago and later beat up a county cop for trying to close it after hours. Other county joints are the crummy Probus Tavern, the Copacabana, where a couple of professionals shot it out last year (personal grudge), and the Oasis.

Everything opens up during Derby Week to clip the touristas;

you trip over the tables as you walk in through the front door. The operators expostulate you can't buy talent like Benny Fields and Beatrice Kaye by selling sandwiches, even at four bucks apiece. The cops and the sheriff never find gambling, despite numerous "investigations" during the big week.

Sheriff Bernie Bax does as he pleases, including putting his family on the payroll. His boys don't win many elections, but they swing enough Democratic votes so the organization can't risk wrist-slapping. The local papers charged that two deputy sheriffs are ex-cons, but when they delved into police files to prove it they found the records had mysteriously disappeared. They raised such a row that they were as mysteriously returned. The men are ex-cons. They are also still deputy sheriffs.

Henderson County, on the Ohio River in western Kentucky, about two hundred miles downriver, has long been wide open, which is not denied in official circles. The Henderson Ministerial Association·has made sporadic efforts to curb violations. But indictments, when any, have been few and ineffective. Many county nightspots lie along U.S. 41, between Henderson and Evansville, in what is known as "The Strip." This includes a neck of land near the Kentucky-Indiana state line, north of the river. Officers of both states leave it alone. Big clubs along The Strip usually have dozens of slots, also big dice tables, roulette, blackjack, chuck-a-luck and beat-the-dealer. Biggest are the Trocadero, the Dells, Riverview Gardens, Commando, Kentucky Tavern and Midway Club.

There just is no public official to whom the honest citizen who would protest against crime or political corruption can go.

Radio station WAVE was tipped off to a big-time cock fight scheduled to be held outside Henderson city limits last Dec. 22 in the barn of "Hooter" Crawford, sponsored by Clarence Wood of the local Trocadero and Henry Sales of Evansville. The station's newsroom staff laid it on the door of Governor Wetherby, who turned it over to the state police chief.

Search warrants were signed secretly without previous warning to the magistrate, but the Commonwealth Attorney insisted on notifying the County Attorney. When the convoy of raiders arrived at the appointed spot they were in time to see the last two trucks being loaded hastily with birds, feed and equipment.

Louisville is lovely, with gracious old buildings and wide avenues lined by beautiful shade trees. Third Street is ancient and aristocratic. Downtown is not bustling, except when the Derby brings in sheep for the shearing. Kentuckians walk slowly, live leisurely, do not overwork.

The jail is on Liberty Street and there's a bookmaker around the corner. For prisoners who can pay they send out for steak dinners or dames. Everyone is affable and easygoing. The ante-bellum families still comport themselves like feudal lords. They are proud of everything about Kentucky except that Abe Lincoln was born there.

22. KEFAUVER CON CONFIDENTIAL

NOT SINCE Andrew Jackson has a national hero arisen from the blood-soaked soil of Tennessee. And then, in the last week of February, 1950, came one a-riding not on a horse, but on a hoax. It was the junior Senator and now the self-summoned Presidential candidate, Hon. Estes Kefauver, the television champ from Chattanooga. Few people knew Kefauver from Hickenlooper. He had campaigned among the hillbillies in a coonskin cap and had won a few paragraphs as a supposed boss-buster who had "defied" Ed Crump of Memphis. He settled down to voting as a New Deal hack, living convivially, unburdened with heavy committees as all freshmen are, dribbling out crumbs of patronage and generating no lightning. Then lightning found him.

The night was clear and there was no forecast of any electrical flash from on high. The Senator was in repose, in his bed, ready to read himself to sleep. He picked up a book. It was *Chicago Confidential*. Instead of barbiturate, it was an eye-opener. Here was a detailed exposure of crime, vice and political debauchery, not only in Chicago, which is the capital of the world to Tennesseeans, but laying forth the brutal facts of the national Syndicate with its heart in New York and its sticky tentacles grasping and gripping almost the entire nation. Here was the quick big chance.

We were in the capital doing the groundwork for *Washington Confidential*. He sought us out. He asked dumb questions and we gave him wise answers—yes, it was all true and enough left over for more volumes.

By a custom, a member of Congress who successfully enters a resolution for a special committee is appointed its chairman. Such a unit to investigate crime is something few legislators would dare to oppose. The sensational Kefauver Committee came into being.

We were not exultant. We write as reporters, not as informers or reformers. Of course if anyone wants to follow up what we publish, that is his affair from then on. We had numerous confabs with the new chairman of the new committee. We parted cordially. But in *Washington Confidential,* published one week before the Kefauver circus hit the big town and the big video, two months after our last page was locked up, we had written:

"The plan, as this went to press, was to save all the fireworks for a final blowout in New York at which the glamour pusses of the underworld, such as Virginia Hill, dubbed by us 'Mafia Rose' would be called for the publicity value. Virginia was served with much ballyhoo in September, but was saved six months to 'hypo' the last act. Frank Costello was also slated to be called if he 'cared to talk.' "

Many thought we had hit a winner with a long-shot guess. It was a little more scientific than that. We knew Kefauver. We knew Rudy Halley. And we knew show business.

Estes followed our script to the letter. The great American medicine show unfolded just as we had said it would. And look what it did for him!

The sight of busty Virginia, scowling Costello with his hands, a good trick, and a sweating United States ambassador writhing on the witness stand was sensational theatrical hokum. As any showman knew it must, it distracted the eyes of the audience from the lack of plot; the customers in the $2 seats remembered only the high spots and forgot that the committee had disclosed nothing not already known; that it had initiated no curative legislation; had not successfully questioned one of the ruling clique of the Mafia; had conducted no investigations in the states or surrounding areas of the five Senators; had not gone into the serious crimes or the infiltration of legitimate business by hoodlums; and had not either by question, accusation or statement so much as inferred that organized vice was tied up with the Democratic National Committee or the Democratic Department of Justice.

The startling disclosures of corruption in high office now flashing across the front pages are being made by other committees. The goods was there in *Washington Confidential,* but Estes got out when he thought the getting was good—which was before he had to step on tender toes. He became a sort of Messiah. Gals swooned over his handsome profile. He was soon the highest-paid lecturer on the American coffee-and-roquefort circuit. He did a movie and got radio dates, wrote articles and books and was cut in on profits of a film about processes which were public property.

Though the committee's work was far from done, Estes knew he couldn't top his New York premiere. Like a canny showman, he bowed out before the audience tired of the turn. Dull and plodding Senator Herbert O'Conor, sadly in need of a boost for a Maryland election he then intended to risk, inherited the mantle.

With stars in his eyes, Estes no longer was interested in the stodgy task of being a Senator. Literature called to him. Even before his committee had issued its report, he overflowed into print in a *Saturday Evening Post* series, for which he and his ghost-writer, Sid Shallet of the *New York Times,* split fifty grand. The services of government employes, government expenses, transportation, hotel and incidental vouchers for himself and staff that he had approved all had gone into collecting and writing material for private pay.

Kefauver, a grandson of a Baptist dominie, has a flexible Tennessee conscience. He was not embarrassed by the use of confidential and nonprivileged testimony from the committee's files for his own articles, denied to newspaper and radio people who earn their livings getting and writing copy. When reporters for the *Chicago Sun-Times* and the *Indianapolis Star* secured and published confidential transcripts, Kefauver threatened them with contempt for that which he himself not only did but overdid.

With an eye for dramatic effects, Estes' ghost-writer told the *Post's* readers that Kefauver had been approached with a bribe offer to lay off a certain prospective witness. Federal statutes make it a felony for a member of either house of Congress to fail to report immediately a bribe bid to the United States Attorney. Estes has refused to name the alleged corruptionist. We say there was no such offer made. Kefauver and his ghost invented it for the publicity value. If Kefauver denies this we demand he publish the names of the parties involved, as the law requires.

Kefauver and his alter ego wrote the book, *Crime in America.* It was a dud, though the government printing office sent out circulars plugging it. Kefauver had spent $265,000 of the taxpayers' money to help him prepare these literary cribbings. While he was writing the *Post* series, one hundred and one persons were employed by the committee, including stenographers (who had to be pretty), out-of-work Democrats and deserving relatives of Rudy Halley. Over his personal signature he approved, among others, the following disbursals from the Treasury for expenses for four months for gathering information and material which found its way into his article and the $3.50 book, before it was released free to the Senate, press and public:

Expense account (no itemization appeared in the Congressional Record): $18,703.78; Transportation, $9,965.79; Telephone and Telegraph, $4,665.96. (Note: Many of Kefauver's personal wires were sent at government expense. We have a few.) Miscellaneous, including newspapers, $3,442.93. (Kefauver subscribed to a press clipping service for his notices.)

Despite all this, his gumshoes couldn't afford to give Tennessee a glance. Without subpoena power and with little time there we found plenty. We won't keep it confidential or charge it on a swindle-sheet.

Kefauver represented the third Tennessee district in Congress from 1938 until 1948. Polk County, included in this district, was controlled by ex-Sheriff Burch Biggs, whose political machine was vulturine with venality. Kefauver was a dear friend of Biggs. He was elected and re-elected every time with Biggs's support. This is an illustration of how valuable that was in the 1940 primaries. Kefauver got 3,323 votes in Polk County while his two opponents got only 30 votes between them. In 1946 his opponent did better. He got 40 votes. But Kefauver got 3,444. Figure all that out.

Kefauver's circle of friends was peculiar. Had he been on the witness stand instead of Ambassador O'Dwyer, he might have found it difficult to explain how he had been a close friend and yachting companion of Herbert Brody for twenty-five years without knowing Brody was king of the lottery in Knoxville. Brody's wife made a considerable contribution to Kefauver's 1948 senatorial campaign. (No righteousness, Senator Tobey?)

A shrewd interrogator might have made political capital, as Kefauver did in a similar circumstance, of the fact his sworn statement of campaign expenses in 1948 shows expenditures of $17,498.96, whereas Section 2,269 of the Tennesse Code makes it a crime to spend more than $10,000 in a campaign for U.S. Senator. Actually, hundreds of thousands were spent for him, circuitously.

Kefauver first came to the public eye when Silliman Evans, fat, pompous, and egotistical publisher of the *Nashville Tennesseean,* a New Deal errand-boy who pulled the paper out of the deep red with government dough, plugged Estes as the logical choice to contest the senatorship against the candidate of Boss Crump, of Memphis. Tennessee, long an impoverished border state with sub-standard incomes and living conditions, now had

chicken in every pot and two cars on every Tobacco Road. The
Tennesse Valley Authority, which was industrializing the state,
was bringing in Northerners, including dregs from the big cities.
It had set up a large group of parasites living on the government
payroll or on government handouts, and construction workers
who were paid premium union wages at U.S. expense. They could
be expected to vote socialistic and New Deal; and that was
Kefauver.

Then came the atomic energy plant at Oak Ridge, near Knoxville. The state spiraled into a new and dizzy boom. Oak Ridge
brought highly-paid skilled workers. They were followed by out-
of-state sharks, gamblers and prostitutes. The pickings were too
good to leave to the aging boss of Memphis. The 1948 campaign
was merely a falling out between allies over the inflated spoils.
Washington sent out the word and the cash flowed for Kefauver.
To his cheering section he is the champ who kayoed wicked Boss
Crump. Not so. Crump is still monarch of all he surveys in
Memphis. Crump and the Kefauver factions have made a secret
peace and are now fighting side by side to keep it all in the family.

To complete the record of the Senate Crime Investigating Committee, which apparently did not have the facilities to do so, we
append herewith a confidential report of a flying trip to Kefauver's
home town, Chattanooga.

A. Chattanooga—Uncle Estes' Cabin

This is the home town of Senator Ester Kefauver, the Hercules
who set forth to clean up all the dark and smelly American stables
and wound up with a shovelful of what is usually found in stables.

We knew, of course, that his place of origin would be pure and
sweet.

The hell it was!

And Estes, who didn't "probe" here, doesn't have to, for as late
as last fall—months after the demise of his crime committee—big-
time gambling was running openly in the ritzy Lookout Mountain Hotel in Chattanooga, which Estes frequently visited. He was
to have been given an award for something there a couple of
months ago, but the ceremony had to be shifted at the last moment because Feds put a lien on all the gambling equipment. It is
now closed for the season.

We would like to give you a snapshot of the city where Estes
Hercules still practices law. It was a pokey Southern town, off the
beaten track, hard to get to, and few came except nearby Tennes-

seeans, Georgians and Alabamans, for whom it was a jobbing and merchandizing center. It had a local aristocracy of snobs who wore shoes. The rest were poor whites and Negroes. Class and racial distinctions were sharp. Kefauver, of the snooty stratum, was educated at Yale and married the daughter of a Scottish peer.

The matriarch was the *Chattanooga Times,* which gave Adolph Ochs to New York. It is now run by heirs and their husbands. The *Times* is as stuffy and stodgy as the giant metropolitan *Times.* Like it, it does not think any news of evil is fit to print. Until the recent great engulfment, the Chattanooga paper was conservative Democratic. Now, like the New York fountainhead, it leans more and more to New Deal nostrums, chuckleheaded coddling of minorities and home-reliefers. Its columns are so consistently overburdened with that type of hearts-and-handouts, it can find no space for the things we are going to tell you.

The same whims of geography and the lines of communications which set the city up as a trading center for an isolated three-state area made it the crime and gambling headquarters for that area. Betting layoffs from the huge government plant at Oak Ridge are made in Chattanooga. That is why this is more than a local situation.

At the top of the political heap is aged Will Cummings, now in his eighties, a former judge who still knows how to pull a political wire if need be. But the most active political boss is the former criminal lawyer, Judge Raulston Schoolfield, official Democratic wheel, an intimate of Kefauver, whom he supported for the Senate.

Next in the political hierarchy comes County Judge Wilkes Thrasher. Parallel to him in influence is labor boss Stanton Smith, also a Kefauver crony. Unions are immensely powerful in this part of the South, with pressure from the government, which requires contractors to employ organized labor, which has Chattanooga hogtied. Without Smith's okay you can't run a peanut stand.

Another power is Maurice Weaver, an attorney who often represents the more important bad boys when they get in trouble.

On the operating end, Chattanooga is run by Police Chief Ed Ricketts, so powerful he overrules the police commission and the mayor. He has the Negro vote in his pocket. He was once indicted on charges involving the disappearance of confiscated whiskey, but was acquitted on a directed verdict.

The police department is crooked almost all the way along. A city commissioner recently and openly admitted he paid off political debts by appointing cops. A noted gambler brags that the chief was his appointee. A high police official, a power in Darktown, owns and operates several colored whore-houses. Some cops have such sticky hands, the upper echelons couldn't trust the captains, who were diverting too much of the take into their own pockets and not passing enough of it upstairs. So now the payoffs are made directly above the captains.

During 1951, while Kefauver was castigating the rest of the nation for its lawlessness, his home town had twice as many homicides as there were in 1950—sixteen in the first six months—which, if projected, would be the equivalent of eight hundred murders a year in Chicago—which leads the nation with less than three hundred—or sixteen hundred in New York, which has fewer per capita than Chicago.

All other major crime, such as robbery, burglary and assault, increased in kind, much higher in percentage than that for the nation as a whole.

Murder means little. No important person is ever convicted. Juries are packed. Even defendants without any fix usually get no more than three years, and that's called "the book."

An important judge imported a hired killer to murder Fred Gill, the gambler. No one went to jail. Gill's son, Fred "Rock" Gill, is now operating. He got his nickname because he's so tough.

We hadn't been in Chattanooga more than an hour before we discovered gambling was running. The only time they ever close it is before an election. We saw gamblers at 15 East 9th, in back of a store. We saw gamblers at Stubby's on 4th, noted for its wine and women. We saw them over Bennett's place, on Main Street. We saw gamblers taking bets in back of Bill's Place, a barbershop on West 9th Street. We saw others in the rear of 104 East 6th. The front store is a blind with nothing in the window. Gamblers hang out in the beer joint next door where a man was killed. You can pick up girls there and take them upstairs a couple of doors away, near the jail and courthouse.

W. Ed Alley has been arrested several times, but never convicted, as a policy operator. He once shot at and pistol-whipped a man. He is a nephew of Divorce Judge W. R. Miller, with some kind of a case record east of Reno. Chattanooga is the divorce mill for the adjoining Georgia counties, and, in a neat switch, Rossville, which adjoins, is the Gretna Green for marrying Tennesseeans in the region where Daniel Boone carried his shotgun.

They call numbers and policy "stock" here, because the payoff digits are a combination of New York Stock Exchange sales. Big winners are often slugged if they won't stand for being chiseled.

Nolan Dunn is an important spoke in the policy wheel. And why not?

C. L. Renner is another gambling figure. He associates with Neil McClary and Jeff Hope.

Kefauver's friend who ran the gambling at Lookout Mountain came to Chattanooga from Miami. His name is S. J. Littlegreen.

Lester Deitch, who operates from the Green Derby, lives in a mansion like the ones in the old plantation movies.

South Side gambling is controlled by Leonard Lane, whose newsstand is frequently raided, but stays open. Lane's wife, Alma, manages the State Hotel. Most of the big gamblers have rooms at the St. George Hotel.

At this writing, slot-machines were confined to union halls, VFW and Legion posts and Elks, Moose and Eagles lodges, which also sold mixed drinks, and the ultra Mountain City Club. Littlegreen had the slot-machine monopoly before he got in trouble with the government.

Most striking to the visitor is the number of pin-ball machines, most of which pay off in cash. They are illegal in New York and Los Angeles, even for merchandise. Some locations, like five-by-ten stationery and cigar stores, will have as many as eight machines, though they can't keep more than one busy. The contraptions are owned by a syndicate, tied up with the cops and political interests. Unless you take what they assign you, blue-coats will dig up a violation on your premise. One joint, called Jack's Place, at 300 West Main Street, has scores. It is a small, cheap bar, employing six B-girls who shill for the machines. They bum change from customers to play the pin-balls and juke-boxes, for which they are paid $10 a week and all they can steal, and hustle after work. Jack's runs a standing "For Sale" ad. When chumps come down from the hills with dad's bankroll to buy it, the loreleis go to work on them.

Pin-ball bosses are Joe Bunch, Frank Stile and Clyde Hughes, all three of whom allied themselves into a labor union, with an AFL charter, and made the distribution a closed-shop union activity protected by law. They recently gave up their AFL charter and now have their own union, with thirty-five members. Wayne Richey, a brother of Sheriff Rex Richey, is a member. The machines come from Chicago, which also supplies financing and strong-arm men. The only independent operator we could learn about was Gene Chambers, who may still be alive when this book reaches print.

Kefauver's friend, Police Chief Ed Ricketts, was quoted as saying, "There is no organized gambling inside the city limits of Chattanooga," on the day we observed the action noted above.

The Tennessee liquor law provides that hooch must be bought in stores, open until 11 P.M., whereas taverns, open until 1 A.M. may sell only beer. So the state is full of speakeasies, blind pigs and moonshiners. The organized underworld, which Kefauver was to obliterate, has taken $100,000,000 in profits on untaxed liquor out of Estes' state, under the eyes of the Treasury's ATU.

Block for block, Chattanooga is as low and scummy as any town in the country.

Beer taverns like Pack's, Sportland and the Silver Dollar, all on West 9th, are patronized by the dirtiest of broads, bums and bookmakers.

South Market is a skidrow that turns the stomach of hardened skidrow experts like your reporters. Whores and pimps work the bar of the Plaza Cafe, not to be confused with the Plaza Hotel. A bawdy house operates next door to the Sterling Sales Company. Girls are easy at Jim's Cafe, and you take them to rooms at 1217½ South Market. The sign known to locals is a Negro sitting in front, who hustles business like a puller-inner for a ghetto second-hand clothing store. The Dixie Hotel on S. Market is much favored.

Madame Ma Roddy and her daughter are noted citizens of West 17th Street. At 940 Douglas Street white men are accommodated with wenches. There's a good old-fashioned red light in the window. Whites can get colored girls and whiskey at Christine's, on West 10th.

One of the best-known bagnios has been running for years at 303 West 16th, in two adjoining buildings. You choose your date in one and take her through the passage to the other—$5 and up. How come we found this out the first night without subpoenas, TV or an appropriation?

The best house in town is on West 9th, near the hospital.

Traveling salesmen, visiting politicians and national magazine writers who come down to interview Kefauver are taken care of by colored porters and bellboys at the Patten Hotel, most of whom have several white "connections" whom they send to the rooms.

The surrounding area is like the city, from ritzy Lookout

Mountain, an independent suburb, to the Lee Highway. Society kids who live on Lookout Mountain are tough brats. Many destroy property, belong to sex-clubs and smoke reefers.

Girls hang out in honkytonks on the Lee Highway and Ringold Road, and at the Wagon Wheel, Cascades and Butterfly. After you make a pickup, you take them to a motel on U.S. 41. Such tourist courts as Paul's, the Knotty Pines and the Okey-Doke charge $5 for a couple of hours.

If an honest census were taken it would show more Negroes in Chattanooga than whites. The local chapter of the NAACP is one of the most obnoxiously vociferous in the country. The *Chattanooga Times* staunchly sticks up for the rights of Negroes to "fully express themselves," which means they are not supposed to be subject to the laws that govern whites.

There are so many gamblers, most colored, that fifty-five took out Federal tax stamps during the first month—seven times as many as the grand total for New York City. There were 247 in Estes' state. New York State had less than twenty. Even after their names were published the coppers did not bother them too much.

The Negroes vote—always in a bloc, always right—which means for Kefauver and the ballot-box-stuffing machine. So the authorities give them anything they want. They take their orders from Bill Grossman, a white man, and from Walter Robinson, the West Side Negro boss. Both represent Judge Schoolfield. Governor Fuller Warren of Florida charged Grossman was helped in an income tax case by Kefauver. He also said Grossman sells dope.

White streetwalkers are arrested on sight, because they compete with houses, taverns and hotels that contribute, but ambulating Elizas have rarely been known to be picked up. East 9th Street is hot Harlem, with dice-games in back rooms, all-night bars, dope, anything. The favorite card game is called "skin," something like poker. Negro sections are spreading all over town. There's a huge one on West 9th, almost in the center of the business district. Douglas and 9th is very tough. Muggers attack the colored and whites alike, drag them into alleys and leave the bodies after they've stripped them naked. Bootleggers openly work on Flynn Street. There's a house on the corner of West 3rd and Pine, run by Negroes, which sells whiskey at all hours to whites, and will deliver to your home.

Chattanooga seems to have more colored homosexuals than white ones. The few Caucasian fairies are forced to cross racial lines and go for colored fags. There's a little house on Douglas near 9th where the intermediates intermingle. Colored pansies swish all over town, one indication of what happens when living gets too easy. When men no longer fight for existence, but live luxuriously on handouts, as women always have done, they lose their manliness and become "females." In reverse, the same phenomenon is masculinizing the new generation of "independent" working women. The lily-whites swish at 7th and Market.

On that note we say au revoir to beautiful, moral, charming Chattanooga, the home of our new national hero, Hercules Kefauver.

B. Memphis—Cramped by Crump

About the last of the old-line political monopolists is aged Ed Crump, who at one time could swing Tennessee, packed more pull in Arkansas and Louisiana than Huey Long, and still rules Memphis, which was the wildest point between Chicago and New Orleans.

But in his dotage the boss got religion. We were astonished. We hadn't been in Memphis in years. We had heard everything ran and everybody paid off.

The most elementary sources of information in a strange town are taxi-drivers and bellboys. They can take you or steer you and you can verify most of what they tell you.

The bellhops were cautious, but when they saw Yankee currency they said they could get us a quart or two after closing hours, and, since we had a suite, they could quietly sneak in some dames at rather steep prices. We asked whether we couldn't go out and find some ourselves. They shook their heads; it could be arranged only by telephone and there wasn't much of it.

We went out and hailed a cabbie. We stopped him on a dark side street, offered a tempting bill and told him we were traveling men from New York out for a high time, so what was doing?

"Nothing," he groaned. "You can go to church, to the movies or to bed." Good, honest profanity sounds great with a Dixie dialect, and he let loose with some. "Before the war," he added, "a man could make an honest living steering to houses and games. Why, I made so much on the side, I often forgot to pick up my pay check. Now I'm starving."

When hackmen don't know what's running, nothing is.

Independent research convinced us Memphis hackies were right. The town is shuttered tight. They locked the doors and threw the key into the Mississippi. It's been that way for years, since Crump went pious after the deaths of his mother and son.

Memphis is a one-man benevolent dictatorship, like Jersey City was under Boss Hague. The boys swiped everything but the sidewalks, but Hague was personally a puritan.

When Crump says no go, it doesn't.

Booster signs proclaim:

"Memphis is the cleanest city in the world."

"Memphis is the safest city in the world."

"Memphis is the quietest city in the world."

And believe us, it is—especially the last. The streets are deserted before midnight. The place is so holy, they call the vice detail the Police Purity Squad. Kefauver fought Crump, whose town is so clean the sports go to Estes'burg for action.

Memphis is long on tradition, but its purple passages are completely of the past. Once people wrote songs about Beale Street. It's still the black belt playground, but not for white men.

Crump didn't grow up a bluenose. For years he let everything roar and got rich on the proceeds. He likes to take a drink or bet on a horse or roll the cubes, but he goes to Hot Springs for such relaxations.

In the lurid past, traveling men arranged their itineraries so they could spend their weekends in Memphis. Now they duck it like Philadelphia. The citizens think this is carrying things to extremes, but Crump is adamant. There's no gambling and few bookies, and about the only pastime for the workingman is poker in private clubs, where the fee is a buck a month and they kitty out for sandwiches and beer.

Taverns are allowed to sell beer, and that's all they sell. You may buy liquor in bottle stores and carry it with you, but you can't get a set-up after hours, even if you wanted to stay up that late. In Crump Stadium they pinch you if you carry a bottle, though that is legal under state law.

Unescorted dames are not permitted at bars. From time to time the coppers make wholesale arrests. Lonesome GIs have to play shuffleboard or pingpong at servicemen's centers or sit around beer taverns where there are no women—not even B-girls—and get drunk on brew. But not even Crump can veto nature's laws, so they make contact, furtively, with cautious streetwalkers who hang around the bus terminals and on Linden and Vance Streets, and take them to cheap hotels and motels.

The voters let Crump get away with this because he gives them so much in the way of parks and public improvements. They love him, though they know no one gets a building contract unless the insurance is written by an approved firm. By coincidence, Crump is in the insurance and building business.

For those who fear they'll explode there's a safety valve. That's wide open West Memphis, right across the river in Arkansas, where Fair Deal Governor McMath knows gamblers and saloon-keepers always vote Democratic.

In West Memphis they sell liquor on Sunday. You can always place a bet there. Those who want dirty burlesque go to the Joy Theatre. Nearby Forest City caters to spenders with luxury gambling spots like the Black Fish Club, temporarily closed during our sojourn. But even in West Memphis there's a limit. McMath turned thumbs down on a race-track there. It might interfere with the handle in gangster-dominated Hot Springs.

When we said Memphis is sapolioed till it shines, we meant white Memphis. Special handling for colored voters requires that Beale Street be permitted to sell liquor and broads—both hard—dope and gambling.

The artificial moral atmosphere imposed by Crump's fiat is not all to the good. When people can't drink or flirt or gamble outside, they do it in homes. And they set horrible examples for their kids. The town has had some of the worst school scandals in the country. Many more are about to break, involving students who have jumped sexual traces as well as gone on dope. One non-virgin club was broken at Treadwell High, but two have gone underground.

There are things in Memphis even bigger than Crump. It has one of the largest colonies of the Sicilian Mafia in the country. Crump has been forced to grant asylum through an agreement that they will lay off street vice.

Most of the groceries are owned by Italians. The Black Hand shakes them down and assigns locations. The Mafia, protected here, makes it a switchboard for its operation in nearby states. And cuts in on the ground floor of liquor smuggling and moonshining in the dry counties of Tennessee and Arkansas.

The Sicilian boss is Pete Minacora (alias Marcello), from New Orleans.

Kefauver did not disclose that the Memphis Black Hand is tied up with labor unions and protection rackets. It is active in wholesale robbery of the giant Memphis Army Supply Depot, physically and through finagling of the books and records, with connivance of military and civilian personnel.

The other super-power in Memphis is the Red-dominated local

of the Distributive, Processing and Office Workers Union of
America, recently kicked out of the Memphis Council of the CIO.
This outfit, which meets on sympathetic business levels with the
Mafia, is infiltrating many of the key industries in the Memphis
area, and there's nothing Crump can do about it.

He is a sad figure, "the last leaf upon the tree" that grew fruity
giants.

C. Top Secret—They Make More Than
Atomic Energy at Oak Ridge!

The atomic energy project is supposed to be our most closely
guarded secret. Billions have been appropriated by Congress for
such installations as Oak Ridge near Knoxville, in Tennessee,
where the AEC has a blank check to construct what it desires and
to spend what it wants, virtually without an accounting to the
taxpayers, because this is "top secret."

The atom plants are our most "sensitive" nerves. Employes,
contractors and merchant-concessionaires are given careful security checks. The plants are private cities—owned by the government—and everyone in them, employes and businessmen alike,
lives on government property and is there by government suf-
ferance.

The payrolls are tremendous. Wherever there is transient labor
earning big pay, rackets are sure to spring up. Oak Ridge is no
exception.

Nothing can transpire on the reservation without the knowledge and at least passive connivance of government project managers and the officials of the Atomic Energy Commission. But
much does happen at Oak Ridge. And many government men are
being paid off so that it can.

On May 20, 1950, a committee of public-spirited local lawyers
addressed a round robin letter to Senator Estes Kefauver, which
contained the following statements:

"There are indications that the forces which our government
has chosen to guard atomic secrets at Oak Ridge, Tennessee, are
in close connection, and are working in conjunction with a nationally controlled crime syndicate.

"It is felt by the signers of this letter, all of whom are practicing
attorneys in Anderson County, Tennessee, that the very foundation of the security program at Oak Ridge is being undermined
by the forces of organized crime. Already these lawless individuals
have a hold in Anderson County in all types of business activities,

including legal and illegal. Of this, along with the other statements made in this letter, proof can and will be furnished to your
committee upon your request.

"Proof as to time, dates, names, places and circumstances surrounding the crime wave in Anderson County and Oak Ridge can
be furnished by the four undersigned attorneys, who have made
an exhaustive investigation. . . ."

It was signed by W. B. Lewallen, Howard Vincent, J. R. Har-
rington and James Weaver.

Under date of May 24, 1950, Kefauver replied as follows:

"I shall be glad to see you any time you come and if I am not
here I suggest you see Mr. Rudolph Halley. He will be glad to
hear your story any time you are here."

But the very next day, before Kefauver's letter had been received in Oak Ridge, he penned another letter. He had talked to
someone in the meantime.

This letter, written twenty-four hours later, read:

"With further reference to your letter it appears upon first impression a matter for local law enforcement. Also, it is quite apparent we cannot undertake to go into the matters of local law
enforcement in every community in the country."

Kefauver then suggested they take it up with the local officials—
the ones they were trying to expose. (We have the originals of
both letters.)

Estes did not hesitate to stick his snoot into local matters, like
corruption in the New York City Fire Department, when it got
publicity. But he shied away from corruption on government
property when it got too close to home.

So desperate Oak Ridge citizens wrote to Senator Wiley (Rep.)
of Wisconsin, a member of the committee. Wiley replied:

"I will immediately look into the matter. In view of the fact
that Oak Ridge is within Chairman Kefauver's own state, I will
confer with him particularly closely on his reactions to the situation."

The reactions were negative.

After which the crusaders wrote for help to the United States
Atomic Energy Commission, suggesting the law-breakers be
bounced from government property.

In a long, legalistic alibi, Fred W. Ford, director of the Office
of Community Affairs, replied:

"In normal, democratic, American cities, the landlord, as a general rule does not attempt to invade the law enforcement field

through such use of the covenants in his agreements with his tenant. The fact that, due to our peculiar situation in Oak Ridge, the Government happens to find itself concerned with both landlord functions and law enforcement activities does not, in our opinion, justify a radical departure from the practices generally prevailing in other communities between landlord and tenant."

Nothing has been done since, except by local vigilante action. We did not find Oak Ridge, or any place in Tennessee, for that matter, in the index of the Kefauver Committee reports.

And day by day the situation is growing worse.

Pete Licavoli of Detroit, the Chicago Fischettis and the Milanos of Cleveland made a deal with the Tennessee Democratic machine—Kefauver's—and split up the jackpot with slots, numbers, gambling and dope, operated by henchmen slipped into government reservations and often on government payrolls. The gambling is so high and wide that many top plant officials are in hock and softened up for Red spies who pay well. Others are on the weed and opium, introduced there by the mobsters and sold out to the Commies, who are blackmailing for top secrets.

The people of Oak Ridge are a captive community, helpless to help themselves. Here is the sad story, as transmitted to Senator Kefauver and other officials and authorities:

Oak Ridge is a government reservation of fifty thousand acres, administered by the Atomic Energy Commission run by Senator Brien McMahon and his former law partner who are members of Connecticut's crooked and Red dominated Democratic party. Its residents can vote for Federal, state and county officials (they live either in Roane or Anderson Counties, which the reservation straddles), but not for city officials.

The sites are closed except to workers, but anyone can come to work and live in the town if he can find employment. The government will allot him a house.

During the war, when the Army was in control, there was little corruption, gambling, vice, etc., because smart, tough Mike McDermott, former New York police inspector who died recently, was chief security officer.

There were some prostitutes in the colored huts, a few knifings, and much policy (they call it "butter and eggs").

The Army's tenure was terminated by the Atomic Energy Act and David Lilienthal took over. All military officials were replaced by civilians. Some Army officers, sensing the heavy sugar bound to be floating around in boom peacetimes, retired and returned as civilians.

Thomas Rentenbach, a major, became a contractor in Knoxville and was awarded a substantial deal for construction of security installations. Bill Bonnet, an assistant area engineer, stayed on and became deputy town manager, in charge of most municipal functions. Bonnet helped hand out contracts for building security installations, new apartment houses, etc.

Taft Moody, of the Crump machine, operated a beer-selling concession and ice cream factory in Oak Ridge during the war, gotten through connections with the right Army officials, notably Captain Philip Anderson.

The colored district is off by itself in one small area of the project. It is as easy to buy a numbers ticket there as it is to get a woman. Wenches get working permits as maids, housekeepers, etc., and set up shop in the two-room cottages the government provides, by paying off to Bonnet's friends.

After the AEC took over, hoodlums began moving into Anderson County. Grant Lawson, formerly of Chicago, with some men from Sandusky, Ohio, made an arrangement to operate slot-machines, policy and baseball pools on the Oak Ridge government area. Bookmakers were going strong, but their activities have subsided. The headquarters of one was in a sandwich shop in the Jefferson part of Oak Ridge.

Lawson and his boys placed their machines in several Oak Ridge clubs, notably the Amvets and the American Legion. So strong was their hold on local officials that when a group of independent citizens attempted to get them to raid the clubs there was no cooperation. Sheriff Bernard Vandergriff was friendly with Lawson. On another occasion, two young lawyers discovered slot-machines in a building just outside the Elza Gate. They demanded that the larceny-boxes be destroyed, but Vandergriff refused. The citizens took matters into their own hands and smashed them. On May 17, 1950, when the Amvets Club was slated to be raided the next day, the postmaster of Oak Ridge, Van D. Hicks, prominent in Anderson County politics, warned the management. Howard Vincent, the crusading lawyer, was fired on twice as he sat in his front yard.

Mark Melman, formerly of Charleston, West Virginia, who had operated gambling houses there until 1949, turned up in Oak Ridge as the manager of the Oak Terrace restaurant. The preceding manager was Bob Phillips, who had been convicted in West Virginia of gambling and operating a gambling house; he departed to serve another West Virginia sentence. Oak Terrace was owned by Harry Shapiro, of Charleston, and Roscoe Stevens, who ran a restaurant there. They brought J. R. Price, a gambler in their home town, to Oak Ridge, and installed him in a house on West Outer Drive.

Houses can be allotted only by contractors for the government, under government rules. Price had no ostensible means of justifying his having a house in Oak Ridge, but he was given one immediately. He began running nightly card games, which were attended by high government personnel, among them Clark Center, project manager for Carbide and Carbon Chemicals Corporation, the chief contractor for the government. Center is the most important man on the project. His company does most of the research and all the production. He, too, is from Charleston.

Also seen frequently in the gambling house was M. M. Marshall, supervisor of the Roane-Anderson Company Concessions Department, a government contractor, in charge of granting business concessions of the area to outside merchants. Lieutenant Charles Fehr, of the Oak Ridge police department, was in the gambling house occasionally—maybe on business.

In the middle of 1949 the weed-pushers moved in. A former Los Angeles gambler was the chief wholesaler, distributing reefers and junk to Negroes, who resold them to atom plant personnel.

Baseball lottery tickets are on sale in most of the Oak Ridge plants, in clubs such as the Moose, Eagles, Amvets and Legion, and in the snack shop in the Jefferson area. The lottery was netting $5,000 weekly. A key figure in the Powerhouse at K-25 area, one of the most vital installations, is a boss of the lottery.

Other characters finding government lodgings on the Oak Ridge scene, built and operated at your expense, are:

John Boring, former bootlegger who passed out poll tax receipts and whiskey in Gordon Browning's successful campaign for Governor, supported by Kefauver.

Fred Hooker, former patrolman, now bartender at the Recreation Hall in Jefferson Center, who operates a baseball lottery and runs a teletype machine for race results.

Joe Young, manager of a Jefferson Recreation Hall, former bootlegger from Jackson County, Tennessee.

Jimmy Davis, convicted numbers racketeer, twice indicted for possessing slot-machines. Once ran numbers in Edgewood restaurant, which was owned by W. E. "Bill Hatfield, executive with AIT, the Oak Ridge bus line, a prominent project official.

The political boss of the town is Sheriff Vandergriff's father, who okays everything. Under him in succession of control is

C. C. Hayes, a CIO local vice-president, in charge of local CIO labor relations. Hayes has been indicted, charged with a vote fraud. His stand-ins are B. F. Standifer, CIO labor relations assistant, and Earl Drinnon, ditto of the AFL.

No one can get on the project unless the unions say so. They okayed these respected citizens, who live in government-owned lodgings (meant for atom plant workers) and operate on U.S. property.

Pop Campbell, 61 Club operator, a convicted bootlegger.

Herb Shadwick, Pop's partner, on parole from Morgan County.

Tom Henderson, West End Cafe operator, indicted in the murder of John Henry Russell.

John Justice, father of Bob, who runs the Willow Grove. John was twice tried for murder and acquitted.

Joe Young, of the Jefferson Recreation Hall; his brother is a two-time murder loser.

Roby Hicks, sandwich shop operator; has had beer license revoked.

Mickey Dwyer, tended bar at Eagles. Convicted on white slavery charge.

Bubber Arnold, of Bob's Tavern. Has twenty-seven Oak Ridge arrests.

But we're running out of paper. You get the idea.

23. THE BIBLE BELT

PUT YOUR pencil on the map in the middle of Iowa and draw a flowing curve through Nebraska, Kansas, Oklahoma, Arkansas, Mississippi and Alabama, through the cracker-country of Georgia, the Carolinas and western Virginia, with overlaps into Kentucky, Tennessee and Missouri. You will have outlined the Bible Belt.

The millions who live within it have little in common. Mississippi is the poorest state and Iowa is the most prosperous; Oklahoma is bone dry and Nebraska is pickled in alcohol. But, except for Birmingham, the Belt is predominantly agricultural. Most of its whites are Anglo-Saxon, hard-shelled Baptists in the South, graduating to Methodism north and west.

The one common factor is seventh-day observance. From Des

Moines to Tuscaloosa, Sunday belongs to the church. On the other
days, the statute of limitations has run out on the other nine
Commandments.

We give you the Bible Belt. And you can have it.

A. Iowa—In and Out of Death Moines

We didn't expect good hunting in the dreary state of the tall
corn. But we needed a day of rest, though it was not Sunday. So we
descended on Des Moines: no whiskey at the bars, but plenty of
Iowans, from teen-agers up, both sexes, stinko or getting that way
on beer; unrestrained burlesque houses as lewd as those in Indianapolis; trollops on the sidewalks and on call—five dollars—
country-fed and apple-cheeked.

The new sheriff of Polk County is in but a short time. The new
courthouse gang has not yet found what makes the cash-register
jingle. The new City Charter government is run by a nonpartisan
group of solid but ingenuous businessmen, with a city manager,
just getting the new form of government in working order. So
nothing there has taken form yet.

These circumstances are not favorable for a wide open town,
but they frame the big chance for cheaters. So far, few have to pay
graft. Crusading Police Chief Frank Mabee, appointed by the new
city manager, was a captain. When gambling ran openly, he followed orders—that's why he was promoted.

The new administration is touchy. After a farmer got rolled
and robbed in the Cargill Hotel, cops raided it. Now the whores
who lived there operate on call instead of bringing clients home.
Des Moines is a piker town; streetwalkers take $5 and under, call
girls ask $5 and up. But it costs $50 to have one visit you in the
city lock-up.

Much of downtown looks like a skidrow, with cheap pick-up
bars and hotels. Few ask questions. The favorites of the transients
are the Como, the Westside, the Grand and the East. Streetwalkers
are pinched but not jailed, fined five to ten dollars.

The best-looking broads hang out on Grant Avenue, between
5th and 8th. The sportiest are at the Theatre Lounge restaurant
and the Carnival Club. The in-betweens frequent taverns on Mul-
berry, from 5th to 8th. The cheesiest tarts work East 5th and 6th,
around Grant and Walnut. We saw good-time gals working in
front of the East Walnut Club, on 6th, and the Corner Tavern, on
5th. Patrons who want to be served in their rooms look up "bath
parlors" and phone for "therapists."

Iowa prohibits the sale of hard liquor at bars, but about every bar in town sells booze, including the best hotels, except during drives. Periodic arrests are made, but licenses are never revoked. Tavernkeepers are fined from $100 to $300. Whiskey is sold in the local calaboose.

Iowa is a possession of the Chicago Mafia. The local operating head is Lew Farrell, who used to be known as Luigi Fratto in Chicago. He brought the Capone beer into Iowa and he recently went into the railroad-siding business with a Sicilian from Omaha. Pete Rand, or Randa, a relative of Farrell, runs the Polk County Italian set-up. Little Italy, not large, is in South Des Moines. But its members own most of the law-breaking taverns, hooker-houses and clip-joints.

The sporty crowd hangs out at Critelli's Tavern, where you see the prettiest girls.

Normally, law-breaking is assessed rather than penalized. The record is satisfied by an arrest, the authorities impose a small shakedown, the municipal treasury takes the fine and everybody is happy. This system works to perfection with gambling. After a pinch, each player is fined $5 and the operators are nailed for from $100 to $1,000, depending on the size of the game. By gentlemen's agreement they are free to run for three months without another collar. So-called fraternal organizations are never disturbed. Open draw poker games run around the clock.

Iowa is Republican, but the Des Moines metropolitan area frequently votes Democratic and is responsible for sending such a joker as Gillette to the Senate. Frank Comfort, an attorney, is his wire into Washington, and you talk to him if you want anything from Uncle Sam. Some years ago, local boondogglers got a dam for the Des Moines River, built by WPA and architected by bright boys in Washington who apparently learned their business from correspondence school. They put the dam up all right, but forgot the spillway. So the works are getting clogged with silt and refuse, and the river may overflow any day.

Des Moines has an active Negro section on Center Street, never bothered, because whenever a colored man is arrested for anything the noisy local branch of the NAACP yells murder. A distinguishing mark of Center Street is its many queer Negroes, for some reason a local specialty. They mix freely with white fairies. They flirt with each other on the library lawn, but have no regular tavern meeting place, moving from bar to bar as word goes out in advance. Drags are held in a house on Terrace Road, in the west end.

This is a rich community, with virtually no underprivileged, no ghettos or slums. But there is much juvenile delinquency, kept out of the papers by wealthier parents of students of Roosevelt High School, where a sin club is operating now with all the trappings of sex, perversion and reefers.

Des Moines is the state capital. When the legislature is in session, there are high jinks at the Fort Des Moines and Savery hotels, where the public utilities lobby and the beer lobby run open house with women and whiskey. The brewery lobby's chief function is to prevent the sale of mixed drinks at bars. The church lobby comes up with an assist.

Hookers hang out also around Lefty's Tavern, East 5th Street, so near the capitol the solons have no trouble finding it no matter how drunk.

Des Moines is the reflection of most of Iowa. Keokuk is wild; all the river towns are wide open. And in the rural communities there is little law for farmers, where hick cops work with justices of the peace, who don't turn in fines and split them with the police. But everyone goes to church and Sunday is sacred.

B. Omaha—Beef and Bookies

Omaha has six hundred saloons, the largest number of gin-mills per capita in the country. Nebraska has the highest per capita hard liquor rate in the U.S. Other than that it hasn't much to speak of.

Surrounded on all sides by important provincial headquarters of the International Mafia—Chicago, Kansas City, Denver and Minneapolis—it is common ground where they meet to transact interstate affairs.

Sicilians constantly flow into Omaha, where the black market in meat is fed with a nod from crooks in OPS.

Visiting hot-money boys dine at good eating places like Johnny's Steak House, in South Omaha, and Caniglia's, where they rub shoulders with local politicians and Alex Marino, local gambler, the front man for the Syndicate.

When we arrived at the airport we noticed that every cab carried an ad on the back reading, "Visit your church on Sunday." So we got ready to beat it on the first plane. Our hack-man induced us to stay.

"Whatta you wanna do?" he asked. "Places to bet? Just go to Chet's cigar store across the street from the Burlington bus terminal. Or try the Rocket on Farnam St." We did.

Other books operated at the Peggy cigar store and the Sportsman in South Omaha. Maxie Abrams is the little king of the local books. Instead of pinching bookmakers, cops close down on penny-gum machines that pay off with trinkets.

There was a flurry after the new U.S. tax law, but that's forgotten.

When public opinion requires a collar, the usual fine is $25. Smart gamblers retain the Boyles, three lawyers, who like to try their cases before Judge Denny O'Brien. They are very clever on technicalities.

After one local gambling crackdown, the town was flooded with leaflets reading, "Make your bets direct by Western Union," with the address of a Chicago bookmaker. Traveling crap games operate in the county, moving from one night club to another, with the word out in advance. The Wish Bone, a chicken joint, is one location.

More powerful even than the underworld is Ak-Sar-Ben (Nebraska spelled backward). This is a charitable organization which rules the state. Its executives, who control its huge finances, are more potent than the Governor or the chief Blackhander.

Ak-Sar-Ben owns the horse-track, outside Omaha. Its profits paid for a private bridge which Ak-Sar-Ben turned over to the public. It runs operas and concerts and ladles out hundreds of thousands elsewhere. When Ak-Sar-Ben operates, all bookies' wires are cut so that chumps have to go out to the track and lose their money on the pari-mutuel machines. These machines bleed the public white, then Ak-Sar-Ben has to turn around and dole out more charitable relief, all of which is according to best Bible Belt practice. The Kefauver Committee pulled out fast when embarrassing testimony might have shown how Big Mob money is laid off at Ak-Sar-Ben.

Omaha's monopoly newspaper, the *World-Herald,* always sees it through rose-colored glasses. It denies crime exists. But there are streetwalkers at 16th and Jackson. The high-class chippies work around the Bell Hotel, 15th and Dodge. There's a call service near the Castle Hotel, on 16th, which supplies girls for cattlemen who frequent that hostelry.

During Ak-Sar-Ben festivals and at convention time extras come from Denver. Prices are high, because the cow-hands are loaded with folding money. Streetwalkers ask $10. Hotel call-girls ask $100. Twenty is the minimum.

Instead of enforcing the law, many members of the police morals squad are the fixers who handle the ice. Otherwise the squad does little else except occasionally pinch Negro after-hour spots, such as the Porters' and Waiters' Club, Jim Bell's and the Harlem Pool Hall, in South Omaha, all set-ups designed to make the record look good. The defendants get off with minimum fines.

Like most stockyard towns, Omaha has a large, tough Negro population. Dives around the South Omaha stockyards are plenty low. Willy Caunce operates a colored pick-up establishment in South Omaha.

Lou Pollard runs a black-and-white house on Hamilton Street. One of his white girls was in bed with a black sweetheart. Her other Negro boy friend got jealous and turned in a false alarm which was answered by three fire trucks, the chief's car, the arson squad, a police cruiser and a press car. She was ginned up when the firemen busted in and she told them to get the hell out of her boudoir.

Another tough colored neighborhood is North 24th Street where kids buy reefers. Dope is freely obtainable at 16th and Cass and on lower Douglas.

Something different is an Indian skidrow. Omaha's lousiest bums are so-called noble Red Men. They are responsible for its major crimes. These are Winnebagos and Omahas, from fifty miles away, who work as common laborers when they do. Their hangout is 16th Street, where they guzzle, gamble and dissect each other with knives. It's against the law to sell booze to an Indian, so they get white tramps to buy cheap domestic wine for them, which they drink by the gallon instead of fire water. Most of their women are whores, whom they pimp for. The women look awful and smell worse. They operate at 16th and Cass and 16th and Chicago and take their patrons into alleys, price $2. Then they pull the old badger game. A brave follows and threatens to scalp the paleface for "fooling around with my squaw."

Omaha is so typically a dirty-minded Bible Belt town. One of its most popular pastimes is stag-parties at private clubs—$1 a ticket with naked broads and dirty movies brought in from Kansas City.

Another kind of party which is open to the public is the annual ball of the Policemen and Firemen's Post, VFW, inactive all year except for one month when it imports a high-powered Chicago promoter. Few refuse to buy tickets. Police Sgt. Howard McArdle, the man behind the scenes, keeps the books.

Even in rugged Omaha men are no longer men. Fags hang out at the Frolics and many live in the YMCA.

If you were pinched for anything we would advise you to get in touch with what the courthouse gang affectionately calls "The Unholy Trio." They are Bob Cornett, a bondsman, George Vanous, his assistant, and Phil Abboud, an attorney.

One really does not need a fix to get sprung. They call Sheriff Collins "Open the door, Richard" because the Douglas County Jail is so easy to crack. Recently there were two jail breaks three months apart. A charwoman reported one to a deputy sheriff, who replied, "Don't give me that crap," and went back to his racing form. Collins dresses his deputies like cowboys. Whores and dope are freely peddled and "furloughs" are for sale.

This is a GOP state but if you want anything in Washington, you talk to Ed McKim, the insurance man, or Frank Matthews, Ambassador to Ireland and chief poohbah of the Fair Deal in Nebraska.

We forgot to tell you, a couple of suites at the old Fontenelle Hotel are gotten up real swanky for visiting cow-magnates who entertain their babes in living rooms decorated like fairy seraglios. These are the classiest layouts in the country, with telephones in the john, next to the throne.

Council Bluffs, Iowa, is contiguous. Its operations are tied up with Omaha. Geographically they're one town. Benny Barone, who runs the Last Chance, where they sell mixed drinks contrary to Iowa law, is one of the top boys of the area. But everyone sells mixed drinks there including the Ruby Room of the Chieftain Hotel.

They book horse in the Empire Grill. Eddie Barich, who had the shuttered Chez Paree, is the wire service man when it operates. Tiny Burris, who ran the Stork, has, like many other gamblers, gone into the drive-in business. That crowd is also in the new Gourmet, on the west side.

P.S. Omaha is dry on Sunday. If you're caught short, Frank Mason, the 14th Street barber, has more than bay rum.

C. Bloody Kansas—Silos and Sex

From 1880 until 1948 Kansas was bone dry. Then it amended its constitution to permit by local option the sale of hard liquor in bottle stores only. Taverns are still limited to beer.

What happened in Kansas was a miniature history of the United States since 1933. The richest men in the state had been its bootleggers. After the fabulous profits were cut off they went into gambling, narcotics, rum-running into dry states and counties, moonshining to avoid payment of Federal taxes, and the operation of dives and after-hour spots which cater to floozies. They also invested in legitimate businesses.

The rackets were controlled by the partners, Bob Carnahan, Max Cohen, Ralph Polk and Lee Young. The latter two were in the Federal hospital prison in Springfield, Missouri, a soft touch for convicts. Others long identified with these activities are Joe LaSalle, a former bodyguard, Robert Brunch, Dean Pricer, Al Hester, Robert L. "Little Steve" Stevens, Link Ramsey and Charlie Rank.

Kansas was and is a dependency of the Pendergast mobs. Bootleg liquor was sent overland by the "Rock Boys" of St. Louis, who picked it up in nearby Cairo, Illinois.

Kansas was the only state in the union which availed itself of the provision in the Repeal amendment making it a Federal crime to transport into a dry state against its wishes. But Uncle Sam policed it with only one administrator and four agents of the Alcoholic Tax Unit. These five ATU men had to crack down on internal producers as well as guard thousands of miles of Kansas border against runners. Kansas City let it be known in Washington that five revenuers would be enough. It was so ordered.

Today, under Repeal, former bootleggers Cohen, Bobby Carnahan and Fred "Red" Clemens are the Missouri interests' representatives in gambling which, despite the Federal tax law, is one of the most profitable sources of revenue in Kansas because of the huge influx of highly paid defense workers. This trio also represents the Syndicate on other fronts and is itself a heavy investor in Las Vegas hotel and gambling house property.

Bloody Kansas has always had a rich tradition of outlawry and criminality. Pro-slavery and abolitionist forces clashed to establish the state government. Civil War guerillas raped and robbed. Towns like Wichita and Topeka were rowdy hell-holes.

Once again this is boom country. Wichita is the fastest growing city in the United States. Its population increased by 50 per cent in the last decade, making it Kansas' chief metropolis.

Defense workers flivvered in from Arkansas and Oklahoma. Many of them are completely illiterate. They sign their pay-checks with X's. They live in trailers and jungle villages, dress in slacks and eat hamburgers. Their newly found wealth from inflated salaries—as high as $150 a week—is dissipated on gambling, liquor and dames.

When Ernie Warden, star reporter of the Levand Bros.' enterprising *Beacon,* discovered a sex-lottery in the Douglas plant, citizens laughed at him. They said it wasn't possible. Who would be dumb enough to spend $2 for a chance to win a girl when you could have all you want for nothing?

That lottery is closed, thanks to Ernie, but others are running. The prize includes a weekend with a babe in a cabin furnished with all the liquor you can drink and all the steak you can eat. The girls sell five hundred tickets on themselves at two bucks a throw, a thousand a week net, but it shrinks to $300 after payment for fixings and the 50 per cent net cutbacks to a union shop steward.

Meanwhile amateur sexing goes on twenty-four hours a day in the plane plants. They run three shifts around the clock. During rest periods loving couples shack up in packing boxes and unfinished bodies of B-29s.

In order to take care of swing shift employes many joints in Wichita and round about keep open all night to sell mixed drinks. One is the Tepee, in the county. The Key Club, supposed to be a private bottle party, also mixes liquor. The Tepee has the distinction of running one of rawest strip-tease shows in the United States. Girls are recruited from Chicago's dives, which are low, then when they reach Wichita they are told to "get dirty."

It is not difficult to get a date in town, either. Many call-girls live in the Coronado Hotel, directly across the street from the police station and City Hall, which makes it easier for all concerned. They also patronize the Kerstin Hotel.

Gals hang out in all taverns and aren't a bit shy. The bobby-soxers and victory girls go to the Cowboy. Reefers are peddled nearby. The lowest whores frequent the North Main St. and East Douglas tenderloin and skidrow.

Kansas didn't obey Federal and state prohibition. It is not worried about the present heat on gambling. Bookies operate in the Brown Building. Incidentally, there is no interest in horse betting, all odds being quoted on baseball, football and basketball games. Football parlay cards are controlled by Wheeler and Kelly. Until the Federal tax on punchboards they ran openly all over town.

TIP FOR ACTION: Phone 29330 and ask for the odds and point spread.

If you want to find a crap game try the colored section. Reefers there and in Little Mexico at Mosley and 9th.

We offer as proof that America is being feminized the fact that tough and isolated Kansas is going homo. When Kansas does anything, it means the rest of the country did it years ago. Wichita

cops are said to have a list of the names of 1000 fairies who live in
the city. That is more than 1 per cent of the total male population. Officers admit they miss ten for every one. So maybe Kinsey wasn't wrong.

You can find them mincing into the Blue Lantern or Curley's
Round House. The biggest fag parties are held in an apartment
over a business building in the 1200 block of East Douglas. You
go through three doors to an inner sanctum where a fat old fairy
in a Japanese kimono makes like a geisha girl.

The guy to see for anything is Ty Lockett, Democratic Sheriff
of the wide-open county. In Washington they listen to "Buzz"
Hill, the Federal Judge, and Postmaster C. M. Fitzwilliams. A lord
of all he surveys is Jimmy Comeau, a recent arrival from Kansas
City's Little Italy. His reports go back there.

Now come with us to Pittsburg, Kansas. That is the mother
lode of the home-made, or "deep shaft" as against imported, whiskey. America is accustomed to thinking of illegally distilled drinks
as "moonshine" or "white mule." Pittsburg, Kansas, is far ahead
of that. It has distilleries almost as large as those in Peoria or
Louisville. In these the best imitations of cordials, gins, brandies
and whiskeys in the world are made. Many a connoisseur cannot
tell the difference between Canadian Club made in Ottawa and
"Canadian Club" made in Pittsburg.

These products are exported to a large part of the United
States and even to France as originals. Labels and government
stamps are forged, the work done by superlative craftsmen. This
enterprise has been functioning for more than sixty years and
keeps a large portion of the population, slightly under 20,000,
employed. It is controlled by emigrants from Palermo, who also
operate in nearby Frontenac, Galena and other parts of the so-
called Kansas "Balkans."

Naturally, since no tax of any kind is paid, these goods can be
and are sold at terrific profit and they offer lively competition to
the bona fide stuff hauled in from beyond the borders. The Pittsburg output also is assessed at various points of distribution, but
not as heavily as the hoodlums' hooch, which is described in
Kansas as "foreign."

D. The Arkies

One of the more important subjects overlooked by Kefauver's committee was the nature of the tie-up between the organized
underworld and the Arkansas authorities which permits Hot

Springs to operate as a year-around refuge and resort for out-of-state gangsters.

Many times during the lengthy and costly hearings we thought Halley was getting hot, but he and the Senators always failed to follow the leads which might have led to pay-dirt. And they might also have pointed straight to a couple of very deserving Fair Deal Democrats.

The casual traveler through Arkansas pictures the entire state like Little Rock, its capital and sole metropolis, where they roll the sidewalks in at midnight. It's not much different earlier, either.

Fifty miles away, in Hot Springs, no sidewalks are rolled—there it is the dice and the customers. Gambling and skulduggery are open and unafraid in the Springs, where there is a constant stream of important Mafistas from all over the country coming to take the healing baths. Strange how so many have rheumatism. "Lucky" Luciano hid out there until Dewey found him.

Hot Springs' revered citizen is Owney "The Killer" Madden, the underworld's elder statesman. Through his good offices Senator J. William Fulbright, the Arkansas Rhodes scholar, expedited an RFC loan to construct the $2,000,000 Jack Tar Hotel in this gambling haven. This was before Fulbright discovered others were using influence to ease RFC loans along the proper paths.

What went on in Hot Springs (and still does) made Saratoga look like piker money. But there were no probes to lay the shocking facts before a startled TV audience. That was because Saratoga is in a Republican state. But Arkansas is strictly Democratic and so is Madden, who bankrolls the kitty collected from the hoods to sweeten the campaign coffers of Fulbright and Governor Sid McMath, Truman's chief tub-thumper.

That fine old tradition of the most exclusive gentleman's club in the world, Senatorial courtesy, was invoked to steer the Kefauver sleuths elsewhere, and Deacon Tobey, nominally a Republican, went along with his Democratic colleagues because the tit-for-tat boiled down to this: You lay off Arkansas and I'll wash up the RFC probe. (One of Tobey's sons was due to be subpoenaed before the Fulbright committee.)

Arkansas' vital statistics might be catalogued thusly:

Principal income: entertaining visiting hoods.

Chief industry: moonshining.

Citizens' hobbies: shooting revenooers and raping their own daughters.

In the hills there is no draft, no census, no taxes, no schools and no law. The only time the hill folk come to town is for relief checks and to vote for Governor McMath. When there are no relief checks there is no crime in the cities because no one can buy whiskey. The hillbillies return to the hills for home-made corn. Except for murder and incest, accepted social customs, the Arkie is pleasant and honest.

Madden, sage of Hot Springs, was one of New York's Big Three public enemies during Prohibition. When he shied from syndication the Mafia sent him to Sing Sing, from which he was out on a ticket of leave for an earlier homicide. Owney saw the light. He turned his rackets over to the Sicilians. They got him out on parole with permission to move to Hot Springs for his health.

The Syndicate rewarded his noble self-abnegation by supporting him in high style. As the years mellowed the hoodlums into middle-aged business tycoons, more and more they called on Owney for advice. In his Elba he is a moving spirit of the crime cartel.

Circuit Judge "Babe" Huff is political boss of Hot Springs. But Madden decides what goes and what doesn't. The mob has investments in the Southern and Pine Clubs, elaborate gaming casinos with a nominal "$1.00 membership fee." There are eight smaller joints. Ironically, the last time Frank Costello went to Hot Springs for "his health," he got so much publicity that Governor McMath, who never closed them before, was forced to order a temporary shutdown. Costello always stays at Senator Fulbright's project, the Jack Tar.

One of the Senator's letters, to Chauncey W. Dodds, RFC Loan Manager, dated in August, 1948, follows:

"I am informed that the Jack Tar Courts, one of the finest establishments of its kind in Hot Springs, Arkansas, has applied for a loan from the RFC. It is expected that the application will reach Washington in the near future.

"I am planning to go to Italy for a conference. Therefore I am writing you before I leave.

"I hope you will give close attention to this application upon its arrival and facilitate its consideration by the board."

Needless to say, the loan was granted. But this was not all Uncle Sam did to help develop the gangsters' health and gambling spot. The Department of the Interior pumps government-owned medicinal waters into hotels so gouty New York hoodlums will not be forced to mingle with the riffraff.

We always figured Fulbright was too good to be true. He is disagreeable and supercilious, an Arky snob. We did a little job on the bright lad. He is the spoiled son of a wealthy mother who got his boost into Congress when she used her small-town newspaper to plug him. He was unheard of until his famous Peace Resolution—ghosted by Justice Owen Roberts.

Though a knight-errant in Washington, Fulbright glosses over the crooked machine, supported by Madden and the Hot Springs gamblers, that gives him office.

McMath and Fulbright are sickening Fair Dealers, but you heard no howls when a contractor named Buckton, who gets all the choice government building handouts, refused to hire Negroes on the Pine Bluff Arsenal. When proceedings were brought to compel him to do so, Federal Judge Trimble, also a good Truman Democrat, dismissed the case. McMath's income tax was under scrutiny while this was being written. An investigation into kickbacks and favoritism in the Highway Department will rock the state.

Little Rock is a city of churches, where the residents invoke the Almighty but forget to ask him to clean up the low and dirty street-level vice which is set up for visiting farmers and hillbillies.

We don't suppose we should bother telling you this at all, because it certainly isn't confidential in Little Rock that females are a commodity easy to buy or get for nothing. You can ask any girl on the street or in any beer tavern. If she isn't a professional the odds are she will do it for a drink. Guys take them to cheap hotels like the Lincoln or the Texas Stanley Rooming House.

A recently arrested whore was found to be suffering from a virulent case of venereal disease. Following the common procedure, police asked her for the names of her recent customers so they could warn them to take proper precautionary measures. In her address book were thirteen members of the legislature. We hope the cops told them. If not, we'll be glad to supply the names so they can go to their doctors.

Just as there are no closed seasons on whoring, so there is no age limit. Young girls from the hills start when they're eleven. The other day cops picked up a sixty-nine-year-old hustler.

Even in this country where sex is common and cheap, there are homosexuals. You find them at beer parlors on Markham and Louisiana Streets. These Arkie fairies were nurtured on moonshine—no poets, artists, interior decorators or fashion designers are among these mis-sexed L'il Abners.

The gracious old Marion Hotel has had its face lifted. When the bellboy took us to our room we noted a gold plaque on the door, where the number should have been. It read, "Presidential Suite, Harry S. Truman slept here, June 10, 1949." Naturally, being the Truman Suite, it had a private bar.

E. Drought in Oklahoma

To two-thirds of the nation, Prohibition is something that went out in 1933, leaving memories of an era giddy with surreptitious sinning and dramatic tales that the oldsters still tell about speakeasies, bootleggers, hijackers, rum-runners, gangsters and murderous "torpedoes" who massacred for the barons of verboten beer and booze.

But for one-third of the nation, Prohibition is a grim, living fact today, with most of its old-time by-products of licentiousness, hoodlumism and homicide.

More than 25,000,000 of your fellow-citizens live in areas which got no relief with the death-rattle of the 18th Amendment, because liquor was thumbed down through state, county, city and even precinct laws, now in force, though by no means enforced. And 25,000,000 others live where the sale of spirits is sanctioned, but so circumscribed by ridiculous rules, usually compromised to assuage extremists on both ends, that there is neither red nor green light, neither license nor liberty, only larceny and debauchery.

Wherever the strong dike of the law is broken, the waters rush in and on their tide they carry the waves of vice, violence, juvenile delinquency and a cold contempt for all morals.

These reporters were active during the life of the Volstead Act. They thought they had seen everything that Prohibition in America can do. They flew back shaking their heads and rubbing their eyes, for they had seen in Tulsa, Oklahoma City and smaller cities devices and conditions which had never reached the side streets of Manhattan or the dark environs of the Loop when some of the sharpest minds in our brotherhood were concentrating on how to keep a liquorless country drunk.

These are comparatively unreported sections; their date-lines are not page 1 copy per se, as they generate no national glamor and are not largely populated by glittering names, so virtually nothing about the conditions in these arid and semi-arid regions hits the telegraph wires. All that these two reporters knew was that there were parts of this country where statutory Prohibition, some of it much older than the 18th Amendment, some of it arriving in sprinkles since Repeal, was on the books.

The United Drys, as the successors to the unlamented Anti-Saloon League are now called, and the W.C.T.U. are attracting millions in contributions. No small part thereof comes from internal industrialists, many of whom have their clubs and their cellars well stocked, but who believe Prohibition promotes employe efficiency.

However, the richest and most generous bankrollers for sustaining and broadening Prohibition are the master whiskey-smugglers and others down the line in the forbidden and therefore fabulous trade.

There are thirty-seven states that have Prohibition by local option, in which localities can bar sale and in many instances possession or transportation of alcoholic beverages. In these states the percentage of population in dry territories ranges from a huge 68.3 in North Carolina to a mere .2 in Nebraska. Kentucky, as famed for its bourbon as it is for its horses, is 61.1 per cent dry.

In clap-trap juke-joints and roadside honkytonks, usually fringing around the immediate outskirts of the cities, we found children reeling, girls who did not appear to be more than fourteen with boys of about the same age or a bit older. They carried cheap doctored stuff in half-pint bottles. These are sold by scores of peddlers of grammar school age, who hustle outside schoolhouses. This kind of liquor is also on sale in many school bookstores. The kids go forth in jalopies or public buses to dance to the jazz records and consume their poison mixed with soft drinks. The boys are known as "hip cats" because they carry their bottles in their pockets.

Around these noisy and crummy traps there is always weedy or woody unoccupied land. And, in pairs, arms around each other, the immature fledglings weave and stagger into hiding. Some smooch in cars even more conspicuously. Men and women pass out, immobile, sprawl on the floors and the roadways. Cockeyed soldiers in uniform, raising pints and fifths, drink to good old Prohibition.

After this there is only one greater kick—dope!

Through strange, dumb overlapping of laws, while possession of a thimbleful of beverage alcohol is a crime, the government's ATU openly and officially sells stamps authorizing such possession. The stamp not only does not immunize one against prosecution, but by statute it is prima facie evidence of a state violation.

However, a stamp is a complete defense against Federal prosecution for violating the national law against bringing liquor into a dry state.

Oklahoma, rich with oil and cattle and millionaire Indians, is dry by law but so wet it could float. Oklahoma City and Tulsa are wide open and Muskogee County is screaming.

Most of the liquor sold in Oklahoma is legal bonded stuff brought in from Texas, Louisiana, Colorado, Arkansas and Illinois. Little moonshine is consumed except by Negroes.

Nothing stronger than 3.2 beer is permitted by law, and if you have a beer license you are not allowed to have dancing or a cabaret—except hotels. The result is like the old New York Raines law. Every night club and dance hall has a few hotel rooms attached and the natural result is that these rooms are rented out for whoring.

Bootleggers advertise by card and by direct mail. Cards are distributed by school kids on the streets and are put in mail boxes. They have the bootlegger's name, address, phone number, price list and guaranteed ten-minute delivery any time of the day or night. Prices are extremely moderate, running on the average about 125 per cent of the price in legal states. Sometimes they meet competition, because there is no state tax. In Tulsa, where drinks are sold openly over bars, you can buy them for as little as 50 cents. This is cheaper, of course, than in New York.

Liquor comes into Oklahoma by truck and by airplane. The syndicate operates planes into an abandoned airport known as Tulakes Airport. The stuff is flown from Shreveport, Louisiana, and carries no state tax.

When a group of constables raided an Oklahoma City night club patronized by the better people, the constables were indicted. The cops said they had taken some of the club's fixtures as well as the evidence.

Law enforcement officers favor Prohibition. When they confiscate a truck, only a quarter of the contents shows up as evidence. The cops sequester the rest for their personal use or sell it to other bootleggers who are on the accredited list, a form of legal hijack. Other hijackers include GI's from nearby posts who borrow weapons from their arsenals and gang up on shipments.

Nothing goes in Tulsa unless Sheriff George Blaine says so.

Bootleg is the state's chief industry, probably bigger than oil. Kids who start in their schooldays handing out printed price lists go through high school delivering orders. Colonized football stars at Tulsa and Oklahoma universities are given the prize appointments to work their way through college as campus bootleggers.

Some of these towns in the dry states have more and gayer night life than those in surrounding wet states. Tulsa provides all-night eating, dancing, and drinking at the Orchid and Stardust clubs. The Club Jericho at 3rd and Driscoll stays open till four. The Casa Dell, where bootleggers sell to dancers, remains open all night. The Flamingo, a Negro joint, advertises, "10:30 till—" The unfilled portion of the promise is as late as the last customer remains.

Tulsa is practically lawless. The same cops who refuse to enforce the state prohibition law enforce nothing else. For instance, the Pearl Hotel, where the babes congregate, does business on a twenty-four-hour basis. Most of the rooms in the three-story Corona Hotel are occupied by high class call girls. Many steam-bath houses are bagnios. Even the Negroes have their own. Chippies hang out at the bus station.

There's a gambler on every corner, in almost every cigar store and hotel lobby. Wagering is no more heinous an offense than liquor. There are card tables in the back of the Veteran's Bar on 2nd Street. You can get action at Blair's. Bookies hang out at the Orpheum Cigar Store.

Gambling is controlled by "Skinny" Gargotta and Tony Belillo, who came from Kansas City to organize it, and Nick Cascio. Tony Marnares, one of the peers of the underworld, runs around with Supreme Court Justice Tom Clark's gang of cronies from Texas.

Clarence Love's Lounge, at Archer and Greenwood, is an all-night Negro joint. Red Morgan is king of the colored bootleggers. The Mexicans live in the northeast section of town where you get your tequilla; and Indians, all over.

Oklahoma's chief drum beater for prohibition is Harry Truman's millionaire pal, Senator Bob Kerr, who votes bleeding heart unless it interferes with the oil or natural gas business. That's his business. He is Truman's contact man with big industry and an active candidate to succeed Barkley.

24. OHIO CONFIDENTIAL

THIS IS a state of irreconcilable lights and shadows. Though it is still largely agricultural, it is dotted with more sizable cities and overgrown towns than any other of the forty-eight. It is unromanticized though it is across the river from that poetic apotheosis, Kentucky. It sends Republicans to the Senate and remains Democratic at home. Its stuffiness was exemplified by William McKinley, who refused to budge from his front porch in Canton and "sat" rather than "ran" for President. Yet, it has produced some of the filthiest scandals in our history, the most brazen of bosses, and within the last quarter of a century the most pitiless and powerful Mafia contingent on the map, not surpassed even by its blood cousins in Brooklyn and Chicago.

In political tradition the Ohio Gang brings to mind the unfortunate Harding and the diabolical Daugherty. But when wise officers of the law and hep mobsters speak of the Ohio Gang, they mean that alliance of dealers in death and extortion which was born with the old Mayfield Road Gang, and which through alliances, relentless conquest and expropriation has muscled to preeminence in the overcrowded, competitive field.

The fact that Ohio, the mother of Presidents, has spawned so many and such murderous public enemies is no open issue with its two strangely contrasted political giants, Senator Robert A. Taft and Governor Frank Lausche.

Taft, aristocratic and conservative, finds his main strength and support on the farms, in the villages and small towns, in the merchants' and bankers' clubs, and in old-fashioned, nonpartisan Cincinnati.

Lausche, a firebrand and a maverick Democrat, is a product of the Cleveland machine—a mesalliance between one of the greatest gangster concentrations on earth and the remnants of the La Follette movement. Cleveland is lousy with independents, unioneers, Fair Dealers and other splinters of malcontents, nuts, pinks and even outright and regimented groups of Reds, with cells in all the Slav neighborhoods near the factories.

For some years Ohio has been sending Republicans to the Senate, but it usually votes Democratic in state and municipal contests. Lausche was mayor of Cleveland before he rose to the executive mansion. Neither as Mayor nor as Governor has Lausche ever expressed himself on the control of his state, from border to border, by the Mafia.

The U.S. Treasury's list of the ninety-two most important Sicilians in the country includes several citizens of Ohio. They are Frank Milano, Akron; Ray Scalise, Youngstown; Nick Nitta, Cleveland; Nick Vitali, Cleveland; Joe De Carlo, Youngstown; Victor Aiello, Youngstown; Frank Palento, Mahoning County.

The membership list of the international Grand Council of the Mafia, secretly supplied by the U.S. Bureau of Narcotics to the Kefauver Committee, and quickly pigeonholed by orders from higher up, included the following:

Charles Vizzini, Youngstown; Charles Cavallaro, Youngstown; Ignacio Amato, Youngstown; Fred Angersola, Cleveland; John Angersola, Cleveland; Vincent Antona, 2832 East Boulevard, Cleveland; John Bertolino, Cleveland; Frank Bruno, Youngstown; Joe Contrera, 4805 Barkwell, Cleveland; William Cordona, Youngstown; Alfonso Creamo, Youngstown; Vincenzo Crisafi, Youngstown; Joe Gallo, 5468 Greenlawn, Cleveland; Stefano Giglio, 875 Longview, Akron; Nino Mingrione, 3767 E. 151st Street, Cleveland; Joseph Morello, Youngstown; Angelo Nappi, Youngstown; Frank Secangula, Cleveland, and Micalino Tamburello, 284 E. Federal, Youngstown.

During the first month of the new Federal gambling tax, two hundred and nineteen bookmakers applied for stamps in northeastern Ohio alone. The total in all New York state was less than twenty. Though Cleveland newspapers published the names and addresses of every applicant, there is no record at this writing that any were molested by local cops or State Troopers.

Because of Ohio's strategic location in the heart of the greatest industrial belt on earth, the Mafia has been able to spread its talons to such surrounding areas as western Pennsylvania, Kentucky, West Virginia, Indiana, Michigan and Ontario, all of which are subsidiary to the great gangster domain of Ohio.

At every end of the state, except on the Cincinnati side, neighbors pour in across the border for the superior kind of knavery which is generally offered in Ohio. Gambling runs in such varied locations as Toledo, Canton, and Steubenville. Lausche, while these words were being typed, announced that he had finally closed the last casino in Ohio. But during all the years they were running under his nose—for three terms—he never attempted to shutter them. And it is not true that they are closed now. They merely move, always tipped off in advance of impending raids by Lausche's troopers, and save their apparatus.

Steubenville is the crime and whore mecca for Pittsburgh. A standard joke in Pittsburgh burlesque is to call Steubenville "Boys Town."

Under the administration of former Mayor Mike Di Salle, the self-nominated Democratic candidate for Senator, Toledo became known as the best action town in the country. It is only minutes from Detroit. Toledo has a swarming Sicilian Black Hand population, which always voted solidly for Mike before he went to the OPS in Washington, which he always appreciated. In Di Salle's OPS office in Washington, in an obscure position, was a member of the Mafia. OPS regulations, as it chanced, turned distribution of the nation's beef over to Italian blacketeers. Mobsters, speculating in all controlled commodities, can flaunt the controls with impunity. All Italian business is given special handling. In Cleveland the OPS occupies an entire building on the most valuable part of Euclid Avenue next to the Statler, in the heart of the elite shopping district. Uncle Sam is paying some deserving Democrat ground-floor rentals for a display store front—empty except for bundles of government handout propaganda.

A. Cleveland—Hard Heart of Hickland

This could well be the typical American city, with its old underlayer of wholesome, ambitious Midwestern progress, overwhelmed like so many others by onrushes of the industrial backwash of predatory paupers, the scum of the Atlantic seaboard and the deep South, and through-traffic mid-European immigration.

This is the least distinctive and distinguished of all our cities, with surface symbolisms of them all, in this day of metamorphosis which routed our norms everywhere since the collapse of the Hoover philosophy.

Cleveland is left-wing and it is crooked. Cleveland was the only big city in the country which supported the old man La Follette for President in 1924. It has a loud and voluble extremist population which reads the *Cleveland Press,* the only pinkish paper in the Scripps-Howard chain, which is permitted to be so because that's where the gravy is in this bowl. Like all political entities governed by so-called progressives, Cleveland has always held out a welcome for gangsters and criminals. The entire history of the political labor movement in this country, as well as in England, shows that Socialists cannot acquire office without the support of

an organized underworld. Cleveland has a great Communist concentration, too, in the Slav sections, where the factory workers
live. The Slavs have their own hoodlums, who do business with
the Mafia on a higher level. At election time they all support the
Democratic candidate.

There is no class or taste here. Vice is shabby stuff. Rich mobsters own homes in Florida and seldom return to Cleveland, except for business. Respectable people move to the suburbs when
they can. The rich who went to Shaker Heights washed their
hands of Cleveland, allowing the mobsters to take over. Bloated
Black Handers followed the aristocracy to the suburbs and bought
and built mansions alongside those who had fled from them.

Now the voters are Negroes, Poles, Hunkies, Italians and hillbillies—the latter the newest tidal wave carrying rubbish to the
northern factories.

Each group has its own bosses, its own hoods and its own politicians, and votes as directed. With no politically adult electoral
group left to act as a check, Cleveland has been turned over to the
highest bidder.

An example: Arthur McBride, who inherited the nationwide
horse-race service after the murder of James M. Ragen, also owns
the Cleveland Yellow Cab Company, which has a monopoly by
law in the city and all suburbs. No independents are permitted.
Cops, acting under orders, drove war veterans out. McBride's
Yellow also has a civil aeronautics franchise to begin an air-taxi
service. He owns a radio station.

Though associated with the top hoods when he ran Continental
Press, McBride is one of Cleveland's most important citizens. He
owns its pro football team. He says his son, Edward Jr., took over the
pony information service.

Suppose you pick up one of his Yellows and ask the driver
what's going. These are some of the things he'll show you and tell
you about:

Numbers are wide open in the colored districts. Bookies, with
and without stamps, operate all over town. There's action on 9th
Street, mostly the Greek baruit game, and roulette and craps at
40th and Scovil.

The main drag of Little Harlem is 55th Street. But the colored
cousins are spreading all over town. They're taking over in the
105th Street area, block-busting into squares of fine and expensive
property. These are the aristocrats among the Negroes. The poorer
ones call them "White Niggers."

Some 90 per cent of the crime is committed by Negroes, though the papers put it at 55 per cent. The colored population is now probably 40 per cent of Cleveland's total, though that is not admitted; the Central area is the most depressed, with more than one hundred thousand. As fast as the Fair Dealers can do it, they tear down slums and build new housing projects for the colored. Central Federal Housing is a paradise compared to any layout for whites. The biggest dope-peddlers and the most active whores live in it. The latter pick up customers on the street and take them to their bedrooms while their husbands read the evening papers in the living rooms.

The Majestic Hotel is the Waldorf of colored hostelries. The black streetwalkers work in front of it. McBride's cab-drivers take white customers. When the wenches see them they hail the cab. The girl's price is $5, which includes her $2 kickback to the driver, who usually gets a tip from the passenger, too.

Policemen, black or white, refuse to patrol singly. It is impractical to use two white officers, because they are mobbed if they make arrests. Two Negro officers won't do, either, because they shake down their own people. So all teams now include one white and one black, to watch the black and protect the white.

Negroes are seldom pinched, almost never for what they do to each other. If they assault a white man, he is arrested if he can still stand. The Negroes have too many votes to be treated like Caucasians. Joe Allen is the colored boss. What he says goes. And that's what he says.

The races mix openly all over. Leo's Casino, on Central, is a hot-spot. Negroes pick up white girls who come for jive at the Sky Bar and Celebrity Bar, on Euclid. Disc jockeys hang out at the Tia Juana. Other black-and-tan resorts are the Mercury, Gold Coast, Society Bar and Towne Casino. You can get anything at any hour at 6107 Hawthorne.

The sable horde swept over Cleveland so fast, it engulfed the tenderloin before the whites were able to move out. For instance, the hotel Doanbrooke, now surrounded by colored enterprises, is where chorus girls and fast models live. The Haddam Hotel, also white, at the otherwise completely black corner of 105th and Euclid, is the residence of many pimps, dope-pushers and queers, frequently pinched there. Lonesome wolves often visit the Alhambra Tavern and the Merry Widow bar, nearby, or Sam's Bar, at 107th, where they find gals who usually don't say no. They take them to such easy hotels as the Regent, at 82nd and Euclid, or the Colonial, Jefferson or Gilsey House, on Prospect, where they don't ask for a marriage certificate.

But the prime pick-ups are in the cocktail lounges of the big hotels. They go for fun or money. Professional hookers work the airport.

The Prospect area, downtown, is a little Chicago—tough, brazen, with dirty shows and B-girls. Koury's Bar runs South Clark Street-type shows, with continuous "entertainment" on a raised platform, supplied by "exotic dancers" who solicit drinks from bar customers between their turns. These women get $60 a week plus tips. There is no commission on drinks, differing from the Chicago practice; but there the girls get only $35. Cleveland hustlers must shill good business between acts to hold their show jobs. The Gay Nineties is a similar spot. You can find such girls also at the Roxy Musical Bar, El Bolero and the Howdy.

In Cleveland, clip joints are called "cheat spots."

Gray's drug store, at Euclid and 105th, is the only one in town always open. So pimps, old whores, narcotics salesmen and fairies hang around it. But the chief concentration point for the queers is the Greyhound bus terminal at Euclid and 107th; they meet in the rest-room. We did not find out whether it's the gents' or the ladies'.

Cleveland is easy for dope addicts as well as sellers. It is so easy to buy junk and reefers, a tie-up between local cops and the mobs is likely. The hottest dope corners are 55th and Central, and 55th and Scovil.

The hillbillies come up from Kentucky and Tennessee by the tens of thousands, tough mountaineers with knives. In Cleveland they locate near Negroes, and they are the only people the blacks are afraid of. The newcomers take no back talk from them. They handle them the Southern way. They have taken over the entire Hough area, where it is no longer safe to go into a beer joint. They bring young mountain girls who whore while their men carve each other and strangers with bowie knives. We saw mountaineers who looked as if they had just left Dogpatch at Dave's bar, on Hough, and the Colonial Garden, Bill's and the Tip Top, on 79th. Also at Phil's, on Euclid.

Cleveland has one of the most verminous skidrows in the country, on Superior Street, where winos, frowsy old bags and down-and-out bums hang around such notorious joints as Mack & Jerry's and the Hut. Clevelanders can't say they don't know about them.

because these dives are in the center of town, across the street from the Cleveland Hotel.

The prime minister of Cleveland is Ray T. Miller, Democratic boss. Other powers are Ben Green, Dan Duffy and Tom Terrell. The latter two control the election board. When Jury Commissioner Louis Bascik talks, he gets attention too. The white-collar segment of the Dems is dominated by Professor Henry Miller Busch, of Cleveland College, in charge of the big-dome vote; Allen Reeves, of the OPS, who rounds up the businessmen, and Albert A. Woldman, state director of industrial relations, who can be very troublesome to recalcitrant industrialists.

But these people are only the cabinet. The king, no benevolent monarch, is pink Jack Kroll, Ohio CIO boss, who not only runs Cleveland, but dictates to the State administration despite his 9th inning strike-out in 1950 when Taft was re-elected. But after all, all Federal, the statewide, and most municipal offices, are still held by Democrats beholden to the labor czars.

Through the close tie-up between crooked and left-wing unions, Democrats, coppers, and the Italians who have outgrown the Sicilian slums on Mayfield Road, local underworld activities were pirated from the Jewish mob, which dominated them. The Jewish bosses had to give up 50 per cent to the Mafia for protection, and the right to operate in Newport and Covington, Kentucky, the swank new Desert Inn in Las Vegas, and much hotel property in Miami.

While the Kefauver Committee treated Cleveland Italian leaders once over lightly, orders came down from the Sicilians, through the Democratic state committee, to make the non-Italians the goats, a procedure followed through at the hearings.

It costs $1,000 to get on the Cleveland police force, and the same for a promotion. You can square a murder for ten Gs and a manslaughter rap for one which is the price to have them docketed as "accidental."

Estes drooled and dribbled with praise for the municipal administration. It's Democratic. There's never been a President from Chattanooga.

B. Cincinnati—You Go There to Get Away From It

The Queen City, once the butt of burlesque comedians who lampooned its brewers, pork packers and strange classical name, was long a stately yet sporty center with some claims to culture. Now it has no consistently active theatre except one which presents the most shamelessly suggestive depravities in the same medium to which it once lent such broad, low comedy—burlesque.

This is the town where the rubber-soled sports from Indiana, Ohio, Pennsylvania and Michigan come to commute to the fun in Kentucky, across the bridge. It is one of the few big tourist and convention cities that has nothing to offer itself. Cincinnati thrives on the lawlessness in Kentucky counties, which have no hotels to accommodate the visitors, so everything is hunky-dory for everyone. The good trade crosses the river, leaving only cheap bums, drunks and streetwalkers on the Cincinnati side.

At midnight the town is unconscious. Not a soul on the streets. You can' walk ten blocks and not see life, but when the bars close, at two-thirty, they spew inebriates who stagger around until they are absorbed into the dullness.

We have seen better trollops elsewhere. With the class on the Kentucky side, only the worst of the old viragos are left for the winos, the strays and the sailors. We saw two policemen watching a broad pick up a drunk at 6th and Sycamore. She followed him for a block, tried to make a contact. He kept pushing her away. Finally she dragged him bodily into a hallway at 220 No. 6th, over which a sign said "Furnished Rooms." Most of these bims solicit around 7th and Vine and take their trade to assignation hotels on E. 5th.

Girls in the show at the House of Rinck and the Cat and Fiddle mix with the customers. After that it's up to you. But the prettiest girls are apparently the lonesomest and hang out at the bar of the famous old Gibson Hotel. Others are to be found at the Garfield Club and Hi-Hat on E. 6th.

For escorts—male or female—lonely visitors phone GA-2666.

Because of the wide-open competition across the Ohio, professional gambling in Cincinnati is minor league stuff, mainly runners to lay off piker bets or sell a five-cent policy slip. A new wrinkle is a mobile handbook, worked in an auto. The bookmaker tips off his customers he'll be at a certain intersection at a specific time. He picks up the bets there and moves on to the next location, then phones the bets by radio-phone.

Ike Hyams, a "retired" gambler, is still fairly important in the little action that runs. But on the whole it's pretty sad. We saw two bookies outside the King's newsstand, with no customers. They were betting each other to kill time.

Eliza was not the first wench who crossed from slave to free territory. Cincinnati has always had a big dark population and it's growing every day. The big sections are on Central Avenue, back of City Hall, and Plum Street, in the West End. They are tough people who show their independence by bumping whites off sidewalks. Kentucky Negroes, who have to kowtow at home, come to Cincinnati on excursions to maul and insult white folks, who don't talk back because if they do they'll get slugged and the cops will rule them wrong.

Anyway, that's how it was until the first of the year. Cincinnati's "nonpartisan" *burgermeister* was a New Deal equal-rightser. He was licked in November by a Republican. But the state is still Democratic and so is the nation. Bill Harlow, of the Murdock Plumbing Company, and Bill Leonard, the insurance man, are the Democrats who fix little things in Cincinnati. Big things, too.

25. NEW JERSEY — THE UPTOWN FLORIDA

THERE IS no such place as New Jersey. It is a breeding bed, playground and refuse dump for New York and Philadelphia and a refuge for their criminals. It is a highway between the two great cities. Few who use it ever stop off or look behind its billboards. If they did, they'd see plenty of ugliness.

Jersey has always been that way, since stage-coaches traveled between New York and Philly. Later the railroads moved in and took it over, and now the state has taken the roads over by imposing confiscatory taxes which relieve the citizens of paying any.

Freebooters were welcomed even as far back as the days when Wall Street, not the Mafia, did the robbing, and Jersey passed special laws which permitted incorporation of the giant octopi which became known as trusts.

When Jim Fisk stole the Erie Railroad he was sheltered in Jersey City while counterfeiting Erie shares. As late as Jimmy Walker's day, his bagman hid out across the Hudson, successfully defying New York probers. He was never questioned since.

There is so much vice and venality in Jersey that it is always in a ferment. The state has no independent underworld rulers of its own. The northern half is for all practical purposes a part of New York; the southern, including Atlantic City, is a part of Philadelphia.

Trenton, the capital, is halfway between and neutral, with both factions meeting there on common ground to bribe the legislature—price 100 per cent higher than in many other Eastern states, because of competition from the industries.

A Burke's peerage of New Jersey's underworld would be repetitious. The names are in the New York and Pennsylvania chapters.

The only individual unique to the state is Abner (Longie) Zwillman, giant of Prohibition days, who falsely pretends to be retired. Zwillman is so powerful he controls the political destinies of both major parties and acts as foreman of the works for the absentee owners from both ends.

Longie is one of the six non-Italians in the country permitted to operate in the exalted upper strata of the Big Mob. The others are Ralph Pierce, Murray Humphreys and Jake Guzik of Chicago, Meyer Lanksy of New York and Phil Kastel, New Orleans.

Longie's only superior in New Jersey is Tony Boy Boiardio, son of Prohibition king Ritchie Boiardio. Before the big merger Longie and Ritchie headed different mobs. When a witness inadvertently mentioned Boiardio's name before the Kefauver Committee, the chairman quickly changed the subject. The only reference to him in all the minutes is this notation in the Index: "Boiardo, Mr., Part 7, page 648." The probers did not know his first name and spelled his surname wrong. But they were aware he was a power at election time.

For many years Jersey has really had a one-party government, though both pretend to fight it out at the polls. This was a natural jelling, cooked up in the early days when Boss Hague, Jersey City's Democratic czar, cemented an understanding with his Republican opposite numbers, who ran the state. So, regardless of who sat in Trenton, there were no changes made anywhere; and that is the state of the state now, despite a highly advertised crime probe—which resulted in the conviction of Western Union on gambling charges and the incarceration of Joe Adonis as a bookie.

Jersey is doubly subject to such temblors because it is shaken up whenever New York or Philly gets hot. This "clean-up" dates to action in Gotham. The New York hoods were doing their business and keeping their books in Bergen County, as the Philadelphia mobsters always do in Camden and thereabouts.

The "drive" gave the Trenton bureaucrats an excuse to jug

a few enemies, get rid of some political opponents, and dust off the hand-set headline type. But little has changed. And little will.

This is just a brief rundown of some of the things rolling at this moment in Newark, the state's largest:

Uncle Joe's, on Halsey Street, and the Grotto in the Italian First Ward are running all night as usual. The Grotto is patronized by the hoodlum aristocracy, which makes the plans there that are sealed the next day in Bernie's Black Out, across the street from City Hall, where all fixes are made, municipally, stateside and Federal, as well as those with labor leaders.

One such in the works at this writing is a deal whereby Sal Moretti's boys will take over the book in the new Wright Aeronautical plant outside Paterson and kick back pro rata to the unioneers.

Jersey continues to harbor most of the top hoodlums of the area. When wanted for questioning, Zwillman, Irving Sherman or Mafistas are as safe in Bergen as at the top of Mount Everest. Newspapermen, including us, publish the addresses of their hideouts, but the Jersey state troopers can't find them just as they couldn't find or didn't want the two Mafia thugs who slugged Mortimer in Fort Lee.

The Kefauver Committee gave the state the brush-off, except to try to harass Jersey City's Mayor John V. Kenny, who licked Hague to a frazzle. The committee was anxious to get him for two reasons—because Hague is vice-chairman of the Democratic National Committee and Kefauver wants his support for President, and because John Winberry, who was on the Kefauver payroll as a special consultant, is a Hague outrider. The rest of the state got the committee go-by because too painstaking a probe might have shown up how extensive were the holdings of the Jersey mobsters in the Hudson & Manhattan R.R., connecting New York and Jersey City, and other big Jersey industries. Longie, caught in a jam, had been forced to admit under oath that he was a security holder in H & M. But the story ended right there—Rudy Halley had been chief counsel of the road until he was fired the day before he joined Kefauver and Dame Fortune.

Longie and other Jersey mobsters have long been used by the national crime cartel to handle its investments in legitimate— and some illegitimate—industries.

Jimmy "Nig" Rutkin, one of Longie's boys, sued Seagram's for $22,000,000, plus an accounting. Joe Nunan, a former U.S.

Commissioner of Internal Revenue, came to see him, warned that if he proceeded with his case Jimmy would be indicted on a tax rap. He was—twenty-four hours before the expiration on the statute of limitations.

Thereupon Uncle Sam threw the full power of the Treasury into the case (note the zealousness to prosecute those who pay off wrong) and Jimmy was convicted on evidence supplied by the defendants in his civil suit. But Rutkin, one of Broadway's best liked, refuses to be the goat.

There is one thing high class in Jersey. It's Ray Dillman's Casino-in-the-Park in Jersey City, just about the swellest refectory in the whole damn country—strictly out of place in the grimy factory town across the Hudson.

When Jersey City was a pocket possession of Hague, the boss, a puritan at heart, forbade night clubs, public dancing and entertainment, though he offered a haven to Manhattan gamblers, bookmakers and thieves to keep their books and divide their take. After the demise of the Hague machine three years ago, the new administration legalized terpsichore in a town where the art had been dead for more than three decades.

Dillman, a sui generis individual who had been manager of New York's super-swank El Morocco, was a Jersey boy at heart; he opened the first and only dance palace in the town, the classiest joint west of the Hudson. Its cellar grill is the unofficial city hall where Kenny's troops map the strategy to shear the unspeakable Hague machine of its last vestiges of power.

Can't think of a nicer way to do it, either.

PART THREE

THE LOWDOWN ON THE BIG TOWNS
(*Confidential!*)

26. NEW YORK CONFIDENTIAL – ACT II

HERE, embattled and betrayed, still stands our last citadel of civilization.

New York, the wonder of the world, is beset with self-seeking sharpers and their grubby, grabbing adherents, their eleemosynary morons and their missionaries of malcontent. But it has weathered siege and storm and remains our one surviving fortress of post-anthropoid existence. It contains the remnants of our art, culture, education, theatre and elegant living.

The same social termite elements that toppled San Francisco and New Orleans from their gracious cosmopolitan witcheries have gnawed at New York, but it is too big for them and it is founded on granite.

The inroads of the three R's—respectability, relief and radicalism—have been heavy, but New York has not yet struck its colors.

And there is high hope, because it draws the talent, the brains, the guts and the energy of the fading world.

Tammany, for centuries the emblem of our misrule, yet always a force for growth and progress in feeding its own grafting avarice, is in a coma of disrepute and desuetude. Our principal officials are nonpartisan, which means they must grovel before the deserting stragglers of all parties. Twenty years of Rooseveltism has tainted us with the noxious virus of vote-catching ordure that desensitized the olfactory perception which was an American gift for self-preservation. We are bedeviled by labor, racial and class groups which combine for only their own ends, contemptuous of the rest of us. All this has befallen us in a score of years.

It was not so until the reflex vibrations of the Great Panic ricocheted and drove the timid and the terrified to cover. They came out, hands up, to sell their souls for immediate pottage. A golden-tongued sorcerer fed it to the weaklings. And the American spirit of game battle was drowned in it.

That was, aptly, the period of the fall of Mayor Jimmy Walker, who became a sacrificial goat because he was the symbol of the city-of-light. Sure, Jimmy played along with the lads under the sign of the Tiger. Sure, he signed anything placed before him, for his nights were long and his days were short. Sure, grateful characters shoved bonds down in his pocket. Sure. But he was New York. He was urbane, scintillant, fastidious, epicurean; his latest quip was a laugh for the millions; his latest peccadillo was a wink and a grin for them; spokesman for the metropolis, he drew cheers and tears from them. Our Jimmy he was. Our Jimmy in the hockshops, in the club-houses and in the cathedrals. He loved the burg and he scorned blue-noses and the apostles of living by bread alone. He went for sports and beauty and music and champagne and carnival.

He was our last, lost dream.

Thereupon, after a year of transition (McKee and O'Brien) the revolution of the polyglot proletariat took over with the strident, greasy and pharisaical Little Flower, La Guardia. He assumed office on January 1, 1934. Only twenty-six days earlier, the Great Experiment had come to an end.

Never before or since, in the memory of living man, was the metropolis so wide open. Though the legal liquor closing hour was and is 4 A.M., no effort was made to shutter anything that stood right with the cops, City Hall, or, strangely enough, Tammany, though Fiorello was elected as a Tiger-killer.

Harlem had one of the greatest booms of its existence. During Prohibition no one had bothered Negro speaks if they bought their liquor from "Dutch" Schultz, whose booze domain extended there from the Bronx. By 1934, the colored inhabitants had reached such proportions that, voting in a bloc, they could well turn a city election. Though La Guardia had beaten (on a religious issue) Joseph V. McKee, the hand-picked candidate of Roosevelt and Ed Flynn, the blue-veined FDR quickly took the gutter idol into his fold—the alliance having been promoted by Eleanor, who, with Mrs. Perkins, Harry Hopkins and the rest of the settlement-house bunch, was an old slum-coddling companion of Fiorello's. He had her undercover support during his campaign, which showed professional Democrats—including FDR—that she was the Boss Tweed of the party.

The Roosevelts and La Guardia set about to take the Negroes, traditional Lincoln Republicans, into the fold. La Guardia not only set up the rule that no Negro was to be arrested for anything —but that police patrolling Harlem could not carry night sticks.

(That special pandering to colored criminals is still with us. While these pages were being typed, the police commissioner, on the representation of Negro groups, withdrew half the mounted police stationed in Harlem and promised to take the rest out soon. Horse-cops are a common sight all over midtown New York where they are not only welcome, but considered by citizens one of the labels of our city. But colored leaders said they frightened Negroes, made them think of cossacks.)

(The reason Harlem wants no mounted cops is simple. Foot patrolmen refuse to work there, except in pairs; even then they goldbrick and remain in the precinct houses [with approval of higher-ups] because their lives aren't safe. Motorized cops aren't much better off, because to be effective in breaking up riots or making pinches they must get out of their cars. But mounties are dreams for this kind of work. Educated police horses can go wherever a man can go. They can charge into sidewalk crowds, pursue fugitives up alleys, etc. And the man on the horse always has control of the situation.)

So Harlem became the big town's first nightlife Mecca after Repeal. Your authors remember trips to smoke-filled cabarets that did not open their doors until after 4 A.M., and ran until noon or as late as a chump could take it. Police cars were parked outside of brightly lighted clubs which were defying all the codes. One of the best known at the time was Dickey Wells, in a cellar, patronized by the theatrical elite. Dickey is dead now, but he recently got some posthumous fame in the trial of Tallulah Bankhead's ex-maid, when she testified that Dickey sold dope for her former mistress.

Everyone liked Wells, though he was known even in the thirties as a junk pusher. He sold it openly in his cafe. And Fiorello's flatfeet took payoffs, most of which went up along the line.

So brazen were the law-breakers under the Little Flower that they didn't hesitate to run illegally in mid-Manhattan. One of the nostalgic after-hour spots was the Kit Kat, on E. 55th Street, run by Julie Podell, who was a Costello boy then, and La Guardia knew it. But La G let it roll though its first show started at 4 A.M. Another midtown law-breaker was Dan Healy's Broadway Room on 54th Street, ten feet from Broadway, on the second floor of a building owned by the late Big Bill Dwyer, king of the bootleggers. Dwyer's offices were right above it. Costello put up the dough for the deadfall and La Guardia's minions were skunked—couldn't shut, couldn't shake.

Down in the Village Jimmy Kelly's famed club was running and it still is. Kelly is dead now, a great loss to New York nightlife, and his assigns close promptly at the legal hour. But Jimmy, an Italian, was a Tammany district leader and, strangely enough, all during the reign of La Guardia, who pretended to be Tammany's scourge, he was allowed to go all night. He had to begin to obey the law only when a Democrat came in.

It was at this time that the nucleus of the world-wide crime syndicate was being conceived in New York. The big boys had left Prohibition behind with billions; now they were looking for new enterprises and investments. LaGuardia was held forth as a bitter enemy of gangsters, but under his protection and with his encouragement the Mob was allowed to grow, congeal and become the Great Crime Cartel.

Before 1932, crime was local. Save for Chicago, the Black Hand gangs were subservient to older, non-Italian ones, for whom they acted as torpedoes.

LaGuardia was elected in 1933; he officiated until 1946. Costello is no subsequent creation of the past six years. The Italian mob had cleaned up all opposition by the late 1930's, after the rub-out of "Dutch" Schultz, who was the last of the nonaffiliated Prohibition kings still active. All this happened while La Guardia was orating every Sunday on the radio about "Let's drive the tinhorns out"—meaning Costello and Erickson—and then dining with Costello every Thursday night in the back room of a West 46th Street spaghetti house. The broadcasts and occasional publicized arrests of big shots (always discharged in court) were swell window-dressing and kept LaGuardia in office for three terms, during which the city was taken over by the underworld.

Parts of Harlem and East Harlem were still white, largely Italian. "Three Finger Brown" Luchese got the gambling. Joey Rao got the pimping and protection. Police Inspector Martini was put in command of the district, which proved so profitable that, before he was forced to resign and sacrifice his pension, he had salted away millions in Italy. Unfortunately for him this was before the war. His fortune was lost during hostilities.

La Guardia had been an attorney for Sidney Hillman's Amalgamated Clothing Workers and he retained his contacts with him and the ILGWU's Dubinsky, permitting the capitulation of the garment center to unioneers working with gangsters. Never before or since was there so much crime in the city.

Midtown assaults became so common, newspapers stopped reporting them unless prominent people were concerned. One who was attacked and got away with his life, though seriously injured, was George Jean Nathan, dean of drama critics, who was set upon by two muggers in W. 46th Street, within sight of Broadway.

Whoring went almost as open as in tenderloin days. Polly Adler, most famed of American madames, flourished, protected by the Sicilian mob. Hundreds of whoring flats were set up on Park Avenue, Central Park West and in the 50's.

Nowhere does the law give so much authority to a Mayor as the charter of the City of New York grants. He has full charge of law enforcement, free from uncooperative commissioners, sheriffs, state troopers, etc. The sheriff has only nominal, civil duties. He is not a peace officer. State police are not permitted within the city. New York's finest are the only coppers, and their commissioner is a personal appointee of the Mayor, not subject to confirmation, serving at his pleasure. Through the commissioner, the Mayor approves every promotion, demotion or act of discipline.

County judges and district attorneys receive pay from the city. The judges of the inferior courts are appointed by the Mayor without confirmation. The Mayor is ex-officio the chief magistrate and may hold court or set up an inquiry. One of his personal cabinet, also serving at the Mayor's pleasure, is a commissioner of investigation, with subpoena power, who may inquire into the affairs of any city or county office-holder, including district attorneys, of which there are five—one for each of the five component counties which make up the city. The Mayor may require prosecutors to report to him. The Mayor assumes complete responsibility and can be held to blame (and removed by the Governor) for failure of his subordinates. For ten of Fiorello's twelve years as Mayor, the Governor was bewildered Herbert Lehman.

Now, regardless of what you heard or read elsewhere, we will tell you what really happened when Fate stepped in and handed Bill O'Dwyer Murder Inc., on a platter. The new prosecutor immediately realized what he had when Al Aman, veteran U.S. nar-

cotics agent in Chicago, ran into a couple of unaccounted-for
bodies in the Catskills, while working on a mob junk lead. Aman
is one of the brainiest men in the bureau. When he had finished
with his case, he had worked up evidence on Murder Inc., which
O'Dwyer foresaw was the biggest thing since Dewey had sent
Luciano to Sing Sing. O'Dwyer is not infallible nor a saint, but regardless of what hit-and-run lenshounds like Tobey, Kefauver and
Halley say, he did break up Murder, Inc., and kept New York
clean of labor protection murders for years.

Unwittingly, he played into the Mafia's hands, because Lepke
and Gurrah were the last of the important Jewish criminals in
the East. Though nominally subject to the Sicilians, they were
too big and powerful for the comfort of the black-handers, who
preferred them out of the way.

O'Dwyer attempted to cash in on the destruction of Murder
Inc., and in 1941, while still district attorney of Kings, he ran for
Mayor against La Guardia, who was seeking his third term. La G
won by a small plurality. O'Dwyer returned to his duties in
Brooklyn and began to work on something so spectacular that he
would have to get his dream fulfilled in the future.

Bill O'Dwyer told us himself at Gracie Mansion, shortly before he resigned to become Ambassador to Mexico, in the presence of Gene Fowler and his daughter and Johnny O'Connor,
musicians' agent, a story which has never been printed before.
For years there had been rumors hinting at what O'Dwyer finally
confirmed for us.

On December 7, 1941, he said, one month after La Guardia
had been re-elected, O'Dwyer was finally prepared to bring before the grand jury first-degree murder charges against La Guardia
and Sidney Hillman, after investigating a killing in the 1920's, an
era of mob murders in the men's clothing industry, whose union
was owned by Hillman. O'Dwyer said he had evidence that Hillman had ordered several murders of recalcitrants and that La-
Guardia, as the union's lawyer, had suborned perjury and squared
the killings after the fact, which would make him a principal
accessory.

O'Dwyer said he was working in his Brooklyn study on that
memorable Sunday, December 7, on the final testimony he planned
to bring before the grand jury the next day, when he heard of the
attack on Pearl Harbor. That night, Bill said, he got a call from
Washington, apparently placed by the President personally, because no operator came on first.

To get the drama of this situation, you must realize war had broken on us a few hours earlier. We had sustained the greatest military defeat in our history. But the President of the United States called him, according to O'Dwyer. This is a free version of the conversation:

"Bill, as you know, we are at war. Everything must be placed aside for its successful completion. I heard yesterday through the grapevine that you were going to try to indict LaGuardia and Hillman. I do not know the merits of the case. But I consider these men vital to the war effort. We must keep the Italians in line because we are fighting Italy, so I can have nothing happen to LaGuardia. And I need Hillman to see that the unions will join ranks for the country too. So as your commander in chief I call on you to do nothing now that will conflict with those objectives."

Bill did nothing. He did not mention further conversations, if any, but obviously there were some. O'Dwyer took a leave of absence as D.A., accepted an Army commission and rose to become a brigadier general and a military governor of Italy.

He came back in time to run for Mayor in 1945. Tammany pals tell us La Guardia understood he better not run against Bill, or else. La Guardia not only did not run, but did not back the regular Republican candidate, putting a third party up as a stalking horse, the candidate, young Newbold Morris, a silk-stocking with little ability, personality or following. But he took enough votes from O'Dwyer's opposition to guarantee Bill's election.

O'Dwyer was no tin angel. But during his five years as Mayor, New York was cleaner than it had been in decades. La Guardia, a socialist, was a cop-hater. Under him there was no morale in the ranks. But O'Dwyer, an ex-policeman, understood police mentality, and he sparked a new spirit.

Most of the big madames left town.

Street vice was cut in half. White people were discouraged from going to Harlem, where police had been issued nightsticks again and were reinforced by mounted men. Many of the more flagrant after-hour spots were shut down. Table gambling was virtually eliminated. New York had not suddenly gone purist. It never was and we hope it never will be. People are alike all over the world. For the sins they are denied they adopt others, which eager and scheming men are always prepared to offer and exploit.

The Mafia had become so firmly entrenched that even had O'Dwyer been disposed to run it out he could not. We contend no one can do that anywhere any more, because the Crime Cartel has become a super-secret government, more powerful than the elected ones. All officials and all parties must function within the framework.

O'Dwyer was not and is not well. He grew tired. We believe he was comparatively poor. His physician advised him to take it easy for a couple of years. O'Dwyer was inclined to accept an offer as president of the Translux theatre chain, at $100,000 a year, until he could return and pursue his real ambition—to run for Governor of New York.

Outside pressures again changed the course of Bill's life. A special election for U.S. Senator had been called. Lehman was the Democratic candidate. State chairman Flynn feared Lehman would take a licking, as he had from Ives, unless a strong candidate ran for Mayor of New York on the ticket. So he and Truman insisted O'Dwyer stick for the sake of the party, and they promised to "support him for Governor" later. O'Dwyer ran, won and pulled in Lehman. But the next year, for similar reasons in reverse, he had to step out. No one had envisioned that Tom Dewey would run for Governor again. When he did decide, the Democrats knew that in even-year elections, when strong New Deal Democratic New York City has no important contests, upstate Republican votes usually decide the issue.

So Bill, a recent bridegroom, was given his chance to rest up. He had always dreamed of being an ambassador. He loved Mexico. Truman sent him there—to make a special election in New York City. The timing was shrewdly schemed so no primary could be held for the mayoralty candidates. The organization handpicked Justice Ferdinand Pecora. It was charged in the campaign that he was Frank Costello's personal choice.

Council President Vincent Impellitteri, who was acting Mayor after O'Dwyer quit, thought he was entitled to the promotion. Many others thought so too. So he ran as an independent. So powerful had the Italian vote become in New York that the Republicans also nominated an Italian nonentity, splitting it up three ways. Charges were freely passed that all three candidates had at various times been seen at public and social gatherings with noted gangsters. Though Impy was said to be on close terms with Luchese, and a night club visitor with Adonis, the voters gave him the job.

At about this time the present wave against bookmaking and the consequent revelation of fixing of law-enforcement officers that always follows began to break into a major scandal. It seemed fortunate to O'Dwyer's friends that he had resigned when he did. Though O'Dwyer had inherited the headache from La-Guardia, under whose administration bookmaking and policy-selling had become tremendous industries, O'Dwyer's enemies tried to make him appear as the instigator of the sell-out to the underworld. He was particularly the victim of the venom of Judge Leibowitz, who had hated O'Dwyer ever since Bill took the nomination for Kings County district attorney from him. Leibo-witz's big ambition had always been to be prosecutor, not judge; he is at his height before the bar, fighting spectacular cases.

In days when Leibowitz was New York's leading criminal at-torney, he specialized in springing murderers. Only one of his clients was unfortunate enough to burn, and that wasn't Sam's fault. He handled many top mobsters and with uniform good luck turned them back into circulation. When he had amassed sufficient means from the underworld to live comfortably for life, his profound ambition took hold. He didn't make it, but as a judge he has been the antithesis of the defense counselor. He is the toughest on the bench, handing out severe sentences, prod-ding grand juries, crusading against crime.

When O'Dwyer resigned to become Mayor, his first assistant, by long custom, stepped up. The Gross gambling scandal began to break. Leibowitz lit the spark which forced the new Kings County district attorney to tear into the former Mayor, at first reluctantly, because he was loyal to his old chief.

Which brings us to New York Confidential, circa 1952.

A. Sidewalks of New York

East Side, West Side, all around the town, the hoods play ring-a-rosie in duplex penthouses, luxury hotels and private clubs in converted mansions.

Only down below is New York comparatively quiet, because, no matter what is said or read about our police force, we still have the finest in the country, probably in the world. There are crooks in every walk of life, so some got on the force, where pay is so low and temptations are so great. After all the hullabaloo, not more than one per cent of the roster was exposed, with more suspicion than evidence against most of them. New York has al-most 20,000 coppers. One per cent of that is 200—it makes a big splash. Three policemen caught stealing in a force of 300 doesn't raise a ripple. But New York derelictions burn up the wires because the legions of little lost lummoxes in the interior smack their lips over sin in Gotham, where they'd all love to live.

Much that is not tolerated in New York is accepted as general custom in the Bible Belt. We do not legally permit strip-teasers or nudes in our clubs and we have banned burlesque. The few peelers who work New York keep on more than you see at the beaches. Our dicks are murder on B-girls. Few night clubs will even take the chance of letting legitimate performers sit out with male friends, including their husbands. Many bars will not permit unescorted women or any women even with men at the bar. There is cheating, but it isn't general.

Gambling, a basic human vice, breaks out covertly. At the present, bookmaking is underground, as it is all over the country, being handled as described heretofore, by phone, union shop foremen and runners who pretend to be taking "social" bets.

Since the departure of O'Dwyer, who would not tolerate open table gambling, the Italian boys took up where they left off when La Guardia went out. The same concessions have been resumed, with Tommy Luchese having the monopoly for Manhattan card and crap games. Most of them run in his East Harlem bailiwick, one of the largest in a flat house at 103rd and Lexington. Chumps are transported in limousines stationed at strategic locations around Times Square—in front of the Piccadilly Hotel, the Victoria, and night clubs where some captains act as steerers. The gambling runs in the heart of ex-Representative Marcantonio's district. Marcantonio appointed Luchese's son to West Point in 1946.

Regardless of election outcomes, the Mafia, which backs all parties, is solid, politically and financially. It owns several of the largest hotels and at least one of the members of the syndicate which bought the Empire State Building from the Raskob estate is a frontman who invests underworld millions in legitimate enterprises.

Of course, many of the new owners are entirely legitimate.

Colonel Henry Crown, of Chicago, the new chairman of the Empire State, was an associate of Jake Arvey in a shady real estate grab in Chicago, to buy property which they knew was to be condemned for a new super-highway. Arvey is the Illinois Democratic boss, a frequent companion of the Fischettis and Capones. We have often seen them dining with him at the Chez Paree. Another stockholder is a New England relative of Sam Bronfman, of Montreal, described before a Senate committee as "the world's richest bootlegger."

The political arm of Costello was Ed Flynn, Bronx boss, former chairman of the Democratic National Committee and right-hand man of FDR, who nominated him to be Minister to Australia. But a usually subservient Senate turned him down when it was brought out that Flynn had diverted city property and city-paid help to pave the courtyard of his country estate.

The Manhattan Democratic leader, boss of Tammany Hall, is Carmine De Sapio, with whom Impy broke when he ran for Mayor as an independent. Impy hates De Sapio so bitterly he has refused all truce offers. So the Tammany leader has gone into a secret alliance with Rudy Halley, who is being groomed by Dave Dubinsky as the next Mayor of New York. De Sapio promised his support in the primaries. He, too, is a close friend of Costello.

Halley, elected president of the city council as a splinter-party choice, advertised as a crime-buster, was backed by criminals. The underworld knows politicians, to be elected, occasionally must make goats of gangsters, pretend they are fighting them.

The Manhattan borough president is young Robert Wagner, ambitious son of the smug author of the Wagner Labor Relations Act. This job is a Costello perquisite. The last occupant, Hugo Rogers, was an admitted friend of both Costello and Marcantonio. He fell with O'Dwyer and young Wagner was put in as a cover. Rogers went on Wagner's payroll with a $10,000 job.

Halley had to make a bluff about following up some of the things the Kefauver Committee had chosen to expose. Rogers' name had figured frequently. Halley demanded his dismissal. As we have frequently pointed out, there are many expendables in the underworld—but Halley neglected to inquire into the bona fides of Borough President Wagner himself, who got a lift from Costello and employed a press agent who publicized Costello and Representative F. D. Roosevelt, Jr., also.

Since his induction, Halley's urge for political preferment has kept him before the public like a sideshow freak. With a little-dictator complex typical of political pipsqueaks, Rudy clamped down "security regulations," ostracizing the press from talking to any of his employes without permission. This wave of bureaucratic censorship conflicts strangely with his attitude during the Kefauver hearings, when he insisted the public was entitled to information, even at the expense of the constitutional rights of witnesses. For his handling of the Kefauver investigation, the

New York State Bar Association adopted a resolution condemning Halley's actions requiring witnesses "to testify against their will before television, newsreel, kleig lights, flash bulbs and nation-wide radio." It asserted this had given rise to "grave questions of constitutional law and public policy."

The great power of the underworld in New York is concentrated even more in the courts than in administrative bodies and is guaranteed by "bi-partisan" nominations. The Costello influence is found on the Federal and state benches. Despite the Kefauver hearings, it is still potent, as the following story will indicate.

When the Kefauver Committee cited Costello for contempt of Congress, the case was referred to U.S. Attorney Irving Saypol, who was affectionately known to his subordinates as Irving Cesspool. Saypol is a close friend of Generoso Pope, publisher of the big Italian language newspaper, *Il Progresso,* who is also a multi-millionaire contractor. Pope is a close friend of Costello. While Saypol was U.S. Attorney, his wife practiced law and her firm handled many cases referred by Pope and his associates. At the time of the Kefauver hearings in New York in March, 1951, Saypol said he would prosecute Costello for contempt and perjury. At this writing no perjury indictment had been returned, though a contempt indictment—a misdemeanor at the most—was returned. Later it proved faulty.

Thereafter, Democratic district leader John Merli, frequently linked with Costello, obtained a New York Supreme Court nomination for Saypol. He was elected last fall and resigned from the U.S. attorney's office. His successor, Myles Lane, one of the few U.S. attorneys whom we could find with no gangster affiliations, went back to the grand jury and got a new contempt indictment against Costello. It was tried but the jury disagreed. We predict he will never serve time.

Most New Yorkers have already forgotten Costello's $100-a-plate Salvation Army party at the Copacabana, attended by a score of high judges, among them Halley's sponsor, Pecora. But not all of Costello's boys on the bench showed up. A few couldn't make it; one, luckily, got the directions mixed and arrived after it was all over.

The Mafia is thick also with more than half of New York City's twenty-three-man congressional delegation. Representative Klein, an unpleasantly loud-mouthed reformer and spokesman of scum, appointed the son of one of our most notorious gamblers to West Point last year. During the war, Klein got priorities for some

Costello enterprises. He is a pal of the crowd behind Yonkers Raceway. Representative Celler, of Brooklyn, another bleeding heart, slipped through a joker to try to bring 50,000 more Sicilians into the United States. This would have strengthened the shock troops of the Black Hand.

One of the most eye-lifting situations which turned up in years was the appointment of Samuel Kaufman to the Federal bench. As an attorney, Kaufman had not only represented Serge Rubenstein, the draft evader, but had handled numerous clients who were close to Costello and Flynn. A couple of years ago, Flynn and other Democrats found themselves faced with a complicated situation. They were interested in two cases due to come up shortly in the Federal court. One was the reorganization and bankruptcy of the Third Avenue Transit System, in which Flynn and a clique of mobsters were known to hold securities. The other was the trial of Alger Hiss, which the White House had called a red herring. The Administration wanted an acquittal.

There was a vacancy for a Federal judge in the Southern District of New York. Kaufman, without any pronounced qualifications, was nominated for it by Truman. A couple of weeks later, while he was sitting in the calendar part, he assigned the Third Avenue and the Hiss cases to himself, a procedure practically unprecedented in the Federal courts of this district.

His conduct of the first Hiss trial caused a tempest. The papers reported how he continually favored the defense and tried to belittle the government's chief prosecution witness, Whittaker Chambers. He refused to let the government cross-examine many defense witnesses, and by facial gestures and otherwise, tried before the jury to discredit witnesses against Hiss.

In his handling of the Third Avenue bankruptcy he consistently ruled in favor of the Flynn-Costello mob, issuing illegal injunctions against the unions, which were vacated by higher courts, and proposing higher fares, though, as a liberal Fair Deal Democrat who bent backward to favor Communist-traitor Hiss, he should have shown more regard for the fare-paying proletariat.

In another part of this book we ran down the list of the top members of the Unione Siciliano, most of whom operated as absentee owners from New York and Brooklyn. When they aren't swanking it at the Waldorf you can usually find them dining in the Patio Bruno, a fine bistro in the Rockefeller project in W. 55th Street near 5th Avenue.

The top local working gangsters who seem to bear charmed

lives at investigation time are headed by the infamous Vito Genovese, who also holds a membership on the Grand Council, and Tommy "Three Finger Brown" Luchese.

The Sicilian hierarchy—which now names or vetoes all political nominations—includes the following representatives of 300 others:

"Fat Joe" Albano. J. Alfano, 1328 70th St., Brooklyn. Jimmy "Blue Eyes" Alo. Alphonse Attardi, 400 E. 11th St. Joe Biondo, 7712 35th St., Jackson Heights. Joe Bedellia, alias Bedeli, also Beverly and Catalano. Tony (The Chief) Bonasira, 1117 83rd St., Brooklyn. Frank Carbo, king of the fight racket. Little Augie Carfano. Joseph Ciarella, alias Joe Martello. Albert J. Contento, alias Al Howard. Trigger Mike Coppola (International List 052). Alex and Tony de Bellis. Joseph De Giovanni, alias Joe Chick. Tony Guarino. Joe (Socks) Lanza. Mike LiMandri, 325 E. 58th St. (International List 187). John "Bath Beach" Oddo. Joey Rao. Vito Sisto, 6619 10th St., Brooklyn. Anthony Strollo, alias Tony Bender. Joe Tocco, 315 E. 114th St.

As already stated, street vice is not popular in this town. The citizens don't like it. We are sophisticated, prefer our sins and immorality amid the silks, satins and fine linens, amid surroundings many of us can afford. And cheap chippies on the loose are bad for legitimate businesses like hotels, department stores, the many fine restaurants and other upper-bracket institutions which make New York unique. Even the top gangsters want to keep New York this way. They live here, raise their families here, are men about town who patronize the opera, first nights and cafes. Our silk-lined ace hoodlums are not flatnosed torpedoes with cauliflower ears, but conservatively groomed men, whom you would mistake for bankers, which many of them now are.

Where side-street sin is organized, the big boys of the Crime Cartel have no hand in it themselves, but hand it out for cigarette money to poor relatives. That is why Greenwich Village can get away with almost anything—it is run by Alan Bono, a cousin of Joe Adonis.

We cannot give you here a compendium on what goes. The following paragraphs are a few, at random, as they occurred to us:

The fairy situation is a pronounced problem, the more so because, in addition to our own, we get the pick of the nation's pansy crop. Like everything else in New York, our homosexuals are divided into three geographic strata—downtown, the West Side, and the East Side. The Greenwich Village she-males are supposed to be the artistic set in an esoteric bohemian colony where everyone knows everyone else. One of their favorite gathering places is the Moroccan Village, on West 8th Street. They can be found also at almost every bar on Third Street, where Lesbians, too, foregather.

The most famous fag joint in town was the 181, at that number
on Second Avenue. After we wrote about it, City Hall was reluctantly forced to shutter it; but it was allowed to reopen sans
liquor license, ostensibly as a hot jive place, but actually to steer
customers to the Rainbow Inn, around the corner, where the gay
girls and boys moved, show and all. As a patron enters the recon-
structed 181, he is told "We only sell cokes; there's no show."
When the customer's face falls, he is handed a card for the
Rainbow.

The West Side fairy contingent is comprised of bums who prey
on lonesome servicemen. They mince around Times Square and
as far east as Bryant Park bars, where a fat fag known as Tiny,
is a front man for the lush workers. Nances work out of Times
Square and infest cafeterias, flea circuses and grind movies under
the eyes of the Navy Shore Patrol and the MPs. Another popular
homo hangout is the Chase cafeteria on 42nd Street.

Fifth Avenue bisects New York. Everything east of it is worlds
apart from the West Side. The East Side is where you find the
wealth, splendor, magnificence and discrimination, as well as the
interesting people, the aristocrats, the entertainment stars and
that most recherche of all cafes, John Perona's El Morocco.

So it is understandable that the East Side homos should be a
cut above those in the other parts of town. We have two breeds
East of the Avenue—the streetwalkers, who parade along Lexington Avenue, from 45th to 59th, and the swish-swells. The streetwalkers are college boys and young "intellectuals" who prance
Lexington, arm in arm, or try to make pick-ups, usually accosting
Negroes. There are some twenty or thirty cocktail lounges along
the avenue and adjoining side streets, all patronized almost exclusively by fairies, and it is not uncommon to see as many as a hundred young near-men packed up against the bar without a woman
on the premises. One of the most patronized is the Golden Pheasant, on 45th just east of Lexington. Another is the beautiful Chan-
delle Bar, on E. 48th.

New York's colleges, special schools and art, music and dramatic
classes abound with queers. Young "men" work their way through
college by such prostitution. Many live at the West 63rd Street
YMCA, where the 9th and 10th floors are notorious as a homosexual whorehouse.

As for our upper-crust blunders of nature—stage stars, millionaires, politicians, diplomats, rounders—you'd be amazed if we told
you their names because they include some of the biggest people

in the United States. They and their opposite numbers, the Lesbians, are usually careful to keep their tendencies private. They mix and associate in top social sets. Many are married, many are parents.

Lexington Avenue is also the chief parade ground of our small contingent of female streetwalkers. We mean small in proportion to all other towns. They are conspicuous on Lexington, where they compete with the boys for the trade of the many well-heeled visitors who stay in East Side hotels. There are no parlor houses in Manhattan and assignation hotels are few because of the housing shortage. So, if you pick up a dame, you've gotta have a place to take her. Few hotels interfere with their patrons' private pleasures if they're quiet about them, though they are on the alert to guard customers from broads who slip them knockout drops and roll them without even coming across.

A lower type of sidewalk solicitor can be found walking along a figure "U" with 7th Avenue, from 52nd to 42nd as one arm, then across 42nd to 8th, and back up to 52nd, along that thoroughfare. These are old, flowsy hookers. If you have no place to go, they will turn a trick in a doorway or take you to a cheap fleabag on Dream Street—47th between 6th and 7th.

Dope is easily obtainable all over town. Puerto Ricans, who have overflowed the boundaries of East Harlem, are now spread into all sectors; and wherever they go they sell narcotics. Broadway, from 50th to 52nd and around the corner of 7th Avenue, is now a Little San Juan, as dark as 110th Street and 5th Avenue. Narcotics agents frequently make arrests in the La Salle Cafeteria, on 51st and 7th, and up and down the adjoining streets, including half the dives on Swing Lane—52nd Street—where only Leon & Eddie's and the 21 Club remain monuments to the days of its decency and glory. Dope buys are made also at the Silver Dollar Cafeteria, on 7th Avenue, where bobby-sox pick-ups and V-girls, some thirteen, give you the eye. They hang out at 50th and 8th, too.

Conditions in Harlem and East Harlem are indescribably frightful. This is the most ghastly ghetto in the world, yet more Negroes and Puerto Ricans flock in, by hundreds of thousands, every year. In one calendar year 101,000 Puerto Ricans arrived by air, alone. There is and there can be no attempt at law enforcement in the area. It is a jungle practically unpoliced. If you don't get killed first you can buy a dame or dope at any corner. There is nothing in the land as terrifying as what police call the "Catacombs," a series of cellars connected by secret subterranean passages running for about a half-mile in the vicinity of 111th and 112th, west of Fifth. Hundreds of dope-fiends sleep underground there, with rats crawling over them. They fight each other like the rats for money to buy junk. They take "mainliners," jagging open the artery with an eye-dropper sharpened to a point or with a piece of broken glass. Nowhere are humans so degraded as the Negroes and Puerto Ricans in the Catacombs—thousands of the tens of thousands in the area, who are on relief or get welfare handouts, with which they buy dope.

These animals have been fed on propaganda so long, they assume the community owes them not only a living, but junk-money. The problem is so bad, two deputy police commissioners have been assigned to cooperate with the Department of Welfare to eradicate the wave of assaults and threats to which welfare investigators have been subjected; many have been beaten and maimed by women and men demanding higher handouts, enforcing perjured claims with threats, demanding cocaine as "medicine."

While bookmaking in other parts of the city has temporarily gone underground, police are making no attempt to stop the sale of numbers tickets, one of Harlem's chief industries. These rackets are run at the operating level by colored people, but are controlled at the top by the Italians.

A Negro newspaper, the *New York Age,* warned that its people throughout the country are supporting the new Italian occupation of Somaliland, in Africa, with war materials bought from the proceeds of the cheap lottery racket. The paper complains that the Italians have pushed Negro policy-bank operators out of the picture. This was long regarded as a Negro monopoly. James R. Lawson, president of the United Africa Nationalist movement, reported to the police about threats made by Italian gangsters in the bar of the Hotel Theresa, warning Negroes to lay off.

The Age said all but two Negroes in Harlem have been pushed out of the numbers by the Black Hand. It named Luciano as the power behind the throne in Italy, who dictates to Premier de Gasperi.

New Yorkers, smartest of all people, are amazingly lackadaisical over local politics and crime. They are easily taken in by left-wingers. To generate excitement a clean-up on a scandalous scale alone works. That often shoots someone up to high office. But no one stays interested long. New Yorkers are not puritans. Our police try hard, but the job is too big for them and they are not always free to do it.

The amateur crime-hunters are usually worse than useless. Some businessmen recently got together and formed the New York Anti-Crime Committee, a pallid copy of Virgil Peterson's vigorous Chicago Crime Commission. The chairman of the New York outfit is former ambassador Spruille Braden, unsophisticated and egotistical. He is surrounded by a staff which includes former members of the unfortunate Kefauver Committee and others who either don't know their way around or are otherwise incompetent.

One of the few far-seeing locals is State Senator Seymour Halpern, who, though a Republican, is perennially re-elected from a Democratic district with the highest plurality for any office on either ticket. Even before Kefauver introduced his resolution in Washington, Halpern had advocated a select committee of the New York Legislature to investigate organized crime in the state and its ties with syndicated crime in other states, as well as its Wall Street banking connections and local financial and real estate operations.

Governor Dewey, himself an old crime-fighter of renown, turned thumbs down; but shortly thereafter he appointed an executive commission to investigate. Its members are either nonentities or aged. Former Judge Proskauer, chairman, will soon be seventy-five. Another member is former police commissioner and state Liquor Authority head Mulrooney, who ran both offices with a loose hand.

New York's liquor laws are among the most liberal in the nation. We have a late closing—4 A.M.—which makes it unprofitable for after-hour spots, of which there are now only a few. The average Gothamite has lost his capacity for staying awake so late. The best-known "bottle club" is Jimmy Carr's Club Carr, now in an E. 69th Street mansion, catering to the swells. The Gold Key, on 56th Street, between 5th and 6th (next door to Blair House) gets away with everything. One of the most brazen dives is the Lilac, on the second floor of an old private house at 56 E. 56th Street. It was started by Nick Bates, former owner of the Merry-Go-Round, who seemed to have an "in" in the proper places. Suckers paid $35 membership fees to keep a bottle in the "club," then saw that anyone who didn't look like trouble could drink all night in the place at a buck a throw for diluted Scotch and rye. It is dangerous to fall asleep in the joint, which has soft, drowsy lights.

In the Murray Hill district there's the Kane Club, on 38th, between Lexington and Park. Several dives deal wild near Broadway, catering to late musicians; but their main trade is in reefers.
There are no rules for Italian all-night spots in Greenwich Village or the lower East Side. But these, like the dens in Harlem
and East Harlem, are seldom patronized by any but their own
groups. Which is just as well, because you wouldn't want to go
anyway.

B. The Empire State

This is a brush-off on outlying New York State, a sample of
what goes—and what doesn't—in one of America's principal concentrations of wealth and people.

New York, giant among cities, is but half of the great, huge
Empire State.

The second city, Buffalo, ranks fifteenth in the United States,
with 600,000 population. We think of it as a village. New York
has nine cities with more than 100,000. Westchester and Nassau
counties are, for all practical purposes, municipalities, each with
a population of about 500,000. The New York non-metropolitan
area is larger in size and population than many important European powers—surpassing all three Scandinavian countries combined. Westchester County, north of the Bronx line, has the highest per capita wealth in the world. And a good deal of it passes
through the hands of Tony Milo, of Yonkers, its top Sicilian.

As one goes farther up along the Hudson he hits Albany, with
its tributary cities of Troy and Schenectady. Most other state capi-
tals go heavy on bagnios for rubes who come in during sessions,
but Troy is so near Albany that the hayseeds drive the ten miles
to where they won't be seen, and patronize some of the lowest cottage whore-houses left in the country. All Albany is the fief of the
O'Connell Democratic machine, the strongest of the few left in
the country. Though Albany has barely more than 150,000 population, the O'Connells beat Governor Tom Dewey when he committed himself to run them out. Dewey superseded the O'Connell
district attorney with a special prosecutor who breathed fire and
brimstone, but suddenly let the grand jury investigation die.
Rumors passed through the corridors of the capitol that the
O'Connells had threatened to accuse U.S. Senator Irving Ives,
then an influential Republican State Senator, and Lieutenant
Governor Joe Hanley in unnamed matters.

Ives, now a sanctimonious teetotaler in Washington, and a Republican me-tooer who supports all Fair Deal measures, used to be a convivial hell-raiser in Albany; and back in Norwich, New York, he was considered quite a cut-up.

Ive's conversion to the left-turn radical fringe is so pronounced that he has hired the blathering John F. Carter, who writes under the pen name of Jay Franklin to ghostwrite his campaign speeches this fall when he stands for re-election.

In the 1930's Carter served as a research assistant to Rex Tugwell, a darling of the pinks, on the socialist resettlement project. He worked as a ghost and paid propagandist for FDR and Truman and wrote most of Harry's speeches in 1948. Carter plugged for a soft policy against Russia.

Marxian-apologist Carter's salary will be paid by the New York State Republican Committee!

Policy is wide open in the mainline towns of Syracuse, Rochester and Buffalo, and everything is handily nonpartisan in Catskill and Adirondack resort regions, handled by the Cole Syndicate of Syracuse.

Upstate New York Sicilian strength is recognized as a political factor by Democrats and Republicans alike. The smaller towns as well as the jaspers usually vote GOP, whereas many of the cities are Democratic in Republican counties.

Regardless of how they appear on the ballot, to be elected a candidate must be cleared by these Italian hierarchs, whose nod can open or close a community:

(NOTE: While these lines were being typed, Joe Di Carlo's Buffalo principality was in the throes of a "clean-up." When the laundry comes back it will be found as dirty as ever.)

Domenico and Giuseppe Aida, Rochester. Patsy Amico, 1315 Culver, Rochester. Giuseppe Anello, Buffalo. Frank Barrata, Buffalo. John Camizzo, 529 N. Salina, Syracuse. Alfonso Catalano, 822 Niagara, Buffalo. Giovanni Catanzaro, Niagara Falls. Tony D'Agortino, East Rochester. Joe and Jerry di Carlo, Buffalo. Phil Gimoreno, Lockwood Avenue, Yonkers. Carlo Mancino, Buffalo. Rocco Pellegrino, Rochester. Joseph Quintano, 21 Court St., Buffalo.

The reigning upstate Sicilian Grand Duke is Stephen Magardino, 1809 Whitney Ave., Niagara Falls.

27. CHICAGO CONFIDENTIAL (ACT II)

*T*HEY CAN'T say we did Chicago on the fly. Lait lived there during twenty-five of his most active years. Mortimer was born and raised there. Both have winnowed their old home town and state, looking for something new, something different, something to tell you as a postscript to our thick book about it. But nothing to speak of showed up.

This Gulliver on the Lake is still captive to the mobsters and political thieves, as it has been since Mike McDonald tied it up. Both big parties have had their innings, changed its putative leadership, and left it unchanged.

If Chicago goes Democratic, Cook County swings Republican. And when the state is thrown one way, the city offsets it. Now and again a reformer gets into office; he is chucked out quickly or he is absorbed. Upsets and turnovers rate a flash and a shrug and then the old platter sings the same old sour melody.

Dissolute, vulgar and carnal, Chicago is the national abattoir not only for its traditional commodities but for all that is fine and soft and sweet. Its virile men and lovely women have passed on and left behind descendants without pride of birth or love of place; most of them have fled into the suburbs or further away, leaving the city to the children of alien blood and stultified spirit. Its fighting motto was "I Will!" Now it is "Stick 'em Up!"

This is the picture of Chicago two years after the publication of *Chicago Confidential:*

Tom Connelly and the late Bill Drury were bounced as police captains because they arrested Al Capone's bagman, Jake Guzik, for the murder of James Ragen, the wire service king who wouldn't scare. They appealed through the state courts to the U.S. Supreme Court, but their dismissal stood.

The captain of a police district which covers a honkytonk area admitted last year that he had taken large payments from a gambling racketeer. He was tried and ordered discharged by the civil service commission. But when he appealed to the Illinois courts, he was ordered reinstated.

That speaks for the administration of justice in Illinois.

Drury, bravest of the bulls, was ambushed and slain while he was cooperating with the Republican candidate for sheriff. In Illinois, the sheriff is the chief peace officer and may supersede the local authorities, though he seldom does so. The Democratic candidate was former police captain Dan Gilbert, for many years chief of the state's attorney's investigation staff, regarded as the real boss of Chicago's police department, of which then Commissioner Pendergrast was a figurehead. Gilbert was the richest policeman in the world. He instigated the dismissal of the two honest coppers.

The odor of the local Democrats was so putrid after Drury's murder that John Babb, the Republican, walked in. Gilbert retired to manage his private enterprises. Among these is a monopoly on the hiring of all racetrack employes, which aware Chicagoans knew he had during all his years on the force. But few Chicagoans know that Gilbert is the dictator of Cook County's labor unions, most of which are brazenly and openly owned by Mafistas or by business managers subservient to them.

Long before Gilbert became a policeman he was a labor slugger; and his opponent charged he had never been prosecuted for a killing in one such labor gang war. During his years on the coppers, Gilbert kept his ties and improved and strengthened them. By the time he was ready to retire, his alliance with the Unione Siciliano was so strong, the fat ex-flatfoot became the big boss of all Chicago's organized workers.

Babb, the new sheriff, went into office proclaiming a crusade against sin. As usual, the Republican found his teammate was a Democrat, State's Attorney Boyle. The Babb promises turned to water, like those of other politicians. So Bill Drury died in vain. Conditions continued so lousy that, a few months ago the Chicago Crime Commission forced Boyle and Babb to appear at a public hearing where they were grilled. Embarrassing questions were asked. A flurry of surface clean-ups in the county followed. None in the city, naturally, because reform Mayor Kennelly trumpets that it is clean.

But Cicero and Calumet City, two of the stinkingest spots on earth, were not bothered. Attention was focused on Ralph's Place, a gambling hell run by Ralph Capone (who now spells it Caponi) in Northfield township. It was forced to move a few miles over the borderline into Lake County; but while this was being written the game moved back into Cook County on a traveling basis, openly advertised, which means the sheriff should know, too.

Austin Wyman, chairman of the Chicago Crime Commission,

said that professional gamblers will not operate a high stake game unless they are in a position to guarantee their patrons they will suffer no embarrassment from law enforcement officials. This syndicate apparently has such a guarantee.

Perhaps one reason why gambling continues to flourish under the new sheriff is that he acquired the services of a press agent firm which announces to newspapers when he is going to raid suspected premises.

Generally speaking, nothing has changed in Chicago since *Chicago Confidential*. The situation on gambling and girls operating out of cocktail lounges is as it was. The same madames operate the same call services at the same phone numbers.

Bookmaking, as elsewhere, is running on a temporary sneak basis while the boys are waiting to see what happens.

But lottery and policy have not been bothered, because they keep thousands of Negroes. The center for this billion-dollar racket is in the 2nd Ward, where all the policy wheels have their headquarters. The Democratic committeeman there is Representative William L. Dawson, colored, a former Republican but a howling New Dealer, chairman of the mighty Committee on Appropriations. Nothing runs in his ward without Dawson's knowledge. It houses also the Chicago operations of the dope ring. Both rackets are highly specialized and protected by Democratic politicians. Down the line, they employ mostly Negroes in Chicago, but the big mob owns the works and has the top jobs.

The headquarters of the Syndicate are in the adjoining 1st Ward (or Loop district), which is bossed politically by Pete Fosco. Another strong Chicago Democrat is Arthur X. Elrod, chairman of the West Side 24th Ward. Bill Drury gave Babb material on Elrod a few hours before he was murdered.

The world wide managing headquarters of the Mafia continues to flourish in Chicago. The gullible were told Kefauver had driven the mobsters into the lake. He never even tried. The original script called for the brush-off treatment in the Windy City. They couldn't stick to the scenario because our *Chicago Confidential* was a best-seller. Then the Drury murder, a sensation, spiked the plans, too. Still Kefauver and Halley dogged it for the local Democrats, whose standard-bearer, Scott Lucas, majority leader of the Senate, was fighting for his political life.

But when a reporter for the *Sun-Times* stole the minutes of the secret hearings, the lid blew off. Kefauver blustered, threatened to cite him for contempt, though he himself never hesitated to publish and sell confidential material. Even the secret hearings were intended to be a whitewash. But George White, on loan from the Narcotics Bureau as an investigator, bomb-shelled the frame-up by rubbing Democratic dirt on to the record. White has been in bad ever since.

The result was a stunning defeat for the Democrats. When Estes saw the damage was done he did some fast thinking and jumped back on, pretending it was his idea to expose his own party. He sold that bill so well that to this day Lucas blames his defeat on Kefauver and refuses to talk to him. This is a confidential memo to former Senator Lucas: You are wrong, pal. Apologize to Estes. He was and is your friend. He had your best interests at heart all the time. If the investigation hadn't gotten out of hand, no metal would have touched you.

As it is, the Chicago mob got off unsinged. A few phony contempt citations were made and quickly thrown out by the courts. No one was bothered. No business, legal or illegal, of the Chicago hoodlums was touched. Chicago continues to be their Eden—the Mafia has a desk in City Hall, where you must talk to its agent before you see the Mayor—if they let you. Kennelly, a publicity-crazed old bachelor with social ambitions, thinks he's Mayor. He never was. The Mayor was Charlie Fischetti, until he died. Charlie, a cousin of Al Capone, was the No. 2 operator of the national Mafia. When the Kefauver Committee pretended it was going to call him, Halley informed the papers days in advance, so Charlie beat it. Then the committee couldn't find him, though he was ringsiding nightly in Miami. Always in the best of health, Charlie suddenly and mysteriously began to ail. He died a "natural death," strangely and mysteriously in the same week Sam Maceo of Galveston also died in bed, and Phil Mangano of Brooklyn was found in an empty lot—robbing the top ranks of three executives.

Fischetti had a big funeral in Brooklyn, after which his two surviving brothers, Rocco and young Joe, continued to carry on the empire. Tony Accardo, former enforcer, moved up one step into Fischetti's place as the Chicago president. This is the common practice in the Black Hand. Johnny Torrio was Jim Colosimo's enforcer. When Colosimo was killed Torrio became boss, with Capone his enforcer. Al shot Torrio's face half off and he fled to Italy. Then Al moved up. When he went to the can, his enforcer, Frank Nitti, took over until he was executed, when Charlie Fischetti was promoted. There is some reason to believe that if Fischetti met with foul play, Accardo knows the score.

After candidate Kefauver departed, Chicago crime jumped 15.34 per cent, all of it protected by the hoods he couldn't find.

One of the great powers of the Mafia is a non-Italian, Guzik, who was Capone's paymaster and continues to be in control of the mob treasury. Instead of waning, along with other Jews in the mob, Guzik is growing.

Ralph Capone, also, is coming up fast. Many think him a figure-head tolerated because he was Al's kid brother. But Virgil Peterson, of the Chicago Crime Commission, tags Ralph as No. 3 in Chicago and possibly—secretly—No. 1.

Little else has changed. The strippers still peel to their all in W. Madison, S. State and N. Clark, but if there aren't as many it's not because of the law; business is punk.

Among the more notorious joints running raw are:

West Side:
Club Aloha, 2443 W. Madison Street.
L & L Cafe, 1316 W. Madison Street.
Soho, 1124 W. Madison Street.
Flamingo, 1359 W. Madison Street.
South Side:
Trocadero, (all-girl revue) 525 S. State Street.
Follies Theatre, State and Congress (Lotus Du Bois).
North Side:
Post Time Club, 357 N. Clark Street.
McGovern's Liberty Inn, 661 N. Clark Street.
The Play House, 550 N. Clark Street.
Miscellaneous:
Silver Frolics, 400 N. Wabash Avenue.
Silver Palm, 1117 Wilson Avenue.

After these words were in type, a few of the foregoing were momentarily shuttered. Not for indecency—they had forgotten to renew their licenses.

And that old stand-by, the 606, on S. Wabash, which runs come war or peace, Dems or GOP, and probably will still be wide open if Stalin takes over. They covered the nudes only one night—the night we were there and they spotted us.

Since the last cop captain was nailed, Rush Street is comparatively quiet. Most of the call-girls and B-girls moved back to the Loop or further north, into the quiet hotel cocktail lounges along Lincoln Park, though Nick & Ollie Arnstein still sell flesh at the

Devonshire, as they did when we reported it in *Chicago Confidential!*

But the Walton Club, on Rush Street, is still a protected bookie hangout and gambler's steer joint. Nor has any effort been made or campaign been started to eradicate the 26 game. This is a form of gambling unique to Chicago, where dice girls work openly and with some alleged pretense of legality, in almost every cocktail lounge, bar, tavern, cigar store and hotel lobby.

As this page was put to bed, killers in the employ of Dems—the party of Stevenson, Douglas and Kennelly—slew a GOP candidate to keep him out of an election!

A. Chicagoland Confidential

Col. Bertie McCormick's World's Greatest Newspaper has annexed the six central-western states into a huge *lebensraum* for the circulation and sale of the Chicago *Trib*. Downstate Illinois naturally falls into what the WGN calls Chicagoland; but the rugged individualistic farmers down there loathe and despise Chicago. Nevertheless Chicago runs all Illinois through its mobsters, who regard the rest of the state about as English barons thought of their lands in Ireland.

As we stated before—except on issues of international politics —Illinois is actually a nonpartisan state, always controlled by the same criminal clique which ties up with unions, Reds and Negro padrones to swing elections. The late Mayor Kelly was one of the most rapacious of all politicians in the history of the city where venality is accepted like the rain. Under the guise of being a friend of labor he improved on corruption in politics to such a degree that his technique provided the script for the Washington Raw Deal.

Though Chicago was and is Democratic, the state, under Governor Green, was nominally Republican. But no attorneys general, state troopers, peace officers or investigators ever disturbed the sanctity of Cook County or East St. Louis, the Democratic sink at the other end. Under the Springfield GOP, bribery and felony were tolerated and protected in the finest any-party tradition. It ran as openly in Democratic bailiwicks as it did in Republican Peoria or Cairo, where the rum-running trust built up the world's largest port of export for untaxed liquors.

Green was the nemesis of Al Capone. As special United States prosecutor, he sent him to the pen, eventual destination Alcatraz—much more than either he or Al had bargained for. The

deal was for Al to plead guilty and take eighteen months on misde-
meanors; but tough Judge Wilkerson warned Al that if he took
the fall he would get the limit. Capone withdrew his plea, was
convicted and got the tough sentence that barely ended in time
for him to die a free man.

Green was Deweyed out of Springfield in the 1948 Truman surprise, to be succeeded by Democratic Adlai Stevenson, high society and all that, a descendant of a former Veep. Stevenson just
about knows he's Governor, but he's not sure of what state. His appointments were on a new low, Democratic committeemen and
crooks getting the best. Under him the legislature went wild, dozens of its members joining other state office-holders on the payroll
of racing associations or being voted stock. Stevenson, like so many
sons of prominent people, is a thoroughgoing left-winger and
visionary. When he vetoed the controversial bill making membership in the Communist party unlawful, which he may or may not
have decided on its merits, as many sincere opponents of the Reds
are opposed to driving them underground, he gratuitously added,
"I know full well this veto will be distorted and misunderstood,
even as telling the truth of what I knew about the reputation of
Alger Hiss was distorted and misunderstood."

Most of us had forgotten that Stevenson was a character witness for the convicted traitor.

But the most controversial figure in Illinois politics at the moment is Senator Paul Douglas, who, because of a strictly inter-
party rebellion against the President on a matter of low, petty
patronage, fooled many Republicans into thinking he is sincere.
We see Douglas roughly as a Democratic Tobey. That's rough
enough. He is a former college professor, always thick with the
pinkos. He is married to a driving and pushing wife who, herself,
sat in Congress for a term and voted the straight Soviet-friend-
ship line. She is pushing him on and up and he likes it. He will
do anything to hold public office.

A lot of thinly sliced salami has appeared in print about this
new public hero, which shows how easy it is to befuddle the
voters, even some of our best-informed GOP friends, who plug
for him. Well, here is the Douglas rundown:

Many Chicagoans do not know this is not the Senator's maiden
run in politics. Many years ago he served in the Chicago City
Council. Get this—he ran and was elected on Ed Kelly's ticket and
gave the criminal boss faithful support. He got his senatorial
nomination from the evil Kelly-Nash-Arvey machine, with lib-

eral campaign contributions from the late Charlie Fischetti. Back here in the East, most of us don't know much about Jake Arvey, Douglas' political sponsor.

Since the defeat of most of the big city Democratic machines, Jake's Cook County organization is the last big-town boss-ridden outfit still in power. Arvey is a pal of the Fischettis and we have seen him with them. He has been castigated by Chicago newspapers for taking advantage of his position as County Commissioner to profit on public projects. We showed in *Washington Confidential* that he is secretly tied up with Louis Johnson, former Secretary of Defense, and through him has made millions on alien property, RFC and other smelly deals.

Another Arvey associate is Colonel Henry R. Crown, Chicago building contractor, who was completely unknown until two years ago when he provided the millions for Hilton to acquire the Waldorf-Astoria. Crown apparently had made his money on Cook County public projects. Arvey was chairman of the county commissioners.

In the last three years the Chicago mystery man not only acquired the Waldorf, but bought working control of the Rock Island Railroad (25 per cent), the Chicago Mercantile Building, and is the leading member of the syndicate that bought the Empire State Building.

Paul Douglas' recent show of independence against the President must be considered in the light of this background—Douglas was not opposed to the President's appointees per se; he threw a monkey-wrench into the deal for only one reason. He wanted Truman to appoint Arvey, the representative of the most corrupt political machine on earth, to a Federal judgeship. Arvey, a millionaire, wanted that judgeship passionately. He resigned his Cook County Democratic chairmanship in 1950 to make himself available. But little Harry never forgets. He remembered that Jake had been one of the first to call for him to quit in 1948, though later Arvey jumped in with mob millions to fight for Harry. So, when the issue was joined, Douglas, the "crusader," fought the President's nomination for his own reasons, but hadn't nerve enough to enter Arvey. He put up figureheads, knowing they stood no chance, because Harry would rather leave those judgeships vacant forever than appoint Douglas nominees, which now accounts for all the Douglas "independence."

The Senator is a typical college crank who has tried everything including Quakerism, Ickesism and New Dealism. He changes from fad to fad with his emotions. If you study his physiognomy you notice the flabby lips and mouth and the glaring, staring eyes of the zealot. His goal, as he has frequently stated, is the welfare state. He justifies accepting support from anyone, including killers, rapists, pimps, and Reds toward that end.

His emotional instability was never so well demonstrated as on the recent occasion when he hysterically ran out of the Senate and collapsed in the cloakroom. Colleagues who thought he was ill were surprised to see him back in his seat an hour later as if he hadn't created a scene in the dignified chamber. "He was talking emotionally—hysterically, like a woman," one Senator who sat with him in the cloakroom said.

Because of his long residence on the pink University of Chicago campus, Illinoisians think their senior Senator is a savant, but, like Tobey, he garbles quotations and scrambles rhetoric. One of his most recent malapropisms was: "I am standing like Stonewall Jackson—they shall not pass."

The political mountebanks of Illinois have fooled many otherwise intelligent people, who have no conception of the tight collaboration which has long linked the "reformers" and the racketeers.

Evil East St. Louis is an illustration. The city usually votes Democratic. The county votes Republican. On statewide or Federal elections it can swing either way. For that reason it gets the green light from Springfield, regardless of who's running the state. The East St. Louis rackets are tied up with St. Louis, which is a division of the Fischetti-Capone mob of Chicago, so the go-ahead now goes through Arvey to Stevenson, as Paul Douglas looks the other way.

The winning factor in an East St. Louis election is the Negro vote, which is always cast in a bloc. These are the children of the Southern darkies dragooned to break a packing-house strike. They still remember bitterly the East St. Louis riots, when dozens were lynched and burning bodies could be smelled twenty miles away. The old-timers are joined by newcomers, just up from Dixie down river, and they all strut their politically insured independence. East St. Louis is one of the few big Negro concentrations where the Reds have made a notable inroad. The mobsters work with any contingent that can deliver, so here they do business with the Reds, who bargain for what they want, then support Democratic or Republican candidates. Dan McGlynn, an attorney, is the GOP Elephant boy, but he plays in the Democratic backroom, too, under the ambidextrous alignment.

East St. Louis is one of the wildest spots in the nation, the playground for St. Louis, Missouri, across the Mississippi bridges.

The East Side hot shots are the Workman boys, who took over from the old Rock Boys after they shot off most of their heads. The few who remain are now snugly syndicated in the mob which the Workmans run as local representatives for the Fischettis. Buster Workman's pride and joy is the Paddock Club, which cost $300,000 to build. When the heat is off there's gambling in the backroom. At all times most of the waitresses solicit male customers—much better than B-girls, because it's not as obvious. The janes take their trade outside and upstairs to rooms in the same building, through another door.

One of the times we were there was when Kefauver was reported to be looking for Buster. The papers said investigators had searched for him high and low. That night we saw him behind the cash register in the Paddock.

Another Workman enterprise is Bowman's, also a gambling joint. When the heat is on for local political reasons, everything runs across the St. Clair county line, and vice versa—with the Empire and Tattle Tale defying all probes. Workman, of course.

East St. Louis crawls with whores, streetwalkers and pick-up gals, who work around the corner from the city hall. St. Louis cabbies drive their trade there, get commissions from the clubs and houses. We saw hookers even at Democratic Club No. 14, which sports a bar. Crap games run as openly as movies. The "Whiskey Chute," a gambling den in back of a bar across from the stockyards, runs all night if there's business.

East St. Louis is so proud of its fairy joints that they advertise in the Missouri papers. One of the most notorious is the Torch Club, where hillbilly queers from miles around congregate.

The town's little Harlem is called the Valley, and when it runs there is no place quite like it on earth. In a depressed swamp under the railroad tracks and bridge approach are cribs and dives with whores, reefers and craps, as lowdown as the rivertowns knew seventy-five years ago, but which public indignation long since wiped out elsewhere.

All this is guarded from interference by the colored wardheelers, who throw the balance in votes to Douglas, Stevenson and the self-perpetuating Fair Deal.

This is in the heart of Chicagoland, the fabulously rich agricultural and industrial interior prairie empire hacked out of wilderness by the best and bravest of our founding forebears.

28. WASHINGTON CONFIDENTIAL (ACT II)

A. The White House Gang—Past and Present

*B*EGINNING with the reign of King Franklin the First and his omnipotent consort, Queen Eleanor, it has been considered unsportsmanlike, un-American and unethical to pan the Administration. The heir apparent (too apparent), Harry the Little, punishes lese majeste with dirty letters and toilet-wall words. We are prepared for the Tower.

We got pretty friendly with the former royal family. Our newspaper beats frequently take us to the ginmills. That's where most Roosevelt princelings play. The dowager goes in through the back door. We frequently ran into her at day-time chorus rehearsals in the old Paradise night club, one of gangster "Chink" Sherman's enterprises. Eleanor was interested in the career of a protégé, a cute teen-ager from the Pennsylvania mines.

The Broadway crowd had contributed to the elevation of her brood. The late President was elected Governor of New York with the support of numbers-sellers, dope-peddlers, bookies, "Dutch" Schultz and Jimmy Hines. Hines remained a member of the FDR braintrust until Dewey sent him to the pokey. In 1932, Hines and Frank Costello shared a suite at Chicago's Drake Hotel, where they helped in the convention fight which resulted in FDR's presidential nomination. In return, Roosevelt gave the boys immunity.

Saratoga ran wide open in the Roosevelt and Lehman—"my good right arm"—days as Governors. There were no pari-mutuels then. Gambling at the track was illegal. But bookmakers operated openly with their names over stalls, provided for them unlawfully by the racing associations. Lehman had a box at Saratoga. We frequently saw him at the races. We know he knew the law was being violated.

The two-way tie-up with the underworld worked both ways. James (Jimmy Got It) Roosevelt was in the juke-box business, in partnership with the Mills Novelty Company, manufacturers of Frank Costello's slot-machines. Anna Roosevelt borrowed some of the bankroll to start her newspaper in Phoenix from Charles Ward, millionaire ex-convict. She stiffed him.

Young Frank's former law-partner, Charles Poletti, could tell plenty about the underworld tie-up between Costello and his friend Marcantonio, if he were asked and if he'd talk. When Junior ran for Congress, an intermediary asked Costello to keep out of his district until after election. Costello complied.

Elliot's unsavory business associations would fill this book.

Jimmy, oldest of the boys, was first to cash in on the good thing. It seems so long ago that he got that $500,000 a year for selling insurance to government contractors. It was. And he and his mother are still getting it. In the late thirties Jimmy amplified his insurance income by dabbling in the movie business. That's when he made a deal with the Costello boys to put out juke-box films. He also produced a couple of feature-length pictures on the West Coast with dough put up by Joe Schenck. Sometime thereafter Schenck wove himself into a strange web of intrigue and conspiracy involving shakedown payments to officials in Capone-dominated movie unions. After Westbrook Pegler and Arthur Ungar, late editor of *Daily Variety,* exposed the deal, Uncle Sam could no longer sidestep prosecution.

A conference was held in the President's office, attended by the Treasury agents who had made the case, the Attorney General and the U.S. Attorney from the district in which the trial was to take place. Roosevelt was advised of the circumstances and reminded that Schenck had lent $50,000 to Eleanor for Jimmy's movie deal. Roosevelt was asked, "What shall we do, Mr. President?" He replied, "I'd just as soon have you forget it."

The prosecutor said, "If you order me to lay off, I must. But in that case I will submit my resignation tomorrow and tell the newspapers I failed to prosecute Schenck and the gangsters because you wouldn't let me."

The prosecution went forward. Schenck, the unfortunate victim elected to take the fall for the industry, went into a prison hospital, then back to civilian life. And the real criminals were secretly paroled before their terms expired.

And did anyone point out that Charles Daggett, who refused to answer whether he was a Communist, was Jimmy Roosevelt's ghost writer in the last campaign?

Which brings us to the drug-store cowboy from Kansas City and the grafters, grifters, poker-players, bourbon-drinkers and influence-peddlers who comprise the present White House Gang.

President Truman recently remarked that 95 per cent of all government employes are honest and loyal. Figuring 2,500,000 on the payroll, that would give us a round figure of 125,000 crooks and traitors. Perhaps it is no coincidence that the kitchen cabinet includes such as Johnny Maragon, Harry Vaughan, Donald Dawson and Merle Young and a host of other less publicized triflers.

No one ever accused the late FDR of being a piker with other people's money, though he and his wife were known to have rubbed the face off a penny if it was their own. But Harry, who never saw $5,000 in a lump sum unless it was in Boss Pendergast's hand, nicked Uncle Sam for $1,500,000 to run the White House. None is accounted for. This is not to be confused with the President's controversial tax-exempt personal expense fund. And it doubles the Roosevelt take.

A lot of inspired detail has been printed about the President's family. His wife is a gracious and self-effacing lady, a great relief from the loud-mouthed trouble-maker who preceded her. His daughter, Margaret, is a charming and friendly young lady. The law provides for the protection of the immediate family of the President. That means his wife and children. Most President's children don't require Secret Service men when they barnstorm for their own private paid ends and enterprises. Wherever and whenever Margaret travels—whether it's a pleasure trip to Europe or a commercially sponsored concert tour to 100 cities—she is accompanied by three Secret Service men whose salaries and all expenses are paid for by the government though she earns more than the President. Miss Truman also rates a personal secretary, government-paid, who travels with her at government expense on her sponsored concert tours and helps her with make-up, presses her dresses and runs her errands.

Whenever Miss Truman comes to a city her Secret Service escort rounds up the local cops and gets a crew of detectives as an auxiliary guard. In New York, at Hotel Carlyle, the U.S. rents rooms on the same floor for her retinue. The city of New York has to put four detectives on an around-the-clock watch in another expensive room.

Truman decided that the Secret Service should extend protection to his maiden sister, Mary Jane. He assigned a detail to protect her at her home in Grand View, Missouri, and drive her around in a government-owned Cadillac limousine.

The duties of the guards assigned to Margaret are more arduous than the public thinks. Margaret is a lady, doesn't drink. But some of her artistic friends in New York are not so abstemious. She mingles in advanced Bohemian circles and she seems to get a kick out of strange people. At such times she is often accompanied by Blevins Davis, old family friend, who inherited millions after he married a wealthy widow much older than himself, who died and left him a railroad fortune. Now he sponsors plays and haute monde art. When Davis is not squiring the President's daughter he is often seen with representatives of Chicago coin-machine manufacturers—slot-machines are also coin-machines.

P.S.—Truman's poker-playing crony, Johnny Maragon, who had to take the rap or else, got fixed up swell as the prison librarian at Lorting, though he is practically illiterate. He was also given special night-out passes. His attorney, Irving Goldstein, who left the Department of Justice to defend him, is back in the D. J. with a higher rating. Maragon has been in the White House many times since his conviction.

B. The Pentagonians

The most perfect plane target in the United States is the giant Pentagon—the heart and core and communications center of our Defense Department. This bait for an enemy attacker was built that way by the same kind of overeducated theorists and gargantuan grafters who have been running our government ever since that fateful March 4th, 1933.

Long sitting in the ducal room of the Pentagon with more power than any military man ever held before, including Caesar or Napoleon, was General of the Army George C. Marshall. To rank-loving Harry Truman, Marshall is the greatest living human —an infallible wizard who can solve all problems—and who insisted only a couple of years ago that the Chinese Reds were only "agrarian reformers."

As Chief of Staff during World War II, and under the orders of a Red-dominated Administration, Marshall prolonged the war in the Pacific from April, when the Japanese were begging for peace, until August, 1945, to give Stalin time to come in and claim spoils in North China. This is the genius who could not remember where he was the night before Pearl Harbor, nor did he know how it happened that he had not warned ground-troops in Hawaii of the impending attack, though Army Intelligence sources had warned him about it weeks before.

Marshall has been retired as Secretary of Defense with high honors, succeeded by Robert A. Lovett, a colorless New York banker without particular talent, who thinks he is the boss, but is actually only an understudy for Anna Rosenberg, Assistant Secretary of Defense. Mrs. Rosenberg is Dean Acheson's line into the Pentagon. Marshall always played Trilby to Acheson's Svengali. Mrs. Rosenberg, America's first woman War Lord, was given her position under Marshall when the aging general began to show his senility. After Marshall retired, Lovett was chosen because Washington knew he could not withstand a character like Mrs. Rosenberg.

There are as many officers and civilians employed in Washington by the Armed Forces now as there were during World War II. Our Armed Forces at this writing are less than 4,000,000, compared with 15,000,000 in 1945. These officers and higher civilians have formed themselves into a Prussianized military caste, along the lines of the famous German General Staff, and are a law unto themselves.

The Defense Department employs more than 3,000 press agents at annual salaries in excess of $10,000,000, to help perpetuate themselves and their successors in office. Once this country prided itself on the subservience of the military to the civilian. Before 1914 we had a peace-time Army of less than 50,000. Now, as a result of a couple of wars and a police action, we have been taken over by military high brass and it is unpatriotic to mention the fact.

Douglas MacArthur is the only military man with guts enough to fight the trend. His call for less power for the professional soldiers and more for the civilians went unheeded. For saying what we are saying here, he is a traitor to the brass.

There are many valid arguments for and against Universal Military Training in peacetime, though there are none against conscription in time of war or emergency. Many who are troubled about UMT recognize its great value but fear it will result in a Prussianized America, in which everyone will have been militarily indoctrinated in his youth to respect the authority of generals. That is one reason why the Pentagon is fighting so vigorously for UMT, not for patriotic reasons, but because it will mean more and higher ranks and bigger pay and larger military establishments to play with and more money to kick around, at all times.

The military services are as money-mad as other segments of this government. At this writing billions had been appropriated for the defense of ourselves and our allies. Only a trickle went out. Now we are outmoded in the air by the backward Chinee, forced to use obsolete planes. Defense plants which have turned out nothing have been working on double and triple shifts, making nothing, while appropriations which have been bleeding the country go for bribes to officers and civilian purchasing agents and inspectors, kickbacks, entertainment, country-club accommodations complete with running hot and cold water and WACS for colonels and generals, chauffeur-driven limousines, mansions and castles abroad for flag officers and Defense Department overseers.

This topheavy Defense Department, which is ending up with more officers and noncoms than privates, is falling apart, with serious rifts between the services, all fighting for the billions in graft and handouts. Unification, supposed to end this friction, has increased it. In the old days each service came before Congress on its own and fought for itself and stood or fell on the demonstration it put up. Now all the boodle is apportioned in air-conditioned, Oriental-carpeted rooms in the Pentagon, where a couple of braintrusters decide who is going to spend what.

To further the military conspiracy to dominate the nation, the self-perpetuating General Staff is attempting to absorb the National Guard, the last defense of Americans against the ambitions of a grasping central government. Though HST is himself an old militia man, he enthusiastically supports this undercover drive on the Guard because he realizes that once it is absorbed it will mark the complete end of state sovereignty. That the militia is established by the Constitution is of no consequence any more. The UMT lobby and the National Guard absorption are special pets of Mrs. Rosenberg.

Washington newspapermen are asking what happened to the threatened perjury prosecutions of De Sola and Friedman, who had charged before a Congressional committee that Anna is a former Communist. When all hell broke loose, the Senators got panicky and voted to confirm her in a fast whitewash. The committee then moved for the indictment of the two. The Attorney General thundered they would be in jail within the fortnight.

Thereupon the sensational story was forgotten by the newspapers. You and we and the rest of the chumps figured these villains had been taken care of by now, and were paying the price for defaming the good name of the untouchable Rosenberg. You may still think so, but we investigated. This is what happened:

A few days after the hue and cry, General Marshall secretly called Attorney General McGrath and spoke to this effect:

"Howard, I was thinking. If you indict those men they will hire shyster lawyers who will insist on subpoenaing Mrs. Rosenberg.

As you know, we are in the midst of a national emergency. I cannot spare Mrs. Rosenberg for even two hours. Let's forget the whole thing."

To which McGrath replied something like this:

"General, I agree."

He did not press for an indictment. The grand jury expired without action. The men whom Marshall, McGrath, the President and Mrs. Rosenberg had accused of bearing false witness, were not molested. They are at large. Mrs. Rosenberg did not demand a court hearing to vindicate her name.

The Defense Department under the Marshall-Lovett-Rosenberg axis is not pretty. There are scandals in almost every post in the country, in addition to the highly publicized affairs at Rossford Depot, near Toledo, and in the Army Engineers. Wherever there are military posts there are gambling, whoring, after-hour guzzling, narcotics and homosexuality. This runs in collusion with MPs, who pay off to provost marshals, and up through a chain like a city police department to commanding officers, area commanders and inspectors from Washington.

Glorious West Point, which could afford to colonize 90 men for its football team with the full knowledge and approval of the upper brass and the War Department, was unable to supply more than 400 officers during the last year. Almost 52,000 came from other sources, many politically appointed.

Procurement officers are in the clutch of bookmakers and gamblers, so they must steal to pay their "debts of honor." Many officers in vital installations are in hock for gambling debts or narcotics and are easy prey to blackmailing Communists, who gouge them to give up military secrets. A dozen or so have been removed for crooked dealings, but most of those accused were merely transferred to other posts. Thousands of incidents have not been made public.

One which was, and got a lot of publicity, was the case of Brigadier General David Crawford, commander of the Detroit Tank Automotive Center, who said a contractor had picked up the tab for his two-day stay at the Congressional Hotel, in Washington. Crawford was a goat. Four years earlier, when Brigadier General Elliot Roosevelt testified that his hotel bill, wedding and honeymoon expenses and gift to his bride, Faye Emerson, had been paid for by Howard Hughes, who was negotiating with General Roosevelt on an airplane contract, it was thought cute.

Many posts have self-installed gambling set-ups, usually run by an enlisted man who was a professional in private life. His bud-

dies do not know they are losing to a pro. The gamblers cut back
to higher-ups. In many posts you can place horse-bets and buy
policy tickets with approval and connivance of COs. In some, especially in isolated areas, officers supply prostitutes, and not only
for morale. Many so-called girl-shows which are flown in know
what they are supposed to do.

There are rackets even in supplying legitimate entertainment
to GIs. The Air Force has a profitable transportation business—
for certain officers. It moves entire theatrical companies in planes
needed for military purposes. These shows save thousands by slipping a few hundred to a transportation officer and agreeing to do
a quickie free show at some nearby post. At least one New York
theatrical company performed free on Long Island, and then obtained transportation of company and luggage in two four-
motored planes to play gambling-houses in Las Vegas. This
happens frequently.

War jobs on construction work as well as on posts go to racketeers. If you do business with the right hoodlum, you get a military job even with a bad security record. It takes months before
anything is checked. Three men in the air force know in advance
where bases are to be built in Europe; their friends cash in on the
knowledge.

If you can't stand this blundering and corruption and you
happen to get a nervous breakdown worrying about it and go to
the hospital—even there you're sunk. There is a racket in the
Army hospital business, too. Commanding officers get rank and allowances based on the number of beds in their institutions. They
never let go of a case if there is any chance of enlarging their
capacity. Cured patients may be kept months or years without
being discharged or returned to duty. Every dodge is employed,
including long leaves of absence with orders to report every ten
days, so the records show high "occupancy." Many in hospitals
are suffering from hospitalization.

The whole military establishment is ingrown, with a policy of
silence and mutual protection for profit and advancement. Upright patriots are snowed under. The freemasonry of the uniform
is thrown over thieves and traitors. Strike up the band—these are
the defenders of our shores and our honor!

C. Probe Bono Publico

Pandemonium struck on the Potomac. The tax boys had been
caught with their hands in the jam and the watchdogs, instead of
tearing them to pieces, were licking their fingers.

In an election year the Internal Revenue and Justice Departments were in flagrant disgrace. And Truman couldn't cry "red herring."

The man who had fired his General of the Army in the midst of a war could not fire his Attorney General in the midst of a scandal. J. Howard McGrath packed too much party power.

But the Pendergast curriculum had taught our President that a man on his back can still use his feet. So he aimed his kicks against an expendable public servant, whose downfall would draw the eyes from his own, and he could arise again, a fighter and a winner. He chose Tom Murphy. He was anathema to the appeasers and the sycophants of Roosevelt-Truman socialization, had defied the White House and convicted Alger Hiss, the darling of Dean Acheson. HST would assign this incorruptible to run the rascals out. Not even the blackest Republican could doubt his qualifications.

But he knew the tortuous processes of our procedures, which safeguard the presumption of innocence. That would give the Administration time—time enough to let the excitement cool; time enough so that in the coming campaign he could whine:

"I did my best. I threw out all political considerations. But Murphy didn't deliver."

Murphy, now a Federal judge, reneged.

So Harry, having made the noble gesture, fell back on the hoary thimblerigging subterfuge: he ruled that McGrath should investigate himself, his own department, and show himself up; slap his left hand with his right hand.

With no impetuous haste, as winter turned to spring, the Attorney General was impaneling special grand juries in all the judicial districts. The panels were to be selected and steered by McGrath's subordinates, appointees of Truman and their Democratic district manipulators.

Finally Newbold Morris got the nod—as McGrath's assistant, with no subpoena power, to probe McGrath. This was an encomium to power-hungry Morris, a perennial candidate for mayor, for supporting Rudy Halley when that White House favorite was elected President of the New York City Council, a job Morris himself held under La Guardia. Morris' first action as official prober was to invite Louis Yavner to act as his chief investigator. Yavner, another La Guardia minion, was Halley's campaign manager. He is the author of the unspeakable bill to elect members of the Board of Education, instead of appointing them, so left wing splinter groups, like Dave Dubinsky's Liberal party which plumped for Halley and Marcantonio's American Laborites, can bullet-vote Reds and agitators onto the board. Yavner turned it down.

Morris announced he would "investigate, not prosecute." A New Dealer and a bleeding heart—attorney for the La Guardia estate—publicly accused of having played with Communist fronts, Morris was himself castigated on the floor of Congress at the time of his appointment for his part in the Maritime Commission scandals (first brought to light in *Washington Confidential*).

Morris may huff and puff and bluff, but we who know Newbold can hear the Democrats chuckling.

Strangely, Tom Murphy, innocent of the ways of politics, had declined the "honor" on advice of U.S. Judge Learned Hand—who is Newbold Morris' father-in-law.

At the same time the House Judiciary Committee voted out a watered-down bill to scrutinize the Department of Justice; weakened with a curious proviso inserted by Chairman Celler limiting the investigation to "proof, not accusations," as if you can prove anything if you don't have indictments first. Celler maintained that his zealousness to protect McGrath had nothing to do with the fact that McGrath had within a few days retained four of Celler's law partners at a fee of $30,000 to handle the sale of securities in an alien property custodianship, which in itself was being investigated by another congressional committee.

We know Celler, too. We know of the tie-ups between his political machine and the worst Brooklyn hoodlums who regularly return him to office. Cellar is also a close personal friend of the about-to-be-whitewashed attorney general.

A few easy touches will be marked for indictments and headlines and campaign oratory. Prosecutions can be stalled and will be, with possibly a handful of exceptions, until after November.

So we predict:

1—Many will be accused, few will be indicted.

2—Most of the indictments will be pigeon-holed to die a natural "statute" death.

3—The few indictments brought to trial will be found faulty.

4—The fewer convicted will be given suspended or light sentences.

5—No important politician, gangster or malefactor will be jeopardized or discommoded, except by publicity.

The onward rush of events may make it necessary for Truman

to remove McGrath, but the foregoing chain of sequences will not be radically altered regardless of who probes how. The congressional investigation of the Justice Department is also under orders to go easy. McGrath has too much on too many, and "runaway" hearings like the Kefauver and King Committees have a way of suddenly petering out.

Next to the Kefauver Committee, the tax bureau investigations of Congressman Cecil King were the best show of the last Congress. Though the King body accomplished more, there was a peculiar affinity between the methods of both. In the millions of words of twaddle about the Treasury hearings nothing told how it began. This is the confidential story of that hearing:

A little clique of well-placed lawyers was monopolizing the processing of tax cases by the Treasury and Justice, through connections with Caudle and Oliphant, who cleared routine dispositions as well as "special treatment." Most other tax attorneys, both the honest and the crooked, were out in the cold. Such eminent lawyers as Randolph Paul, a former undersecretary of the Treasury and dean of the tax bar, were denied crumbs. Paul knew troubled clients were being steered elsewhere. Adrian deWind, a busy specialist a few years before, was also behind the eight-ball. Representative King, whose office represented California businessmen, got the chill.

Those with grievances real and imagined, honest men and crooks, got together and pooled their power and information to drive the rascals out—they didn't mean all the rascals in the government; just Caudle, Oliphant and a few other uncooperative bureaucrats who made it tough for them.

When King introduced his resolution for the vendetta and set up his committee with deWind as counsel, neither dreamed it would lead where it did. Paul's office supplied the data. But the hearings got out of hand. King was the most surprised man in Washington. He is an Administration wheel horse. Did you then notice the soft pedal?

In January, King told another Congressman he would give his right arm to get out of the mess. King hadn't counted on the monkey-business in the collection end of the Treasury that would be turned up. It hurt in the bread basket. The accused Collectors of Internal Revenue were politically appointed by Roosevelt and Truman, and were selling favors for votes as well as cash. Even now the votes haven't been mentioned.

When the hearings ran away, the emphasis was quickly switched to provide a couple of goats, smear the rest for headlines, then get out and back to normal.

Gullible citizens may think King turned up something. But the record shows this: A handful of petty crooks were indicted and a few convicted. Two or three not too important office-holders were bounced. No prosecutions. But what was turned up beyond a few mink coats bought at wholesale? Many "smart" people always buy them wholesale. These were marks who thought they got price breaks and probably paid as much as they would have in stores.

But no committee asked for the records of Max Koch, a wholesale furrier doing business on Seventh Avenue, in New York, who sells minks to cabinet officers, judges and White House cronies. His affairs are legal. We'd like to see who pays the bills. Incidentally, his son-in-law is a Federal judge.

Not one big gangster, black marketeer, businessman or politician was involved in the tax scandals. None will be. The present program of the committee is to hold hearings in New York early in March, the week this book is published. Though we are not in the confidence of the committee we can tell you confidentially that it has had agents here for weeks trying to find one star victim who will make the front pages like Kefauver did with O'Dwyer, Virginia Hill and Costello. King, who votes left-wing, is hoping to develop a big and respected merchant or banker to be the chump and show that "Wall Street is to blame." Then he will run for Senator this year.

Costello's tax may be mentioned. He may be quizzed. But that's all. The returns of no Mafista will be checked more than perfunctorily, if at all. Joe Nunan, a tax lawyer for the mobsters, who was the Commissioner of Internal Revenue during the department's most odoriferous days, will walk out smiling after a few days of sweating on the stand for the cameras and the citizens.

The committee will fold up with "recommendations" and bows for having done its duty by exposing the pattern.

Congress may have authorized Truman's slick political blockbuster to make all collectors civil service employes. That looks swell on the surface. It is one of the biggest steals of the century. It will freeze for life a lot of deserving Democrats who would be canned if and when a Republican is elected.

The same thing happened in the Post Office when FDR was acclaimed for taking Class 1 postmasterships out of politics and putting them under civil service. The unthinking do not realize the appointing authority still has the right to pick its own choices from those who qualify. The questions are made so easy, even a Democratic office-holder can answer them. For instance, Al Goldman, protégé of Boss Ed Flynn, was postmaster of New York. When the boys decided to steal the post offices he managed to pass the civil service test and nail down the job for life. That happened all over the country. The post offices were taken out of politics—and handed to Democratic politicians.

The consideration for drawing the curtain on the tax investigation was the appointment by Truman of Charles W. Davis as general counsel of the Internal Revenue Bureau to succeed the unfortunate Oliphant. Davis is a young man with practically no experience. Almost his entire professional career has been in the service of the House Ways and Means Committee, which is conducting the investigation, as a clerk. The Washington pipeline says King dictated this appointment as the price of peace. Now he and his crowd run the legal end of the bureau.

An unhappy result of the probe was the discrediting of the rank and file of the tax-collecting machinery.

When the heat hit Roosevelt and Truman political appointees, trained publicity seals swung the wordage around to make it look as if the Internal Revenue structure itself was faithless instead of fixing the responsibility where it belonged, on the shoulders of Treasury Secretary Snyder, Attorney General McGrath and the Democratic National Committee.

Now every one of the 57,000 tax employes is under a blanket stigma. Hundreds were and are guilty, but they are a fraction of the total. Honest men and women had been trying to do as good a job as they could with orders from above to lay off favorites.

The investigation has failed to demonstrate that the important fixes were arranged above. After tax men made some cases, they got lost somewhere in the higher echelons of the Treasury or in Justice, which refused to prosecute or had U.S. attorneys lose them until after the statute of limitations had tolled. There are more than 16,500 hot squeals now iced away. These affect sacred cows who will never be nailed for evasions.

The honest, fearless and hardworking intelligence unit of the Treasury was also smeared under the general plan, though in the final showdown it came through cleared. The public was not so informed. The big shots resented efforts of the "U-boats," which they are called in police lingo, to get Frank Costello (they're working on him now) and decided to undermine the special agents. These men, who got Al Capone, Nocky Johnson and

Henry Lustig after all other cops failed, have been building a file on the Mafia for years. First Kefauver and Halley spilled the beans through premature disclosures; now the King press agents have hampered their effectiveness by placing them under a cloud. Yet, while the comic opera sleuths and committee gumshoes were looking for goats, veteran Special Agents working under keen, determined James Guthrie and John J. McIntyre were given the green light by Internal Revenue Commissioner Dunlap to get Costello and other important racketeers. Dunlap, a former Brigadier General, was brought in "to clean it up." He is trying, but whatever his boys find, Justice and his own superiors in the Treasury will file away or scramble up so that, regardless of the evidence, few important Mafistas will see the inside of jails on tax charges.

Prosecutions of campaign contributors are to be avoided except if one publicized case can be used to bamboozle laymen. But the major disgraceful public corruption is to be skillfully skipped over by Democratic wheelhorses, as this recent bit of non sequitur from the stammering lips of New York's Park Avenue junior Senator, Herbert Lehman, indicates:

In referring to the present wave of dishonesty, Lehman said it resulted from "persistent attacks on the right of government servants to think independently."

In other words, he means they are so mad because we won't let them be Communists, they're stealing from the till.

D. Truman Sickness

The strange epidemic that has been depopulating Washington may be likened by future historians to the great plagues of London. For want of another name this mysterious visitation is known as Truman poisoning, because just before the death rattle Harry always expresses his confidence in the next victim. Before it runs its course many whose names appear herein may be hauled away in their political coffins, some between the time this is written and when it reaches print, so fast is the course of the fatal malady.

This treatise will not recapitulate the peculations and spoliations exposed, but seldom punished. General Vaughan, John F. Maragon, Donald Dawson are no longer confidential. Nor are the deep-freezes, mink coats, deals to empty Federal prisons, black-marketing, Kansas City election steals, campaign funds from Erickson and Costello, tax-forgiveness of Mafia mobsters, influence-peddling, RFC loans to sharpers through sharks and Justice

Department whitewashes involving known and itemized looting of the Federal cash-drawer ten times in excess of the whole Federal budget in the year of Tea Pot Dome.

A few chumps have been sacrificed, a few others indicted for newspaper field-days. But the same gang of bag-and-boodle boys still runs the works, insulated by beaming bureaucrats, social workers, party plugs and eurythmic dancers, all with their fingers in the government pie. Their thefts are beginning to break the bank. Federal tax collections last year were more than fifty billion dollars—seventeen times that which was extorted in 1934. And yet the government operated at a deficit. Collections were the equivalent of all the earnings of the total population of every state west of the Mississippi. Some was spent to study such things as neurosis in animals and the courtship secrets of Indian tribes.

In his first six years in office, Truman spent one-third of all the money ever spent by the United States in its entire history. All Federal tax collections from 1789 to June 30, 1945, were $254,000,000,000. Truman collected $262,000,000,000 from July 1, 1945, to July 1, 1951. He wants $84,000,000,000 this year.

This picture of Washington, D.C., circa 1952, tells you what you got for your money. It is a primer of departments and agencies mired in mud beyond conceivable extrication. Not a hundred Hoovers and Murphys and no Morrises ever could clear it up.

Tens of thousands of costly government press agents disseminate handouts, publish books, throw expensive cocktail parties, provide girls and gin at government expense to drum-beat for their agencies, solidify themselves in jobs and whitewash their superiors' betrayals of the people. They have propagandized for socialized medicine, public housing, state insurance and every imaginable and some not imaginable forms of boondoggling designed to increase the fat in the pork barrel that already supports a privileged ruling caste of 2,500,000 with U.S. government checks and millions more who swill from state and municipal troughs.

Influence runs the whole price scale. Tips and theatre tickets will take care of secretaries. Gay parties for executives or gifts for their wives do cheap business upstairs. But big deals—in contracts, financing, locations of plants and Federal cantonments—cost what the traffic will bear.

Meanwhile, the government clamps a news blackout on all malfeasance, at first pretending it doesn't exist, then, when it breaks, saying it's an isolated case and shouldn't be talked about anyway, because it violates secrecy.

Washington is verminous with spies, agents-provocateur, conspirators, whores and fairies, all seeking to get something on everyone else. The State Department spies on Congressmen. High State Department officials spend government money attempting to frame lawmakers so they won't vote against State's pet measures or men. State Department agents try to bribe newspapermen with exclusive handouts, bids to select parties, trips on official junkets at government expense, or cash. When all that doesn't work, they try dames—even queers. If it's still no go, they have agents trailing them.

So brazen are Acheson's cloak-and-dagger boys, they've had a tail on J. Edgar Hoover, of all people, hoping to catch him in something. Hoover and his great FBI are the nemesis of State, whose boss refused to turn his back on Alger Hiss.

Jokers slipped through in routine legislation set up laws whereby the government can jail factory workers if they talk against Truman or his union satellites. Federal judges try to muzzle newspapers guilty only of exposing corruption.

While it curtails the freedom of speech and movement of its opponents, the mammoth central government pays radio commentators to slant their talks to the infamous bureaucracy, already so dug in that administrations come and go but they go on forever. These bureaus, commissions, independent committees, authorities and other alphabetical incubi are largely independent and indestructible. Congresses have surrendered most of their control over them. They have wide discretionary power to fix wages, prices, rents; to determine rates for public utilities and transportation companies; to allocate routes; radio channels; award contracts, give subsidies, lend money, compete with private business, collect taxes, regulate or forbid the sale of securities, determine the ingredients of foods and drugs, prosecute for alleged anti-trust violations—in fact Congress has yielded to them almost all its powers except the right to appropriate, and that is now negligible because each of these government agencies employs hundreds of press agents and lobbyists to cajole or bribe Congress to spend more.

Congress surrendered even its right to be bribed! The gravy accrues to the agencies. Congressmen get little now but free booze.

The Executive department runs 20,000 autos—mostly chauffeur-driven. This does not include Defense. Many of these cars are turned over to private citizens and friends of officials or are at the disposal of influential syndicated columnists or newspapermen who may be able to put in a plug for an upcoming appropriation.

So insatiable are the bureaucrats for appropriations that when they can no longer think of legitimate excuses to get money, after having every possible request taken care of by a Congress that no longer cares, they dream up tricks to start new money gushing.

These are just a few:

U.S. servicemen and women in Britain are to get free wigs if they're embarrassed by growing bald. An unpublicized Army order said the toupees are to offset psychiatric disorders caused by vanishing hair.

The Air Force bought coffee from the Army at 67 cents a pound, then used it to hold down the dust while sweeping up the floors.

Government funds were provided by the National Institute of Mental Health to permit Professor Robert W. Finch, of Northwestern University, to study the "unconscious factors governing courtship and mate selection."

The Economic Stabilization Agency helped to stabilize the economics of the furniture industry with $155 easy chairs and $286 davenports. Now executives can romance their secretaries in style.

When the GSA moved into the old Interior Building it cost 14 Gs to tear out the secret wiring which had been installed there by Harold Ickes. The Ick had a penchant for listening in on the conversations of his underlings. Some of what he heard from the powder-room must have burned his ears.

The Bureau of Indian Affairs, under Honest Harold, smelled no sweeter than it does now under Secretary Chapman, also a thoroughgoing boobycrat. Bribery is rampant. Certain lawyers have the monopoly to represent Indians. Concessions are peddled on a high bid basis and undertable currency to traders, who get the green light to put the simple Redmen in hock. Rich Indians can't touch their dough. They are wards of the government. But the Bureau's Indian guardians have a picnic living off the aborigines' wealth, disguising it with twisted bookkeeping.

The Public Roads Administration is called the Paupers' Relief Administration. Thomas H. MacDonald, its head, lives in the faintly pinkish and literary Cosmos Club. When the Alcan Highway was under construction, army personnel employed on it got $21 a month for a fourteen-to-eighteen-hour day, slept in tents, had no furloughs. The PRA men worked side by side. Its politically appointed, draft-exempt employes got $150 a week for the same work—on an eight-hour day, plus pay to and from their jobs, per diem allowances, vacations and prefab houses.

One of the colossal racket nests is the Veterans Administration, with a graduated shakedown price list which includes kickbacks from approved trade schools, kickbacks for approval of textbooks and tools, and every other possible grafting device.

The Post Office, long America's pride, is riddled with inefficiency, favoritism and payoffs. Even the famed postal inspectors have been reached. It is as easy to tamper with the mails as it was to fix a tax case. Rank and file, hard-working, underpaid employes are disgusted as they see funds poured into crooked contracts, swollen subsidies, overpriced purchases. Good jobs are for sale. The Post Office raised rates and crimped services, but it openly admitted it wastes millions. A figure of $45,000,000 wastage was given for twenty offices. The total amount that could be saved, according to insiders, runs to $150,000,000 or $200,000,000.

The Department of Justice's Immigration Service is one of the most lucrative shakedown sources in the government. Conservative Congressional estimates indicated there are 5,000,000 illegally-entered aliens in the country. The names of most of them are known—they remain through political influence, payoffs, union pressure, or, in the case of Reds or left-wingers, intervention by high government officials, Congressmen, the Roosevelts and certain New Deal newspapers like the *St. Louis Post-Dispatch,* which led the fight for Ellen Knauth, who, though adjudged a security risk, was finally allowed to remain.

Smuggled aliens are divided into two groups—subversives and enemy agents in one; criminals in the other. The same ring handles the details for both. The aliens are concentrated in Havana or Windsor, Ontario. Should they be arrested after arrival in the U.S., the law firms of certain Congressmen are retained. Among the most active in this field are Representatives F. D. Roosevelt, Jr., and Jacob Javits, of New York, and James Morrison, of Louisiana. Many Congressmen introduce private bills to permit such aliens to remain in the country or become citizens.

The Federal Housing Administration is one of the most fertile fields for feathering the nest of politicians who are on the right side. The President's brother heads the Kansas City office. This gold-plated pay-car has been streamlined so deserving Democrats can collect two ways. Here's how it generally works:

Suppose you are planning to build a project which is going to cost $1,000,000. The FHA lends you $1,250,000. The extra $250,-000 goes into the promoter's pocket as salary, financing-expenses, commissions and bonus, which he splits fifty-fifty with FHA expediters. He pays construction costs to companies he owns under different names at inflated prices with the remaining million. Long before the project is completed, the fly-by-night corporation which got the government loan goes bankrupt, having been milked of its assets by the crooks and politicians. The government thereupon forecloses its mortgage, takes over the structure and resells it at a bargain to other crooks. Sometimes the same ones get it back again for practically nothing—then borrow big dough on it all over again.

The ill-fated OPS is a shakedown organization. A merchant who wants higher prices has to pay for them. People who are in bad politically are threatened with prosecution. Employers who don't cooperate with unions get nothing. The chief enforcement officer of OPS is Edward P. Morgan, who has two claims to fame. He was the counsel for the Pearl Harbor whitewash and once again for the Tydings Committee whitewash. His OPS enforcement is on a par with both. There were 10,000 employes of OPS at this writing, and they were increasing by the minute, with salaries up to $15,000 a year, plus side-money, of course.

Another scandal is ready for disclosure any time a Senator wants to go into pardons and paroles. These have been for sale for years, beginning with the first Roosevelt Administration, when mobsters and campaign contributors were never allowed to languish long in cells. There is a regular graduated list of prices for jails and penitentiaries. Other prices apply for soft jobs in the jails and frequent vacations.

But you don't need to go to jail. With the proper payoff the Department of Justice stalls the prosecution until the statute of limitations begins to work.

One of the big blowoffs is taking place in the office of the Alien Property Custodian, where a favored few are robbing former German and Japanese properties. Many law firms are on the favored list for heavy fees, including Fulton, Walter & (Rudy) Halley.

Through a curious chain of coincidences, the Alien Property Custodian is the landlord—through the General Aniline & Film Corporation—of the gangster-owned Chicago night club, the Chez Paree. Halley received fees from General. Other large fees were paid to Louis Johnson, former Secretary of Defense. The Halley law firm also cut itself a melon for pleadings before the SEC, ICC and FCC. The latter potent body is the supreme authority in connection with the granting of radio and TV channels and stations. The Halley connection there is through Frieda Hennock, blonde commissioner, who like Rudy is a protégé of Ferdinand Pecora, former New York Supreme Court Justice who was defeated for Mayor after it was charged he was Frank Costello's choice. While Halley's firm was defending a station owner accused of bias and anti-Semitism before the FCC, your authors saw him and Commissioner Hennock together socially, despite legal ethics. Truman nominated Frieda to the Federal bench, the first woman so honored, but the bar associations shrieked about her after-hour occupations so loudly that the Senate by-passed her and she withdrew.

Halley was once a counsel for the Truman Committee. There are many others who cashed in on their connections with the White House. Clark M. Clifford, Truman's ghost-writer, is legal and economic adviser to the Indonesian Government, which is receiving handouts from the United States. He represented Howard Hughes' TWA on a deal awaiting the President's decision. He was retained as counsel for the Capitol Transit Company, in Washington, about whose financing there is much mystery, inasmuch as its present controlling stockholder took part in a political slush fund kitty that included a representative of Chicago's Capone mob. Clifford got the Brazilians a raise in the price of coffee. He charged $25,000 per consultation in the White House, where he practiced law while on the U.S. payroll. He received a fee from two Chinese accused by their government of looting the Chinese bank account.

Leon Henderson, a darling of the New Deal, makes plenty peddling influence and advice, through his supposed control of the Americans for Democratic Action. The last time we saw him he was exuberant at El Morocco, dancing a jig with Baroness von Stackleburg, whose husband got his job with the World Bank through Leon. Now that he's out of that organization, he and his wife use their social prestige to push the Florida Citrus industry, with Henderson's covert assistance.

Wilson Wyatt, who was Federal Housing Administrator and now practices law, is the undercover brains of the ADA. His firm cashes in accordingly. Charles S. Murphy, the President's lawyer, is another big whig in ADA and pulls the strings that make the pressure group dance as the Fair Deal wishes.

Anna Rosenberg and Oscar Ewing are also represented on the

brain trust. They are close friends personally. Washington gagsters call them "Mr. Rosenberg and Miss Ewing," because she
always walks ahead, pushes open the doors and sits down last.

Boondoggling with other people's money affects every branch
of the Raw Deal, even in overseas installations. U.S. High Commissioner John J. McCloy soaked the German Government $725,-
000 to remodel and furnish his house in Bonn. He is building a
$9,000,000 housing project in which 458 Americans can live in
style with snack bars, bowling alleys, night clubs and a putting
green. All apartments will be furnished, from the forty-two single-
bedroom suites for "male and female bachelors" to the de luxe
layout with four double bedrooms, dining room, living room,
kitchen and two baths. The equipment will include pillows, glass-
ware, table silver, dishes, flat-irons and percolators. Food will be
provided by the Army Quartermaster.

Government officials in Washington fly all over the country and
all over the world in official planes. The Treasury commands its
own through the Coast Guard, and there is no way to tell how
much money has been wasted on junkets provided for officials and
their families. Undersecretary Edward H. Foley and Comptroller
of the Currency Preston Delano, a Roosevelt leftover, took their
wives to Sun Valley for a four-day visit while the plane's crew of
six lived at the resort on government expense. This happens continually up and down the line of Washington officialdom.

No Congressman arises to question it, because the members are
themselves the worst chiselers of free transportation, with the notable exception of Vice-President Barkley, who took his wife
along on a joyride to Japan. During the last Congressional recess
more than a hundred Congressmen took flyers to Japan, China,
the South Seas, South America, Scandinavia, England, France,
Italy and the Middle East.

One of the most profitable sources of graft is in perquisites reserved for the Senate and the House, such as the private police
force, page boys and staffers. Millions have been stolen from Congressional funds by pals of the Vice-President. They are not questioned. Les Biffle is the patronage dispenser for the Senate. Among
the jobs at his disposal is that of the chaplain, also a political
plum because it boosts the dominie's stock in his own church.
The present chaplain is the Reverend Frederick Brown Harris,
an unctuous politician with an incurable social yen. Dr. Harris,
though a snob, did not hesitate to pull plenty of strings to get his
job.

On the staff of the Senate Sergeant at Arms is a gentleman whose sole purpose appears to be procuring women for Senators. Many are so old they require young girls only for company. Before the Vice-President remarried, he liked pretty girls to talk to. The Senate Sergeant at Arms also employs undercover agents. Through them Barkley knows so much that few dare question or cross him. The Vice-President accepted $5,000 lecture dates from those with causes to plead before the Senate, but the lobby investigating committee kept far away from the subject.

After Roosevelt's court packing, the Supreme Court of the United States gradually lost the prestige and honor it had earned since the days of John Marshall. Many cases are no longer decided on the law or on their merits, but for political, economic, social or other reasons even less judicial. As of this writing the nine men who compose the court of last resort are:

Chief Justice Fred M. Vinson, who was Federal Loan administrator when deserving Democrats borrowed millions. He served as Secretary of the Treasury during the period many of the great frauds now being uncovered took place. His best friend, Thurman Arnold, calls him "Flannel-mouth Fred" to his face.

Hugo Lafayette Black, of Birmingham, Alabama, a cracker and former Ku Kluxer, appointed by Roosevelt in 1937 in a fit of anger after the Senate turned down the court packing plan. He has become a devoted left-winger.

Dull and dreary Stanley Forman Reed was a character witness for Alger Hiss.

Felix Frankfurter, brains of the New Deal, evil genius of the socialist revolution, godfather of Acheson and Hiss and the whole nest of appeasers, left-wingers, welfare-staters, do-gooders and queer intellectuals. He, too, was a Hiss character witness. He is arrogant, self-centered, a pink Napoleon.

William Orville Douglas is a poseur, a social butterfly and party-goer. He is frustrated with ambitions for high office. He was accused on the floor of Congress as having given "aid and comfort" to America's enemies on many occasions.

Robert H. Jackson, political bed-fellow of FDR, onetime general counsel for the Bureau of Internal Revenue and Attorney General of the United States when the mobsters took over both departments.

Harold Hitz Burton, a nonentity from Cleveland.

Tom C. Clark, Attorney General before McGrath, who inherited the most crooked department in the United States government from him. He is a Texas rough-neck trying to become legitimate. Gagsters say he actually looked at a lawbook last year.

Sherman Minton, thoroughgoing Indiana Democrat, rewarded for his loyalty to Frank McHale, national committeeman, with this exalted seat. His reasoning is devious, he is trying to be left of Black.

Judy Coplon thinks they're all great.

E. Politics as Usual—How to Win by Losing

The Country and the Administration are going to hell, but there is no moratorium on politics in Washington—especially in a Presidential year.

Every deal, every move, every act, every whisper is measured to votes. Appointments, firings, indictments, convictions, Supreme Court decisions and trial balloons all have political significance. Nine-tenths of the "lowdown" is rumor—but rumor has a mighty function in the capital—to test the public's reaction to what may come later.

As 1951 waned, it appeared evident to Truman that unless the anti-Administration trend, which began with the Korean fiasco and went into high with disclosures of corruption in government, was halted, the party might be up against it in the up-coming election.

Truman wanted and will always want to stay in the White House. But he is a cagey little codger who cut his teeth on the Pendergast Ring. He had no intention of quitting at the beginning of 1952, hoping to reverse the GOP upsurge, as he had done before, by something dramatic—like good news from abroad or a phony drive on crooks in government. He would send a couple of office-holders to the can—if it would help him hang on at 1600 Pennsylvania Ave.

Other Democrats who thought they saw the handwriting on the wall had their own ideas on how to save the party, and at the same time, their own political skins.

To one group Estes Kefauver was the answer. The Tennessee terror had been campaigning ever since he dropped his bill to investigate crime into the Senate hopper. Early in 1950 we wrote that he was yearning for the Vice-Presidency. Estes was flattered but asked us as a personal favor to lay off. "The boss in the White House won't like it," he said. And shuddered. But that gave him a bug.

The current Kefauver strategy is aimed at accidentals. Estes will come into the convention with delegates and prestige. He will settle for the Vice-Presidency and not be disappointed if he gets nothing, because he is really thinking of 1956. Many who are cool toward Truman are for him. Ed Flynn, notorious New York boss and Frank Costello ally, is secretly plugging for Estes as a payoff for the Kefauver Committee's carelessness in not calling him. The Los Angeles police department provided Kefauver with indisputable evidence that Flynn and White House crony Teddy Hayes were tied up with Costello in a plan to take over the Mexican National Lottery. We have seen correspondence between L.A. cops and Kefauver Committee attachés in which an investigation was promised. It never came off.

Another group of Democrat dissidents were sitting on the most complicated political scheme ever hatched in our history.

Briefly, the plan, which grew more sinister with every refinement, was this:

To plug Ike Eisenhower for the GOP nomination. If he got it, then, when the Democrats met, two weeks later, to move that Ike's nomination be made unanimous. The fine scheming presumed that if Eisenhower were the "national unity" candidate of both parties he would appoint a coalition cabinet, retaining many Democrat spoilsmen. In the event of such a "nonpolitical" administration, the new President probably would not fire the hold-over bureaucrats. Even more frightening was the carefully thought-up plan that, with no contest for the Presidency, few voters would go to the polls, leaving the incumbent Senators and Congressmen in, thus assuring Democratic control of the next Congress. And Harry would be the elder statesman, the strong man to whom all winners would be beholden.

By the time these words appear in print this scheme may have foundered. Anyway, that is what the boys were playing with when we went to press.

Democrats believed Ike would look favorably on such a double nomination. The General has no stomach for rough-and-tumble party warfare and its mudslinging. Or so it is said.

His bi-party nomination would be an endorsement of Harry's foreign policies. Ike would be expected to retain the Acheson axis in State and the Marshall mummies in Defense.

That was the deal Truman put up to Ike last winter when the *New York Times'* Arthur Krock got a slightly garbled version that Eisenhower had been offered the Democratic nomination. Though Harry denied it, Krock was right so far—but not far enough.

The plan was hatching in Washington and throughout the

U. S. A. CONFIDENTIAL

country all winter. Subtle feelers were put out here and there. Senator Paul Douglas, reputed to be an anti-Administration Democrat, but actually tightly tied up with Democratic crooks through the Jake Arvey Chicago machine, was used as a sounding-board for a two-party nomination. As the year progressed other feelers went out to see whether the road was clear for the greatest political steal since Napoleon became First Consul.

This desperate, grandiose scheme, which would sabotage America's two-party system forever, had the enthusiastic, if covert, support of the huge professional military machine, which envisioned the perfect set-up, in a one-party government with a general at its head. They reasoned that, regardless of his simplicity, good humor and "humanity," Ike is a West Pointer, a professional soldier and a member of the elite corps.

Many Eastern Republican backers of Eisenhower were conversant with the deal. Some came from states like Massachusetts and Rhode Island, which have a disconcerting way of going Democratic in presidential years. No longer hoping to win a national election themselves, these Republicans prefer to sell out to Democrats rather than face starvation—an orthodox political maneuver which has its roots in big cities, where the opposition party usually puts up a weak sister in municipal campaigns, then is rewarded with plums and appointments by the "ins."

Many Republicans are afraid the GOP may win. As "outs," they run their own local machines; but if a GOPer sits in the White House, he will dictate all down the line, reshaping Republican state organizations that were hostile to him before the convention, by patronage. Few politicians have patriotic illusions. They would rather stick in office as Governors or Senators than sit on the sidelines for the good of their party. This was even more evident in the South, where Republican committeemen have no patronage, local or Federal. They get handouts from their Democratic opposite numbers.

As the presidential year dawned, there was broad indecision and defeatism in the GOP, sparked by Democrats who had been infiltrated into the enemy camp. These fifth columnists were operating boldly in Washington, where at the League for Republican Women Voters CIO union literature was distributed. A picture of left-wing Helen Gahagan Douglas, defeated for the Senate as a Red-supporter, hung on the wall. Officials said they wanted to present both sides.

Democrats were active on their own front. Mike Di Salle used

OPS transportation to sell the Fair Deal. Navy Secretary Kimball spends more of the taxpayers' money fighting Republicans than he does Communists. Labor Secretary Maurice Tobin is supposed to have the union and New England vote in the bag—but Uncle Sam pays for it. Oscar Ewing, the blubber-head from the Bronx, sells the party along with his socialized medicine, which he campaigns for with taxes to which members of the American Medical Association contribute.

The full sixty-one billion bucks for arms and foreign relief, already appropriated but sadly delayed, is getting under way now. When the money was voted last year, the braintrust planned it that way—nuts with Korea or the North Atlantic Treaty. The idea was to build up a terrific backlog, then let the reservoir overflow this spring and summer, flooding the country with fast money and guaranteeing a Democratic victory in the fall.

In the meantime, the boodle bund also counts on another reservoir of votes. Recent figures of the Department of Commerce show that annual government payrolls—Federal, state and municipal—are more than $30 billion, with pay checks to nine million families.

Inasmuch as the Democrats control the national government, run half the states and almost all the big cities, 80 per cent of these are expected to vote that way.

Democratic bigwigs also count mightily on the vote power of the 17,000,000 checks mailed out each month by Uncle Sam—not including those to servicemen; among these—one out of nine of the population—are U.S. payrolls, relief, farmers' and businessmen's handouts and pensions, social security payments, etc.

To insure the triumph of the right, word is now being passed along to all of Uncle Sam's 2,500,000 employes that votes can be traced and they had better vote Democratic or else. Even those who come from states using voting machines have been advised that the boys know who votes how.

At the same time a plot is being hatched by the Democratic command to steal the absentee ballots of servicemen—a comparatively simple procedure to substitute Democratic ballots wherever needed. The stunt was tried with great effect during FDR's last campaign, when the service vote was counted almost unanimously his way.

Politicians of both parties have been wooing the so-called minority vote all year. The Administration has had apoplexy over the "shabby" treatment of the Mexican "wetbacks" who work as

itinerant laborers on American farms. The Latin-American vote
is powerful now, especially in New York, New Jersey, Michigan
and California, and there are more Mexican voters in New
Mexico than whites—in an uncertain state.

Italian voters whose blocs are vital to success in New York,
Pennsylvania, Connecticut, Ohio and Illinois are being wooed
with grants in aid to Italy of billions, plus many juicy appointments here of Americans of Italian descent. Both parties are fighting for this plum. New York's left-wing Republican Congressman
Jacob Javits, who usually votes with the Democrats, is yelling for
admission of 500,000 more aliens—mostly from Italy. (His law
firm finds immigration work highly profitable.)

The Humphrey civil rights bills are catch-alls designed to keep
Negroes Democratic and to seduce all other minorities. Seven
Fair Deal Democrats and one Fair Deal Republican joined as co-
sponsors. They are Douglas, of Illinois, called an "honest dreamer,"
but actually a product of the stinkingest political machine in the
world; Benton, of Connecticut, a fanatic for queer radical ideas;
Lehman, of New York, a senile social stuffed shirt who needs a
guide to show him to the men's room; Magnuson, of Washington,
playboy of the Senate; Murray, of Montana, who stayed on the
cuff at a Miami hotel which he had helped to get an RFC loan;
Neely, of West Virginia, backed by the crooks, and Pastore, of
Rhode Island, chosen by the Mafia. The lone Republican, who
is no such thing, is Morse of Oregon, a socialist schemer.

Another political gimmick similar to the dispersal of industries
to "hostile" localities is found in the construction of public
housing. By plot and by plan, first conceived by the sainted Roosevelt's stooges, like the despicable Harry Hopkins, public housing
developments are erected in Republican districts. As everyone
knows, tenants must get political clearance to move into such a
development. Most people who do are unioneers, Negroes, slum
rabble and precinct handymen who will vote as they are told.

These projects are tax exempt, while the home owners in the
pre-empted neighborhoods must pay increased assessments as they
see their own values ruined—all this by design to expunge the
middle class.

But the prize political steal of them all was dreamed up by
Harry Truman to kid the public into forgetting the income tax
scandals. He proposed making all the collectors civil service. That
would mean freezing the crooks for life onto the payroll and into
pensions, so the Republicans, if they ever get in, have to keep

them. Roosevelt did it with postmasters. He was praised for "taking them out of politics." What he did was obligate forever 22,000 deserving Democrats.

And not one Republican that we can find has been chosen to be frozen since—despite civil service.

F. The District of Confusion

As we predicted it would be, in *Washington Confidential,* home rule again had hard sledding. Even the most ardent Northern shrieker for leveling us all grew thoughtful in the face of the figures we printed, that at least half of Washington's population is Negro. We were reviled but not contradicted by the same "liberals" who suddenly grew queasy at the thought of the obvious possibility that the first elected Mayor of the nation's capital might be black. The watered down bill reported out provided for an appointed Mayor.

The residents of the District are voteless. They are governed by a three-man commission appointed by the President. They live in a community as boss-ridden as any major metropolis in the land. The czar and Boss Hague is Milton Kronheim, very rich wholesale liquor dealer. Kronheim once settled a Federal OPA assessment by tossing 250 Grand notes on a table. He made his son a municipal court judge. Last year he elevated his son's law partner to the potent position of District Commissioner. The new commissioner, Jiggs Donohue, at once became king of the three-man body, as Kronheim ordered. Commissioner John Russell Young, the former strong man, went into an immediate political decline.

In order to clinch the victory the Kronheim faction initiated another investigation of District crime, which, instead of being such, actually was gimmicked up to "get" Young, no difficult job at that, as the record of his unbelievably corrupt administration showed. A secondary object was the elimination of unorganized gamblers who fought the Syndicate.

The probe was conducted by a Senate sub-committee headed by Matt Neely, of West Virginia, a political servant and ally of Bill Lias, Wheeling gambler who owes Uncle Sam $2,000,000 in back taxes. The other Democrats on the inquisition were Pastore of Rhode Island, elected with the aid of Mafia votes, and Hunt of Wyoming, the little dentist who wasn't there most of the time on the Kefauver Committee.

The chief counsel of this new expense to the taxpayers was one

Arnold Baumann, a hitherto unknown New York attorney, who is a protégé of Carmine De Sapio, leader of Tammany Hall and close personal friend of Frank Costello, whose Whitely Liquors does business with the senior Kronheim.

The new committee had as reference the complete record of the intelligent probe of District conditions conducted last year by Hyman Fischbach, counsel for a House committee. He did a terrific job with little money or publicity. Baumann also had *Washington Confidential* in front of him. After reckless expenditures, the Senate committee found nothing that Fischbach or we had not already printed.

After making its two main points, i.e., to smear Young, which was a cinch, and to blast local unaffiliated hoods who were standing in the way of a complete take-over of local vice by criminals from out-of-town, the interest of the investigators waned.

Kronheim's immense power began in 1948. He contributed $25,000 to Truman's campaign fund when the President found touches tough. Five Grand was in Donohue's name. Kronheim has frequently sweetened the Democratic kitty since then.

Also a Donohue client was Emmit Warring, notorious Washington gambler whose life and times we had recorded.

Another lawyer with whom Kronheim had business dealings was T. Lamar Caudle, deposed tax-prosecutor. Caudle frequently borrowed money from Kronheim while Kronheim's suit for tax overpayments was before the U.S. courts.

Commissioner Donohue's first act was to call Lait and Mortimer categorical liars. He denied there were gangsters, gamblers, whores, after-hour spots and other skulduggery at the street level.

We stopped over in his immaculate burg and went over familiar ground. We had told the truth the first time. And here is what we found a year later:

Since Donohue took office, a new U.S. attorney and police chief were installed. The scandals in the police department were worse than those in New York. Chief Barrett quit under fire—Truman sickness—after he had failed in Federal court to halt an order forcing policemen to fill out questionnaires as to their wealth. The new chief was Barrett's assistant, buddy and whip-cracker.

Despite the changes, the city is as wide open as before *Washington Confidential*, rather more so. Every after-hour ginmill we mentioned is still going, except the Hideaway, which shuttered after a murder and reopened as a Negro swing-and-jive joint—

where dope-peddlers congregate and sell weeds out in front, on the street.

There are at least 500 such alleged bottle-clubs operating openly, every one with coppers on the payroll. Of them all only one obeys the regulations—the Lyre's Club.

The infamous Gold Key is roaring again—this is General Vaughan's favorite spot, where broads are available in front and games go on in the rear—but Donohue pretends not to know about it. The Atlas, a few blocks from the White House, also runs all night—with craps on the top floor.

Streetwalkers still promenade, especially at 13th and New York, and take their customers to cheap hotels. The bars we wrote about still break the same laws with the same floozies—or fairies.

Call-girls are available if you wink to bellboys at the Carlton, Statler, Willard, Shoreham, Wardman and dozens of others. Numbers and policy are as big as ever, with betting agents and commissioners working right in the District government building as well as the Senate and House office buildings.

Bets are laid off on the wires of a bookmaker with a suite in the Dorchester Hotel or phoned across the line to Virginia and Maryland. The new Federal tax act is a dead letter. Washington never went strong for horses. Policy is not being bothered by the tax boys because it supports so many Negroes.

Some of the surrounding Maryland counties have clamped down, so their fairy and prostitute trade moved into the capital. Prince Georges officials made strippers put on panties. Now a dozen cabarets in the District present nudes—lowdown dirty ones —and advertise naked girls openly in the dailies. There was only one such in Washington last year.

When we were in the capital last, Donohue attended a stag birthday party for Jimmy Lake, local fight referee. Donohue's patron, Kronheim, Sr., was with him. Others in the party, which Jiggs called "the most amazing demonstration I've seen," included Mush Alos, a bookmaker; Pete Gianeris, listed by us in *Washington Confidential* as the kingpin gambler, and Al Brown, owner of the Gold Key Club, which openly breaks the law seven nights a week. These and other pet hoods, gamblers, racketeers and thieves sat with Donohue while Sally Rand and other nudes stripped for the honored guests.

Some time after the publication of the Washington book, authorities issued a proclamation saying there were only about twenty-five narcotics addicts in the District. A few days later, a

less-publicized statement announced that seventy-seven heroin
peddlers had been arrested in one hour in one neighborhood. More
than three sellers per user sounds like government contract technique.

Washington topped every city in the country in felonious assaults—not only per capita, but by total number. It had one-third
as many murders as Chicago, with one-sixth the population, the
per capita top for the country. First at last in the American
League!

29. BALTIMORE CONFIDENTIAL
(ACT II)

WE POURED it in with a 10,000-word chapter in *Washington Confidential* about Baltimore. We named names, gave addresses and phone numbers of cheating gamblers, madames and
dope-peddlers, and listed the evil Sicilians who protect them. We
traced political alliances from ward-heelers to Baltimore's Mayor
Tom D'Alesandro. He was re-elected in a breeze last year, despite
such exposures. We knocked the lid off the State Democratic machine, of which Senator Herbert O'Conor remains the chief pooh-
bah. Such accusations could invite libel actions, which we do not
want; none were filed.

Some time after the publication, we journeyed to Baltimore on
a routine assignment to make a television appearance. We learned
no station dared carry the broadcast. The one which had scheduled it got chicken and canceled. The press agent then arranged
for us to wax a platter for a radio broadcast next day. This, too,
was silenced. Protests to the Federal Communications Commission were filed and forgotten. Senator O'Conor is also a member
of the Committee on Interstate and Foreign Commerce, which
votes the funds for the FCC.

We resurveyed Baltimore to see whether the Kefauver Committee (O'Conor was its chairman at the end) and our book had made
any changes in dirt and degeneracy. We were startled to discover
they had.

Nude photos had been ordered out of the novelty store windows! But they were still on sale inside.

That was all. Everything else was the same. The girls who

stripped at the Oasis, the Miami, Kay's and the other dives still peeled down to their complete all, saving the expense of G-strings and net bras. They still worked at table level, instead of on raised stages or in back of bars as they do even in Chicago, and still rubbed their fannies in the faces of ringside customers who craved such clean fun.

Most of the store windows of the "Block," E. Baltimore Street's skidrow, openly displayed rubber goods. Streetwalkers swung their big red handbags in front—asking price $10, taking as low as $2. B-girls still work in most of the saloons and brashly solicit customers to buy drinks. You can place a bet on a nag, buy a policy slip or latch onto reefers or hard junk on almost any corner and if you get pinched you can do all three in jail.

But Baltimore is not unique among the communities of the Free State. The last time we checked with the Commissioner of Internal Revenue we found more than 4,000 Maryland citizens had purchased U.S. tax stamps for such gaming devices as one-armed bandits. These names are available to all for the asking, even Senator O'Conor.

Many Maryland counties had "legalized" slot-machines by "local option," though the state law forbids them and state courts have ruled that county "local option" has no legal basis. Baltimore, an independent city in no county, cannot even use that subterfuge. But license fees were paid for the swindle-machines by more than 1,000 there.

Even Maryland Republicans are in the Free State tradition. The new Governor, elected in the landslide that defeated Red-whitewasher Tydings, is silent, though under Maryland law he appoints the Baltimore police commissioner. The legislature is strongly stacked with Dems and the Governor cannot function unless he plays house with O'Conor's chosen. And leading all these is Jack Pollack, a former bootlegger once arrested on a murder charge. When he split with Bill "Boss" Curran and threw his weight to the Republican candidate, Theodore Roosevelt McKeldin was elected chief executive. Pollack and Baltimore Mayor D'Alesandro are like Siamese twins. The third man in the local triumvirate is O'Conor, who did not dare run for re-election this fall. Painfully aware of what had happened to his colleague, Millard Tydings, who carried the ball for Owen Lattimore's apologists, O'Conor turned Commie-fighter. But it was too late.

Baltimore's large Italian population always voted as a unit.

We listed the undercover kingpins of Little Sicily as Frank Gattuso, James Caranna, Tom Lafata, Joe Pallozolla and John Maurice. Their desires are conveyed to proper circles by D'Alesandro, a former New Deal yes-man in Congress, now Mayor of the offal of what was once charmingly salty but stately, beautiful Baltimore.

The venal nature of machine politics in Maryland and its integration into the nationwide underworld syndicate had long alarmed law enforcement officers everywhere. The state is a favorite hide-out for crooks on the lam, who can buy protection there against extradition warrants. But respectable citizens were unaware of what was occurring under their noses until they read *Washington Confidential*. Then they demanded that the Kefauver Committee come in. Estes replied he knew of no skulduggery in Baltimore. Thus was the deal between the five Senators on the committee—not to intrude into each other's dark closets—honored.

Kefauver, the born ringmaster, has a fine sense of timing. He withdrew from the chairmanship after his sock video appearance, side-stepping the thud of the anticlimax. He suspected that his adoring public would soon start asking questions, such as what was accomplished beyond pinning horns on a few high-smelling goats. Estes turned the roadshow No. 2 company over to O'Conor.

After O'Conor's ascension he, too, parried his home state's demand for an investigation until he was forced into a two-day brush-off at which no individual named by us was questioned or even remotely mentioned in others' testimony. There was no full-scale probe of crime conditions in Baltimore and Maryland. Mafistas were immune. O'Conor confined it to nailing a "gentleman" bookmaker at North Beach.

Though O'Conor has been on the public payroll ever since his graduation from law school, this Chesapeake Bay Horatio Alger-boy is now a comparatively wealthy man. The highest-paid job he ever held is U.S. Senator, $15,000 per annum—including expenses. He first suckled from the public nipple as People's Counsel for the Public Service Commission, right after his graduation. He was supposed to represent the constituency against the greedy interests. No public utility companies starved. He was rewarded by sub-rosa contributions to the piggy-bank which made him State's (District) Attorney of Baltimore in 1923 and kept him there eleven years, during which period the local underworld had seven field days every week. The big mob made its gains in Baltimore and dug in, while unorganized wrong-doers were sent to the

penitentiary by prosecutor O'Conor in the golden years of Prohibition. The nauseating conditions which now grip the nation's
sixth city are a direct outgrowth of the political policies of the
O'Conor regime.

Such a man could only go up. He did—State Attorney General
in 1934, and Governor in 1938. The Governor then, too, named
the Baltimore police head; he could clean the town up. Did he?
During his two terms in the state house in Annapolis, Baltimore
was as wicked and scummy as it is now.

Nor was there any law enforcement crackdown in any other
part of the state. His state troopers did not clean up Jimmy Fon-
taine's swank gambling hell, across the street from the Washington, D.C., city limits. Emboldened by the hands-off attitude at
home, Maryland's rich and bloated underworld reached across
the border and took over Washington, too. The profits filtered
back into the Free State and some trickled into the campaign
coffers of O'Conor's Democratic party.

In 1946 Governor O'Conor was ready to carry Maryland's torch
of freedom to illuminate the national scene. He was elected U.S.
Senator by less than 2,000 votes, all of them contested, with the
financial aid of one of the crookedest crime-politico tie-ups in the
history of the country. Charges of wholesale vote-buying and in-
timidation by Sicilian Black Handers have never been disproved.

In the upper house O'Conor was no Calhoun. He is a firm be-
liever in allowing dead dogs to lie—in Maryland, anyway. In that
laudable ambition he was joined by the three other Democrats
in Maryland's Congressional delegation—the Hon. Edward A.
Garmatz, of Baltimore, a former police magistrate and member
of the state racing commission, which tolerates unbelievable
crooked business at some of the half-mile tracks; the Hon. George
H. Fallon, also of Baltimore, a member of the Democratic state
central committee, which does not look a Mafia contribution in
the mouth; and the Hon. Lansdale G. Sasscer, of Upper Marlboro,
who is returned to office by the votes of the harlots, slot-machine
operators, gamblers and procurers of Prince Georges County.
(There are so many, Sasscer plans to run for O'Conor's seat.)
They and Mayor D'Alesandro are the only Democrats left in important offices in the Free State. They banded together to keep it
free. But not equal. The underworld is a privileged class.

Again we returned to Baltimore while preparing these pages,
to see whether something had not been accomplished, after all.
Sho' 'nuff! We saw a stripper in the Oasis wearing a G-string. It

had only the thickness of violin cat-gut, but it was a G-string. We went to the Miami and, lo and behold, a peeler there stopped taking off when she still had a wisp of diaphanous net the size of a postage stamp, covering her last vestigial rampart of virtue at bay.

Coppers heard we were in town and pulled a few raids. But the judge sternly rebuked them. "How come you just discovered this after all these years?" asked the court—then he discharged the maiden who had been arrested for shimmying her bare backside at a cash customer.

We also dug a little deeper this time and found names we didn't know before. We discovered that the most important Sicilian in the state is Tony Lionello. The Corbis—Pat, Eddie, Frank and Joe—and the Fallanos and Carlottas and the rest are under him.

When Frank Costello or other New York businessmen drive to Baltimore for conferences, you see big, black bullet-proof sedans with New York and New Jersey plates in front of one of the Corbis' restaurants. And you always find Lionello there. He is rated the richest man on the E. Baltimore Street skidrow and tenderloin, silent partner and owner of six of the toughest bars. Recently, one of Lionello's managers was arrested for seven violations. A police sergeant threatened the complainant with jail on a trumped-up charge. This sergeant gets a $250-a-week payoff from one gambling place on E. Baltimore Street.

Lionello's drag goes through Jack Pollack, who controls the State liquor examining board, and Judge Joseph Dimenenico, who sits on the bench to placate the Italian vote.

Because of a criminal record Lionello was unable to obtain liquor licenses even in Maryland where everything has a price tag. Former Governor Lane, a Democrat, gave the green light in 1947 after hearing from Pollack.

Now Lionello has virtually cornered the operation of downtown dives where girls mingle, sailors are robbed, drinks are watered and dope is peddled. The cops are his boys. Should a customer be unwise enough to squawk he gets arrested for disorderly conduct.

Most of his bars are operated by others as fronts. Joe Munafo is on the Gay White Way license. Crystal Bar, hangout of the pimps, is run by Sam Holtzman.

Sam Munafo is on the permit for Dubner's restaurant, a high class eating place, nevertheless.

The racket in the nearby bars was so good last year that the hookers who work them were rewarded by the proprietors with Christmas gifts, including stockings, make-up kits and expensive boxes of candy. These girls are not employes, but volunteers who bring their trade in. Those who did especially well were given diamond trinkets and, in some cases, fur coats.

But no minks. They are reserved for the Washington whores.

PART FOUR

THE EMPIRE
(*Confidential!*)

THE EMPIRE CONFIDENTIAL

OUR IMPERIAL system consists of two incorporated territories, Alaska and Hawaii; Puerto Rico which is a combination territory, self-governing commonwealth and enemy nation; and several minor possessions such as Guam, the Virgin Islands, Samoa, etc., with varying forms of government, but all under the boondoggling, graft-ridden, self-serving and socialist-minded U.S. Department of the Interior.

Alaska and Hawaii plug for statehood but probably will never get it; Puerto Rico indignantly turns it down, but may end up in the union because Puerto Ricans on the mainland have votes and are the balance of power in New York state. Few care what happens to the minor possessions, therefore they are rare hunting for expropriators from Washington.

30. HALF-BAKED ALASKA

LARGER THAN Texas, populated by less than 150,000 including Eskimos, Indians and walruses, is Alaska, a wilderness frontier. The only signs of civilization are occasional outposts with unpaved streets and one- and two-story shanties.

Its distances are so vast that travelers between two points often find it more convenient to return to the mainland and start all over again. There are millions of acres without habitation, inaccessible even by plane.

Residents are not concerned about statehood. All they want is lower living costs and more and cheaper women. The loudest shouters for representation are New Deal carpetbaggers who have descended by the thousands to rob and ruin the territory. Its governor, judges and important officials are appointed in Washington. These leeches know a Republican administration will replace them with good, faithful and hungry GOPers. To prevent such a calamity statehood is proposed. In that event the Democrats, who now greatly outnumber Republicans in Alaska, would be able to set up their own government, elect their own governor and keep all the plums for themselves. They don't give a damn for the two senators they'd be able to send to Washington; what they want is to dip their hands into the fabulous public lands and natural resources, now a Federal trust, which would be turned over to the new state.

The Alaska Railroad, government owned, is operated by Colonel J. P. Johnson, a New Deal appointee and pal of Governor Gruening. The railroad pays more for supplies than do privately owned companies. To do business with the road, contractors must be okayed by the proper Dems.

Up in the great frozen north a man needs a pal and a dog. Friendship is a mighty fine thing here. For instance—

Stanley McCutcheon is the attorney for the Alaska Airways. He is also a crony of Governor Gruening. When the airline applied for new routes—directly competitive with old established routes held by Republicans—it got them.

Federal Judge Anthony J. Dimond, former delegate to Congress, is the short-cut to Washington. Being his friend helps a lot. He is a kind jurist. He gives light sentences—especially to left-wingers and hoodlums.

The Mt. McKinley Hotel, between Anchorage and Fairbanks, cost millions to build only six years ago—when the Department of the Interior decided to develop Alaska as a tourist resort. The real purpose was to reward the proper contractors. Now the government is anxious to lease it for a dollar a year to anyone. No takers. The heating bill is $7,000 a month. Mt. McKinley is a sweet hide-out for VIPs and their babes—who pretend they're hunting—at government expense, of course.

Among Alaska's fantastic natural resources is enough wood to supply the newspaper wants of the world for the next thousand years. Paper could be produced there easily and cheaply if Uncle Sam spent the merest fraction of what he's throwing away elsewhere. But Truman and the Fair Deal boys do not want to help newspapers. They want to break them through a paper shortage. Eventually newsprint will be rationed, as in Peron's Argentina, where it is given to the proper publishers. Meanwhile, Alaska is losing an excellent opportunity for industrialization.

The Indian Affairs Bureau is loaded with Reds, bureaucrats, do-gooders, nuts and just plain lazy bums. There are so many of the latter they say there are more Indian Affairs men than there are Indians in Alaska.

Governor Gruening is an original Ickes man. You know what that means. An Ickes-Eleanor Roosevelt brainchild was the Matanuska Valley Settlement. Whole communities were transported from the states to make this a green and verdant paradise. Most of the settlers were ne'er-do-wells and tramps their home communities wanted to bounce, anyway. The government gave them land and okayed their credit. After running up big bills 75 per cent of them beat it. Most of the farmers who remained recently walked off to go to work in the local military projects at big dough.

The new Palmer Airport at Matanuska was tundra and farm, owned by one Bert Snodgrass. He got it for nothing fifteen years ago as a government homesteader. Until recently it was worth no more than $10,000, but it sold for $300,000, of which one-half was paid by the territory and one-half by Uncle Sam.

But see what happened to Northwest Airlines' great-circle route to the Orient, which depended on government weather stations spread out across the north Pacific isles. The maintenance cost was practically nil, yet the Defense Department ordered them shut, allegedly for economy, actually to handicap our air force bases near Siberia as a favor to Russia.

Economy is an unknown word. Meanwhile we spend billions building these bases. More than 30 per cent ends up in the hands of crooks, grafters, politicians, labor racketeers, etc. Every plan, every installation and every troop movement is made available to Russian spies who live in profusion in Anchorage, Fairbanks, Juneau and other towns, tolerated and protected by Interior, State and Defense.

You can't get a job on a government project without an OK from the Reds and labor goons.

Larry Moore, of New York, represents the Contractors' Association. He squares with the unions. All specifications go through his hands.

Reds are in on everything from fish-packing on Bristol Bay to sensitive key civilian jobs. Not all government employes in Alaska are Commies, but most assist the Commies, because everyone drinks too much and talks too much. The bar of the Westward Hotel is a miniature Washington Mayflower. If you hang around long enough you can learn all the military secrets. Communists also use whores and dope to seduce lonesome soldiers, government construction workers and important civilians.

Almost any female can make $1,000 a night!

Alaska has a new gold rush. Only this time the prospectors aren't men, and their precious metal isn't coming from the ground.

Rip-roaring, hell-raising Anchorage, on America's last frontier, has been taken over by another type of gold-digger—blondes, redheads and brunettes, who sing, dance, strip and supply the hunger for feminine company. Their "strike" is as rich as the Klondike or the Yukon ever produced.

Underpaid chorines, who don't rate $50 per in the States, are dragging down $125 and expenses in this dame-starved and amusement-famished golconda. And that's a trifle compared to what they garner "on the side."

One doll, after hoofing for twenty weeks in an Anchorage gin-mill, is reported to have returned to New York with $100,000!

Anchorage's population is said to have quadrupled in the past year, mostly construction workers, who reap a bonanza. But, along with them come card sharks and shady characters, then pigeons with big eyes and taking ways.

You can leave Seattle after lunch by Northwest Airlines and be in Anchorage for supper, and it's only a matter of hours from Broadway, where the "smart set" is studying timetables since hearing about the pickings.

A line of blonde hoofers from San Francisco labored at the appropriately named Last Chance, owned by Gruening's friend, Larry Stewart. The girls were in for four weeks, but wanted to stay a year where chumps paid a hundred for what some used to do for nothing.

The native females, who are called "klutches" (pronounced klootches) and look just like it, are also-ran competition for Stateside girls, which partially accounts for the inflated rates. A big night for most is not wine, women and song, but hooch, klutch and a broken phonograph record.

EMPLOYMENT NOTE: If you're bored, poor or neglected

on Broadway, honey, head for Anchorage. The nuggets are crying to be picked up by gals up thataway.

Most of the professional harlots are colored, flown up by plane loads. They occupy most of the seats on the scheduled flights. Pimps charter full planes and pack them with gals. The CAB winks an eye and gives up seats needed for troops, construction workers and the Korean air ferry.

You'd think you were in Harlem, you see so many colored gents in Cadillac convertibles, imported at great expense from the Mainland in space needed for food and military supplies. The ten richest men in Anchorage today are Afro-Americans.

Whores run to all kinds, types, colors, and sizes, but they are all expensive. Fourth Street is Anchorage's main drag. Hustlers work the bars. The Federal and the Mint are klutch hangouts. Prospective customers take them in cabs to the outskirts of town where they are serviced in the back of the car. No place in Anchorage is ever put off bounds because of women, dope or moonshine. The only time the MPs declare a place off limits is for dirty kitchens.

After the 1 A.M. closing, which is seldom observed, everyone dashes out to the city limits, only four or five blocks away. There is no law of any kind on the tundra. There are only four U.S. marshals to police the entire sub-continent. They have eleven fewer deputies today than they did before the beginning of the New Deal twenty years ago, and the reason for that is obvious. The lawbreakers want it that way.

Outside of town the Green Lantern, known affectionately as the Green Latrine, sells whores of the lowest type. Larry Starn's Fort Starn is a cheap saloon and night club with dormitories set up in a semicircle in the rear yard, resembling a tourist court or motel. It is called Fort Starn because it is in fact a fort where Larry's armed thugs are barricaded to fight off any possible assault by peace officers, who never come.

The Alibi, owned by Starn, is one of the toughest joints in the whole world. It is not unusual for dead bodies to be left right in the middle of the room after a gun or knife fight while the rest of the customers go on drinking. This is one of the few spots actually off limits for servicemen and it is patronized by bums and hobos, drunks from the mines and oldtime siwashes and their klutches. There's gambling in the back room.

Brown's Chicken Shack is another with rear dormitories where the complement of girls is about 75 per cent black and 25 per cent white.

The House of Joy is a Negro brothel outside of town. Most cabbies are pimps. During the warmer months they set their whores up on beds in the woods in the outskirts, because of the housing shortage.

Madames fly girls in bush-planes to lonely outposts where the price is $150 a man or a thousand bucks for the night. Town whores get $20 a go or $500 for the night. The desperate Air Force imported 300 cute civilian workers for just one purpose. The Air Base is now known as the Snatch Patch.

Whores sell reefers and heroin packaged in Mexico. One minor dope peddler was arrested as he stepped off our plane. He was importing it at the rate of a million a year. Anchorage is a focal point for distribution of heroin and marijuana. Marijuana cigarettes are showing in the small villages along the coastline and wreaking havoc with Eskimos and Indians.

Reds and the underworld work in close harmony, infiltrating all Army and Air Force posts. Teen-age servicemen are addicts. Stories like the following appear daily in the Alaska newspapers:

"Ft. Richardson soldiers left a Matanuska Valley bus in shambles one morning in an outbreak of what the transportation firm termed 'senseless, outrageous vandalism.' "

Dope is expensive, five to ten times as high as in the States. Heroin sells for $10 a cap and marijuana cigarettes for $4 each. Anchorage is plagued with muggings, hold-ups, highway robberies and house-breakings, a merry sport engaged in by servicemen as well as civilians. To the disgust of the honest-to-goodness sourdoughs left over from the Klondike, nothing then was as bad as now.

During the past year the government has been robbed of millions in accounts of post exchanges. When this story breaks, if it ever does, it will go right to the Pentagon in Washington.

Where there are so few women and so many men homosexuals are in clover. Such is encouraged by many officials who themselves like it. The only female flesh seen by most of the servicemen in the remote outposts is in occasional USO shows flown in. A new gimmick in the USO is flying dance-partners instead of actresses. Though it will be denied, many do more than dance with servicemen. A smart girl can pick up $50,000 on a two-month trip to the backwoods, but she will have to split part of this with army officers and some of the boys in the USO. High brass is supposed to be taken care of first and for nothing.

Gambling is big business in Alaska. The Union Club, on 4th, strictly a dive, makes no attempt to hide the card games going on inside. At Chester Creek in back of the Green Latrine, the guards wear 45s in holsters to protect the game.

There are different laws for Eskimos, whites and Negroes. A colored man is seldom arrested and never prosecuted. Whites get pinched, but get off easy if they have a fix. Eskimos get the works.

The body of an Eskimo woman was found in the stands of a local ball park. She had been stabbed to death. They didn't bother with a coroner's hearing. But two servicemen got the book for killing a caribou.

A white cab-driver got ten months for manslaughter. The same day in the same court a Kodiak Eskimo was given eighteen months for breaking and entering. Another Eskimo got eight years for shooting a white man in the leg.

Eskimos are mentioned only when brain-trusters want something from Washington. A. C. Newell acts for the Federal Home Finance Agency in Alaska, offering loans to Eskimos. They may borrow up to $500 to install floors, roofs and sidewalks around their ice huts, which they don't want. By the time the lawyers and fixers and government agents force them to take it they get about $100 and the other guys take the rest. A wag calls it the Igloo Owners Loan Corp.

31. HAWAII: HULAS AND HAOLES

*O*NLY TAHITI has been pictured as ecstatically as Hawaii, the Pearl of the Pacific. With hard steel guitar wailing and soft ukulele strumming, our island possession has been set to music recognized as its own around the world. Immortals have strained their descriptive powers to convey its idyllic appeal and a Tin Pan Alley Byron attained his nadir by rhyming "Hawaii" with "How Are You?"

That is all gratuitous. Topping it for something like a century have been the commercialized advertising and hyperbolic paeans for the transportation lines and the tourist hotels.

The attack on Pearl Harbor made its big moment in history and Honolulu became an international page one dateline. The inevitable travelers' tales and novels with Hawaiian locale were a by-product of the war that followed.

So we flew there. We even had a drawing-room, a luxury not

afforded to us in any other of our flights over some 75,000 miles.
We landed in great good humor—

On a day not drenched in sunshine; it was drenched with rain,
Presently the soft Hawaiian moon peeped out. That was the time
to first behold Waikiki Beach. We beheld it—about twenty feet
wide and two miles long. It was too cold for bathing and no bare-
foot maidens wiggling it in grass skirts were dancing.

We went back to our hotel. And our sleep was torn through
the "languorous" night by the chatter of mynah birds. But we still
had hopes. We, from the harsh precincts of the hard mainland,
would go among the simple, unspoiled native children of nature,
the carefree cousins we had adopted but never assimilated.

We found those who were not living off visitors grouchy, pre-
occupied with making mundane money at humdrum tasks. Those
around the hotels and other tourist traps had the hands we had
expected to see undulating to the barbaric rhythms out, palms up,
for tips—in bills, not silver. The only smiles we got were the
stereotyped professional grimaces shaped with the same facial
muscles that formed for us wherever we had set down our bags.
The stiff-necked manager was aloof and the cashier, who had never
heard of us, seemed suspicious. He may have thought we were
burglars; the rates they charged made the feeling mutual.

Mortimer is married to a girl who was born, reared and uni-
versity-educated in Hawaii. So, for the record, we will note that
the young women are attractive. We will then return to facts.

Missionaries came to Hawaii to do good. They remained and
did well. They took the natives' land and left them Bibles.

The descendants of five became an oligarchy through inter-
marriages, interlocking directorates and social connections. Like
such groups everywhere, the Big Five is now a shell, paralyzed by
taxes and gone to pot through natural leveling processes. But it
is still the whipping boy of Communists, union agitators and
malcontents. Until recently the Big Five strangled the Islands
through ownership of the shipping lines and franchises, which
gave them exclusive distributorships and agencies for all mainland and imported products and services. But the wedge has been
driven and mass force is at work. The new king is Communist
Harry Bridges. The princelings are union bosses. The new
wealth is that of the rich Japanese and Chinese "huis," Hawaiian
for syndicates.

The air age ended Hawaii's isolation and the steamers' monopoly. Three scheduled airlines fly more passengers in a day

than ships carried in a month. Mainland underworld money is coming in to build and buy hotels. Chinese merchants organized two banks, breaking the money control. But the triumph of the rabble is unhealthy. The civil population continues to decline. It was down to 460,000 in 1951. These figures do not tell it all. Thousands of Negroes have taken the places of Islanders, who moved to the mainland with its greater opportunities and its more virile life.

Unemployment reached an all-time high last year, with as many as 35,000 workers without jobs. This does not include the tens of thousands almost always on strike in one or the other of Bridges' three big unions—sugar, pineapples and shipping.

The government withdrew the entire military establishment in a brutal blow to Hawaii's economy. At one time it provided a third of its income. Since Korea, there is a small reactivation, only a drop in the bucket compared to pre-Pearl Harbor days.

Japan knew that whoever controlled Hawaii controlled America's West Coast. The Soviet is eyeing it now. Russia accomplished what Japan could never do, though Hawaii's largest population group is Japanese. Communists infiltrated through Red unions to such an extent the Islands are now a Soviet bastion in the Pacific. Communism tried a new formula of conquest here and won. It was done with the knowledge and connivance of official Washington. While some branches of the Federal government gave aid and comfort to Bridges in his fight to strangle the Hawaiian economy, other coordinate branches withdrew troops who protected the Pacific. Reds openly captured the local Democratic party organization and were rewarded with patronage, including high territorial offices.

Since the troop dispersal, Hawaii has but three sources of revenue. Bridges controls all. Pineapple and sugar culture each account for one-third of the income. Bridges' longshore union organized both. Tourism and transportation provide the only other income. That depends on ship movements. Bridges has the last word. The Islands' food, clothing and fuel supply is dependent on his whim. Nothing is manufactured locally. Even refined sugar may not be exported under a Federal statute which decrees it may be shipped to the mainland only in raw bulk—a nod to U.S. sugar refinery workers.

Hawaii was the Paradise of the Pacific. For those with wealth there was no more magnificent Eden. Of the poor there were few.

Tropical fruits and easy living for all made life joyous without the tensions of civilized society.

Hawaii's so-called racial tolerance is more evident in the writings of boosters than in actual practice. Every one of the major groups has its own prejudices against others, and they all agree on disliking Negroes, who are barred at most bars and restaurants. Orientals have petitioned the Island legislature not to enact a local FEPC. Japanese make up a third of the population. Most employment ads say "Japanese preferred."

Until recently, the Island government restricted races in the public schools with a cute gag called "standard English schools." The reasoning behind it was that children of alien Orientals did not speak as good English as did whites; if they were put together, they would contaminate the language. Theoretically, Orientals who spoke perfect English were eligible for standard English schools, housed in better buildings, with superior faculties and facilities. As it was meant to work out, few Orientals applied because the standard schools were built in white neighborhoods, inconvenient to them. Standard English schools have been discontinued. Segregation goes along with standard English classes held separately from general classes.

The old resident kamaainas dressed well, held their liquor and were gentlemen. Now Coast Haoles—native slang for mainland whites—have taken over with aloha shirts, fat dames in mink coats and side-of-the-mouth-talking gamblers and sports. They have driven out the old-time ways.

The Negro influx is Hawaii's great tragedy. During the war, the Navy brought them in large numbers from Southern plantations and jails. Negroes were able to pass as Tahitians or Samoans. They wrote home to their relatives and brought on their families. Now they have taken over most of the Islands' vice. The principal trouble-makers formerly were Filipino farm-workers, unencumbered with wives or families, who spent their money on gambling, cock-fighting and whoring. They did not go for major crimes, which the Negroes imported.

Chinese are congenital big gamblers and opium smugglers. This generation is educated, intelligent, well fixed and law-abiding. The police chief of Honolulu is Dan Liu, a young Chinese, efficient and fearless. Honolulu's command was not always that way. After scandals in the twenties, the city imported a professor of police administration from a mainland college to be chief. Mac-Arthur borrowed him, figuring he knew how to handle Japanese.

While he was in Tokyo the Honolulu grand jury looked into his affairs. The disclosures were so shocking, he was forced out. During his tenure gambling was wide open. Honolulu had one of the most notorious red light districts in the world.

What gives Honolulu any sort of vice uniqueness is gambling on high school games. It is not unusual for a capacity crowd of 25,000 to be on hand for a non-championship high school football game in an eight team league. That's 10 per cent of the population, equivalent to 800,000 in New York. College games at the University of Hawaii draw less than 12,000, which makes high school sports big business.

There have been rumors of "juice" before . . . that's native slang for a rigged or thrown game . . . but the cops found no evidence until early 1952 when four were arrested for fixing two games on point spreads, then acquitted. McKinley, Kamehameha and Roosevelt High Schools were involved, three of the eight.

In addition to being the only city in the U.S. where fixing high school games is major business (the weekly betting turnover runs to $500,000) Honolulu is the only town where fixing of pro football games has been proven.

The Territory is normally and by tradition Republican. Honolulu usually votes Democratic and corrupt. The Governor and the higher officers and judges are appointed by the President. For the past twenty years they have been Democratic and New Deal, and have so loaded the civil service.

The present Governor is Oren E. Long. He was promoted from Secretary of the Territory. He had been Superintendent of the Department of Public Instruction. He is a typical teacher, a pleasant fuddy-duddy. The big boys continually put things over. He was supposed to belong to the middle-of-the-road faction of the Democratic party, but he is a pushover for Reds and lefties.

Former Governor Ingram M. Stainback, an old hand with the Ickes bunch in Interior, was pushed upstairs last year to the Federal court. The Island public was yelling because he had appointed Communists and their supporters to high jobs. Stainback, like many territorial officials, is a carpetbagger from the mainland, handed the governorship as a political payoff.

Malihinis from the mainland come over and load the payroll with pals from back home. Then they get to like the place, the power and position, and decide to stay, becoming firm supporters of statehood, figuring that if they help push it through the voters will reward them with fat state jobs. But many Islanders are freezing up on the statehood idea. They'd like a tax-free deal like Puerto Rico's instead.

The spectacular career of William B. Brown, recently appointed by Truman to the circuit court for the county of Maui, is typical of the rise of a carpetbagger. Brown came from Chilicothe, Ohio, where he was tied up with the local New Deal outfit. In 1943, six years after he had graduated from Harvard Law School—than which there is no better way of procuring political preference under the present regime—he came to Hawaii to join the local OPA. He became its price attorney in 1945. And when that bureau closed, he was made Territorial Treasurer until he became a judge.

In political and Army brass circles, Hawaii is regarded as something like conquered territory, or like British careermen used to think of India. High officers and their wives ride around in government-owned touring cars, behind uniformed sergeants. Civil officers throw favors to military, and vice versa. For instance, Louis Le Baron, associate justice of the Territorial Supreme Court, left Hawaii on June 8 last year on a cruiser, a guest of the Navy, for a mainland vacation. He returned on the military transport *General Daniel I. Sultan* as a guest of the Army—and you.

The advantages of being a Democrat are so self-evident that many hungry Republican politicians jump the traces and declare themselves members of the reigning party. One of the most recent was William J. Nobriga, a Republican member of the Territorial Senate, whose switch gave the GOP a bare eight-to-seven majority.

The only Territory-wide elected official is the Delegate to Congress, now and for many terms Joseph Rider Farrington, a Republican with a fine record. He is the publisher of the *Honolulu Star-Bulletin*, whose famed editor, Riley H. Allen, often puts up a one-man fight against turning the Islands over to mainland crooks and thugs.

Hawaii is an example of what happens in a dictatorial welfare state. Office-holders are divided between screwballs and thieves. You may pick which put over Honolulu's new Federal Building, designed in Washington. It was built with a reinforced roof "to hold snow." It has a heavy-duty boiler and plant for central heating. The coldest day ever is about 60°.

They built some Federal housing in Hilo, at $9,000 a unit, exactly twice the cost of the same dwellings built by private operators. Some years ago, a tidal wave washed away a large part of Hilo's waterfront. A repetition is so much a possibility that a warning siren to announce one, like air-raid signals on the mainland, is tested every week. Yet the bright lads from Harvard, who had never been to Hilo, ordered a new road along the beach front on land cleared away by the last tidal wave. This multi-million-dollar highway, a major military artery, is completely at the mercy of the ocean and the elements and has since been shut down several times when the sea came in.

Many refused to work, because it's so easy to live as a beachcomber on a pittance. Those on relief tell the administrators they will not stoop to toil. Negroes are on the handout rolls as soon as they arrive. The largest Honolulu building in floor-space is that of the Welfare Department.

Known Communists control many of the unions. Those named before Congressional committees as pinks or Red-lovers have been appointed to public office by droves. For every one forced to resign, a score remain in important places, many openly.

Edward Berman, judge of the Territorial Court of Tax Appeals, was accused under oath before a Congressional committee of being a Communist. He declared, "There is no factual basis." But he resigned. He had been appointed during the administration of Governor Stainback. U.S. Judge Metzger has been an open sympathizer of Communists and Reds. He recently made a wholesale jail delivery when he freed thirty-nine alleged Communists of contempt charges.

Reds try to seduce servicemen and workers in government projects with the usual lures—girls and dope. Ninety-nine per cent of the dope seized by Treasury agents is carried by men in Bridges' shipping unions. The rest comes by mail, bound in the bindings of books. A kickback from this filthy trade goes to the Red unions. The money is sent back behind the Iron Curtain, whence the dope originates, after the organized underworld, which handles retail distribution, collects its share.

Negro and Puerto Rican sailors sell vacuum sealed cans each containing 600 marijuana seeds, which are avidly bought up by local youths and planted in marginal lands near plantations. Waves of arrests of teen-agers indicate that reefer cultivation may soon rival that of pine and sugar, and you can bet it will be unionized by Bridges.

Island unions are so brazen that the Hawaiian Government Employes Association officially and as a matter of record stood up for crooked policemen caught red-handed taking bribes.

The machinations of Bridges are supported by office-holders.

Hawaii County Chairman James Kealoha permitted the ILWU to store rice and other commodities in free space in county buildings in preparation for a strike against plantation-owners.

Not all unions in Hawaii are Red, but all unions in Hawaii get special handling. After the National Production Authority declared an emergency which forbade construction of unnecessary buildings requiring steel, Local 677 of the American Federation of Musicians sought and obtained a special permit to build a $57,000 practice hall and business office in Honolulu, requiring more than twenty-five tons of steel. Fred R. Kingman, district manager of the NPA, said music was important for morale. The flowery announcement stated, "One feature of the auditorium will be that it will be equipped for making recordings. Practicing groups can play back the results of their practice, detect flaws and then correct them."

Hotel Street, in downtown Honolulu, is honkytonk lane where servicemen go to get dames in taxi dance-halls and bars. Streetwalkers amble along Smith and Pauahu. Many prostitutes are Negroes, whose pimps sell reefers and policy slips. Smith Street, once the center of Chinatown, is going black.

Hawaii has a tradition for whoring. It does not fall down. J. D. Charles was recently arrested on the complaint of a twenty-six-year-old woman, who said she worked as a prostitute for him for five years and turned over in that time more than $200,000. She was a glutton for work. Other panderers carry nude photographs of their merchandise and pass them out in the bars.

During the late war, the Navy Department imported mainland prosties to supplement the local supply. All harridans arrested in San Francisco were given the alternative of going to the can or working for three months in Honolulu as indentured courtesans. We didn't hear of any who chose jail. The terms of the contract provided that the gals would live on a restricted street—Queen Emma, which they could not leave. The queues of servicemen were so great, many girls returned to California with $50,000.

But the descendants of the missionaries squawked their heads off, so the Navy shipped the hussies home. This opened up new avenues of wealth for the local madames. Jean O'Hara not only became a millionaire, she wrote a bootlegged book describing her career, which later became the basis for a novel by Bill Huie, *The Revolt of Mamie Stover*. Dorothy McCreedy had a chain of parlor-houses across the Pacific. Her principal one was in Hawaii, where she was an institution for years. She owned the only open Cadillac in town when President Roosevelt visited, and it was commandeered by the Secret Service for FDR's triumphant parade. The whole town knew that car. Roosevelt never knew why the cheers were diluted with laughs.

Though the end of the Navy's Operation Tart spelled wealth for the city madames, the nonpros found it difficult to cash in, because a military curfew cleared the streets at sundown; designed to protect the native wenches from a fate that used to be worse than death. Yet there are many young hapa-haoles (half-whites) growing up today.

With the exception of Negro numbers and Filipino cockfights, gambling is pretty much an Oriental monopoly. The big Chinese gamblers operate on Mauna Kea Street. Narcotics were a problem only among the Chinese, who smoked the pipe. Until this generation Japanese never used dope. But the Negroes have flooded Hawaii with marijuana. Servicemen are prime targets. The dope gang is popularizing a native root called "awa," chewed by rural Hawaiians for a narcotic effect. It is now being sold in cities and to servicemen. Plans are under way to export it to the mainland.

After the war, Hawaii was overrun by smart boys who came to trade in government surplus. This was a Mafia syndicate operation. Many other suspicious characters are infiltrating. Charles Paul Swartz, from Chicago, was arrested in connection with trying to introduce a national football lottery, but, as so frequently happens, the prosecutor quickly dismissed the charge. Along with Swartz came one Joe Torrio.

Another character the Honolulu police are tailing is Salvatore Terrano, who was on friendly terms with members of the Purple Gang in Detroit. Other Sicilians, recent arrivals in the Island Paradise, are Ralph de Sopa, a man with many arrests, and John de Sopa, who had a lengthy record even before he operated the Twin State gambling club in Reno and the Midtown Tavern in San Francisco.

Jerry Zucker now owns the Niumalu Hotel, where the sporty crowd goes. Zucker ran the Tradewinds, on Hotel Street, during the war and was in trouble with military authorities. He has been arrested on gambling charges.

The newest mainland hot shot is Harry Maundrell, who operates a sleek and expensive restaurant and cocktail lounge on Kalakaua Avenue, on the Royal Hawaiian grounds. Before he came to Hawaii and built his $250,000 luxury resort, Maundrell worked for a modest salary in San Francisco as office manager for Elmer (Bones) Remmer, king of the San Francisco gamblers.

This was a success story in the Horatio Alger tradition, for after the slaying of Bugsy Siegel, Remmer's interests suddenly expanded and the boss took his employe in as a partner, giving him an interest in the gambling dives El Cerrito and the Willows in San Mateo.

Remmer was in Honolulu on September 20, 1947, vacationing at the Royal with two San Francisco police captains as his guests. Shortly after that work got under way on the Maundrell Restaurant. Maundrell lives in a mansion on Diamond Head Terrace and this will probably be news to him: that Dan Liu's efficient sleuths check the names of all mainland hoods who visit him in either place.

The tourists' Hawaii is Waikiki, three miles from downtown, beginning at Kau Kau Korner, drive-in restaurant remembered with affection by all GIs who served in the Pacific. Waikiki has the better restaurants as well as the clip joints and almost all the night clubs, including the most beautiful one in the world—Waikiki Lau Yee Chai.

Waikiki is the hangout of the mahus (fairies), who meet their soldier sweethearts there.

The Outrigger Canoe Club, between the Royal and the Moana Hotel, is lily-white, except for blooded Hawaiians. The remaining Hawaiians are either menials or high society descendants of the royal families. The Moana is old and gracious, with a lovely banyan tree covering the oceanside court. It's for schoolteachers and old ladies, and, surprisingly, pick-ups. The Royal, also owned by the Matson Navigation Company, is sleek and modern, out of place in the tropics, expensive and snob-crazy.

Yet a tourist has little choice. The line controls the biggest hotels and makes it difficult for those bound for other hotels to get accommodations on the S. S. Lurline, which, despite the slick-paper advertising, is only a road show company of an Atlantic luxury liner.

Bridges' union help on board, which includes stewards and barkeeps, is impertinent and truculent. And those propensities pervade almost everyone who deals with strangers in and around what was the hospitable, childlike Pearl of the Pacific—which has been switched for a five-and-dime imitation.

32. PUERTO RICO -- MANHATTAN'S INCUBATOR

WE WERE there. We saw, we listened, we smelled. The reactions of all the senses were familiar. Because we are New Yorkers.
In the last twenty years some 600,000 of the little Brown Brothers
have been funneled into our town, mostly in East Harlem.

For these are fellow-citizens, an automatic status granted by
Congress, which chose to make this Caribbean island a possession
in contrast to Cuba and the Philippines, to which we had pledged
eventual independence.

Not for more than thirty years did a mainland political shark
visualize the political possibilities of more than 2,000,000 ready-
made voters who could be bought and shipped for nickels. That
protagonist of the common man—the commoner the better—
Fiorello H. La Guardia, was the political prodigy who fell on and
immediately began to work this gold-mine. He began the only pre-
designed mass piping of qualified voters from beyond our borders.
The lure—and it took little to bring them streaming from their
overcrowded native grounds with its miserable economic conditions to the fabled metropolis—was relief. Before they set foot on
the continent, they had been penciled in on the dole. And since
that could be cut off by a wave of the hand, they voted in a body,
successively Republican, Democratic and La Guardia's own creation, the American Labor Party.

Now they are in their second New York generation. Some of
their children even speak English. They are precious. Many influential people and institutions feel that, by accepting our public
gratuities, they have become our foster children. Their privileges
have become vested rights. Mustn't say anything unflattering about
them, though they have become the most vicious element in New
York life.

With fifty scheduled non-stop flights a week from Puerto Rico—
carrying more than 3,000 passengers—and scores of non-skeds
daily, Puerto Rico is now a suburb of Manhattan.

Your confidential reporters will not bother to list the dives along
San Juan's waterfront, nor the joints in Santurce, an upper class
suburb.

Nor will we devote space to gambling, which is now legal in the Territory. All Puerto Ricans gamble, especially on the lottery. Games in the better spots and hotels were set up to entice mainland dollars, but the Florida gamblers who put up the dough soon found that few chumps were coming this way.

Nor will we discuss the dirt, the squalor and lack of sanitation found not only in the slums but even in good houses and expensive restaurants, lest Eleanor accuse us of being anti-something. The Puerto Rican Health Department said recently the food in only twenty-four spots in the entire Territory is fit for human consumption. That is not the fault of grasping imperialists.

While on a raid in East Harlem with narcotics officers, we questioned a young Puerto Rican arrested for selling heroin. He had been in the States for seven months and on relief all that time. This was arranged for him in San Juan by an agent of Marcantonio. "He such nice senor," the young fellow said. He arrived in New York in October, a few weeks before election. He voted for Marcantonio, unaware of New York State's requirement of one year's residence. Nor did he know that age 19 was too young to vote. No one told him.

Not all Puerto Ricans are dusky like those in New York, despite the propaganda sold by professional racists of the Roosevelt stamp. There is greater racial discrimination in Puerto Rico, where a third are white, than here.

A few years ago we attended an official government function at La Forteleza, the Governor's palace, a beautiful Spanish colonial gem, built by Ponce de Leon, Puerto Rico's first governor. Five thousand were invited to the ball. Not one was a Negro. Official segregation was so complete that a second edition of the official party was held for Negroes only at a rich Negro's mansion.

Upper-crust Puerto Ricans characterize dark-skinned fellow countrymen as dogs and cattle. They are barred from better night clubs and hotels. Those who live in the cities do menial labor or work as servants and no colored man in Dixie is kicked around as much as pale Puerto Ricans abuse this canaille.

Puerto Rico is a fraud on the American people. Residents of Hawaii and Alaska have all the obligations but none of the privileges of American citizenship, but Puerto Rico elects its own Governor and government and is writing its own constitution. Its residents are exempt from American income and excise taxes. Meanwhile they are American citizens, under the protection of the American flag, and get huge handouts from the politicians in

Washington. That is because Puerto Ricans on the mainland vote
in blocs in strategic locations; but who ever heard of an Eskimo
vote in New York?

Governor Luis Munoz-Marin is a big and handsome brute with
a thrilling, mellifluous voice. Once a poet in Greenwich Village
and a Hollywood bit player, he returned to his native land to follow in the footsteps of his father, a legendary revolutionary hero.
Munoz is a political faker of the Fiorello La Guardia stamp, though
easier on the nose, eyes and ears and probably neater and tidier
at the table. In his time Munoz has been a Nationalist, a Soviet
admirer and a professed Socialist. At present he owns Puerto
Rico's local New Deal party, the Popular Democrats, which in
dictatorial fashion is for all purposes the only one.

Under the late FDR, Puerto Rico was an Eleanor Roosevelt
principality. She had the privilege of naming the Governors. In
return, San Juan's slum development and cooperative stores are
named after her.

She appointed Rexford Guy Tugwell, early New Dealer. With
his settlement house mind he was going to show the natives how
to wash their children and put dimity curtains on their windows.
Instead he built a glass solarium on the roof of the governor's palace and took sunbaths. La Forteleza is a historic shrine, the oldest
building on the Western hemisphere. Tugwell's glass penthouse
stuck out as a tower of miserable taste, spoiling the pure and perfect lines of the palace.

He acquired a fleet of luxurious limousines, at Territorial expense, though cars, tires and gas were rationed for others. He
turned the palace's historic Spanish courtyard into a personal
parking lot, boarding up a 400-year-old well in the center of its
patio.

Though the public may visit the White House, Tugwell barred
the gates of La Forteleza. Its lovely grounds became his private
preserve. He removed a squad from the undermanned Insular
Police to act as chauffeurs and footmen for himself, wife and dog.

When it came time to resign he went on the payroll of the
"liberal" University of Chicago. His highly paid job required
his presence in Chicago only four months a year. Then came
strange coincidences. A part-time chair was set up at the University of Puerto Rico, and with it went a furnished house. Mrs.
Tugwell said she'd help with the decorations—purely as a public
service, you understand. When the trustees named the new professor, who do you think it was? You're right, it was Tugwell.

The big brains in Washington decided the next Governor should be a native-born Puerto Rican. Munoz-Marin was already the island dictator, in fact if not in name.

Even Harry knew an American Senate could not and would not confirm a wild man like Munoz-Marin. At Munoz's suggestion Truman named Jesus T. Pinero, a charming and highly educated and greatly respected Puerto Rican businessman. He was Resident Commissioner in Washington before that. Pinero was a gentleman. He could not stomach Puerto Rican politics. He well knew Munoz was becoming the Island Mussolini. At the end of his short term he was happy to get out.

When the bill to permit Puerto Rico to name its own Governor was slipped through, Munoz was elected almost unanimously. The island has gone further towards socialism than England under the Labour government.

Puerto Rico is under a typical totalitarian reign of terror. Attempts have been made to muzzle the press. Papers have been driven out of business. Secret police spy on political opponents of the ruling party. Enemies of Munoz are arrested on trumped up charges, often booked in rural police stations where lawyers can't find them with writs.

The local government is rotten with corruption. Jobs are for sale. Government property is diverted to private use. Puerto Rican birth certificates are peddled at bargain prices to Communist and criminal aliens who are given sanctuary by crooked officials. By act of Congress, anyone born in Puerto Rico since 1898 is automatically an American citizen.

The misdeeds of the Socialist cabal in La Forteleza are camouflaged by a constant anti-American propaganda campaign, paid for with U.S. taxpayers' money. The English language is no longer required in schools and is taught in practically none. English-speaking Puerto Ricans refuse to use the language. For years there was no English newspaper in this American Territory.

Many high government officials live openly with mistresses, maintaining two families. Their sweethearts are on the public payroll.

This is socialism in flower. Puerto Rico shares the wealth and its politicians take it all.

33. TEMPORARY EMPIRE CONFIDENTIAL -- PROCONSULS IN JAPAN

*B*Y *THE TIME* these words reach print the Japanese Peace Treaty may have been ratified by the United States Senate and our Armed Forces in Nippon will cease to be occupiers, to become guests.

The Army will remain in Japan, no longer as empire builders, but as security troops stationed at bases subject to further mutual negotiation and similar in status to bases in England, France, North Africa, the Philippines, etc.

The Army, of course, does not want to give up its prerogatives or the luxury housing it seized from the Japanese, who plan to repossess it. It does not want to vacate Tokyo with its Yashiwara tradition, bargain shops and good living, but the Japs see no reason why security bases must be located in the capital instead of in remote rural sections. The Army seeks to continue its extra-territorial rights and all its privileges, which included graft, sale of charters, franchises and rights, finagling of the rate of exchange, disposition of relief supplies, resale of military goods and all the other rackets of the mainland, multiplied and amplified.

Army brass wants to continue bossing Japanese officials and summoning their statesmen. The conquerors do not want the "No Japanese Allowed" signs taken down, and they fear more "Off Limits to Foreigners" signs which the natives are determined to spread in their place.

Abuses always follow conquering forces. Japan was no exception. MacArthur, aloof and turreted, had to devote most of his time to matters of top policy, while lower brass, down the line from two-star generals to one-stripe noncoms, pushed their weight around in the unaccustomed roles of Oriental dictators in a land lush with beautiful women and the spoils of an ancient civilization.

After MacArthur's dismissal, conditions got worse, as Washington pets, freed from the fear of MacArthur's terrible wrath if he should discover what was going on, ran wild.

This is a confidential report of post-MacArthur Japan:

A remote village where several thousand American troops are stationed is the most disputed hot spot in Japan at this moment. Bands of rough prostitutes, 300 to 1,000 in each, circle around this area. As there are no housing facilities, the troop commander by compulsion billets them in farmers' homes, over strong objections from the village officials. Rooms used by these girls were remodeled in ostentatious colors without consent of the owners and at U.S. government expense.

Illegal transactions of military notes and goods worth several thousand dollars are conducted in broad daylight. Military notes, transferred to Tokyo by black marketeers, are converted into yen at the rate of 250 per dollar, breaking the level of the official rate by 110 yen.

The sex life of American soldiers in Japan seems to have been unexpectedly developed without disturbing the Japanese community, in contrast with western Germany. The Japanese Government established a special district at the east end of Tokyo, housing licensed prostitutes for use of the occupation forces. As soon as the new constitution went into effect, in May, 1947, prohibiting such a system, the district was wiped out formally and was made "off limits" by occupation authority. Consequently, there emerged street prostitutes called "pan-pan." It is a specific expression meaning prostitute in a native language of South Sea Islanders. This word was brought to Japan by American soldiers.

These pan-pan girls number over 20,000 in Tokyo, alone. They constitute a typical community ruled by pan-pan bosses. Girls who take Americans as permanent companions are called "yo-pan" ("yo" means western, in Japanese.) They number about 5,000. They are very proud of their American soldier sweethearts, even when they are treated as prostitutes by the Japanese community, in contrast to the whores who cater only to Japanese and who are ashamed of their profession. Japanese authorities have tried to sweep out the pan-pans, though recognizing their existence as a bulwark to defend wives and daughters from assault by soldiers. Some Americans picked pan-pan girls as brides and brought them home.

Prostitutes gather around districts like Yokohama, Tachikawa, the Ginza (main street of Tokyo) near the SCAP building, and a military installation near Tachikawa. They can be hired as temporary wives of American soldiers at 20,000 yen per month, or in goods, less than $60. Such a girl has a rented room or house near the barracks where she can receive her "husband" when he is off duty. Soldiers who cannot afford such an outlay pay $4 in cash for a night. A few prostitutes make tremendous fortunes, over a million yen, and are the highest taxpayers in their districts. Miss T. A., whose "husband" is a sergeant in the Air Force, now in Korea, has a large estate and several million yen in a bank deposit.

Officers seldom contact the pan-pan, as most have their wives in Japan or go to the Bacchus Club, off the Ginza, where they buy girls.

Civilians or high brass go to cabarets or bars or geisha houses, where Japanese politicians, officials and leading businessmen entertain their guests. Geisha houses are generally used to corrupt GHQ top officials with saké and girls. A few officers, including colonels and generals, keep Japanese mistresses in secret establishments, commuting to their houses several times a week. These are mostly dancers, interpreters, geishas and widows who lost husbands in the war. They come from good families and are entirely satisfied with their position, despite criticism or contempt from neighbors.

These women are also mediums for illegal transactions. They are connected with Koreans and Chinese who have a wide underground influence in the Tokyo-Yokohama area. The Koreans and Chinese, linked with South Seas smugglers, operate tea houses, cabarets and goods shops on the Ginza, downtown Tokyo. Black marketeers resell dollars and goods which they buy from pan-pans around Tokyo. The Tokyo metropolitan police raided the vital center, Yanagishita, but no evidence was found.

MPs furnish information on police activity to smugglers and law-breakers for a fee, and their officers are at the heart of all rackets here, providing protection and selling military secrets.

Some high brass keep Oriental mistresses who are in the pay of Reds.

Justified by expediency is the importation of American gals (as Wacs, Waves, nurses, civilian employes, entertainers, Red Cross, etc.) but actually to comfort lonesome GIs.

High officers attempt to discourage "fraternizing" with native girls, not only on the espionage angle, but to prevent disorder. Many servicemen, adopting the attitude of swaggering conquerors, rape Japanese girls. Killings have followed. Other GIs make a liaison with a local wench, then refuse to pay her or her pimp. Some Americans have been beaten and maimed in retaliation. Several murders are traceable to this form of gyp.

One of the most closely guarded swindles concerns the whereabouts of a missing $50,000,000. When the so-called SCAP account was transferred to the Japanese government last August 15, the books showed it at $350,000,000. But when the Japanese counted up they discovered $50,000,000 had mysteriously been siphoned off between April, when MacArthur got the boot, and August. Many key officials are believed to have pocketed stray millions and gotten them out of the country through connivance of crooked employes of American banks.

Since the outbreak of the Korean police action, graft really went into high, procurement officers reaping a harvest on contracts for goods supplied to American troops. U.S. purchasing officers and officials are impudent in their outright demands for their share of the profits. If it is refused, improper classifications down-grade the goods to an inferior quality rating, making the manufacturer subject to heavy damages.

A small businessman who delivers machine-tools complained that he is not only busy all day working on the defense orders but that he must stay up all night to entertain officers at Asakusa and Tsukiji, famed geisha-house districts. The minimum kickback to officers is 10 per cent and does not constitute a crime under a never publicized occupation regulation.

There are several thousand American civilians in Tokyo representing trade, insurance and shipping, grouped together by the Japanese under the generic term of "buyer." These turn over tremendous fortunes by importing sugar, coffee and other goods, illegally sold to Korean and Chinese brokers on the black market. This is possible because the Japanese government grants import licenses on the dollar basis to American "buyers" to provide goods for shops especially established for the sole benefit of foreigners. But the American "buyers" sell these license papers or goods to black-market brokers. One American, who occupied a big downtown office, procured for him through a bribe to American occupation authorities, made several billion yen in illegal sugar transactions. When MPs, who were on his payroll, tipped him off that the metropolitan police were after him, he successfully fled Japan on an American Air Force plane, leaving his vast fortune scattered in the names of stand-ins.

The *Reader's Digest* and Central Motion Picture Exchange are two of the most powerful civilian organizations affecting Japanese economy, because of their huge Japanese holdings in yen, which they are not permitted to convert into dollars. Each account runs around five billion yen—so big that it can make or break the Japanese market—and is sought after by banks and brokers for deposit accounts. Some employes of both organizations are pocketing "gifts" in return for seeing that the right Japanese firms or banks get the money. This is illegal by mutual consent of the Japanese government and occupation authorities, but complaints made to SCAP are meaningless because the proper lower levels are taken care of before word reaches the commander in chief.

Chinese and Korean "buyers" use black-market profits to collect U.S. military notes and greenbacks, with which they purchase more sugar, coffee, cars, wrist-watches, etc., from American "buyers" with such goods to sell.

The trade in hot money is intimately tied up with prostitution. The chief means by which American soldiers put dollars into local circulation is through the pan-pans, who sell them to black marketeers. The known trade in American currency distributed through prostitutes runs to $100,000,000 a year.

The illicit trade also revolves around such cheap-jack gifts as costume jewelry, Ingersoll watches, etc. For instance, Japanese women now seem to favor a certain type of American watch which costs $7 when sold in an American store in American money to American nationals. GIs give these to pan-pans, who sell them to Japanese at $30.

Japanese womanhood as a whole will also be most reluctant to see the troop ships sail away. For under the Americans they were treated like ladies for the first time, instead of household slaves, as they were before the occupation. Japanese men know the good old days will never return and they are bitter. Women now vote, hold property, and no longer must they wait until all the menfolk are served before eating.

The females were spoiled by the woman-hungry Americans. Now they find it hard to turn back to Jap men. Consequently, a wave of female homosexualism is sweeping over the islands. Many pan-pan girls take female sweethearts for relaxation; dance-hall girls openly and brazenly make love to other girls; rich Japanese women are usurping the prerogatives of their former lords and masters by patronizing geisha houses and romancing the girls.

Another striking fast-money racket is the illegal trading in American cars by civilians. Japanese may purchase U.S. cars through their Ministry of International Trade on payment of approximately $2,000 in taxes above the market price. Occupation personnel have taken advantage of this by illegally leasing cars to Japanese or Koreans. They buy them at American prices, not subject to Japanese tax, and rent them to Japanese for from $100 to $200 a month, including gas tickets and a charge of $800 for their driver's license. There are 4,700 American cars owned by civilians in Tokyo, registered under the 30,000 license-number series, which means "foreign buyers." Of these 3,000 are illegally leased or sold to Japanese or Koreans, at an annual tax-evasion of $6,-000,000. Half of this sum is the profit made by the Americans. Japanese authorities are helpless. When cars are registered to prominent Americans, no action can be taken.

But why should Tokyo be more honest than Washington?

PART FIVE

"ONE" WORLD
(*Confidential!*)

34. UN -- THE GLOBAL BOONDOGGLE

FROM THE window where your reporters are working they can
see the huge monolith of the United Nations rising above Manhattan's East Side, like a stark gravestone. Laborers and craftsmen
are completing the final embellishments on the massive archi-
tectural monster; a monument to the conquest of the world by
boondogglers.

The doors will soon be opened to the public. Already sightseers
clamber on First Avenue to look at the mammoth mausoleum.
Autograph bugs have deserted first nights, hoping for a Peruvian
delegate or Mrs. Roosevelt. To satisfy the whims of the curious
multitude, the UN thoughtfully provided a sight-seeing concession. Who do you think got it? That's easy—a lady pal of Eleanor.

This sovereign hunk of concrete which comprises UN world
headquarters is a city-state in the heart of the City of New York,
but immune from its laws. Even American employes are exempt
from United States and New York State taxes, which makes it a
snug harbor for harpies, especially since they've been unionized by
a Stalin minion and can no longer be fired, even by the Secretary
General.

These one-world bureaucrats quickly learned all the obnoxious
manners of all bureaucrats all over the world. But they've added
some outrageous ones on international lines. UNers are the bane
of New York cops and cafe-owners. Delegates strut around, refuse
to pay liquor tabs on grounds of "diplomatic immunity," pass
bum checks in shops and squawk "privilege" if there's a come-
back. Their chauffeurs race and speed and maim and kill, and
their chiefs refuse to allow them to submit to arrest. The clerical
and office levels are just as bad. Secretaries, stenos, technicians
and experts get drunk, fight with policemen and beef about
invasion of UN rights. "No Parking" signs in overcrowded Manhattan mean nothing to the UN "peace-on-earth" crowd, who

giggle and gurgle at their bohemian soirees about how they put the dumb cossacks in their places. Reefer-selling and bookmaking go on in the extra-territorial confines of the compound.

The backbone of the secretariat comes from the old UNRRA, which under La Guardia, Lehman and Eleanor Roosevelt was loaded with spies, Communists, fairies, Lesbians and bright young men of the British Foreign Office, which in self-interest plugs for our recognition of Red China.

After-work orgies engaged in by interracial, intersexual groups are held in dim Greenwich Village studios by the world saviors. Reds are infiltrated into every rank, from elevator runners to department heads. More than half of the UN's civil service, as well as brains, is composed of Communists or sympathizers, who torpedo measures before they can be launched.

Though the U.S. contributed all but 6 per cent of the foreign ground troops in Korea, all but 8 per cent of the naval forces, and 98.24 per cent of the air power, our men were purposely and erroneously labeled UN forces—a sop to the one-worlders. The practical result of this swindle was that all affairs relating to the UN's army had to be submitted to the UN and, through it, to the enemy, disclosing troop dispositions, numbers of men employed, kinds of matériel, etc.

The lofty scheming which made this possible came from the same brains that planned the Korean adventure in the first place. Acheson and Marshall, both proponents of the "agrarian" Peoples Republic of China, figured that if we went into Korea we'd be kicked out before reinforcements came, which would give the Reds the opportunity they wanted to get rid of President Synghman Rhee. It would also create an excuse for us to recognize Red China, give Formosa to the Commies, and discredit MacArthur. When he crossed up UN and Washington pinks by holding and going forward, they had to fire him and revise the whole timetable.

Meanwhile, we are being asked to "up" our contribution to the support of UN, to add more law-breakers, degenerates and Communists to New York's already oversized contingent of them.

One of the greatest fiascos of all time was UNRRA, the old United Nations' Relief Organization. Billions of our money were spent to improve living conditions behind the Iron Curtain—but most of the food and supplies it bought never hit the man on the street, because the commissars got it first. Wherever UNRRA sent our wealth it was hoarded by officials or sold in the black market. Dizzy big-domes even sent such necessities as oranges to

Algiers, where they grow, and butter to China, where it is never used.

When UNRRA got too smelly, Washington came up with ECA, which went UNRRA one better in that we put up all the dough instead of only 95 per cent. And we spent more—twelve billion in four years. ECA, under such visionaries as Paul Hoffman, was loaded with social and settlement-house workers, college professors, pipe-smoking sophisticates and just plain Reds, who made all the policy. When this stank worse than UNRRA, Congress abolished it and set up another joker, called the Mutual Security Administration, with $6,500,000,000 to spend the first year. Though Congress specifically repudiated certain characters connected with the old set-up, Director Averill Harriman hired them back again. And under their management the entire aid program is a failure. Pinks and Stalinists, who infiltrated, saw to it that nothing was shipped which might aid Russia's enemies.

Yet the State Department and Mutual Security are still authorizing the shipment of vital supplies behind the Curtain as a "security measure."

As with UNRRA and ECA, that which does get to our friends will be damaged or inferior, or slipped to black-marketeers or grafting politicians, or it will be non-defense matériel like a library to Rome, bathtubs for Egyptians whose king spent $4,000,-000 of our money to renovate his yacht, and tuxedos for Greeks. Heavy merchandise will go to countries with crooked administrations, to be resold to Russians and used against us eventually.

Though absorbed by MSA, the ECAers are still engaged in monkeyshines at this writing. Here are a few current bad ones:

In the Philippines, American officials have entered into collusion with local contractors.

Wives of eighty-five European industrialists were joyridden around America at government expense.

Hundreds of American union officials are taken on junkets to Europe. Some were welcomed behind the Iron Curtain.

Hundreds of laid-up Liberty ships are being broken out to move coal, wheat, foodstuffs and clothing to Europe, free—while we pay inflated prices.

We send our precious newsprint to anti-U.S. and pro-Red newspapers in foreign countries, which use it to attack us. Our supporters abroad can't get any. Truman now threatens to cut American supplies.

Under Point Four—whatever that is—France is using our dough to speed up its postal service, so that if you mail a letter before noon it will be delivered in Paris the same day. Maybe we could get some Point Four relief for New York, where such service can't be had from Manhattan to Brooklyn.

Yet France taxes the United States for army bases and construction projects supposed to protect France. When the U.S. wants to build a road or air strip, we pay about 24 per cent of the total cost to the thrifty French.

ECA agents (now MSA) in Europe conspire with German, French and other foreign industrialists to okay loans from the American government for building projects abroad, in return for a 25 per cent cut. We know of several specific instances where American agents begged foreign industrialists to borrow from Uncle Sam to build resorts, hotels and even gambling casinos.

So much of our dough is being siphoned off by American agents in cahoots with European industrialists that you see more Cadillacs in Vienna than in Washington.

Meanwhile, there are terrible conflicts abroad between representatives of the American military and State Department officials. Europeans are taking advantage and reaping the profits. Harriman, another bemused big businessman who has been seduced by the bureaucrats, is ignorant of all this and continues to make statements that all is well. When his MSA or State's striped-panties don't sell us out, the Military Government does. It contains some of our most thriving thieves. One of the juiciest rackets ever dreamed up is in deals made with Germans to get back property taken from them during the war. For an extra fee, military government men will also sell them property seized from their competitors. McCloy is a stuffed dinner jacket and doesn't know this and plenty more.

We now have 174,000 employes outside the continental limits, exclusive of military personnel. This figure does not include more than 500,000 on construction jobs, etc. off-shore, who also get monthly checks from Uncle Sam.

It does include 81 of wild Oscar Ewing's public health men in Greece, Turkey, Indonesia and Thailand and ten quarantine experts in Paris. There are 117 agriculture experts under Point Four abroad. Public roads in Ethiopia, Costa Rica and Turkey are being developed by 433 Commerce Department civilians.

Our State Department doesn't give a damn whether it helps international relations. It cost us $25,000 to entertain 375 exchange students at luncheons—because at each luncheon there were 15 State Department employes for each three guests—at $9 a plate—for lunch.

State is also liberal with our dough when it comes to hosting foreign diplomats. A crew of official procurers was set up at the recent San Francisco conference to sign the Japanese peace treaty. About $25,000 was paid out of confidential funds for gals for visiting delegates—and boys—for the American contingent.

Even our Central Intelligence Agency has a Communist cell. Many key jobs are filled with those who play in with the enemy. The FBI is handcuffed. Hoover's reports go to the Attorney General and President—where they languish until some courageous Senator brings them up in Congress—and is called a smear artist for fighting the traitors.

Internationalists still press to get us to surrender more sovereignty and more dough. One of the most dangerous of the international groups is a crackpot organization called World Federalists, dangerous because many of its officers are naïve industrialists, civic leaders, clergymen and others with good names who have been taken over by such professionals as Norman Cousins, of the *Saturday Review;* Supreme Court Justice Bill Douglas, Walter Reuther, of the CIO-UAW, and Robert Sherwood, Roosevelt's ghost-writer. The other directors provide the trimming; these do the spade-work to turn the United States into a state in a United World that will be dominated on a popular vote basis by Russia, which now controls more than half the globe's population, directly or indirectly, through alliances with such socialist medicinemen as India's Nehru.

Perhaps your hometown paper didn't report what Chester Bowles, the new Ambassador to India, said the day he arrived there. It was his opinion that peace in Korea "may well be the first step to recognition of Red China." We say Bowles got that from the feed-bag—it is still Administration policy.

*   *   *

L'Envoi Confidential: We have now published four books in forty-four months, a world record for collaborations and for books on current affairs. We have been subjects of attack by members of our craft who felt they had to defend their own localities. Though we have between us seventy-five years of newspaper experience, we expect and ask no favors from our fellow professionals. We know they're honest. But we were chewing up old touches with a retired Chicago dick and he was telling us of a safeblower who crossed up his partner. One of us inquired, "Then you don't believe that oldie about honor among thieves?" And he spat out the answer: "Naw—they ain' no better'n the rest of us!"

INDEX

Place names are not indexed.

Consult Table of Contents for sections in which places are located.

A

Abt, John J., 55
Accardo, Tony, 15, 323
Acheson, Dean, 27, 248, 338, 345, 351, 393
Adamo, Momo, 155, 170
Adler, Polly, 163, 304
Adler, Sanford, 171, 188
Adonis, Joe, 18, 34, 167, 297, 307, 313
Ak-Sar-Ben, 275
Alaska Airways, 367
Alaska Railroad, 367
Alcan Highway, 346
Alibi, The, 370
Alien Property Custodian, 348
Allen, Riley H., 377
Alos, Mush, 359
Aman, Al, 304
Amerasia, 108
American Federation of Musicians, 379
American Guild of Variety Artists, 68
American Labor Party, 55, 339, 382
American Medical Association, 105, 355
American Mercury, 100, 238
American Youth for Democracy, 49
Americans for Democratic Action, 48, 53, 61, 349
Anderson, Clinton H., 157, 167, 171
Angelica, Biaggio, 207
Annenberg, Walter, 221
Anslinger, Harry S., 27, 222
Anti-Saloon League, 285
Arvey, Jake, 309, 327
Atlas, The, 359
Atomic Energy Commission, 266, 267, 268, 269

B

Babb, John, 321, 322
Balestrere, James "Pop," 239, 241

Balestrere, Mario "Crip," 148
Balinese Room, 215, 217, 218
Baltimore Sun, 49
Bankhead, Tallulah, 302
Banks, Tommy, 117, 118, 119, 158
Barkley, Alben W., 16, 247, 248, 287, 350, 351
Barrett, Chief, 358
Baumann, Arnold, 358
Beacon, 279
Beck, Dave, 67, 121, 122, 123, 126
Benton, William, Sen., 53, 107, 108, 356
Berman, Edward, 378
Biffle, Les, 247, 350
Binaggio, Charlie, 170, 190, 235, 236, 239, 242
Bingay, Malcolm, 172
Biscailuz, Eugene, 154
Black, Hugo Lafayette, 351
Blanda, Charles, 183, 200
Blumenfeld, Isidore, 117
Bommarito, Joe "Scarface," 176
Bonanno, Joe, 15
Bonnelli, William, 154
Boston Post, 94
Bowles, Chester, 107, 108, 109, 396
Bowron, Fletcher, 22, 153
Boyle, Bill, 132, 236
Braden, Spruille, 317
Bresslau, Joe, 70
Bridgeport Herald, 111
Bridges, Harry, 53, 69, 140, 168, 373, 381
Brodson, Sidney, 230, 309
Brown, Al, 359
Brown, William B., 377
Brown's Chicken Shack, 370
Brunauer, Esther, 88, 108
Bureau of Indian Affairs, 346, 368
Burton, Harold Hitz, 351
Busch, Mrs. Adolphus, 243

Consult Table of Contents for sections in which place names are located.

Byrd, Harry, Sen., 115
Byrnes, James F., 67, 68

C

Camorra, 10, 147
Cann, Kid, 117, 158
Capitol Transit Company, 349
Capone, Al, 12, 20, 102, 229, 320, 323,
   325, 326
Capone, Ralph, 321, 324
Caputo, 33
Caranna, James, 362
Carnegie Endowment for International
   Peace, 56
Carter, Amon, 192, 210
Caudle, Theron Lamar, 198, 222, 340,
   358
Celler, Emanuel, Rep., 55, 312, 339
Central Intelligence Agency, 396
Central Motion Picture Exchange, 389
Chapman, Oscar L., 346
Chattanooga Times, 258, 262
Chiang Kai-shek, 50
Chicago Confidential, 32, 253, 320, 322,
   325
Chicago Crime Commission, 182, 222,
   317, 321, 324
Chicago Sun-Times, The, 255, 322
Chicago Tribune, 325
Christian Socialists, 51
Chung, Dr. Margaret, 145
Churchill Downs, 247
Ciro's, 167
Clark, Bob, 197
Clark, Joseph S., Jr., 221
Clark, Tom C., 157, 197, 287, 351
Cleveland Press, 290
Clifford, Clark M., 349
Cohen, Mickey, 33, 155, 156, 157, 167,
   194
Collier's, 15, 139, 226
Colosimo, Jim, 323
Columbia University, 47, 51
Connally, Thomas, Sen., 195, 198, 320
Connelly, Tom, 18
Copacabana, 21, 34, 41, 230, 311
Cosmos Club, 346
Costello, Frank, 12, 15, 17, 18, 21, 25,
   29, 31, 49, 70, 71, 73, 79, 80, 82, 105,
   188, 254, 282, 303, 307, 310, 311, 312,
   330, 341, 342, 343, 349, 353, 358, 364
Cousins, Norman, 396

Cow Town, 209
Crawford, Brig. Gen. David, 336
Crime in America, 255
Crown, Col. Henry R., 309, 327
Crump, Ed (Boss) 80, 256, 257, 263, 264,
   265, 266
Crystal Bar, 364
Cummings, Homer S., 106, 198
Curran, Bill "Boss," 361
Currie, Laughlin, 54
Cutty, Tom, 70

D

D'Agostino, Johnny, 222
D'Alesandro, Tom, 360, 362, 363
Dallas Times-Herald, 197
Davis, Blevins, 186, 333
Davis, Charles W., 342
Dawson, Donald, 234, 332, 343
Dawson, William L., 322
Dean, Gordon, 107
de Gasperi, Premier, 27, 316
Delano, Preston, 350
de Lucia, Paul, 15
Denver Post, 185
Department of Defense, 45, 122
DeSapio, Carmine, 310, 358
de Sopa, John, 380
de Sopa, Ralph, 380
Dever, Paul A., 89, 90, 92
Dewey, John, 47, 48
Dewey, Thomas E., 12, 305, 307, 317,
   318, 330
deWind, Adrian, 340
Diamond, Anthony J., 367
Di Giovanni, Peter, 239
Dillinger, John, 131
Dillman, Ray, 299
Dimenenico, Joseph, 364
Dio, Johnny, 70
DiSalle, Michael, 290, 354
Donohue, Jiggs, 357, 358, 359
Douglas, Helen Gahagan, 354
Douglas, Paul, Sen., 51, 53, 326, 327, 328,
   329, 354, 356
Douglas, William O., 185, 351, 396
Dragna, Jack, 15
Dragna, Tom, 156
Drury, Bill, 18, 320, 321, 322
Dubinsky, David, 69, 71, 72, 73, 304,
   310
Dubner's restaurant, 364
Duff, James H., Sen., 219

Consult Table of Contents for sections in which place names are located.

E

ECA, 54, 394, 395
Economic Stabilization Agency, 346
Eisenhower, Dwight D., 51, 220, 353, 354
El Morocco, 125, 217, 243, 299, 314, 349
Elrod, Arthur X., 322
Emerson, Prof. Thomas, 50, 55
Empire State Building, 309
Equitable Life Assurance Co., 204
Erickson, Frank, 102, 247, 343
Evans, Silliman, 256
Ewing, Oscar, 349, 355, 395

F

Fallon, George H., 363
Fanning, Michael (Postmaster of U.S.), 153, 156
Farrington, Joseph Rider, 377
Fast, Howard, 49
Federal, The, 370
Federal Bureau of Investigation, 25, 40, 95, 144, 198, 235, 396
Federal Communications Commission, 20
Federal Home Finance Agency, 372
Federal Housing Administration, 347
Federal Maritime Commission, 68
Field, Frederick V., 108
Finch, Prof. Robert W., 346
Fischbach, Hyman, 358
Fischetti, Charles, 15, 18, 200, 215, 323, 327
Fitzsimons Army Hospital, 186
Fleming, Dorothy B., 36
Flynn, Ed, 301, 307, 310, 312, 342, 353
Foley, Edward H., 350
Ford distributor, 223
Ford Foundation, 48
Ford, Henry, 172, 174
Ford, Henry II, 21
Ford Motor Co., 175
Fort Starn, 370
Fosco, Pete, 322
Fowler, Gene, 305
Francis, Charles, 205
Frankfurter, Felix, 56, 351
Franklin, Jay, 319
Fulbright, J. William, 281, 282, 283

G

Galveston *News*, 214
Galveston *Tribune*, 214

Garmatz, Edward A., 363
Gattuso, Frank, 362
Gay White Way, 364
General Aniline & Film Corporation, 348
Gianeris, Pete, 359
Gilbert, Dan, 321
Gizzo, Tony, 236, 237, 239, 240
Godfrey, Arthur, 176
Gold Key, 359
Goldberg, Louis "Dutch," 12, 13
Goldman, Al, 342
Gon Sam Mue, 146
Graham, Dr. Frank, 50
Gray, Barry, 37, 72
Green, Theodore Francis, 97, 325, 326
Green Lantern, 370
Greenspun, Hank, 191
Gruening, Ernest, 367, 368, 369
GSA, 346
Gulotta, Gasper, 82, 83
Guthrie, James, 343
Guzik, Jake, 297, 320, 324

H

Hague, Boss, 264, 297, 298, 299
Hall, Jack, 69
Halley, Rudolph, 16, 18, 71, 72, 82, 125, 221, 243, 254, 255, 267, 298, 305, 310, 311, 322, 338, 343, 348, 349
Halpern, Seymour, 317
Hammett, Dashiel, 62
Hand, Judge Learned, 339
Hanley, Joe, 318
Hanson, Haldore E., 108
Harper's, 30
Harriman, Averill, 394
Harris, Rev. Frederick Brown, 350
Harvard Law School, 51
Harvard University, 93
Hastie, William Henry, 55
Hauser, Fred, 139
Hayes, Teddy, 353
Hays, Arthur Garfield, 56
Henderson, Leon, 349
Hennock, Frieda, 349
Herman, Pete, 82, 83, 84
Hill, Virginia, 7, 13, 17, 32, 71, 125, 127, 146, 157, 184, 188, 254, 341
Hillman, Sidney, 68, 69, 304, 305, 306
Hilton, Conrad, 327
Hilton hotel chain, 203
Hines, Jimmy, 330
Hiss, Alger, 51, 52, 55, 56, 248, 312, 326, 328, 351

Consult Table of Contents for sections in which place names are located.

Hoffman, Paul, 394
Hogan, Frank, 71
Holcombe, Oscar, 204, 205
Hollywood Life, 166
Honolulu Star-Bulletin, 377
Hoover, J. Edgar, 25, 34, 95, 345, 396
Hopkins, Harry, 106, 238, 301, 356
Hornbeck, Stanley K., 56
House of Joy, 371
Houston Chronicle, 203
Houston Press, 204
Hover, Herman, 167
Howard, Joseph, 131, 132, 133, 135
Hughes, Howard, 125, 193, 204, 205
Hughes, Maury, 157, 197
Huie, Bill, 238
Humphrey, Hubert, 53, 117, 118, 120
Humphreys, Murray, 297
Hunt, H. L., 197
Hunt, Lester C., 17, 24, 357
Hunter College, 43, 49
Hutchins, Robert, 48
Hynes, John B., 89, 91, 92

I

Ickes, Harold, 106, 346
Il Progresso, 311
ILWU, 379
Immigration Service, 347
Impellitteri, Vincent, 307, 310
Indianapolis Star, The, 255
Institute of Pacific Relations, 49, 108
Ives, Irving, 53, 55, 318, 319

J

Jackson, Robert H., 351
Jaffe, Philip, 108
Javits, Jacob K., 55, 347, 356
Jessup, Philip C., 56
Johns Hopkins University, 49, 50
Johnson, Enoch "Nocky," 222
Johnson, Col. J. P., 367
Johnson, Louis, 327, 348
Johnson, Lyndon, 205, 212
Jones, Jesse, 201, 203, 204

K

Kaiser, Henry J., 105
Kansas City Crime Commission, 235
Kansas City Star, 237, 242
Kastel, Dandy Phil, 80, 81, 83, 297

Kaufman, Samuel, 312
Kealoha, James, 379
Kefauver, Estes, 2, 4, 7, 9, 16, 17, 18, 19,
    22, 23, 25, 27, 30, 35, 71, 81, 82, 100,
    102, 111, 112, 114, 139, 140, 148, 154,
    155, 174, 177, 184, 221, 224, 229, 243,
    244, 247, 253, 254, 256, 257, 258, 261-8,
    281, 305, 322, 324, 329, 341, 343, 352,
    353
Kefauver Committee, 215, 220, 268, 275,
    280, 289, 294, 297, 298, 310, 311, 317,
    340, 357, 360, 362
Kelly, Ed, 325, 326
Kelly, Jimmy, 303
Kennelly, Martin, 321, 323
Kenny, John V., 298
Kerr, Senator Bob, 287
Kimball, Dan A., 355
King, Cecil, 340, 341, 343
Kingman, Fred R., 379
Kinsey, Dr. Alfred C., 46, 135, 280
Klein, Alfred, 221
Klein, Arthur G., 311
Knauth, Ellen, 347
Koch, Max, 341
Krock, Arthur, 353
Kronheim, Milton, 357, 358, 359
Ku Klux Klan, 5, 58

L

Lafata, Tom, 362
La Guardia, Fiorello, 29, 61, 301-309,
    382, 384, 393
Lait, Jack, 12, 16, 92, 228, 235, 320, 358
Lane, Myles, 311
Langer, William, 114
Lansky, Meyer, 297
Las Vegas Morning Sun, 191
Lattimore, Owen, 49, 50, 52, 108
Lausche, Governor Frank, 288, 289, 290
Lawrence, David, 224, 225, 226, 227
Lazia, Johnny, 236, 237
Le Baron, Louis, 377
Lee, Mrs. Dorothy McCullough, 127
Lehman, Herbert, 12, 53, 55, 56, 304,
    307, 330, 343, 356, 393
Leibowitz, Judge, 308
Letterman Army Hospital, 150
Levine, Benny, 71
Lewis, John L., 219, 227
Lewisburg Federal Prison, 55
Lias, Bill, 357
Liberal party, 339

Consult Table of Contents for sections in which place names are located.

Licavoli, Pete, 177, 178, 190, 268
Lieberman, Seymour, 206
Lilienthal, David, 268
Lionello, Tony, 364
Liu, Dan, 375, 381
Lodge, Henry Cabot, Jr., 89
Long, Huey, 76, 78, 79, 80, 85, 263
Long, Oren E., 376
Los Angeles Mirror, 163
Lovett, Robert M., 333, 334
Lowall, Gene, 183
Lucas, Scott, 322
Luchese, "Three-Finger Brown," 29, 303, 307, 309
Luciano, Charles (Lucky), 15, 27, 29, 33, 281, 305, 316
Lynch, Jack, 223
Lyre's Club, 359

M

MacArthur, Gen. Douglas, 126, 235, 334, 375, 386, 389, 393
MacBain, Leonard, 243
MacDonald, Thomas H., 346
Maceo, Rosario, 215
Maceo, Sam, 18, 80, 206, 207, 215, 218, 323
Macri, Benjamin, 70, 71
Madden, Owney "The Killer," 13, 102, 201, 282, 283
Mafia, 4, 8, 9, 10, 11, 13, 14, 17, 22, 23, 26, 27, 28, 32, 33, 37, 45, 77, 80, 83, 90, 91, 121, 145, 147, 148, 158, 174, 175, 176, 179, 180, 182, 183, 184, 194, 201, 206, 207, 209, 219, 220, 228, 229, 236, 239, 241, 265, 266, 273, 274, 281, 288, 289, 290, 296, 298, 305, 309, 311, 322, 324, 356
Magardino, Stephen, 319
Magnuson, Warren G., Sen., 53, 114, 122, 125, 356
Magruder, Calvert, 56
Mangano, Phil, 215, 323
Mangano, Vincent, 15
Maragon, John F., 332, 333, 343
Marcantonio, Vito, 28, 51, 55, 61, 62, 98, 168, 309, 310, 331, 383
Marcello, Carlos, 83
Marcus, Stanley, 196
Margardino, Sephano, 15
Margiotti, Charlie, 219, 220
Marshall, Gen. George C., 333, 334, 335, 336, 393

Matanuska Valley Settlement, 368
Maundrell, Harry, 380
Maurice, John, 362
Mayfield Road Gang, 156, 288, 294
McBride, Arthur, 20, 291
McCarran, Pat, Sen., 54
McCarthy, Glenn, 202, 203, 207
McCarthy, Joe, 231
McCloy, John J., 350, 395
McCormick, Col. Bertie, 108, 325
McCreedy, Dorothy, 379
McCutcheon, Stanley, 367
McGrath, J. Howard, 16, 88, 91, 95, 97, 98, 99, 182, 335, 336, 338, 340
McHale, Frank, 132, 352
McIntyre, John J., 343
McKee, Joseph V., 301
McKeldin, Theodore Roosevelt, 361
McKinney, Frank, 131, 132, 133
McKissick, Henry, 236
McLevy, Jasper, 109, 110
McMahon, Brien, Sen., 18, 106, 107, 128, 222, 268
McMath, Sid, 265, 281, 282, 283
Metzger, U. S. Judge, 378
Meyer, Johnny, 125
Milano, Frank, 15, 156, 289
Mills Novelty Company, 330
Milwaukee Journal, 229
Mint, The, 370
Minton, Sherman, 352
Mitchell, Joey, 135
Mitchum, Robert, 159
Mocambo, 167
Moody, Blair, 175
Moody, W. L., Jr., 214, 217
Moore, Larry, 368, 369
Moretti, Willie, 167
Morris, Newbold, 306, 338
Morrison, Charlie, 167
Morrison, De Lesseps, 79
Morrison, James H., 82, 347
Morse, Wayne, 53, 128, 129, 356
Mortimer, Lee, 7, 8, 12, 16, 92, 100, 203, 228, 235, 298, 320, 358
Mt. McKinley Hotel, 367
Muir, Florabel, 166
Munafo, Joe, 364
Munoz-Marin, Luis, 384, 385
Murder, Inc., 69, 71, 188, 304, 305
Murphy, Charles S., 349
Murphy, Frank, 172, 174
Murphy, Tom, 338, 339
Murray, James E., Sen., 356

Consult Table of Contents for sections in which place names are located.

Mutual Security Administration, 394, 395

N

NAACP, 61, 160, 161, 180, 273
Nashville Tennesseean, 256
Nathan, George Jean, 304
National Association for the Advancement of Colored People, *See* NAACP
National Education Association, 48
National Lawyers' Guild, 50, 55, 166
National Production Authority, 379
Neely, Matt, 356, 357
Nehru, Jawaharlal, 396
Neiman-Marcus, 195, 196, 208
New Orleans Daily Item, 79, 85
New Orleans Times-Picayune, 85
New York Age, 316
New York Anti-Crime Committee, 317
New York Compass, 50
New York Daily Mirror, 203
New York State Bar Association, 311
New York Times, 35, 48, 69, 89, 140, 255, 354
New York World, 59
New Yorker, 29, 56
Newell, A. C., 372
Newsom, Bob, 170
Newton, James Quigg, Jr., 181, 185
Niles, David, 54, 103
Nitti, Frank, 323
Nobriga, William J., 377
Nunan, Joseph, 16, 341

O

O'Conor, Herbert, 16, 247, 255, 360-363
O'Dwyer, William, 17, 71, 256, 304, 305, 307, 308, 309, 341
Office of Price Administration, 107, 174
Office of Price Stabilization, 16, 290, 348
O'Hara, Jean, 379
Omaha World-Herald, 26, 275
Omerta, 9, 10
Ossanna, Fred A., 119

P

Pacht, Isaac, 166
Palladino, Rocky, 33, 93, 94
Pallozolla, Joe, 362
Palmer Airport, 368

Palumbo, Frank, 222, 223
Parker, Bill, 153
Pastore, John, 98, 99, 356, 357
Patriarca, Raymond, 98
Paul, Randolph, 340
Payton, Barbara, 159
Pecora, Ferdinand, 17, 307, 311, 349
Pegler, Westbrook, 331
Pendergast, Jim, 236, 239
Pendergast, Tom, 233, 234, 235, 236, 237, 238, 240, 241, 321, 332
Pendergast, Vivian, 240
Perkins, Mrs. Frances, 301
Perona, John, 314
Peterson, Virgil, 182, 222, 317, 324
Philadelphia *Inquirer,* 221
Philadelphia *Morning Telegraph,* 221
Philadelphia *Racing Form,* 221
Pickett, Clarence E., 56
Pierce, Ralph, 297
Pinero, Jesus T., 385
Pinkertons, 219
Poletti, Charles, 12, 331
Pollack, Jack, 361, 364
Pope, Generoso, 311
Post Office, 347
Powell, Adam Clayton, 55
Profaci, Joseph, 15
Providence Journal-Bulletin, 99
Public Roads Administration, 346
Public Service Commission, 362
Puerto Rican Health Department, 383
Purdome, Eugene, 241

R

Ragen, James M., 291, 320
Rand, Sally, 359
Rappaport, Jerome L., 91, 92
Rayburn, Sam, 194
Reader's Digest, 389
Reconstruction Finance Corporation, *See* RFC
Reed, Stanley Forman, 56, 351
Remmer, Elmer (Bones), 148, 381
Reuther, Walter, 67, 172, 173, 174, 396
RFC, 105, 126, 190, 203
Rhee, Synghman, 393
Rice, Downey, 247
Richardson, Dale, 208
Riman, Wolf, 241
Roberts, Owen, 283
Rockingham Park, 102, 103
Romanoff, Mike, 167

Consult Table of Contents for sections in which place names are located.

Roosevelt, Anna, 118, 330
Roosevelt, Eleanor, 48, 52, 56, 61, 67, 172,
   301, 384, 392, 393
Roosevelt, Elliot, 336
Roosevelt, Franklin D., 12, 54, 67, 85,
   102, 106, 122, 301, 302, 310, 319, 330,
   331, 332
Roosevelt, Franklin D., Jr., 53, 55, 310,
   347
Roosevelt, James, 90, 104, 137, 138, 160,
   161, 330
Roosevelt University, 51
Roselli, Johnny, 156, 157
Rosenberg, Anna, 334, 335, 336, 349
Rubenstein, Serge, 107, 312
Rutkin, Jimmy "Nig," 298
Ryan, Clendenin, 19
Ryan, Ray, 230

                    S

Saltonstall, Leverett, 53, 89, 105, 205
Samish, Art, 138, 139, 140, 149, 155, 166
Sasscer, Lansdale G., 363
Saturday Evening Post, The, 255
Saturday Review, 48, 396
Saypol, Irving, 311
Schenck, Joe, 331
SEC, 19, 101
Sedway, Moe, 188
Seven, Toni, 125
Shamrock Hotel, 157, 202, 206, 208, 210
Shenker, Morris, 243, 244
Sherman, Irving, 18, 70, 71, 72, 73, 298
Sherwood, Robert, 396
Shomberg, Pop, 12
Shushan, Abe, 80
Siegel Bugsy, 8, 118, 146, 155, 156, 157,
   166, 168, 171, 188, 191, 381
Sinatra, Frank, 21, 166
Sinclair, Upton, 137
Smaldone, Clyde, 183, 184
Smaldone, Eugene, 183
Smiley, Allen, 157
Smith, Lou, 102, 103
Smith, Margaret Chase, 53, 88, 128
Smith, Paul, 91
Snake Hill, 211
Snodgrass, Bert, 368
South Bay *Daily Breeze,* 168
Southern Methodist University, 200
Spink, J. G. Taylor, 243
Sporting News, 243
St. Louis Post-Dispatch, 347

Stainback, Ingram M., 376, 378
State Department, 44, 45, 88
Stern, David, 85
Stevenson, Adlai, 56, 326, 329
Stone, William Treadwell, 108
Strand, Sheriff Bert, 170
Stretch, Joe, 70
Swartz, Charles Paul, 380
Swope, Gerard, Jr., 56

                    T

Taft, Robert A., 288
Tarantino, Jimmie, 166
Teachers' College, 43, 47
Tennessee Valley Authority, 257
Terrano, Salvatore, 380
Texas Rangers, 193, 206, 209
Third Avenue Transit System, 312
Tobey, Charles, Sen., 7, 17, 30, 53, 87,
   100, 101, 102, 103, 104, 105, 243, 256,
   281, 305, 326, 328
Tobin, Dan, 122, 136
Tobin, Maurice, 90, 91, 355
Topeka Capital, 26
Torrio, Johnny, 323, 379
Triana, Vincenzo, 15
Truman Committee, 349
Truman, Harry S., 2, 3, 31, 50, 54, 55, 67,
   70, 79, 86, 91, 114, 118, 125, 138, 194,
   205, 220, 224, 232, 233, 235, 236, 237,
   238, 240, 241, 248, 287, 307, 312, 319,
   326, 327, 333, 335, 338, 344, 353, 356,
   368, 377, 385
Truman, Margaret, 186, 332
Tugwell, Rexford G., 319, 384
Turner, Lana, 164
TWA, 349
Tydings, Millard, 361

                    U

U. C. L. A., 43
U.S. Bureau of Narcotics, 289
Union Club, 371
United Drys, 285
University of Bridgeport, 111
University of California, 51, 151
University of Chicago, 43, 48, 50, 328,
   384
University of Hawaii, 376
University of Louisville, 250
University of Missouri, 246
University of North Carolina, 50

Consult Table of Contents for sections in which place names are located.

University of Puerto Rico, 384
University of Virginia, 50
University of Washington, 51, 124
University of Wisconsin, 43, 231
UNNRA, 126, 393, 394

V

Vaughan, Gen. Harry, 79, 133, 234, 236, 332, 343, 359
Veterans Administration, 347
Vinson, Fred M., 351

W

Wagner, Robert, 310
Walker, Jimmy, 296, 301
Wallace, Bess (Mrs. Harry S. Truman), 233
Wallgren, Mon, 122, 125, 126
Ward, Charley, 118, 119, 331
Warren, Earl, 22, 138, 139
Warren, Fuller, 262
Warring, Emmit, 358
Washington Confidential, 16, 18, 38, 44, 139, 247, 253, 254, 327, 339, 357, 358, 359, 360, 362
WAVE, 248, 252
W.C.T.U., 285
Weiss, Seymour, 80

Wellesley College, 51, 93
Wells, Dickey, 302
West Point, 48, 49
Wiley, Alexander, 17, 267
Wilkerson, Judge, 326
Williams, Gov. Gerhardt Mennen (Soapy), 172, 175, 178
Wilson, Arlon, 235
Workman, Buster, 329
Wyatt, Wilson, 349
Wyman, Austin, 321

Y

Yale Law School, 50
Yavner, Louis, 338
YMCA, 314
Young, John Russell, 357, 358
Young, Merle, 332
Youngdahl, Luther, 114, 115, 153

Z

Zeidler, Frank P., 230
Zerilli, Joe, 176
Zimmerman, Charles, 72
Zucker, Jerry, 380
Zwillman, Abner (Longie), 18, 56, 297, 298

Consult Table of Contents for sections in which place names are located.